Political Ecology

Political Ecology

Science, Myth and Power

Edited by
Philip Stott and Sian Sullivan
School of Oriental and African Studies,
University of London

A member of the Hodder Headline Group
LONDON

Co-published in the United States of America by
Oxford University Press Inc., New York

First published in Great Britain in 2000 by Arnold,
a member of the Hodder Headline Group,
338 Euston Road, London NW1 3BH
http://www.arnoldpublishers.com

Co-published in the United States of America by
Oxford University Press Inc.,
198 Madison Avenue, New York, NY 10016

British Library Cataloguing in Publication Data
A catalogue record for this book is available from the British Library

Library of Congress Cataloging-in-Publication Data
A catalog record for this book is available from the Library of Congress

ISBN 0 340 76165 2 (hb)
ISBN 0 340 76166 0 (pb)

1 2 3 4 5 6 7 8 9 10

Production Editor: James Rabson
Production Controller: Iain McWilliams
Cover Design: Terry Griffiths

Typeset in 10/12 pt Times by Phoenix Photosetting, Chatham, Kent
Printed and bound in Great Britain by MPG Books Ltd, Bodmin, Cornwall

What do you think about this book? Or any other Arnold title?
Please send your comments to feedback.arnold@hodder.co.uk

Political Ecology

Science, Myth and Power

Edited by
Philip Stott and Sian Sullivan
School of Oriental and African Studies,
University of London

A member of the Hodder Headline Group
LONDON

Co-published in the United States of America by
Oxford University Press Inc., New York

First published in Great Britain in 2000 by Arnold,
a member of the Hodder Headline Group,
338 Euston Road, London NW1 3BH
http://www.arnoldpublishers.com

Co-published in the United States of America by
Oxford University Press Inc.,
198 Madison Avenue, New York, NY10016

British Library Cataloguing in Publication Data
A catalogue record for this book is available from the British Library

Library of Congress Cataloging-in-Publication Data
A catalog record for this book is available from the Library of Congress

ISBN 0 340 76165 2 (hb)
ISBN 0 340 76166 0 (pb)

1 2 3 4 5 6 7 8 9 10

Production Editor: James Rabson
Production Controller: Iain McWilliams
Cover Design: Terry Griffiths

Typeset in 10/12 pt Times by Phoenix Photosetting, Chatham, Kent
Printed and bound in Great Britain by MPG Books Ltd, Bodmin, Cornwall

What do you think about this book? Or any other Arnold title?
Please send your comments to feedback.arnold@hodder.co.uk

Contents

There is a web site for this book at
http://www.arnoldpublishers.com/support/politicalecology/
which includes abstracts and useful resources for the book

Notes on Contributors

J. Anthony Allan is Professor of Geography in the University of London at the School of Oriental and African Studies, UK.

Ren Azuma is Professor of Cultural Geography, Mie University, Japan.

Kathleen M. Baker is a lecturer in the Department of Geography, School of Oriental and African Studies, University of London, UK.

Robert W. Bradnock is Head of the Department of Geography, School of Oriental and African Studies, University of London, UK.

David Crouch is Professor of Cultural Geography, Tourism and Leisure in the School of Tourism at the University of Derby, UK.

Korinna Horta is currently working for the Environmental Defense Fund, Washington, USA.

Sarah Jewitt is a lecturer on environment and development-related issues in the Department of Geography, School of Oriental and African Studies, University of London, UK.

Sanjay Kumar is currently on leave from his post as Conservator of Forests with the Indian Forest Service while he undertakes doctoral research on social capital and community-based resource management in the Jharkhand region at the University of Cambridge, UK.

Deborah Potts is a lecturer in the Department of Geography, School of Oriental and African Studies, University of London, UK.

Patricia L. Saunders is a freelance researcher in development, environment and peace issues in the governmental, intergovernmental, NGO and academic sectors.

Philip Stott is Professor of Biogeography in the University of London at the School of Oriental and African Studies, UK.

Sian Sullivan holds a Post-doctoral Research Fellowship, based in the Departments of Anthropology and Geography, School of Oriental and African Studies, University of London, UK.

Anthony R. Turton is a political scientist at the University of Pretoria, Republic of South Africa.

Jeroen Warner is a researcher at the Flood Hazard Research Centre, Middlesex University, UK.

Richard Wiltshire is a Senior Lecturer in Geography, School of Oriental and African Studies, University of London, UK.

Preface

This book is derived from a two-term Research Seminar Series on 'Political Ecology' held in the Department of Geography, School of Oriental and African Studies (SOAS), University of London, during the academic year 1998–99. Meetings were convened every Tuesday during term time and the final version presented here reflects the interactive inputs of many scholars and students who participated in the lively discussions. The Series was organised by Professor Tony Allan, the then Research Tutor of the Department, who also chaired most of the sessions. Particular thanks must also go to Ms Jacqui Dyer, Dr Eric Patrick and Dr Hiroyuki Yoshida for their strong and stimulating support throughout.

The editors would further like to express their own thanks to all the authors for the prompt delivery of manuscripts and for dealing so amiably with the many requests for additional information sought during editing. They are especially grateful to those authors who work outside SOAS and also to Patricia L. Saunders for her pioneering chapter on the construction of knowledge relating to 'environmental refugees' which was especially commissioned for the book. Finally, they wish to thank most warmly Dr Robert Bradnock, the then Head of the Department of Geography at SOAS, our copy editor Ms Susan Dunsmore, and Ms Luciana O'Flaherty of Arnold for their tremendous support during the process of bringing the final version to print.

Professor Philip Stott
Dr Sian Sullivan
January 2000

List of abbreviations

ANC	African National Congress
AOGCM	Atmosphere Ocean Global Change Models
BSE	bovine spongiform encephalophaly
BWDBP	Bangladesh Water Development Board
CA	Communal Areas
CBD	Convention on Biodiversity
CFU	Commercial Farmers Union
CPI(M)	Communist Party of India (Marxist)
DFID	Department for International Development
DRFN	Desert Research Foundation of Namibia
ENWC	Eastern National Water Carrier
FAO	Food and Agricultural Organization
GAD	Gender and Development
GATT	General Agreement on Trade and Tariffs
GCU	Gambia Cooperative Union
GDP	Gross Domestic Product
GED	Gender, Environment and Development
GEF	Global Environment Facility
GMOs	Genetically Modified Organisms
GTZ	Gesellschaft für Technische Zusammenarbeit
HDRA	Henry Doubleday Research Association
ICRC	International Committee of the Red Cross
IIED	International Institute for Environment and Development
IIMI	International Institute for Irrigation and Management
ILC	International Law Commission
IPCC	Intergovernmental Panel on Climate Change
IR	International Relations
IUCN	World Conservation Union (formerly International Union for the Conservation of Nature)
JFM	Joint Forest Management
KIC	Kuwait Investment Company
LDCs	Less Developed Countries
LGA	Local Government Association

LHWP	Lesotho Highlands Water Project
MAWRD	Ministry of Agriculture, Water and Rural Development
MENA	Middle East and North Africa
MET	Ministry of Tourism
MNC	Multinational Corporation
MZWP	Matebele–Zambezi Water Project
NADC	National Agricultural Data Centre
NAPCOD	Programme to Combat Desertification
NASS	National Agricultural Sample Survey
NATO	North Atlantic Treaty Organization
NEA	National Environmental Agency
NGO	Non-Governmental Organization
NIEO	New International Economic Order
NSALG	National Society of Allotment and Leisure Gardeners
NSC	North–South Carrier
NTFP	Non-Timber Forest Products
ODA	Overseas Development Agency
ODC	Overseas Development Council
OED	Operations Evaluation Department
PIUCN	International Unit for the Conservation of Nature
PRA	Participatory Rural Appraisal
RA	Resettlement Areas
RDP	Reconstruction and Development Programme
SADC	Southern African Development Community
SLEMSA	Soil Loss Estimation Model for Southern Africa
SOAS	School of Oriental and African Studies
TNC	Transnational Corporation
UNCED	United Nations Conference on Environment and Development
UNEP	United Nations Environment Programme
UNHCR	United Nations High Commission for Refugees
UNSRID	United Nations Research Institute for Social Development
USDA	United States Department of Agriculture
WCMC	World Conservation Environment Centre
WED	Women, Environment and Development
WID	Women in Development
WILD	Wildlife Integration for Livelihood Diversification
ZFU	Zimbabwe Farmers Union

Introduction

Philip Stott and Sian Sullivan

In *The Postmodern Condition: A Report on Knowledge*,[1] Jean-François Lyotard (1979; 1984: 25) draws a clear distinction between the language games of an idealised formal science and the language games of narrative knowledge on which social relationships are based. For legitimation, Lyotard argues, formal scientific knowledge requires that one language game – one system of 'denotation' or signification – be retained and all others excluded. A scientific statement's truth-value *within* the language game of science is the only criterion determining its acceptability. The relationship between the sender, referent and addressee depends on what the nineteenth century called 'verification' and the twentieth century 'falsification' within the limits of the formal language game of science. The process is seen as producing a consensus, although not every consensus is ultimately regarded as a sign of truth by those not involved in the original language game.

Scientific knowledge is in this way 'set apart from the language games that combine to form the social bond' because 'it is no longer a direct and shared component of the bond' (Lyotard 1984: 25). But the language games of formal science do not exist in a political or philosophical vacuum. Instead, they are legitimised against the power relations in which they are embedded and through this are able to act in contexts far from the specific locations (laboratories, field experiments, etc.) in which they are built and developed (cf. Latour, 1983). As such, the language games of formal science comprise what Alexander, Burt and Collinson (1995) have called 'Big Talk' – important, male, metonymic, serious, official, correct, objective and emphatic. By contrast, the language games of narrative knowledge have tended to be trivialised as 'Small Talk' – unimportant, female, metaphoric, trivial, popular, incorrect, subjective and phatic. Ironically, however, as discourse theory and its emphasis on the deconstruction of orthodoxy have chipped away at the certainties of what might be termed a modern, structuralist science, its reified 'truths' – its 'grand narratives' – can be seen in some contexts to employ the language games of myth, legend and fable to enable legitimation.

Hence the title of this edited volume of essays: *Political Ecology: Science, Myth and Power*. It is a collection of observations and analyses regarding the creation, legitimisation and contestation of environmental narratives that draw their power by using the 'Big Talk' of a reified 'science'. All the essays investigate consensus views, particularly those informing policy at national and international levels, which draw legitimacy by using the language, if not the practice, of the natural sciences, primarily ecology and hydrology. The focus is on exploring contested narratives in which the methodologies of 'science' can be seen as playing rather a small part in the social bond legitimising such narratives. In other words, the essays reflect the extent to which the 'science' of environment is socially and politically situated, rather than unambiguous or separable from the subjective location of human perception.

In essence, for us this defines contemporary 'political ecology'. It is a concern with tracing the genealogy of narratives concerning 'the environment', with identifying power relationships supported by such narratives, and with asserting the consequences of hegemony over, and within, these narratives for economic and social development, and particularly for constraining possibilities for self-determination. Critical questions in this context are: 'Who decides the conditions of truth?', 'Who has the power to decide for society?' and 'Who is the subject whose prescriptions are norms for those they obligate?' (Lyotard, 1984). As emphasised by Bryant and Bailey (1997: 3), such questions highlight circumstances which may lead to contestation and struggle because they make explicit the need for 'transformation of a series of highly unequal power relationships upon which the present system is based: First/Third Worlds, rich/poor or rulers/ruled'. For wealthy industrialised nations there is some truth in the observation that the name of the 'hero' has become the people: 'the sign of legitimacy is the people's consensus and their mode of creating norms is deliberation' (Lyotard, 1984: 30); cf. the present debates over food scares, such as genetically modified organisms (GMOs) and bovine spongiform encephalophaly (BSE).[2] Given the structural inequalities existing between these nations and those of the developing countries of 'the South', however, our concern here lies primarily in the ways in which the 'citizen sciences' held by an 'environmentalist' populace of the former can exert constraint over the development trajectories of the latter.

This book endeavours to explore such environmental power and legitimation relationships (cf. Stott, 1999) through detailed regional examples that are primarily contextualised within the Less Developed Countries (LDCs) of the South. Thus our dominant questions are: Who currently holds power over influential narratives? How is this power employed and for what political purposes? What is the 'science' within defined narratives? And what are the ideas of morality infusing narratives and their supporting 'science'? We begin here with a brief history and evolution of what might be termed political ecology ideas, followed by a summary of the ensuing chapters.

The enculturation of 'Political Ecology'

'Political ecology', in the sense of politically located ideas of environment and of the 'right' relationships of humans to and within 'it', has existed unconsciously from the moment people started to imagine environmental utopias and dystopias. It can be traced from Virgil's *The Georgics* (29 BC),[3] through the writings of Jean-Jacques Rousseau (1712–78)[4] and Henry David Thoreau (1817–62),[5] to the 'The Shire' and 'Mordor' of J.R.R. Tolkien's *The Lord of the Rings*.[6]

In the context of a mid-twentieth century crisis of faith in technological progress – 'progress' which had brought the Nazi death chambers, Hiroshima, and the indiscriminate use of napalm over the tropical forests of Vietnam – a reactive and 'back-to-nature' environmentalism became increasingly politically vocal. Classic texts informed what was then part of a counterculture, providing it with 'facts and figures' with which to fight what was seen as an expanding frontier of ecological destruction in the name of economic growth.

Pivotal in constructing this grand narrative was Rachel Carson's cult environmentalist text, *Silent Spring* (1962). In a most revealing passage, Carson quite deliberately attempts to legitimise her 'science' by setting up a myth – a utopia clearly echoing *The Little House* books of Laura Ingalls Wilder (1867–1957),[7] but especially the Kansas of Dorothy, Toto, and the Wizard of Oz.[8] The contrasting dystopia is vividly provided by 'The Wicked Witch of the West' – growth, development, industrialization, urbanisation, the use of chemicals in large-scale agriculture, and science itself. Carson wrote:

> 'There was once a town in the heart of America where all life seemed to live in harmony with its surroundings. The town lay in the midst of a checkerboard of prosperous farms, with fields of grain and hillsides of orchards where, in spring, white clouds of bloom drifted above green fields. In autumn, oak and maple and birch set up a blaze of colour that flamed and flickered across a backdrop of pines. The foxes barked in the hills and deer silently crossed the fields, half hidden in the mists of the autumn morning . . . Then a strange blight crept over the area and everything began to change. Some evil spell had settled on the community: mysterious maladies swept the flocks of chickens; the cattle and sheep sickened and died. Everywhere was a shadow of death.'

This, and similar populist myths, continue to inform both film and literature as in, for example, the homely television series, *The Waltons*.[9] Tellingly, they say little about the murder and destruction ('genocide') of previous livelihoods and cultures that accompanied the recent appropriation of land from its former inhabitants, without which Carson's 'checkerboard of prosperous farms' would not have existed.[10]

This reactionary environmentalism of the 'First World' has been legitimised to some extent in the academic political ecology literature, notably in Atkinson's important 1991 text, *Principles of Political Ecology*. This attempted to define a strong political-science theoretical framework for the growth of Western environmentalism and the rise of 'Green politics'. Through doing so, Atkinson accepted, if somewhat uncritically, the dominant environmental narratives of the day, as constructed by, among others, the Ehrlichs' (1969) *The Population Bomb*, Edward Goldsmith's (1972) *A Blueprint for Survival*, Meadows *et al.* (1972) *The Limits to Growth*, and E.F. Schumacher's (1973) *Small is Beautiful*. While focusing on environmental problems caused by capital-intensive production in industrialised societies, Malthusian and Neo-Malthusian concerns regarding anticipated problems of human population growth in the countries of 'the South', particularly in relation to what is viewed as a degrading renewable resource base, were dramatically expressed in this literature.

Emerging from these perspectives were the various international conventions on the environment, which constrain the development actions of their signatories (e.g. the 1992 Rio Conventions on Desertification and Biodiversity, discussed respectively in Chapter 1 by Sullivan and Chapter 8 by Horta). These shape developmental processes and opportunities with a range of concepts which have assumed something of a totemic significance in international donor and policy discourses; among them are ideas of 'sustainability', 'community', 'biodiversity', as well as the various terms describing human-induced environmental 'degradation' ('desertification', 'deforestation', and so on). 'The World Conservation Strategy' of the early 1980s, for example, espoused the concept of 'sustainable development', further popularised in 1987 through the internationally influential deliberations of the Brundtland Commission (World Commission on Environment and Development, 1987). Bramwell (1989; 1994) provides a good critical history of these ideas and concepts, concluding that 'the environment' has become 'the "Northern White Empire" 's last burden, and may be its last crusade' (Bramwell, 1994: 208). In Chapter 6 of this book, Tony Turton explores the implications of a reactionary political ecology, as formulated by Atkinson (1991). He looks particularly at the problems associated with its transfer into the contexts of developing countries in relation to the inherent conflicts of interest between economic development, of the form experienced by the predominantly urbanised/industrialised nations, and environmental conservation.

Increasingly this has become the nub of the problems at the heart of political ecology, i.e. concern with the human rights injustices which can be wrought by the transfer of inappropriate ideas with regard to ecological 'health' and 'integrity' into contexts far from the ecological and political circumstances in which they arose, and the exposure of the interests served by these ideas. Researchers have approached and critiqued these issues from a number of directions. On the one hand, for example, the late 1970s and 1980s saw academic researchers make explicit the political contexts of environmental problems in the developing world. Early uses of the term 'political ecology' are found during this period, as in the two articles, 'Ownership and political ecology' (Wolf, 1972) and 'A critique of political ecology' (Ensenberger, 1974), but also in a book by Cockburn and Ridgeway (1979), the first to carry *Political Ecology* as its title (see Morse and Stocking, 1995, for further comments on the history of the term).

Significant here are Piers Blaikie's 1980s' publications which identified the political circumstances that forced people into activities which caused environmental degradation in the absence of alternative possibilities (see especially *The Political Economy of Soil Erosion in Developing Countries*, 1985, and *Land Degradation and Society* by Blaikie and Brookfield, 1987). This emphasis tended to characterise the literature covering the so-called 'fuelwood crisis' (cf. Leach and Mearns, 1988). A key observation here is that such texts did not normally question the existence of irreversible degradation, nor tease apart the sources and 'evidence' for such environmental narratives. Importantly, however, they did emphasise that people in 'the South' were not degrading 'natural resources' through irrational and carelessly destructive behaviours. 'Putting politics first' is now a recurrent theme, especially with regard to the countries of the South, and nowhere more so than in the work of the political scientist turned human geographer, Raymond Bryant (e.g. 1992; 1997; Bryant and Bailey, 1997). Bryant, in particular, endeavours to bring the local politics of 'Southern contexts' more sharply into focus in environmental narratives and he has thereby exposed to some extent the political nature of such narratives (cf. Chapter 2 by Deborah Potts).

A second crucial strand in the 'political ecology' literature has involved the query and re-framing of accepted environmental narratives, particularly those directed via international environment and development discourses to resource users in 'the South'. Notable in this regard are Thompson *et al.*'s (1986) *Uncertainty on a Himalayan Scale* which comprised a major rethinking of conventional wisdom regarding deforestation and soil erosion in the Himalayas, along with Homewood and Rodgers' (1987) theoretically and data-informed critique of the prevalent accusation of 'overgrazing' directed at African pastoralists using and managing the drylands of that continent. The edited volumes by Behnke *et al.* (1993) *Range Ecology at Disequilibrium* (see also Behnke and Scoones, 1992) and Leach and Mearns' (1996) *The Lie of the Land* can be seen as emerging from this tradition, and in many ways the present volume attempts to pursue some of the themes consolidated by these collections.

As can be seen, the complexity of the issues identified by an awareness of the political underpinnings of ecological ideas and narratives necessitates a creative approach to research; one which transcends disciplinary boundaries so as to foster communication between the natural and social sciences, and one which engages with a range of methodologies (see Homewood (forthcoming) on the possibilities for such 'hybrid' research; also Batterbury and Bebbington, 1999). 'Political ecology' has witnessed a growth in interdisciplinarity and transdisciplinarity using complementary sources of data in an endeavour to build relatively full pictures of dynamic land-use patterns and changing environmental ideas for specific contexts. Key in this respect are emphases on the following: local narratives; the significance of theoretical frameworks and assumptions in constraining the construction of environmental narratives; culturally informed ideas regarding the conceptual separation of people from the environment; and the importance of both the temporal and spatial scales of observation in influencing the 'findings' of environmental research. Furthermore, there has been a growing focus on the significance of history and contingency in guiding both the construction of particular narratives and the ways in which people use or manage both environments and technology. To date, one of the most complete analyses incorporating a range of data and field approaches remains Fairhead and Leach's (1996) *Misreading the African Landscape*, a book which has done much to inspire debate regarding the legitimacy of dominant environmental narratives and to stimulate in-depth research which embraces a range of analytics (see also Fairhead and Leach, 1998).

'Political ecology' and its future

Whither now then 'political ecology'? It is certainly arguable that political ecology over the past 30 years has grown increasingly successful both in illustrating the political dimensions of environmental narratives and in deconstructing particular narratives to suggest that accepted ideas of 'degradation' and 'deterioration' may not be the simple linear trends that tend to predominate in both populist and 'scientific formulations' of people–environmental interactions. In the future, a new challenge for academics in this field might be to make an even more explicit commitment to enable alternative voices and narratives to be heard; that is, to release the 'excluded voices' of Michel Foucault (1990; Rabinow, 1986). Extending from this is an emphasis on the circumstances in which social movements and local resistance to dominant international narratives emerge; Peet and Watts' (1996) *Liberation Ecologies* is a key collection in this regard. Unfortunately, this theme is not fully explored in the present book. Chapter 1 by Sullivan, with its focus on oral testimony and ethnography concerning perceptions of environmental change, attempts to open some space for local 'voices', but the volume is limited in the extent to which it grapples with the contexts in which dissenting voices might be transformed into resistance.

In part, this relates to oral constraints on the endeavour by academic researchers to make their findings and observations accessible within local and policy circumstances, such that they might add support where concordant with local dissent. Key here is the emphasis on academic 'performance' according to set research assessment criteria. This means that publication either at the locale of fieldwork, or in the policy context of research, is not credited or valued even while it may contain possibilities for change in relation to potentially limiting discourses. A further constraint, of course, is what might be considered an in-built resistance to unpalatable research findings, given the needs for implementers and policy-makers to produce outcomes and give the impression of success. Both the present editors have received threats and hate mail in one form or another in this respect.

A second issue is the constraints imposed by a predominantly political science approach to 'political ecology', which, as Sullivan argues in Chapter 1, has perhaps effected a masking of 'ecology' in both theoretical and analytical terms. While acknowledging the critical importance of discourse analysis and a political framing of environmental issues, we consider as invaluable a 'meaningful' engagement with the constructed 'science' (or lack of it) that underscores environmental 'certainties' and 'wisdoms' (see also Chapter 3 by Bradnock and Saunders).

This view is perhaps particularly relevant given developments in what might be termed a 'post-structural science of complexity', that is, one which explicitly acknowledges that complex systems cannot be explained and/or modelled effectively by using reductionist or atomistic analytics (see especially Paul Cilliers' 1998 book, *Complexity and Postmodernism: Understanding Complex Systems*). In other words, we note here the crucial difference between a reductionist experimental analytics, commonly viewed as the norm of 'science' and perhaps dismissed in something of a knee-jerk reaction by extreme relativist theorists, and the integrative approaches to modelling and thinking about complex systems that is, and has been, taking science into new directions for some time now. The 'post-structural science' of the latter assimilates the significance of sophisticated multivariate modelling computer techniques, neural and other networks, Prigogine dissipative structures (i.e. systems characterised by openness, non-equilibrium, and non-linear interactions), historical contingency, and the influence of the latter on the evolutionary trajectories of complex systems.

A final observation we would like to make here relates to the importance of in-depth work in analyses of environmental ideas: namely in revealing and clarifying circumstances whereby differences *within* local 'communities' mean that not all people of a place or context experience environmental ideas in the same way, or hold concordant views. A non-essentialising of 'local actors' has been particularly relevant for the context of gender because of the burgeoning significance of 'Women-In-Development' (WID) and 'Women, Environment and Development' (WED) discourses in international development as a whole. 'Gender analysis' moves away from a position that essentialises women as a unitary category, and particularly one which is somehow considered inherently 'close-to-nature' (as popularised by an ecofeminist position on environmental issues, cf. Shiva (1989) and Mies and Shiva (1993); in this volume, see Chapter 4 by Jewitt and Kumar and Chapter 7 by Baker). As part of a critical feminist 'political ecology', this can make explicit contexts and narratives whereby women tend to be disadvantaged by prevailing views of environment and land-use practices (cf. Jackson, 1993; Rocheleau, 1995; Sullivan, in press (a)). A non-essentialising approach is invaluable for exploring the implications of other axes of difference and identity, such as age and ethnicity, in the experience of, and ability to appropriate beneficially from, environment and development discourses; see, for example, Taylor (1999), Sullivan (in press (b)).

The structure of the book

To review, this book explores instances of mismatch and discontinuity between discourses that have become accepted currency in global and international settings and local contexts and narratives. Given the variety of issues and locales that are addressed, it is hardly surprising that the individual chapters do not share unthinkingly a common approach to 'political ecology'. Rather, they address various local contexts and issues, primarily in 'the South', but also in Japan and the United Kingdom (Chapter 9 by Wiltshire, Crouch and Azuma), as well as the Middle East (Chapter 5 by Allan), employing a wide range of 'political ecologies' reflecting development within the field over the past 30 years. We have organised the book with reference to the crucial dimensions of political ecology identified above, namely science, myth and power. We have already alluded to our approach to the relationships between 'science' and 'myth': namely, that while we recognise the validity of a reductionist analytics in exploration of identified propositional statements, we also consider that many knowledges about 'the environment' are mythologised as scientifically correct while being based on very little 'science' indeed. By 'myth' we refer thus to the grand narratives that embrace and legitimise particular environmental knowledges, and which thereby enable myth to masquerade as 'objective knowledge' – as 'science'. We are particularly interested in the growth of certain 'hegemonic myths', namely those which have been employed to exclude all other myths from policy debate (e.g. see with regard to the construction of 'tropical rain forests', Stott, 1999). Many of these hegemonic myths appear to be Northern, middle class, white, Anglo-Saxon, and male in their origins, perhaps reflecting a view of 'the environment' as 'the "Northern White Empire"'s last burden' (Bramwell, 1994: 208).

All this, of course, in turn relates to 'power' and to certain key questions: 'Who determines environmental narratives?'; 'How do such narratives become currency in international relations discourse?'; and 'What is the potential for challenging the *status quo*, particularly in the light of the processes of globalisation?' This volume addresses all these vital questions through a broad range of research based on case studies taken especially from Asia and Africa, including the oil-rich Middle East and Japan, but more generally situated in the ecologies, ethnographies, geomorphologies, and hydrologies of the developing world.

The chapters are arranged into three main parts. In Part 1 we explore contexts of specific 'scientific' environmental knowledges, the 'evidence' supporting them, alternative explanations for phenomena considered to comprise environmental 'degradation', and local narratives as counterpoints to 'official' discourses. Deborah Potts, for example, convincingly demonstrates that narratives in Zimbabwe regarding the degradation of seasonally waterlogged wetlands and of widespread soil erosion are not upheld by independent research regarding agricultural productivity and are inseparable from the political positions they support. This has resulted in a denigration of the government resettlement programme because it goes against international ideas regarding market forces, commerce, and agricultural efficiency. The consequences are profound for the land-hungry inhabitants of Zimbabwe's rural areas, who remain hamstrung by a continuing situation of gross inequity in land distribution.

This study shares many parallels with the scenario documented for Namibia in Sian Sullivan's chapter where narratives of degradation have been similarly constructed and asserted as 'fact' in the absence of 'evidence' as conceived in a Western or Northern natural science analytics. In these situations it is not necessarily that the science is right or wrong, but that the *praxis* of science has not found its way into the discourse at all. The interesting question here is how such narratives assume the legitimacy of scientific 'fact' when they reflect the subjective and value-laden perceptions of 'expert' observers that are frequently stated without the support of credible 'evidence'. Further, the chapter incorporates oral testimony material from local inhabitants which suggests that while people perceive declines in environmental phenomena (e.g. rainfall), this is frequently linked with observations of damaging socio-political processes over which they have little control. It is suggested that assertions of deterioration in one domain over which people have little control (i.e. climate) become metaphors for frustrations felt regarding the lack of power they are able to exert over other areas of their lives; namely in relation to effecting claims to land in a context of current gross inequality in the distribution of land resulting from a history of devastating economic and political marginalisation.

The two chapters by Robert W. Bradnock and Patricia L. Saunders and by Sarah Jewitt and Sanjay Kumar illustrate these themes further, but with detailed reference to the political contexts of the Indian sub-continent. The first demonstrates how an international grand narrative can be built on the slightest of 'science' foundations and even on a total misunderstanding of the hydrology and geomorphology of the region. The second illuminates clearly the role of gender in the development and expression of environmental narratives, by using critically a 'feminist political ecology' in an analysis of environmental issues, patterns of resource-use and decision-making in the forests of east India.

In Part 2 we have identified the key resource of water as a 'seminal case' via which to explore these issues further. That the book contains this focus on water reflects the existence of the international 'Water Issues Study Group'[11] that meets regularly at the School of Oriental and African Studies (SOAS) and which is headed by Tony Allan. Tony Allan's chapter emphasises the significance of perceptions of risk for environmental policy-making and of the inertia in policy changes that occur when a dominant environmental knowledge persists. In this case, the politicians of the most water-scarce region of the world, i.e. the oil-rich states of the Middle East and North Africa, are able to maintain the illusion that the region is water sufficient because it has access to subsidised 'virtual water' in the form of grain imports via global trade. Such a situation militates against conservative water-use and demand-pricing which tax consumers and, in contrast to the environmental movements of the West, has appeared to prevent the emergence of a regional constituency concerned about the over-exploitation of water resources.

Tony Turton's chapter develops this framework of 'virtual water' from a political science perspective and for a developing country context, namely the provision of water in southern Africa. In this case, circumstances are somewhat different. As a relatively resource-poor region in global terms, the option of importing 'water' in the form of grain imports, while appropriate in both environmental and developmental terms, is problematic. This chapter also incorporates a useful review of recent political ecology thinking from both Atkinson (1991) and Eckersley (1997) as a background against which ideas concerning water management are developed.

In Part 3, 'The Relations of Power, Global to Local', we look more carefully at different scales of world environmental 'power relations'. In doing this we address explicitly implications of the observation that many dominant environmental narratives, including those relating to deforestation, desertification, the loss of biodiversity, and global warming, have become increasingly enforced through international conventions and protocols, mediated via the control and management of donor funding. These conventions, supported by meta-narratives legitimised by a western analytical science, act to constrain certain development activities. Given relationships between North and South, rich and poor, and so on, they can thus maintain and even exacerbate existing structural inequalities.

Kathy Baker's chapter takes a gender analysis approach to identify the structural influences on both men and women's differential ability to produce in the agricultural sector, in a context of a fairly continuous drought over the past 30 years in the West African Sahel, coupled with the demands of internationally led Structural Adjustment policies. The chapter draws out the way in which policy decisions made at national and international levels attenuate the ability of both men and women to act on indigenous knowledge and innovation in local settings. It also accentuates the different roles in agricultural production that are associated with gender and the consequentially differential effects of policy on men and women.

In Korinna Horta's chapter, the relationship between the biodiversity-friendly policy statements and the real existing programmes of two publicly funded international institutions, the World Bank and the Global Environment Facility (GEF), are examined. These are, respectively, the world's most influential development agency and its largest source of financing for global environmental projects. They are intimately linked in that the former is the administrator and implementer of the latter, with its primary concern for the environments and biodiversity of 'the developing South'. Critical here is the observation that a major conflict of interest exists between these two institutions. The World Bank is committed to its shareholders which are dominated by the developed countries of the North, while the GEF, with its primary concern for the environments and biodiversity-rich countries of 'the developing South', is committed to a one-country/one-vote principle. The implications of this for developing countries are profound, amounting to a potential (and actual) disproportional influence by donor countries ('the North') over the receiving countries ('the South') in terms of environmental programmes and policy.

Richard Wiltshire, David Crouch and Ren Azuma bring environmental narratives into an urban setting, examining how allotments are constructed to further political ends. This is an especially interesting contribution in that it compares and contrasts the role of allotments in Japan and the United Kingdom and examines their relationship to Agenda 21 (United Nations Conference on Environment and Development, 1992). In doing so, it analyses the impact of an internationally constructed agenda in specific local contexts.

The history of the international construction of environmentalism and environmental ideas is an area of scholarly activity that is only now beginning to receive the attention it fully deserves. In a fine pioneering study, Patricia L. Saunders evaluates the political construction of the concept of 'environmental refugees' from Thomas Malthus through 31 key documents including the formative contributions of Lester Brown and the Worldwatch Institute. She then assesses the implications of these origins for the usefulness of the construct in analysis and policy-making, suggesting areas for further research. She concludes that the construct is currently being adopted by some 'who would reject many of the assumptions of its originators'.

Finally, Jeroen Warner provides a useful review of related concerns about global environmental security and their implications for environmental narratives, international policy, and the global distribution of power. His chapter is a fitting summary of the significance of political ecology and of environmental concerns for international relations in an increasingly global, but unequally, connected world, where power, myth and science continue to interplay to support the strong against the weak.

Notes

1 This report, *La condition postmoderne: rapport sur le savoir*, on the state of knowledge in the Western world, was first produced in 1979 at the request of the Conseil des Universités of the Government of Quebec. Its object was the study of the condition of knowledge in the most highly developed societies, particularly with regard to incredulity toward metanarratives, such as Marxism.

2 See for example: Julian Morris and Roger Bate (eds) (1999) *Fearing food: risk, health and environment*. Oxford and Woburn, MA: Butterworth-Heinemann.

3 See 'Virgil's *The Georgics*': http://classics.mit.edu/Virgil/georgics.sum/html

4 See, for example, 'Rousseau – the first romantic': http://members.aol.com/Heraklit1/rousseau.htm

5 See especially *Walden: or, Life in the Woods* (first published 1854).

6 The contrasting lands of homely goodness and outright evil brilliantly created in J.R.R. Tolkien's 1950s' classic trilogy, *The Lord of the Rings* (1954–55), voted in some Millennium surveys as the 'Book of the Century'.

7 Laura Ingalls Wilder was born on 7 February 1867, in a tiny log house in the Big Woods of Wisconsin. Her seven *Little House* books, originally written for her daughter, Rose, soon became children's classics, capturing forever the idyllic myths of an earlier and simpler America. The first was *Little House in the Big Woods* (1932, but relating to the years 1871–72); the second, and most famous, was *Little House on the Prairie* (1935, relating to the years 1873–74). See: http://ourworld.compuserve.com/homepages/p_greetham/ingalls/home.html
8 From L. Frank Baum's (1856–1919) original *The Wonderful Wizard of Oz*, first published 1900. There were many 'Oz' books written by Baum until his death in 1919. The characters became universally known through one of the most celebrated films of the twentieth century, *The Wizard of Oz* (1939), starring the child actress, Judy Garland, as Dorothy. See:http://www.eskimo.com/~tiktok/index.html
9 Created by Earl Hamner, *The Waltons* is a long-running television series, the first episode of which was shown in 1972. When asked where Walton's Mountain was, Hamner's sister replied: 'It's a place where my brother was happy.' See: http://www.the-waltons.com/
10 See, for example, Dee Brown's (1970) classic text: *Bury my Heart at Wounded Knee: An Indian History of the American West*. London, Vintage.
11 For more information visit the Group's Website: http://www.soas.ac.uk/geography/waterissues/

References

Alexander, M., Burt, M. and Collinson, A. 1995: Big talk, small talk: BT's strategic use of semiotics in planning its current advertising. *Journal of the Market Research Society* 37(2): 91–102.
Atkinson, A. 1991: *Principles of political ecology*. London: Belhaven Press.
Batterbury, S.P.J. and Bebbington, A.J. 1999: Environmental histories, access to resources and landscape change: an introduction. *Land Degradation and Development* 10: 279–90.
Baum, L.F. 1900: *The Wonderful Wizard of Oz*. Chicago and New York: Geo. M. Hill Co.
Behnke, R.H. and Scoones, I. 1992: *Rethinking range ecology: implications for rangeland management in Africa*. London: Drylands Networks Programme.
Behnke, R.H., Scoones, I. and Kerven, C. (eds) 1993: *Range ecology at disequilibrium*. London: ODI.
Blaikie, P.M. 1985: *The political economy of soil erosion in developing countries*. London: Longman.
Blaikie, P.M. and Brookfield, H.C. (eds) 1987: *Land degradation and society*. London: Methuen.
Bramwell, A. 1989: *Ecology in the twentieth century: a history*. New Haven, CT and London: Yale University Press.
Bramwell, A. 1994: *The fading of the Greens: the decline of environmental politics in the West*. New Haven, CT and London: Yale University Press.
Brown, D. 1970: *Bury my heart at Wounded Knee: an Indian history of the American west*. London: Vintage.
Bryant, R.L. 1992: Political ecology: an emerging research agenda in Third World studies. *Political Geography* 1: 14–36.
Bryant, R.L. 1997: *The political ecology of forestry in Burma 1824–1994*. London: Hurst.
Bryant, R.L. and Bailey, S. 1997: *Third World political ecology*. London and New York: Routledge.
Carson, R. 1962: *Silent spring*. Boston: Houghton Mifflin.
Cilliers, P. 1998: *Complexity and postmodernism: understanding complex systems*. London: Routledge.
Cockburn, A. and Ridgeway, J. (eds) 1979: *Political ecology*. New York: Times Books.
Eckersley, R. 1997: *Environmentalism and political theory*. London: UCL Press.
Ehrlich, P.R. and Ehrlich, A. 1969: *The population bomb*. New York: Ballantine.
Ensenberger, H.M. 1974: A critique of political ecology. *New Left Review* 8: 3–32.
Fairhead, J. and Leach, M. 1996: *Misreading the African landscape: society and ecology in a forest-savanna mosaic*. Cambridge: Cambridge University Press.
Fairhead, J. and Leach, M. 1998: *Reframing deforestation: global analysis and local realities: studies in West Africa*. London and New York: Routledge.

Foucault, M. 1990: *The archaeology of knowledge*. London: Routledge.

Goldsmith, E. 1972: *A blueprint for survival*. [*The Ecologist* **2**.] London.

Homewood, K. forthcoming: *Rural resources and local livelihoods* (provisional title).

Homewood, K. and Rodgers, W.A. 1987: 'Pastoralism, conservation and the overgrazing controversy'. In Anderson, D. and Grove, R. (eds), *Conservation in Africa: people, policies and practice*, Cambridge: Cambridge University Press.

Jackson, C. 1993. Doing what comes naturally? Women and environment in development. *World Development* **21**(12): 1947–63.

Latour, B. 1983: Give me a laboratory and I will raise the world. In Knorr-Cetina, K. and Mulkay, M. (eds), *Science observed*. London: Sage, 141–70.

Leach, G. and Mearns, R. 1988: *Beyond the fuelwood crisis: people, land and trees in Africa*. London: Earthscan.

Leach, M. and Mearns, R. 1996: *The Lie of the Land: challenging received wisdom on the African environment*. London, Oxford and Portsmouth: The International African Institute, James Currey and Heinemann.

Lyotard, J.-F. 1979: *La condition postmoderne: rapport sur le savoir*. Quebec: Les Editions de Minuit.

Lyotard, J.-F. 1984: *The postmodern condition: a report on knowledge* (Theory and History of Literature Vol. 10). Manchester: Manchester University Press.

Meadows, D.H., Meadows, D.L. and Randers, J. 1972: *The limits to growth: a report for the Club of Rome's project for the predicament of mankind*. London: Pan; New York: Universe Books.

Mies, M. and Shiva, V. 1993: *Ecofeminism*. London: Zed Books.

Morris, J. and Bate, R. 1999: *Fearing food: risk, health and environment*. Oxford and Woburn, MA: Butterworth-Heinemann.

Morse, S. and Stocking, M. (eds) 1995: *People and environment*. Vancouver: UBC Press.

Peet, R. and Watts, M. (eds) 1996: *Liberation ecologies: environment, development and social movements*. London and New York: Routledge.

Rabinow, P. (ed.) 1986: *The Foucault reader*. Harmondsworth: Penguin.

Rocheleau, D. 1995: Gender and biodiversity: a feminist political ecology perspective. *IDS Bulletin*. **26**(1): 9–16.

Schumacher, E.F. 1973: *Small is beautiful: economics as if people mattered*. London: Harper and Row.

Shiva, V. 1989: *Staying alive: women, ecology and development*. London: Zed Books.

Stott, P. 1999: *Tropical rain forest: a political ecology of hegemonic mythmaking*. (IEA Studies on the Environment No. 15). London: IEA.

Sullivan, S. in press (a): Perfume and pastoralism: gender, ethnographic myths and community-based conservation in a former Namibian 'homeland'. In Hodgson, D. (ed.), *Rethinking pastoralism in Africa: gender, culture and the myth of the patriarchal pastoralist*. Oxford: James Currey and Ohio University Press.

Sullivan, S. in press (b): How sustainable is the communalising discourse of 'new conservation'? The masking of difference, inequality and aspiration in the fledgling 'conservancies' of Namibia.' In Chatty, D. (ed.), *Displacement, forced settlement and conservation*. Oxford: Berghahn Press.

Taylor, M. 1999: 'You cannot put a tie on a buffalo and say that is development': differing priorities in community conservation, Botswana. Unpublished paper presented at conference on 'African environments – past and present', St Anthony's College, University of Oxford, 5–8 July 1999.

Thompson, M., Warburton, M. and Hatley, T. 1986: *Uncertainty on a Himalayan scale*. London: Ethnographica.

Thoreau, H.D. 1971: *Walden*. Edited by J. Lyndon Shanley. Princeton, NJ: Princeton University Press.

Tolkien, J.R.R. 1953–55: *The Lord of the Rings*. 3 vols. London: George Allen and Unwin.

United Nations Conference on Environment and Development 1992: *Agenda 21*. Rio de Janeiro, 3–14 June 1992, United Nations.

Wolf, E. 1972: Ownership and political ecology. *Anthropological Quarterly* **43**: 201–5.

World Commission on Environment and Development (Brundtland Commission) 1987: *Our common future*. Oxford and New York.

Part 1

Science and Myth

1

Getting the science right, or introducing science in the first place?

Local 'facts', global discourse – 'desertification' in north-west Namibia

Sian Sullivan

1.1 Introduction

Poststructuralist deconstruction of 'received wisdoms' of the environment tends to lay blame at the door of a simplistic and peculiarly western natural science: portrayed as hamstrung by its tendency to bracket research questions from their wider socio-political and historical contexts, yet hegemonic in its ability to assert 'power at a distance' (Murdoch and Clark, 1994 following Latour, 1987, 1993) and thereby constrain people's lives in often brutally repressive ways. The extreme relativist's position is to deny that there can be any validity to scientific analyses of environmental problems, since far from constituting a defensible means of observing 'real-world' phenomena such analyses are embedded in particular individual, social and historical moments and cannot be divorced from the power relations they uphold. In other words, to throw the scientific baby out with the bath-water. To the relativist's amusement, the realist might claim instead that we just have to get the science right: that with new tools and techniques, and with new conceptual influences over data collection and interpretation, the 'truth' will be revealed, allowing rational planning and management of the environment for the common social and environmental good.

In this chapter I argue that both these perspectives ignore a fundamental aspect of many modern environmental narratives, particularly those relating to the 'developing world'. That is, that they have become accepted as 'fact' in the absence of what most natural scientists would today acknowledge as the praxis of science, i.e. the standardised and 'transparent' collection of data to explore propositional or 'testable' statements, and the interpretation of such data within a defendable, albeit changing and contentious, theoretical framework.

My discussion hinges around a particular environmental issue, that of 'desertification' in north-west Namibia, identified as the outcome of disintegration of local-level resource management institutions and considered 'undisputed fact' by the country's donor-funded Programme to Combat Desertification. Most assertions of degradation and imminent system collapse in the area have been made without the support of any 'scientifically derived' data whatsoever, and have certainly occluded local narratives and wider ecological theorising about the environment. Significantly in the context of a post-apartheid southern Africa, where the opportunity exists to formulate radical policy enabling self-determination in the pastoral use and management of existing and expanded communal rangelands, a pervasive discourse of 'desertification' driven by international environmentalist ideals justifies land policies based on increasing control and regulation rather than fostering flexibility in land-use. Several analyses from elsewhere similarly identify links between negative environmental discourses and severely repressive policy (cf. Homewood and Rodgers, 1987; Fairhead and Leach, 1996; Homewood and Brockington, 1999).

Nevertheless, assertions of degradation incorporate a number of propositional truths which are amenable to analysis and potential falsification through the praxis of science within the limits of interpretation imposed by both spatial and temporal scale (Allen and Starr, 1982; Solbrig, 1991; Scoones, 1997; Sullivan, 1999a) and conceptual framework.[1] Institutional alliances, of course, also constrain the interpretation of data. As reviewed here, a critical realist approach in recent independent analyses seems actually to provide little support for specific claims of widespread desertification in north-west Namibia. Not surprisingly, such analyses converge with individual oral testimony accounts of ecological dynamics in the area.

In this case, the question is not about getting the science right, but about introducing science into the debate in the first place. Given the acknowledged strength of 'science' in policy discourse, the implications of this can be profound: if researchers are prepared to allow their choice of publishing outlet to be governed in part by criteria other than academic research assessments, then I would argue that the pathways exist whereby data can strengthen the power and voice of local narratives and concerns in contesting national and global policy debate. In other words, if we as academics are to talk any sense at all about the problems of representing local narratives in regulatory environmental discourses, then we need to complement our political ecology musings with some political engagement. As Peet and Watts (1996: 37–8) acknowledge with their term 'liberation ecology', the challenge is to recognise the emancipatory and 'politically transformative' potential of environmental researches which, they suggest, should include a 'nuanced' and 'thickly textured' empiricism.

There is a second issue here, however. The literature regarding environmental degradation resounds metaphorically with calls for cross-disciplinary and 'hybrid' approaches to research (e.g. Batterbury and Bebbington, 1999), a call echoed in recent meetings on issues relating to 'environment and development.'[2] In other words, towards breaking down the dualisms between natural and social science, realist and relativist analytics. The commitment on the part of both natural scientists and social theorists to learn and take seriously the other's language, however, is conspicuous largely by its absence. A case in point is Atkinson's (1991) reactionary treatise on 'political ecology': dominated by an unproblematised and uncritical acceptance of environmental degradation narratives, with little consideration of either the hegemonic impacts of these northern 'citizen science' discourses on developing country contexts, or of paradigmatic shifts in the biophysical sciences regarding ecological dynamics and complexity.

Put bluntly, and at risk of essentialising categories, while natural scientists are alienated by what they see as the unnecessarily obscuring jargon of poststructuralist analysis, an anti-science humanities (cf. Dunbar, 1995) appears unaware of new models and thinking in the natural sciences, continuing to portray an archaic picture of science as an unreflexive endeavour in which scientists are ignorant of the contexts in which they work. In this chapter I maintain instead that observed discontinuities between data and discourse, as suggested by the case material, point to the identification of greater parallels than are normally acknowledged in the conceptual thinking characterising both an integrative (Holling, 1998: 3) 'realist' science and 'constructivist' social theorising. In other words, that a poststructural political ecology (cf. Escobar, 1996) could do well to give more space to dramatic conceptual shifts occurring in the physical and life sciences (see also Sullivan, under revision). These offer cogent and coherent challenges to what could be termed a temperate-zone Enlightenment foundationalism, built on seemingly fundamental principles of equilibrium, gradual change, and predictability in a relatively constant environment. It is suggested that these tenets will be, and are being, displaced inexorably by a language of non-equilibrium, unpredictable and continual change, contingency and sensitivity to historical processes, and emergent complexity from local level networks. All of these have become crucial concepts in both anthropology and ecology researches of African drylands. By indicating convergences of language and metaphor that introduce possibilities for communication across the apparently impermeable boundaries separating realist 'science' and relativist discourse theory, such thinking might make genuinely possible the hybrid, post-disciplinary arenas of environmental anthropology and political ecology.

1.2. A dryland on the brink of collapse?[3]

1.2.1 Building a discourse

The former Damaraland 'homeland' of north-west Namibia (*see* Fig. 1.1) has been the focus of a long history of assertions of devastating environmental degradation, generally made with reference to human misuse of resources. As long ago as 1786, the explorer Thompson wrote of the region that 'some people who have visited a part of Caffraria[4] have said that it appeared to them to have been a country worn out by time, and had once been fruitful' (in Jill Kinahan, 1990: 44). Reiterating this dismal view, Native Commissioner Hahn (1928: 222) wrote that '[t]here can scarcely be a doubt that this barren coast-girdle gradually increases in breadth and encroaches gradually upon the more fertile parts of the country, which in time will become as barren as the coast-land now is'. In this tradition, and following field visits in the 1950s, an 'ethnologist' for the South African administration wrote of the settlement of Sesfontein that:

> the whole . . . area has been overgrazed so thoroughly that only the large trees remain in a level plain of bare sand. There are no young trees nor can any raise its head owing to the intensive browsing of the numerous cattle, goats and donkeys . . . as the large trees die off one by one and no others take their place it seems that all vegetation must eventually disappear.
> (van Warmelo, 1962: 39)

Consultancy reports from the 1970s similarly maintained that '[a]buse of natural resources in the past has aggravated the problems of the livestock industry in the Homeland . . . severe degradation has occurred' (Loxton *et al.*, 1974: 22).

Since independence in 1990, declarations of degradation and pending environmental collapse have fallen thick and fast. Apparently, 'environmental catastrophe [is] imminent in most of the communal areas' (United Democratic Front, 1991: 5); the 'rural economy in the arid western parts of Namibia has steadily declined over the last few decades, its reserves of pasture depleted to critical levels' (John Kinahan, 1993: 385); 'The ravaged landscape is testimony to mass overgrazing' (Næraa *et al.*, 1993: 82); 'eventually the whole ecosystem

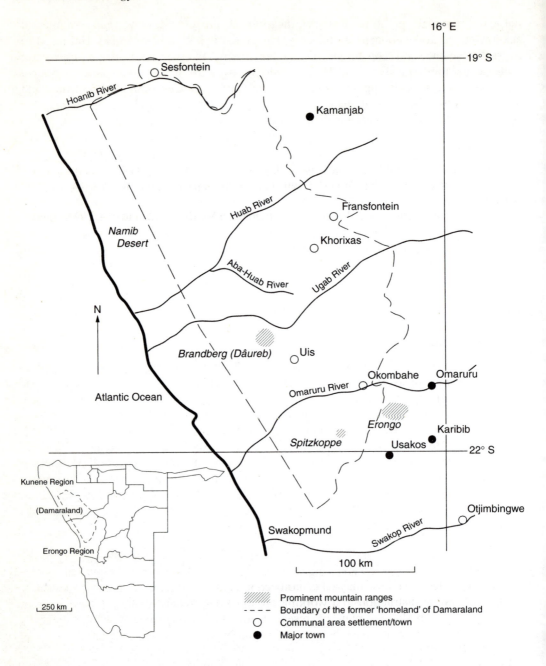

Figure 1.1 Map of Namibia showing the location of the former 'homeland' of Damaraland in relation to post-independence regional boundaries

will suffer severely and collapse' (Infoscience, 1994: 22); 'Reduction in vegetation cover and subsequent soil denudation following overgrazing . . . can be found in all regions, in particular, . . . Kunene' (Seely and Jacobson, 1994: 31; see also Seely *et al.*, 1995: 53); and 'overgrazing has resulted in the virtual disappearance of perennial grass leading to continuous soil erosion' (Giorgis, 1995: 232). A recent head of the Directorate of Resource Management, Ministry of Environment and Tourism, recently summed up this thinking for the Hoanib river catchment in the statement that:

> [this] is now a desert landscape; grass, or for that matter any growth other than huge acacias is nowhere to be seen. All and all, it is an ecological system put off balance and in danger of collapsing altogether. The only way that something can be done about this, is to have fewer . . . livestock.
>
> (quoted in Menges 1992 in Rohde, 1997b: 368)

The former Damaraland is not an isolated case: statements echoing these sentiments can be found for communal areas throughout the country. For example, Malan and Owen-Smith (1974: 140) assert for the Kaokoveld (north Kunene) that severe overgrazing is a problem, particularly in valley areas dominated by woodland savanna, where it is thought to have 'virtually exterminated most perennial grass species' so that 'for much of the year the ground . . . is bare and trampled into a fine dust'. For the Kalahari sandveld of Hereroland it is considered that an increase in livestock numbers, particularly cattle, throughout this century has caused 'overgrazing, soil erosion, and trampling of the rangeland', perceived to 'drastically decrease the grassland productivity' (Kajujaha-Matundu, 1996: 6, 22). Similarly, widespread concern has been expressed regarding vegetation degradation through overgrazing and deforestation in the former Owambo region of north-central Namibia, particularly the central Cuvelai floodplain, leading to the assertion that central Owambo is approaching the limits of its human and livestock carrying capacity under present subsistence strategies (cf. Loxton *et al.*, 1983: 87, 114; Jensen, 1990: 15; Erkkiliä and Siiskonen, 1992: 152–5; Marsh and Seely, 1992: 17, 25; NISER, 1992: ix; Marsh, 1994: 44–50; Soroses *et al.*, 1994: 6–14; Mubita, 1995: 68–70).

In most cases, and certainly with regard to the north-west, these confident assertions were made without reference to a shred of supportive natural science 'evidence'. The praxis of science thus has barely entered the discourse. Nevertheless, these assertions and perceptions by a few 'experts' somehow have assumed the validity and sanction of 'science', to the extent that contextualised research into whether or not desertification processes are occurring, or what form these may take, has been treated as an undertaking of little worth. A case in point is the instruction to a working group of researchers, invited to participate in discussions to formulate a plan of research for the second phase of the country's Desertification Programme (see below), to begin by assuming that desertification has occurred (pers. obs., Planning Workshop, 1995).

Furthermore, and following Leach and Fairhead (1998), assertions and impressions of desertification have gained currency only through the occlusion of significant contexts: of historical circumstances and political processes shaping and constraining land-use by communal area inhabitants (cf. Lau, 1979, 1987; Fuller, 1993), and of local narratives and knowledge concerning landscape and biophysical resources (cf. Sullivan, 1996a, 1999a and b, under revision). In addition, they incorporate little from current academic debate regarding the significance of abiotic factors, primarily rainfall, in driving productivity and land use in dryland environments over and above the density-dependent effects of livestock.[5]

Current fears of 'desertification' in Namibia are institutionalised in the country's 'Programme to Combat Desertification' (NAPCOD): a joint initiative of the Desert Research Foundation of Namibia (DRFN), the Ministry of Environment and Tourism (MET) and the Ministry of Agriculture, Water and Rural Development (MAWRD) (with the DRFN running most of its activities), funded by the Deutsche Gesellschaft für Technische Zusammenarbeit (GTZ) of the Federal Republic of Germany (Seely and Jacobson, 1994; Wolters, 1994; Seely *et al.*, 1995: 57–61; Mouton *et al.*, 1997: 1). Through its media programme NAPCOD has considerable potential to mould a desertification-aware national consciousness, which pervades thinking regarding land reform and natural resources management projects alike. NAPCOD, therefore, can be seen as both a response to, and a cause of, desertification concern. The Programme's position is summarised in its recent policy review which states, '[t]hat land degradation has, and is continuing to, take place at an alarming rate *is an undisputed fact*' (Dewdney, 1996: iii, emphasis added; see also Mouton *et al.*, 1997). Similarly, economic assessments of the impacts of desertification in Namibia, while acknowledged as based on 'assumed and reported, rather than scientifically documented, change' (Quan *et al.*, 1994: foreword), consider it as given that desertification is occurring.

1.2.2. Institutionally-located biophysical research

Since the inauguration of NAPCOD in 1994, a handful of short-term studies incorporating biophysical approaches have been carried out under its auspices. What is interesting about these is, first, that their stated agenda is to document processes of desertification (i.e. desertification is a *fait accompli*), and second, that their findings have been interpreted as indicating processes of desertification without considering alternative, and possibly more parsimonious, explanations. What is perhaps of graver concern is the manner in which these studies are socialising young Namibians to view the land-use practices of their communal area country-folk as environmentally degrading and in need of reform, while inadvertently deflecting interest from over-arching policy issues such as land redistribution.[6]

For example, the 1994–95 DRFN Summer Desertification Project, conducted in arid pro-Namib farmland of southern Kunene and northern Erongo Regions, had as its starting point the consideration that 'farmers of this area are experiencing difficulties with an ever-deteriorating rangeland that makes livestock farming only marginally productive' (Kambatuku *et al.*, 1995: 3). A primary objective of this study was thus to 'gather vital information on desertification' (ibid.: 4). For this reason, two of the eight study sites were located in an area which appeared so desolate and severely degraded that it was given the working name of the 'Moonlandscape'. Not surprisingly given this framework, the project found a number of biophysical 'degradation-correlates' with grazing pressure (see Table 1.1). Overall, it was suggested that reductions in primary productivity and changes in plant species assemblages were occurring as a result of unsustainable grazing pressure, particularly around boreholes, and that these changes may be irreversible at sites considered severely overgrazed.

These conclusions were drawn, however, without appreciation of either the effect on the area of several years of below-average rainfall, or the residual potential for ecosystem productivity given appropriate abiotic conditions. In other words, alternative possible explanations for the research findings were not considered. The complex ecological dynamics of this arid area were forcefully illustrated by the late rains of 1995, occurring only a couple of months after the completion of the DRFN project, which transformed

Table 1.1. 'Findings' and alternative readings of the 1994–95 and 1996–97 Desert Research Foundation of Namibia (DRFN) Summer Desertification Projects conducted in southern Kunene and northern Erongo Regions

1994–95 DRFN Summer Desertification Project

1. The toxic invasive plant *Geigaria ornativa*, interpreted as a sign of heavy grazing pressure, was common at all study sites with sandy soils and intense grazing, although it actually occurred in its highest proportion at the site with the greatest grass cover (Jobst, 1995; 32). Similarly associated with heavy utilisation by livestock close to boreholes was the reduced incidence of perennial grass species and the encroachment of *Acacia mellifera* and *Acacia tortilis*. These factors were interpreted as the possible beginning of piosphere* development and perhaps of 'desertification' (Jobst, 1995: 32–6). Little emphasis, however, was given to the high recorded levels of between-site variability in both species composition and biomass which indicated that factors other than proximity to boreholes and the consequent impacts of livestock might be driving these variables.

2. Soil parameters were also related nonlinearly to distance from boreholes, with higher nutrient levels occurring in the immediate vicinity of waterpoints due to manuring by livestock (Mouton, 1995: 16). No significant differences in these parameters were found for sites on sandy soils under different grazing pressures, and differences between sites on silts were attributed to factors other than grazing (Mouton, 1995: 17). Grazing intensity thus appears a poor predictor of soil factors.

3. High germination rates for planted seeds in soil samples taken from the study sites indicated that plant growth potential was high in all but the two 'Moonlandscape' sites considered to have experienced the most intense grazing history (Kambatuku, 1995: 41). Despite the crusted and compacted silty soils of these sites, however, unexpectedly high productivity following heavy rains in February 1995 points to both the significance of rainfall, and to problems with drawing conclusions of 'the existence of desertification' (Kambatuku, 1995: 52) from biophysical data collected for a single temporal sample falling at the end of a drought period. Biomass production was also lower in sites categorised as heavily utilised, but proximity to a waterpoint, i.e. associated with heavy livestock impact, had no significant effect on germination or productivity (Kambatuku, 1995: 45).

4. Soil samples from sites classified as heavily grazed had lower numbers of both seeds and nematodes, the former representing seed bank status and the latter indicating presence of soil biota required for organic matter decomposition and nutrient cycling (Nghitila, 1995: 55–60). Again, this was interpreted as supporting the case for rangeland degradation in the area, but see comments for point 3 above.

1996–97 DRFN Summer Desertification Project

5. Distance from the communal area settlement of Otjimbingwe had significant negative and positive effects on the height of browse line and distance measured between woody individuals respectively, but had no statistical effect on tree size distribution (Apollus *et al.*, 1997: 4). These results were interpreted as indicating that 'local overgrazing is occurring', exacerbated by higher wood removal closer to the settlement (Apollus *et al.*, 1997: 6). Given that distances of only up to 1200 m from the settlement were measured, the results also indicate that these effects were extremely small scale, and might be considered low in relation to the expected demand for natural resources in this relatively densely populated settlement.

6. No significant differences were observed in grass height either at different distances from Otjimbingwe, or between Otjimbingwe and the neighbouring lightly-stocked commercial farm of Tsaobis (Appollus *et al.*, 1997: 4). This was considered as probably because 'the whole area has been equally overgrazed' (Appolus *et al.*, 1997; 7). The different stocking-levels for the areas studied, however, suggest that a more parsimonious explanation lies in the overarching role of low rainfall in constraining herbaceous productivity in both areas, particularly in view of the fact that this study was conducted towards the end of the dry season.

1996–97 DRFN Summer Desertification Project – *continued*

7. With regard to soil factors, organic carbon content was higher in Otjimbingwe than in the commercial farms, while a range of bioassay measures used to assess fertility displayed no significant differences between the two (Apollus *et al.*, 1997: 4–5). This was considered due to depositions of organic carbon at Otjimbingwe through the flooding of the Swakop River (Apollus *et al.*, 1997: 7). The role of manuring by livestock in raising soil fertility was overlooked (although see Ward *et al.*, 1998: 368), and the results were interpreted as follows:

[t]his is a good indication that the soil in the Otjimbingwe area is not totally exhausted of its nutrients. If the people of the area could be convinced to reduce their livestock numbers, land degradation could be greatly reduced and even reversed. That is, through better land management in the area the vegetation . . . can once again flourish.

(Apollus *et al.*, 1997: 7)

Similarly, '[e]ven though the communal area has 20 times more stock than the commercial farms, the soil is basically the same. Once the stock numbers are reduced, the communal area has great potential to recover' (Apollus *et al.*, 1997: 7). An alternative explanation might be that both soil fertility indices and the high recorded stocking-levels indicate that land-use practices in the Otjimbingwe area in fact are 'sustainable', and that land degradation, in terms of reduced fertility and secondary productivity, is not occurring.

Note: *The growth of degraded areas of land in a circular pattern around waterpoints or settlements, due to 'the radial nature of a point-centred livestock system' in which 'the available grazing resource increases exponentially with distance from a borehole . . . creating annuli of different herbivore use intensites' (Perkins and Thomas, 1993: 184).

the entire study area into a landscape reminiscent of prairie grasslands. Even the 'Moonlandscape' became an unrecognisable sea of palatable *Stipagrostis* spp. grasses (Jacobson and Jacobson, pers. comm.; Jacobson *et al.*, 1995), an outcome which certainly could not have been foreseen within the constraints of the conceptual framework informing the study.

The 1996–97 DRFN Summer Desertification Project similarly focused on the semi-arid farming areas of southern Erongo Region, an area introduced in the following terms:

> More than 100 years of heavy grazing has left much of this region appearing severely degraded. This overgrazing has been caused by a wide variety of factors such as poor management, greed, government subsidies which encouraged overstocking, and local overpopulation. The major problem induced by overgrazing has been denudation of the vegetation, with soil nutrient depletion as possible consequences of this . . . This problem appears particularly acute in the drier areas of this zone, especially around water holes.
>
> (Ward, 1997: 2)

Let's leave aside the ahistorical framing of the research area and issues[7] and focus on the natural science aims of the project. Two of the study objectives were to determine whether degradation increases with proximity to settlement in a communal area, and whether a communal area with high stocking-levels suffers greater degradation than an adjacent commercial farm with lower stocking-levels. These aims were tested using comparisons of a variety of vegetation and soil parameters at the communal area of Otjimbingwe and two commercial farms in Erongo Region (*see* Table 1.1). While the overall conclusion of the project was that 'communal farming . . . is not more destructive to the natural environment than commercial farming' (Apollus *et al.*, 1997: 7), land degradation through overgrazing by livestock was considered as given throughout the study area (Kisco *et al.*, 1997: 1; Munukayumbwa *et al.*, 1997: 1; Ward, 1997: 2). This supported several recommendations for destocking (cf. Apollus *et al.*, 1997: 7–8). Furthermore, and as points 6 and 7 in Table 1.1 indicate, interpretations of the lack of differences in indices for the two areas are distinctly constrained when considered against possible alternative explanations. Interestingly, the apparent lack of a 'tragedy of the commons' in the communal area seems to have supported a reframing of the study's conclusions in an autonomous publication (i.e. with no mention of NAPCOD) which also incorporates an expanded data-set with measures of herbaceous productivity in wet periods as well as dry (Ward *et al.*, 1998). In this, the study findings are interpreted as pointing 'both to the resilience of arid environments to high stocking levels and the over-riding influence of abiotic variables on environmental quality' (Ward *et al.*, 1998: 357).

1.2.3 Independent biophysical research

Significantly, research conducted in this same area but independently of NAPCOD and drawing on ecological theory embracing non-equilibrium and non-linear dynamics, constructs something of a counter-narrative to desertification explanations. For example, a recent study based on analyses of archival landscape photographs for 38 sites matched with recent repeat images, and of matched aerial photographs between 1958 and 1981 corresponding to six of these ground photo sites, increases the time-depth of discussion back to the late nineteenth century (Rohde, 1997a, 1997b). This appears to tell the following

Table 1.2 Output of a simple factorial analysis of variance (ANOVA) of herbaceous vegetation cover abundances by treatment of quadrats as enclosed or unenclosed (i.e. released from, versus subject to, livestock grazing respectively) and by year (i.e. representing different rainfalls) and site location (representing settlement impact). Results significant at less than p = 0.01 are printed in bold and marked with an asterix. Study located in the Sesfontein-Khowarib basin, southern Kunene Region, north-west Namibia (discussed in detail in Sullivan, 1998)

enclosure by year		main effects						interaction		
		enclosure			*year*			*enclosure by year*		
	df	*F*	*p*	*df*	*F*	*p*		*df*	*F*	*p*
total live above-ground biomass	1	0.06	0.8100	1	**79.96**	***0.0005**		1	0.01	0.9410
grasses	1	0.01	0.9450	1	**79.52**	***0.0005**		1	0.01	0.9430
forbs	1	0.67	0.4160	1	**25.02**	***0.0005**		1	0.00	0.9580
plant litter	**1**	**8.12**	***0.005**	1	**17.66**	***0.0005**		1	**6.59**	***0.012**
bare ground	**1**	**11.67**	***0.001**	1	**54.07**	***0.0005**		1	**6.46**	***0.013**

enclosure by site		main effects						interaction		
		enclosure			*site*			*enclosure by site*		
	df	*F*	*p*	*df*	*F*	*p*		*df*	*F*	*p*
total live above-ground biomass	1	0.15	0.6990	5	**5.58**	***0.0005**		5	0.02	1.0000
grasses	1	0.05	0.8310	5	**5.41**	***0.0001**		5	0.02	1.0000
forbs	1	1.37	0.2450	5	**9.44**	***0.0005**		5	0.14	0.9840
plant litter	1	**7.14**	***0.009**	5	**10.57**	***0.0005**		5	0.26	0.9340
bare ground	1	**8.67**	***0.004**	5	**6.59**	***0.0005**		5	0.38	0.8610

Notes

This analysis tested for differences in the means of herbaceous vegetation cover abundances for each of 48 quadrats to assess the extent to which these differences could be explained by enclosure of the plots, growing season and site, as well as the interaction of these with each other. These parameters were entered as factors in a simple factorial analysis of variance model with cover, namely of above-ground live biomass, grasses, forbs, plant litter and bare-ground, as dependent variables. Cover is widely used as a measure of livestock impact and, according to the degradation view, might be expected to be positively related to distance from settlement and exclusion of livestock, with the latter being more pronounced after two years. The proportion of each quadrat recorded as bare ground would be expected to show the opposite pattern.

The output of this analysis listed in Table 1.2 instead suggests the following. First, that the effects of both year and site were highly significant with regard to all of the cover variables. The strength of the relationships (indicated by the F-ratios) were greater for year indicating that temporal variability, reflecting rainfall, had a stronger impact on cover than spatial variability. Conversely, the incidence of livestock grazing was only ever significant for plant litter and bare ground and not for above-ground biomass. This effect of enclosure was maintained only in combination with year and not when tested in combination with site and further analysis indicated that this was due to higher abundances of plant litter within the fenced quadrats in the second year of study.

Overall, the analysis mirrors floristic exploration of the dataset (Sullivan, 1998), confirming that patterns in the dataset were determined by site location and growing season, and emphasising the spatial and temporal patchiness of this dryland environment. In fact, the differences in growing potential represented by the two seasons monitored in this study completely preempted any anticipated effect of exclusion of livestock on above-ground biomass; the clear pattern is one of between-site variability in species composition and productivity in response to a good growing season in 1995, followed by extreme uniformity between sites due to the dry conditions of 1996. High differentials in productivity in relation to variable rainfall have similarly been described for desert dune habitats of the Namib (Seely and Louw, 1980), for *Eragrostis* spp. and *Aristida* spp. in the semi-arid eastern Karoo (360mm a^{-1}) (Hoffman *et al.*, 1990; see also O'Connor and Roux, 1995), and coefficients of variation of >50 per cent were the norm for a range of life history parameters of serotinous plants in the central Namib (Günster, 1994). Drought thus acts as an 'equaliser' in areas that retain the potential to be extremely productive and diverse given appropriate abiotic conditions. It is well-known that productivity in desert ecosystems is dependent on an absolute minimum amount of precipitation (the zero-yield threshold), above which productivity tends to increase linearly with increasing rainfall (cf. Walter, 1939; Noy-Meir, 1973; Seely, 1978; Rutherford, 1980: Hadley and Szarek, 1981; Le Houérou, 1984). In addition, fine-tuned combinations of temperature, precipitation, soil conditions and topography are significant in defining the potential for productivity and allowing the establishment of species (cf. Ludwig and Whitford, 1981; Cox, 1984; Günster, 1995: 107). With this in mind, the herbaceous cover recorded in this study following the 1995 growing season indicates that given the right combination of conditions the nutrient-rich silts of the Hoanib Basin can be extremely productive, despite the long-term use of this area for grazing by communal farmers and despite the tendency for these alluvial soils to have a disproportionately low water-retaining capacity in arid environments (Noy-Meir, 1973; Frost *et al.*, 1986; Van Rooyen *et al.*, 1994). In this case, saturation of the system by torrential rain over a short time period early in February 1995, combined with reduced evaporation due to a run of cloudy days, appear to have been the elements which allowed 'escape' of primary productivity in north-west Namibia during this season.

The build-up of plant litter observed in quadrats where livestock were excluded, however, could indicate that under 'normal' conditions livestock might be having a detrimental effect on soil fertility through preventing the accumulation of plant litter. Such an interpretation should be balanced against evidence for the promotion of soil fertility through manuring by livestock; bioassays carried out for this study, for example, indicated a relatively high potential for plant growth in sites close to settlements where livestock pressure was concentrated (see also Perkins and Thomas, 1993: 188; Mouton, 1995: 16), and increases in soil fertility due to manuring by grazing livestock may also enhance the nutritional value of herbaceous species (cf. Rethman *et al.*, 1971: 57).

story: that an increase in woody vegetation has occurred throughout the region since the first half of this century; that this increase includes species used intensively for browse, firewood and building material, and is independent of degree and type of land-use and of land tenure; and that, when analysed in conjunction with available rainfall data can be attributed to climatic factors over the last 100 years, primarily a period of relatively high rainfall averages during the first few decades of this century (Rohde, 1997a; 1997b: 307–31, 341–75). This analysis seems to contradict 'the stereotypical belief that communal farming and . . . densely populated communal settlements, cause irreversible environmental degradation', and supports a 'case for climate change as the dominant factor affecting trees and shrubs within an inherently resilient environment' (Rohde, 1997a: 135; 1997b: 314, 376). With regard to herbaceous vegetation, these analyses also illustrate 'that dry periods in the past resulted in denuded landscapes' similar to those observed recently (cf. the 'Moonlandscape' referred to above) without apparently hampering the potential for herbaceous productivity in years with above-average rainfall (Rohde, 1997b: 309).

Similar interpretations have been drawn from a recent structured ecological survey of vegetation designed to assess settlement impact in the northern part of Khorixas District, southern Kunene Region (Sullivan, 1998; 1999b). This dataset comprises 2760 woody plant individuals in a stratified sample of 75 transects, and 48 quadrats, half fenced to exclude livestock, in which herbaceous vegetation was monitored over two growing seasons. A number of standard ecological variables, including patterns in community floristics, diversity, cover and population structure, were analysed in relation to measures of use by people and livestock around three focal settlements. In contrast to common expressions of degradation, these data indicate the following. First, none of the measured vegetation variables demonstrated that land-use pressure was having a negative impact on anything but a local scale confined to within settlements. Second, for woody vegetation, widening the scale of analysis from that surveyed in a preliminary study of resource-use impacts in the area (Sullivan and Konstant, 1997) suggested that localised settlement impacts are within the range of variability expressed by a variety of vegetation measures over larger scales, including areas currently experiencing little or no utilisation by people or livestock. Third, that patterns in the woody vegetation dataset at both community and individual-species levels failed to provide consistent evidence for the degrading effects of resource utilisation, even though woody species, through the stability conferred by their longer lifespans, can act as longer-term and more robust indicators of vegetation change. Fourth, that tree populations demonstrate high recruitment and regenerative potential despite assertions that '[t]here are no young trees nor can any raise its head owing to the intensive browsing of the numerous cattle, goats and donkeys' (see above). Finally, that herbaceous productivity is highly resilient under good rainfall conditions, and even in areas under intensive utilisation by livestock. In order to bring some natural science data into this discussion, Fig. 1.2 and Table 1.2 provide, with explanatory notes, some of the 'results' of this analysis.

Despite these findings, much of which are available in Namibia as published and unpublished manuscripts, 'Damaraland' has been selected for further NAPCOD work 'due to *the fact* that desertification in (this) area is progressing rapidly' (Kamwi, 1997: 2, emphasis added). While adhering to principles of participation and support for community action in the sustainable use of natural resources (Kroll and Kruger, 1998; Seely, 1998), environment and development programmes informed by NAPCOD apparently continue to build on an unproblematised acceptance of desertification caused by land-use practices in the communal areas.

1.2.4 National sustaining of a global discourse

The different picture emerging from contextualised and empirical data analyses leads to the question of why environmental collapse through human-induced desertification has remained such an overarching interpretive and explanatory framework in relation to land-use in this part of Namibia (and beyond)? Two offerings are made here in response to this question.

The first identifies effects on national knowledge production of the transmission of a reactive, 'northern' environmentalist worldview, informed by concerns of pending ecological collapse as formulated by 'deep ecology', 'ecophilosophy' and in some calls for a 'political ecology' (cf. Fox, 1990; Atkinson, 1991). This is exported by an international development community via the various UN summits and conventions and donor-funded projects on environment and development, introducing very real constraints to the developing economies of 'the south' who have to demonstrate adherence to 'green' values and policies in order to qualify for support (cf. Davies, 1992 in Leach and Mearns, 1996: 25–6). Importantly for resource-poor countries like Namibia, local scientists who do not

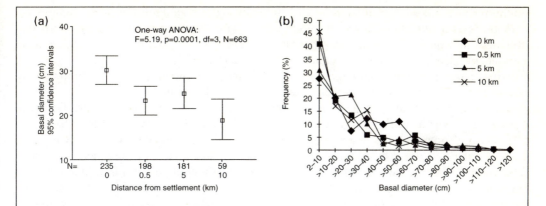

Figure 1.2 Graphical representation of the findings of analysis of the population structure as measured by basal diameter, of the tree *Acacia tortilis* in relation to settlement impact, as reflected indirectly by distance from settlement

Notes

As detailed in section 1.2.1, propositional statements exist regarding the population structure of woody species around specific settlements in northern Khorixas District. For example, the assertions that '[t]here are no young trees nor can any raise its head owing to the intensive browsing of the numerous cattle, goats and donkeys', and that 'as the large trees die off one by one and no others take their place it seems that all vegetation must disappear' (Van Warmelo, 1962: 39), can be tested fairly explicitly using standard ecology or forestry survey tools. Given that perceptions of vegetation degradation inform policies and projects designed to reduce numbers of livestock and otherwise control resource-use activities, I would suggest that some 'data gathering' might be useful for either the affirmation or discrediting of these views: if the latter, then it stands to reason that the findings of such research might be employed in support of local herding economies, and in the contestation of nationally or internationally driven agendas.

In this analysis, and as Fig 1.2a indicates, distance from settlement was significantly related to the size of a basal diameter of *Acacia tortilis*, the most common species (as defined by both formal and folk taxonomies) occurring on the western alluvial plains of the Hoanib River and a tree important locally in the provision of browse, building poles, firewood, medicine and food. The height of individuals of this tree also follows the same pattern (Sullivan, 1999b), namely that the largest individuals occurred within settlements while the smallest individuals occurred in samples furthest from settlement. Direct measures of woody plant utilisation, namely branch removal and browsing by livestock were negatively correlated with distance from settlement ($r = -0.49$ and -0.48 for cutting and browsing respectively, $p = 0.0001$, $N = 663$), suggesting that distance from settlement was indeed useful as a surrogate measure of resource impact.

Interpretation of these results in accordance with the degradation paradigm would suggest that recruitment of juveniles, i.e. of smaller individuals, is adversely affected by settlement pressure, with possibly long-term consequences for the viability of the population. Analysis of the size class distributions of these measures, however, suggests a rather different picture. Fig. 1.2b demonstrate that basal diameter sizes conform well to the reverse J-shaped distribution associated with healthy tree populations that display high recruitment potential. This is true for all distances from settlement, for which the frequencies of individuals in the smaller regeneration size classes were comparable. Fig. 1.2b further shows that the reason for the relatively high mean heights measured for *A. tortilis* within settlements was the greater frequency of extremely tall individuals recorded for these samples; this had the effect of pulling the mean disproportionately upwards and contributing to the significant results produced in the ANOVA. Again, the degradation paradigm might suggest that this is due to the effects of branch cutting in reducing the size of otherwise large individuals. As would be expected from a 'healthy' population, however, height and basal diameter had a strong positive association ($r = 0.8$, $p = 0.0001$, $n = 507$), indicating that levels of cutting are not high enough to reduce the expected relationship between these size measures. This relationship remained significant and positive even when only individuals from within settlements were tested, i.e. those subject to the greatest intensities of utilisation ($r = 0.82$, $p = 0.0001$, $n = 135$).

conform to the agendas of internationally funded programmes find their opportunities for both presenting opposing views and obtaining research-funding to investigate alternative scenarios are seriously compromised (Marais, pers. comm., June 1999). Global–local interlinkages thus amount to the creation of what Escobar (1996: 50) terms an 'ecocracy', in which the north retains dominance via the managerial ethic justified by a normalising environment-development discourse of 'sustainable development'.

Given the demonisation of desert in international 'green' environmental ideals,[8] Namibia, the whole of which 'is rated as potential desert' (UNCOD, 1977; Tyson, 1986: 86), is at a distinct disadvantage. No wonder then that national policy-makers have essentially toed the international policy line by framing a commitment to 'sustainable development' within an overarching 'Green Plan' (Brown, 1992) (something of a contradiction in terms given the short proportion of time annually that most of this arid country could actually be considered 'green'), and focusing concerns regarding the sustainability of development within its institutionalised, and much publicised, efforts to fend off desertification. As such, desertification, although based on specific propositional and potentially falsifiable statements, has to be alternatively understood as a constructed and self-reflexive 'institutional fact' (cf. Thompson *et al.*, 1986), which supports the flow of resources from the international donor community to sustain implementing institutions, and which upholds the validity of intervention by these institutions and associated 'experts' (cf. Roe, 1995: 1066). The situation has not been helped by the sanctioning, until fairly recently, of the apartheid administrations of South Africa and Namibia which, according to Dean *et al.* (1995: 258), has fostered 'research parochialism' and contributed to the twin existence of 'a plethora of opinions' with 'a dearth of published and reliable scientific evidence' in relation to dryland degradation. The sudden flow of research-funding to a post-apartheid southern Africa, to quote a Namibian colleague, has 'created a feeding frenzy in resource-hungry institutions willing to sell their integrity for a few pieces of silver' (Marais, pers comm., June 1999).

Continuing in this Nietzschean/Foucauldian vein of tracing the 'genealogy' of the 'undisputed fact' of desertification brings us to a second identification of 'correlative' power relations masked by this 'truth': namely that institutional appropriation of this international environmental narrative supports the continuation of policies and projects based on the regulation of rural land-use practices in the name of preventing degradation. With regard to pastoralism these include: attempts to persuade pastoralists to destock;[9] adherence to demarcation of communal land into individual holdings as the means of land tenure reform (Republic of Namibia, 1997; i.e. Scoones' 'politics of straight lines' (1996: 44)); and a focus on intervention in local institutions of resource management because the assumed collapse of these is considered to underpin perceived degradation (cf. Sullivan, 1999a). All of these processes have been documented as contributing to increased poverty, landlessness and social tension in drylands throughout Africa (cf. Brokensha and Riley, 1986; Barrow, 1990; Oba, 1992; TGLP Project, 1997). At the same time, the underlying structural inequality in land distribution remains unchanged.

1.2.5 Local narratives: 'And the wind is now our rain'

Unsurprisingly, people using the land have their own opinions about its state of health. But what is particularly revealing is the manner in which ideas and perceptions of landscape are linked with national socio-political processes. This section draws on oral testimony material regarding local individuals' perceptions of ecological dynamics. Selected transcripts are from a broader field project conducted in the first part of 1999 intended to collate the views of Damara-speaking people on a range of contemporary issues, particularly those relating to land and resource management (Sullivan and Ganuses, in preparation). The discussions forming the basis of this fieldwork were open-ended but structured to cover specific issues, such as whether or not people thought there had been changes in their local environment during their lifetime, what form such changes had taken, and what was considered to have caused them. Interviewees included men and women, young and old, and were from a range of locations throughout north-west Namibia: all were known to the interviewers, myself and Suro Ganuses, from several years' fieldwork in the area. It should be noted that this period of discussions took place towards the close of a severely below-average rain season.

Rainfall as the driving force behind dramatic temporal and spatial variations in vegetation is depicted vividly in these interviews. For example:

At this plain the grass comes out when it rains, but the rain isn't falling now; . . . When the rain falls you can't see the ground or the people for the grass. If it is ‖*hao* [i.e. the time when the land is green] you cannot see the children for the grass. When the rain falls the grass and the |*hînis* (*Tribulus* spp.) come out over the whole place and our dresses get yellow [from walking through the yellow flowers of |*hînis*]. When it rains, in the places where people stay the grass comes out like in the past. But if it doesn't rain then there is no grass. There is nothing. At Hurubes where the people are staying with cattle and goats [e.g. Bergsig, Palmfontein etc.] the grass still grows when the rain falls.

(‖Hairo, 14 April 1999; Sesfontein/!Nani‖aus)

The rain that falls [this year] is only half of what it should be and there is nothing growing. The first rain which came [this season] only touched the ground a little bit. After that it hasn't fallen . . . But that year when you were coming and going it rained [1994–95 season]; that rain was good! Yes, if the rain comes, the trees stand alive. If the rain falls things look clean. If there is no rain the leaves get dry, and some of them have no leaves. Only rain makes the ground green and brings the new leaves.

(Habuhege, 19 April 1999; Ani≠gab, !U≠gab River)

When she falls you can see the places where she falls; the sky gets dark while some areas are left out. This year she has cut this place out. And the wind is now our rain. The clouds cover the whole sky so that it is dark and you can see the rain standing in the sky. And the red wind [which brings the sand] comes before the rain and you think the rain is coming. But no, there is nothing; the rain moves off with the wind. The wind breaks through our houses and falls strongly like the rain. But there is no rain. Yes, it is very difficult.

(Meda, 19 April 1999; ‖Gaisoas, !U≠gab River)

When I am in the field with the livestock I see the changes. When I first came to Malansrust the drought was very bad. Then after that we get the rain and it was very good; the ground became green. But now the drought is back again. It is just this area that you can see which is green and otherwise there is no grazing again. There are big differences between the years. The cattle start to die and that is why my boss has taken them to Kamanjab area. The rain moves so that this year it hasn't fallen at this farm but only around it. We see the rain come but it just passes through without falling here. For the whole of this season the rain didn't come to this area. And then last month, when the season is supposed to be over, the rain started falling here and the place became green.

(Willem, 18 April 1999; Malansrust Farm, Aba-‖Huab River)

Overlying the capriciousness of rainfall, however, is a clear sense of things having deteriorated; having become in some sense 'dirty' or 'untidy'. As ǀHairo says, 'it is different now; it is untidy', and as Habuhege iterates, 'first the place was clean but now the place has become poor, shabby'. Generally this is linked to a perception of overall decline in rainfall, coupled with a shift in the distribution of rain such that it seems to occur later in the season. Thus,

> The rain used to fall when the old grass was still there; the old grass would get dark as it became wet from the rain, and the new grass would come up through the old grass. Yes, the rain is not falling as it used to fall. Before, when the rain fell we didn't eat because we couldn't make fire to cook food. When we planted mealies the rain washed the seeds away; also those of watermelons. Sometimes people too were swept away by the water and drowned. It is different. At this time of year we should be living with grass and with everywhere being green and our hearts would be awake. But now it is just the sun which works, and things are not the same . . . it seems that in Sesfontein there is something that has taken the rain away.
>
> (ǀHairo, 14 April 1999; Sesfontein)

> Yes, it is different. Some trees have nothing on them and some trees have something on them. But before they looked healthy. The trees had leaves. Now some of the trees have been burned red by the sun, scorched by the sun so they've died, died out. Yes, it fell much better then and the grass stood about; and the rivers flowed.
>
> (Habuhege, 19 April 1999; Aniǂgab, !Uǂgab River)

> When we had to move here things were better . . . but in about three years' time the area looked different because of severe drought. Yes, when we first came here the rain was falling and the river was flowing. Now the river hasn't flowed for two years. Our things that we brought with us when we first came here died when we got to this place. The cattle are dead, the goats are dead. And because the rain fell only a little in the following years they died like that . . . And the people that remain will also die because of hunger and starvation. To think that our leaders said, 'It's a good land!' Do you see these houses? All of the people have moved out because of the drought.

> In front of this house it gets green when it rains; ǀkînin (*Tribulus* spp.) and grasses come out. But there is nothing like this now. Maybe they will come when it rains, but now there is no rain. Now I don't know if there are still seeds lying in the ground; if God graces us then maybe they will grow again.
>
> (Meda, 19 April 1999; ǁGaisoas, !Uǂgab River)

It is actually rather difficult to establish from existing rainfall records that a decline in rainfall has occurred (cf. Sullivan, 1998).[10] So what are we to make of prevalent perceptions of such a decline, and of its apparent effects on people's lives and livelihoods? I believe that narratives of deteriorating rainfall instead provide a powerful metaphor for portraying the impotence people feel in the face of a century of apartheid-rule, followed by an extremely uncertain policy environment during which quality of life has fallen in real terms for many of Namibia's citizens. Just as rainfall is something that is uncontrollable, so there are a number of social and political processes which appear intractable to many and which constrain options for self-determination. A sense of powerlessness in the face of current change is conveyed by ǀHairo who says:

When we grew up in the past the rain was falling. Now I think, 'what's going on?' The clouds come but they don't bring any water; I think to myself, 'what's happening, what's going on?' When !Nauriseb[11] was here the grass was like this and we would break pieces of *tsaurahain* (*Colophospermum mopane*), *≠âun* (*Grewia* spp. cf. *bicolor* and *flava*), *|homexarebe* (*Geigaria acaulis*), *|ânan* (*Commiphora virgata*), pack them together like a small circular hut and make a fire, and we would stand in the smoke from that fire; the adults that were there would then run to escape the smoke from that fire leaving only !Nauriseb when all the people had moved away, with the fire still making smoke. The old people tell us of these things which happened then at this place. Now none of these rituals are practised and I thought that maybe this is why the rain does not fall the same as before.

Maybe the heart of the people was at one then and is following different paths now, and maybe it is because of this divisiveness that the rain is not falling. Before, the people had the same aims and did the same things but maybe the rain doesn't fall now because of these differences of the heart. Before, the old people would do the same things, but now everyone has got their own heart, from the child up to the adult. It because of the many 'governments' who are trying to change things. When there was just one government things went well; now there are many and everyone wants to get up and have their say. There is no King, and the old government is now finished here in Sesfontein. . . . Even the white people would leave if the King said 'go away'. There used to be one king here and one pastor; a woman would sleep at her parents' house and would only go to her own house when she was married. Now there are so many governments and leaders, how can the rain fall in this chaos?

As an elderly woman |Hairo is clearly nostalgic for a time in the past when people's roles in society were relatively clear-cut and where the settlement's hierarchy was well established and well organised. Perceptions that modernisation processes and a lapse of customs are the ultimate causes of reduced rainfall have similarly been recorded for the Sahel (Cross and Barker, 1994). What |Hairo is also articulating, however, is a feeling of non-involvement – of non-representation in the current plethora – the 'chaos' – of new environment and development initiatives in the area. Although operating with a 'community-based' and 'participatory' rhetoric, many such initiatives rely on local committees which are not perceived as fairly elected and which are considered in many circumstances to proceed with little involvement of the wider 'community' in terms of either consultation or decision-making (Sullivan, in press b). Regarding ideas of coherence and historical continuity Landau (1993: 4) also argues that for inhabitants of Botswana's eastern Tsapang Hills 'rain *apparently fell* only on communities of mutual support'. Rain and fertility are similarly linked to community coherence and stability by Feierman (1990 in Landau, 1993: 10) in his analysis of peasant discourse in Shambaa, Tanzania.

Perceptions of deterioration are in many cases inseparable from feelings of powerlessness in relation to exerting control over the use of land and its resources. As Meda describes:

When the rain fell strongly that time [i.e. 1994–95] then really too many people moved here to ||Gaisoas. Herero people with many cattle, goats and donkeys. With lots of those things they came to this land and when the rain falls and the grass came out they damaged the grass. This makes the land very bad. It empties because the grass didn't grow up and pour out its seeds. But now if the people did not move here in those years when the rain falls then maybe something will remain. Too many people move in even though the rain is half of what it was. In some areas the tufts of perennial grasses are no longer there, but maybe when it rains they will come out again.

Similarly, Willem, a farm labourer for a largely absentee herder at Malansrust Farm[12] states:

> The trees here are better than when I first came but the grass is not here. Because the fences are broken the livestock of other people move in and trample the grass . . . the other day I took more than twenty cattle back to Blaauport Farm but then they moved in again. At night time there are cattle everywhere. This camp here cannot afford to take all the livestock of this area; they finish the grass and trample the ground, and when the rain falls the seeds don't come out, and those that do are blown away by the wind. As we are talking the livestock of the other farms are behind that mountain and they will move in here . . . everyday they move in. And they don't ask; the livestock themselves move in because there are no fences. And if you mend the fences the elephants come and break them down!

In these passages, livestock are quite clearly linked to ideas of land degradation. However, such descriptions only seem to arise in contexts of contested claims to land and grazing, normally associated with instances of recent immigration of herds into an area where others consider themselves to have relatively long-term claims to the land. Namibia's post-independence constitution provides for all Namibians to move to wherever they wish on communal land with the *proviso* that they 'take account of the rights and customs of the local communities living there' (Republic of Namibia, 1991: 28–9). The problem is that there is no institutional basis for monitoring the effects of such movements or for protecting the rights of existing residents. In situations where options for movement are greatest among the wealthy (Rohde, 1993; Sullivan 1996a), and where ethnicity as a major axis of difference tends to conspire against certain groups (cf. Botelle and Rohde, 1995; Twyman, 1999; Taylor, 1999), this otherwise liberal context can be deeply disempowering. Expressing concern over the impacts of livestock on available grazing resources is one way of vocalising anger and frustration at the inequalities supporting such immigration. This is particularly so when some families know themselves to have been blatantly impoverished by the policies of previous years, and who perceive the current situation to be one whereby other Namibians are better able to exploit resources now unavailable to them. A case in point is that of Meda quoted above: her family was evicted in the 1950s from her home area of !Aollaexas (Aukeigas) when it was gazetted as Daan Viljoen Game Park for the use of Windhoek's white inhabitants; their subsequent movement to the marginal environment of the western reaches of the Ugab (!U≠gab) River caused large losses of their primary source of wealth and subsistence, i.e. livestock; and their applications to the new government to have their ancestral lands restored to them have been all but ignored. On top of all this, since 1994 she and other inhabitants of the western Ugab River have had to cope with an influx of elephant to the area.

To sum up, people articulate a view of vegetation changes as driven primarily by extreme rainfall events in a way which resonates strongly with recent non-equilibrium theories of ecological dynamics in drylands. While perceptions of deterioration – in rainfall and productivity – exist in local environmental knowledges, these appear inseparable from expressions of dissatisfaction with wider socio-political processes. As such, statements affirming deterioration are inextricably linked with descriptions of situations which individuals see as being exclusionary and undermining. Instead of being a simple biophysical process, ideas of 'land degradation' thus cogently describe people's concerns over broader land policy, their anxieties over their lack of power to determine how land is used, and their frustrations over long-standing land claims.

1.3 Discussion

People in the 'actual' dryland environments of the south are not passively subject to either the forces of their biophysical environment, or the political power infusing consensual views of environment and development. In contrast, and not surprisingly, people actively manage what are socially and culturally constructed landscapes, as opposed to wild environments of unmediated forces, and access internationally funded environment and development programmes in local and national contexts in opportunistic ways. These actions notwithstanding, however, and as Fairhead and Leach state (1996: 292), the intersection of global environmental discourses with local contexts seems to foster distinct relations of disadvantage whereby resource users are constructed as 'incapable resource stewards' thus 'instilling the imperative to intervene and improve the situation on their behalf'. Today such intervention is justified by the colonising languages of 'sustainable development' and 'degradation', both of which constitute what Escobar (1996: 56) refers to as a 'semiotic conquest of social life by expert discourses and economistic conceptions'.

So, if we have reached some academic consensus that the environmental narratives constructed during a period of modernist colonial expansion, and extended in today's climate of globalising soundbites, are politically driven and conceptually flawed, then what next for 'political ecology'? Turning back to my introduction I would iterate that two routes consistent with a political ecology stance are to consider political engagement ourselves with the issues with which we work, and to embrace a more communicative stance with regard to breaking down disciplinary boundaries, particularly those characterising the natural or realist-social or constructivist divide.

1.3.1 Putting the politics into political ecology

At a conference not long ago I struck up conversation with a scholar of Namibian forestry and historical land tenure issues. On asking him why his potentially emancipatory work was largely unavailable in Namibia – a question prompted by several queries while recently in the country – I was somewhat taken aback by the response that 'Well, it won't do me any favours [to publish in Namibia]'. As academics building a career on the back of deconstructing consensual environmental narratives and emphasising their correlative marginalising effects, I would suggest that our positions become untenable if we do not make the effort to release our work and perspectives into the arenas from which they came, and to which they are (hopefully) relevant. As many of us already do, this means, for example, complementing our academic record by publishing in local academic journals, collaborating with local people and institutions, working with other media such as radio and, perhaps, 'doing consultancy' as a means of 'infiltrating' national and international policy fora. One of the challenges we face in these endeavours, of course, is persuading academic research assessment of the validity of these activities.

A second challenge, however, comes, one might say, from within: from a certain academic posturing which maintains something of a self-reinforcing bubble of cynicism regarding either our ability to engage meaningfully with 'actual actors' in 'actual environments', or our justification in perhaps constructing new environmental orthodoxies to replace the old. Regarding the former, I would maintain that we are subjectively positioned (i.e. actors ourselves) within the global–local interlinkages (i.e. actual environments) we write about and which are infused with myriad environmental knowledges. In other words, we do not have the luxury of locating ourselves outside these contexts because we are already part of them: as Hobart (1996: 20) states regarding anthropological fieldwork in Bali, '[b]efore I had spent a night in the village I was a political issue'. Thus, instead of being naïve to think that our fieldwork and our writings can contribute to debate in a transformative sense, we are perhaps naïve to think otherwise; to think that by being part of a 'northern' academic tradition our research is thereby, or should be, apolitical and divorced from either local contexts or global policy-oriented discourse.

Regarding the latter: if knowledge is now socially constructed, historically located and politically coloured then we could see this as an opportunity to contribute to the construction of knowledges which we feel, as individuals and as academics, are defendable. When we talk about 'received wisdoms' of the environment and their alienating effects, and following Gordon (1998), we are implicitly acknowledging situations whereby it is not simply that 'knowledge is power' (i.e. Foucault; Giddens), but rather that it is power which defines what knowledge is. By extension, it is at least partially the continuing ignorance and occlusion of alternative knowledges – of local environmental and other narratives – which allow the globalising institutions of the north to uphold the hegemonic and normalising discourses they do. As academics, and as emphasised above, we are in a unique position to penetrate these discourses in multiple contexts and at different levels. Perhaps this is a hopelessly optimistic suggestion; but to me it seems infinitely preferable to an ethically nihilistic doctrine of non-engagement posited by the 'philosophies of despair' (Dunbar, 1995: 5) of extreme post-modern relativism.

1.3.2 A role for ecology in political ecology?

Contextualising the production of environmental dogma so that its political implications are clarified is one route to explaining the institutionalisation of degradation 'truths'. A second route points to the now oft-asserted recognition that the so-called 'objective' understandings of environmental and socio-economic phenomena arrived at by 'science' are themselves constrained by historically located cultural ideals peculiar to all aspects of Western Enlightenment thought. In particular, degradation discourses are inseparable from a wider inappropriate application of a language of 'boundary-conventions' constructed to describe closed thermodynamic systems (Shapin and Schaffer, 1985: 342 in Latour, 1993: 16) to the analysis of complex, open systems including living organisms, the abiotic and biotic interactions of ecosystems, and the economic and political 'systems' of people (Jantsch, 1980; Biot *et al.*, 1992; Behnke *et al.*, 1993; Sullivan, 1996b, under revision; Stott, 1997, 1998). The perhaps inevitable outcome has been the construction of an ideology of equilibrium and predictability in which environments are readily conceptualised as degraded because neither they, nor the peoples inhabiting, utilising and constructing them, are seen as dynamic and changing at all scales and in all directions. Within this framework, logical questions and concern focus on optimisation and adaptation, rather than on innovation and diversification; on maintaining stability or equilibrium through constraining activities seen as the source of disturbance; on uni-directional, linear conceptions of (normally negative) change; and on collapse to the most probable, least-ordered state.

Focusing on these flaws in the historical evolution of science, however, does not in itself justify a throwing out of the scientific baby with the poststructuralist bath-water. Not only does this undermine the possibilities for communication latent in the observational empiricism shared by people throughout the world, but this position becomes untenable if it is understood that the ecological or integrative biophysical sciences, or at least elements of them, have themselves moved radically beyond a solely reductionist analytics of living complexes within an unflexive framework of equilibrium thinking.

At risk of drawing imprecise and unjustifiable analogies across disciplinary divides (Sokal and Bricmont, 1998), therefore, I would argue that shifts in realist biophysical sciences, particularly the construction of a 'new' integrative science of complex systems (Jantsch, 1980; Prigogine, 1989; Kauffman, 1993, 1995; Holling, 1998), have a rich potential to interact with a relativist rejection of normative structures (on this see in particular Cilliers, 1998). Moreover, this interchange of concepts and language can constitute part of a more unifying metalanguage, as advocated by Stott (1998: 1), drawing 'key signifiers' (Eco, 1984) from an embracing of non-equilibrial and contingent dynamics. Key to this thinking is a conceptual and formal commitment to resolve the contradictions inherent in accepting that patterns in biological, ecological, social or economic 'aggregates' are both emergent or 'ordered' *and* continually evolving; influenced by historical contingency and often unpredictable from analyses of the local behaviours of individual components.

Perhaps in contrast to a relativist sociology of science, I suggest, therefore, that there might be much room for conceptual exchange between a biophysical science which embraces both form (i.e. structure) and change (i.e. innovation) in living complexes, and an actor-oriented applied social science grappling with conflicts between local dynamics and national or global structures. In furthering political ecology researches of hegemonic environmental discourses, and in better representing currently obstructed environmental knowledges, I believe the fostering of such communication is critical. Africa's drylands are proving a compelling context for this debate. They are variable within time-scales of immediate importance for crucial livelihood decisions. Moreover, this variability is unpredictable. These environments and the lifestyles they support present deep conceptual challenges to a northern Enlightenment worldview founded on notions of predictability, linearity, efficiency and equilibrium. Over the past 15 years these challenges have been grappled with in anthropological researches which emphasise the coherence of seemingly haphazard mobility and herd management strategies among Africans engaging in pastoralism and pastoro-foraging (cf. Sandford, 1983; Coughenour *et al.*, 1985; Homewood and Rodgers, 1987, 1991). These views are now consolidated in what is becoming a paradigmatic 'new ecology' of non-equilibrium focusing on arid and semi-arid environments (cf. Wiens, 1984; Ellis and Swift, 1988; Behnke *et al.*, 1993), which emphasises the significance of abiotically driven variability and draws heavily on anthropological understandings of nomadic and transhumantic pastoralism. Given the profound policy implications of 'new' debate, and the incisive parallels to be found between the critical realism of biophysical research, the actor-oriented approaches of a rather more constructivist social anthropology, and local narratives, it would seem that there is much justification for engaging with, rather than constructing barriers to, a range of analytics.

Acknowledgements

In Namibia, Suro Ganuses from Sesfontein and Phil Hutchinson were my companions and fieldwork would have been impossible without them. Thanks also go to the Damara farmers with whom I talked about landscape, herding and rainfall. Fieldwork funding from the Nuffield Foundation, the Economic and Social Research Centre, and the Desert Research Foundation of Namibia is gratefully acknowledged. The paper has been written with support from a British Academy Post-doctoral Research Fellowship.

Notes

1 See debate regarding the validity of equilibrium and non-equilibrium concepts to arid and semi-arid rangelands in Illius and O'Connor (1999) and Sullivan and Rohde (submitted).
2 E.g. discussion at a workshop on 'constructivism and realism in environment and development' held at the London School of Economics, 14 December 1998, and at a conference on 'African environments – past and present' at Oxford University, 5–8 July 1999.
3 This section draws heavily on ideas expressed as part of a much longer paper which assesses ecological and ethnographic data in relation to narratives of environmental and social collapse in southern Kunene Region, north-west Namibia, within the context of historical and political factors affecting land distribution and current land policy initiatives (Sullivan, under revision).
4 An early name describing the region known today as north-west Namibia and south-west Angola.
5 See, for example, Sandford (1983), Wiens (1984), Coughenour *et al.* (1985, 1990), Caughley *et al.* (1987), Homewood and Rodgers (1987), Ellis and Swift (1988), Warren and Agnew (1988), Westoby *et al.* (1989), Abel and Blaikie (1990), Boonzaier *et al.* (1990), Biot *et al.* (1992), Behnke (1993), Behnke *et al.* (1993), Ellis *et al.* (1993), Dahlberg (1994), Milton and Hoffman (1994), Norbury *et al.* (1994), Thomas and Middleton (1994), Dean *et al.* (1995), Scoones (1995), Sullivan (1996b), Jacobson (1997), and Jacobson and Jacobson (1998).
6 This extends to current uncontextualised interpretations of early ethnographic texts. For example, the classification of Damara-speaking Namibians as 'culturally hunter-gatherers' who have only acquired livestock in very recent times is now considered extremely problematic; see references in Sullivan (in press b), and the 'Kalahari debate' in relation to ahistorical views of Bushman peoples, cf. Wilmsen, 1989). Nevertheless it has been reasserted unproblematically in recent DRFN texts in statements that '[t]he Damara people, who were hunter-gatherers, followed the example of Hereros and became cattle and goat farmers' (Kambatuku *et al.*, 1995: 2).
7 According to which, the impoverishment of regional herding economies over the last few centuries due to mercantile and imperial expansion (Lau, 1987), the devastating effects of rinderpest in 1897 (Bley, 1996) and the persecution of Namibians under German colonial rule and a later apartheid administration (Bley, 1996; Hayes *et al.*, 1998) might never have happened.
8 An Internet search on 'desertification' on 21 July 1999 produced 5047 'hits', providing some indication of the extent of concern regarding this environmental issue.
9 For example, among conservationists it is hoped that a byproduct of increasing the pathways whereby local 'communities' can benefit from revenues generated by wildlife tourism will be a reduction in herd sizes and a corresponding lowering of the risk of environmental degradation (cf. Ashley *et al.*, 1994; Ashley and Garland, 1994; Jones, 1995; Ashley, 1997), while the project manager of a current Ministry of Agriculture, Water and Rural Development Project of the Sesfontein–Khowarib basin, southern Kunene Region, in 1996 maintained that if desertification was to be avoided in the basin then all livestock should be removed from the area.
10 This is indicated, for example, by a lack of correlation between rainfall from one year to the next. In analysis of rainfall data for four stations in north-west Namibia only the data from !Uis had a significant, but relatively weak, serial correlation ($r = -0.52$, $p = 0.03$, N = 18). Data for Fransfontein, Khorixas and Sesfontein were not correlated (r = -0.08, p = 0.58, N = 56; r = -0.09, p = 0.60 N = 37; and r -0.08, p = 0.70, N = 24, respectively) and appeared randomly distributed when plotted graphically.
11 The first Damara leader of Sesfontein/!Nanilaus.
12 The former 'homeland' of Damaraland, the northern portion of which now falls in Kunene Region, consists in part of a number of former commercial farms which were used by settler farmers and then redistributed to communal farmers when the 'homeland' was created in the 1970s. Since then these surveyed and fenced farms have been owned by the state and used as communal land.

References

Abel, N.O.J. and Blaikie, P.M. 1990: Land degradation, stocking rates and conservation policies in the communal rangelands of Botswana and Zimbabwe. *Pastoral Development Network Paper* **29a**. London: Overseas Development Institute.

Allen, T.F.H. and Starr, T.B. 1982: *Hierarchy: perspectives for ecological complexity*. Chicago: Chicago University Press.

Apollus, A., Kathena, J. and Tjiveze, H. 1997: Land degradation in Otjimbingwe and the surrounding commercial farms: an ecological and sociological investigation. In D. Ward (ed.), *Land degradation in the pro-Namib*. Windhoek: Report of the Summer Desertification Project (DRFN) 1996 funded by United States Agency for International Development and Swedish International Development Agency.

Ashley, C. 1997: Wildlife Integration for Livelihood Diversification (WILD) project plan. Draft document.

Ashley, C., Barnes, J. and Healy, T. 1994: Profits, equity, growth and sustainability: the potential role of wildlife enterprises in Caprivi and other communal areas of Namibia. *Research Discussion Paper* **2**. Windhoek: Directorate of Environmental Affairs, Ministry of Environment and Tourism.

Ashley, C. and Garland, E. 1994: Promoting community-based tourism development: why, what and how? *Research Discussion Paper* **4**. Windhoek: Directorate of Environmental Affairs, Ministry of Environment and Tourism.

Atkinson, A. 1991: *Principles of political ecology*. London: Belhaven Press.

Barrow, E. 1990: Usufruct rights to trees: the role of Ekwar in dryland central Turkana, Kenya. *Human Ecology* **18**(2), 163–76.

Batterbury, S.P.J. and Bebbington, A.J. 1999: Environmental histories, access to resources and landscape change: an introduction. *Land Degradation and Development* **10**, 279–88.

Behnke, R. 1993: Natural resource management in pastoral Africa. Paper presented to the UNEP workshop on listening to the people: social aspects of dryland management, December 1993, Nairobi.

Behnke, R.H., Scoones, I. and Kerven, C. (eds) 1993: *Range ecology at disequilibrium: new models of natural variability and pastoral adaptation in African savannas*. London: Overseas Development Institute, International Institute for Environment and Development, Commonwealth Secretariat.

Biot, Y., Lambert, R. and Perkin, S. 1992: What's the problem? An essay on land degradation, science and development in Sub-Saharan Africa. *Discussion Paper* DP 222. Norwich: School of Development Studies, University of East Anglia.

Bley, H. 1996: *Namibia under German rule*. Hamburg: Lit Verlag.

Boonzaier, E.A., Hoffman, M.T., Archer, F.M. and Smith, A.B. 1990: Communal land use and the 'tragedy of the commons': some problems and development perspectives with specific reference to the semi-arid regions of Southern Africa. *Journal of the Grassland Society of Southern Africa* **7**(2), 77–80.

Botelle, A. and Rohde, R. 1995: *Those who live on the land: a socio-economic baseline survey for land use planning in the communal areas of Eastern Otjozondjupa*. Windhoek: Land Use Planning Series Report 1, Ministry of Lands, Resettlement and Rehabilitation.

Brokensha, D. and Riley, B.W. 1986: Changes in uses of plants in Mbeere, Kenya. *Journal of Arid Environments* **11**, 75–80.

Brown, C.J. (ed.) 1992: *Namibia's Green Plan (Environment and Development)*. Windhoek: Ministry of Environment and Tourism.

Caughley, G., Shepherd, N. and Short, J. (eds) 1987: *Kangaroos: their ecology and management in the sheep rangelands of Australia*. Cambridge: Cambridge University Press.

Cilliers, P. 1998: *Complexity and postmodernism: understanding complex systems*. London: Routledge.

Coughenour, M.B., Coppock, D.L. and Ellis, J.E. 1990: Herbaceous forage variability in an arid pastoral region of Kenya: importance of topographic and rainfall gradients. *Journal of Arid Environments* **19**, 147–59.

Coughenour, M.B., Ellis, J.E., Swift, D.M., Coppock, D.L., Galvin, K., McCabe, J.T. and Hart, T.C. 1985: Energy extraction and use in a nomadic pastoral ecosystem. *Science* **230**, 619–24.

Cox, J.R. 1984: Temperature, timing of precipitation and soil texture effects on germination, emergence and seedling survival of South African lovegrasses. *Journal of South African Botany* **50**: 159–70.

Cross, N. and Barker, R. 1994: *At the desert's edge: oral histories from the Sahel.* London: Panos and SOS Sahel.

Dahlberg, A. 1994: Contesting views and changing paradigms: the land degradation debate in Southern Africa. *Discussion Paper 6*, Uppsala: Nordiska Afrikainstitutet.

Davies, S. 1992: Green conditionality and food security: winners and losers from the greening of aid. *Journal of International Development* **4**(2), 151–65.

Dean, W.R.J., Hoffman, M.T., Meadows, M.E. and Milton, S.J. 1995: Desertification in the semi-arid Karoo, South Africa: review and reassessment. *Journal of Arid Environments* **30**, 247–64.

Dewdney, R. 1996: *Policy factors and desertification: analysis and proposals.* Windhoek: Report for Namibian Programme to Combat Desertification.

Dunbar, R. 1995: *The trouble with science.* London: Faber and Faber.

Eco, U. 1984: *Semiotics and the philosophy of language.* London: The Macmillan Press Ltd.

Ellis, J.E., Coughenour, M.B. and Swift, D.M. 1993: Climate variability, ecosystem stability, and the implications for range and livestock development. In R.H. Behnke, I. Scoones and C. Kerven (eds), *Range ecology at disequilibrium: new models of natural variability and pastoral adaptation in African savannas.* London: Overseas Development Institute, International Institute of Environment and Development, Commonwealth Secretariat, 31–41.

Ellis, J.E. and Swift, D.M. 1988: Stability of African pastoral ecosystems: alternative paradigms and implications for development. *Journal of Range Management* **41**, 450–9.

Erkkilä, A. and Siiskonen, M. 1992: *Forestry in Namibia.* Finland: University of Joensuu.

Escobar, A. 1996: Constructing nature: elements for a poststructural political ecology. In Peet, R. and Watts, M. (eds), *Liberation ecologies: environment, development, social movements.* London: Routledge, 46–68.

Fairhead, J. and Leach, M. 1996: *Misreading the African landscape: society and ecology in a Forest-Savanna mosaic.* Cambridge and New York: Cambridge University Press.

Feierman, S. 1990: *Peasant intellectuals: anthropology and history in Tanzania.* Madison: University of Wisconsin Press.

Fox, W. 1990: *Toward a transpersonal ecology: developing new foundations for environmentalism.* Boston and London: Shambhala.

Fuller, B.B. 1993: Institutional appropriation and social change among agropastoralists in central Namibia 1916–1988. Unpublished PhD dissertation, Boston Graduate School.

Giorgis, D.W. 1995: Drought and sustainable development. In Moorsom, R., Franz, J. and Mupotola, M. (eds), *Coping with aridity: drought impacts and preparedness in Namibia.* Frankfurt: Brandes and Apsel Verlag/NEPRU, 227–43.

Frost, P., Medina, E., Menaut, J.C., Solbrig, O., Swift, M. and Walker, B. 1986: Response of savannas to stress and disturbance. *Biological International* (Special Issue) **10**.

Gordon, R.J. 1998: Vagrancy, law and 'shadow knowledge': internal pacification 1915–1939. In Hayes, P., Silvester, J., Wallace, M. and Hartmann, W. (eds), *Namibia under South Africa rule: mobility and containment 1915–1946.* London, Windhoek, Athens: James Currey, Out of Africa, Ohio University Press, 51–76.

Government of the Republic of Namibia 1997: *National land policy.* Windhoek: Government of the Republic of Namibia.

Günster, A. 1994: Variability in life history parameters of four serotinous plants in the Namib Desert. *Vegetatio* **114**, 149–60.

Günster, A. 1995: Grass cover distribution in the central Namib: a rapid method to assess regional and local rainfall patterns of arid regions? *Journal of Arid Environments* **29**, 107–14.

Hadley, N.F. and Szarek, S.R. 1981: Productivity of desert ecosystems. *Bioscience* **31**(10), 747–53.

Hahn, C.H. 1928: Damaraland and the Berg Damaras. *Cape Monthly Magazine*, 218–30, 289–97.

Hayes, P., Silvester, J., Wallace, M. and Hartmann, W. (eds) 1998: *Namibia under South Africa rule: mobility and containment 1915–1946*. London, Windhoek, Athens: James Currey, Out of Africa, Ohio University Press.

Hobart, M. 1996: Ethnography as a practice, or the unimportance of penguins. *Europæa* **II**(1), 3–36.

Hoffman, M.T., Barr, G.D. and Cowling, R.M. 1990: Vegetation dynamics in the semi-arid eastern Karoo, South Africa: the effect of seasonal rainfall and competition on grass and shrub basal cover. *South African Journal of Science* **86**: 462–63.

Holling, C.S. 1998: Two cultures of ecology. *Conservation Ecology* **2**(2), online http://www.consecol.org/vol2/iss2/art4

Homewood, K.M. and Brockington, D. 1999: Biodiversity, conservation and development in Mkomazi, Tanzania. *Global Ecology and Biogeography Letters*.

Homewood, K.M. and Rodgers, W.A. 1987: Pastoralism, conservation and the overgrazing controversy. In Anderson, D. and Grove R. (eds), *Conservation in Africa: people, policies and practice*. Cambridge: Cambridge University Press, 111–28.

Homewood, K.M. and Rodgers, W.A. 1991: *Maasailand ecology: pastoralist development and wildlife conservation in Ngorongoro, Tanzania*. Cambridge: Cambridge University Press.

Illius, A. and O'Connor, T. 1999: 'On the relevance of nonequilibrium concepts to arid and semi-arid grazing systems. *Ecological Applications* **9**(3), 798–813.

Infoscience 1994: *Report on sustainable development in the Sesfontein/Khowarib Basin*. Windhoek: Infoscience.

Jacobson, K.M. 1997: Moisture and substrate stability determine VA-mycorrhizal fungal community distribution and structure in an arid grassland. *Journal of Arid Environments* **35**, 59–75.

Jacobson, K.M. and Jacobson, P.J. 1998: Rainfall regulates the decomposition of buried cellulose in the Namib Desert. *Journal of Arid Enviornments* **38**, 571–83.

Jacobson, P.J. and Jacobson, K. 1995: Personal communication.

Jacobson, P.J., Jacobson, K.M. and Seely, M.K. 1995: *Ephemeral rivers and their catchments: sustaining people and development in western Namibia*. Windhoek: Desert Research Foundation of Namibia, Windhoek and Swedish International Development Agency.

Jantsch, E. 1980: *The self-organising universe: scientific and human implications of the emerging paradigm of evolution*. Oxford: Pergamon Press.

Jensen, A.M. 1990: *Rural development project Owamboland, Namibia: environmental component*. Geneva: LWF.

Jobst, P. 1995: Botanical composition and productivity under different grazing pressures in northwestern Namibia. Occasional Paper 2, 19–38. *Summer desertification project December 1994–January 1995*. Windhoek, Namibia: DRFN.

Jones, B.T.B. 1995: *Wildlife management, utilization and tourism in communal areas: benefits to communities an improved resource management*. Research Discussion Paper 5. Windhoek: Directorate of Environmental Affairs, Ministry of Environmental and Tourism.

Kajujaha-Matundu, O. 1996: *Subsistence farmers' perception of environmental problems and monetary estimates of agricultural and non-agricultural resources in the Okakarara area*. Occasional Paper 5. Windhoek: Desert Research Foundation of Namibia.

Kambatuku, J.R. 1995: The effect of rangeland management on soil productivity: using plant germination and growth rates as a measure of soil productivity. Occasional Paper 2, 39–54. *Summer desertification project December 1994–January 1995*. Windhoek, Namibia: DRFN.

Kambatuku, J.R., Uariua-Kakujaha, K. and Abrams, M.M. 1995: The study in perspective: general introduction. Occasional Paper 2, 2–5. *Summer desertification project December 1994–January 1995*. Windhoek, Namibia: DRFN.

Kamwi. J.A. 1997: *Overview of environmental issues in former 'Damaraland'*. Occasional Paper 7. Windhoek: Desert Research Foundation of Namibia.

Kauffman, S. 1993: *The origins of order: self-organization and selection in evolution*. Oxford: Oxford University Press.

Kauffman, S. 1995: *At home in the universe: the search for the laws of self-organization and complexity*. London: Penguin Books Ltd.

Kinahan, Jill 1990: The impenetrable shield: HMS Nautilis and the Namib Coast in the late 18th century. *Cimbebasia* **12**, 23–61.

Kinahan, John 1993: The rise and fall of nomadic pastoralism in the central Namib Desert. In Shaw T., Sinclair, P., Andali B. and Okpoko A. (eds), *The archaeology of Africa*. London: Routledge, 372–85.

Kisco, M., Simataa, L. and Munukayumbwa, S. 1997: Bush encroachment in the Pro-Namib. In Ward D. (ed.), *Land degradation in the pro-Namib*. Windhoek: Report of the Summer Desertification Project (DRFN) 1996 funded by USAID and SIDA.

Kroll, T. and Kruger, A.S. 1998: Closing the gap: bringing communal farmers and service institutions together for livestock and rangeland development. *Journal of Arid Environments* **39**, 315–23.

Landau, P.S. 1993: When rain falls: rainmaking and community in a Tswana village, c. 1870 to recent times. *The International Journal of African Historical Studies* **26**(1), 1–30.

Latour, B. 1987: *Science in action*. Milton Keynes: Open University Press.

Latour, B. 1993: *We have never been modern*, trans. by Catherine Porter. Hemel Hempstead: Harvester Wheatsheaf.

Lau, B. 1979: A critique of the historical sources and historiography relating to the 'Damaras' in pre-colonial Namibia. Unpublished BA (Hons) dissertation, Dept. of History, University of Cape Town.

Lau, B. 1987: *Southern and central Namibia in Jonker Afrikaner's time*. Windhoek: Windhoek Archives Publication Series 8, National Archives.

Leach, M. and Fairhead, J. 1998: Fashioned forest pasts and the occlusion of history: landscape, conservation and politics in the historiography of West Africa. Paper presented to the Berkeley Workshop on Environmental Politics, Colloquium series on 'Culture, Power, Political Economy', 1998–1999, Institute of International Studies, University of California.

Leach, M. and Mearns, R. 1996: Environmental change and policy: challenging received wisdom in Africa. In Leach, M. and Mearns, R. (eds), *The lie of the land: challenging received wisdom on the African environment*. London, Oxford and Portsmouth: The International African Institute, James Currey and Heinemann, 1–33.

Le Houérou, H.N. 1984: Rain use efficiency: a unifying concept in arid-land ecology. *Journal of Arid Environments* **7**: 213–47.

Loxton, R.F., Hunting and Associates 1974: The natural resources of Damaraland. Pretoria. Unpublished report undertaken for the Department of Bantu Administration and Development.

Loxton, Venn and Associates 1983: Development strategy for Owamboland, Ontwikkelingstrategie vir Owambo. Unpublished consultancy report, Windhoek.

Ludwig, J.A. and Whitford, W.G. 1981: Short-term water and energy flow in arid ecosystems. In Goodall, D.W. and Perreira, R.A. (eds), *Arid land ecosystems*, Vol. 2. Cambridge: Cambridge, University Press, 271–99.

Malan, J.S. and Owen-Smith, G.L. 1974: The ethnobotany of Kaokoland. *Cimbebasia* (B) **2**(5), 131–78.

Marais, E. 1999: Entomologist, National Museum of Namibia, Windhoek.

Marsh, A. 1994: *Trees: threatened lifelines of northern Namibia, the people's perspective*. Windhoek: Gamsberg Macmillan.

Marsh, A. and Seely, M. (eds) 1992: *Oshanas: sustaining people, environment and development in Central Owambo, Namibia*. Windhoek: Desert Research Foundation of Namibia, Windhoek and Swedish International Development Agency.

Menges, W. 1992: What is it worth to keep farming alive in Damaraland? *Tempo Newspaper*. 20 September, Windhoek.

Milton, S.J. and Hoffman, M.T. 1994: The application of state and transition models to rangeland research and management in arid succulent and semi-arid grassy Karoo, South Africa. *African Journal of Range and Forage Science* **11**(1), 18–26.

Mouton, D.P. 1995: Soil characteristics under different grazing regimes in northwestern Namibia.

Occasional Paper 2, 6–18. *Summer desertification project December 1994–January 1995.* Windhoek, Namibia: DRFN.

Mouton, D., Mufeti, T. and Kisting, H. 1997: A preliminary assessment of the land cover and biomass variations in the Huab. In Ward, D. (ed.), *Land degradation in the pro-Namib.* Windhoek: Report of the Summer Desertification Project (DRFN) 1996 funded by United States Agency for International Development and Swedish International Development Agency.

Mubita, O. 1995: Drought effects on forests and woodlands. In Moorsom, R. Franz, J. and Mupotola M. (eds), *Coping with aridity: drought impacts and preparedness in Namibia.* Frankfurt: Brandes and Apsel Verlag/NEPRU, 63–77.

Munukayumbwa, S., Simataa, L. and Kisco, M. 1997: Overgrazing near waterpoints in the Pro-Namib. In Ward, D. (ed.), *Land degradation in the pro-Namib.* Windhoek: Report of the Summer Desertification Project (DRFN) 1996 funded by United States Agency for International Development and Swedish International Development Agency.

Murdoch, J. and Clark, J. 1994: *Sustainable knowledge.* Centre for Rural Economy Working Paper Series **9**. London: Department of Geography University College, London.

Næraa, T., Devereux, S., Frayne, B. and Harnett, P. 1993: *Coping with drought in Namibia: informal social security systems in Caprivi and Erongo, 1992.* NISER Research Report 12. Windhoek: Namibian Institute for Social and Economic Research, Multidisciplinary Research Centre, University of Namibia.

Nghitila, T.M. 1995: Selected soil flora and fauna as indicators of biotic integrity in northwestern Namibia rangelands. Occasional Paper 2, 55–61. *Summer desertification project December 1994–January 1995.* Windhoek, Namibia: DRFN.

NISER 1992: *Namibian household food security report.* Windhoek: University of Namibia.

Norbury, G.L., Norbury, D.C. and Oliver, A.J. 1994: Facultative behaviour in unpredictable environments: mobility of red kangaroos in arid Western Australia. *Journal of Animal Ecology* **63**, 410–18.

Noy-Meir, I. 1973: Desert ecosystems: environment and producers. *Annual Review of Ecological Systematics* **4**: 25–51.

Oba, G. 1992: *Ecological factors in land use conflicts, land administration and food insecurity in Turkana, Kenya.* Pastoral Development Network Paper **33a**. London: Overseas Development Institute.

O'Connor, T.G. and Roux, P.W. 1995: Vegetation changes (1949–1971) in a semi-arid, grassy dwarf shrubland in the Karoo, South Africa: influence of rainfall variability and grazing by sheep. *Journal of Applied Ecology* **32**: 612–26.

Peet, R. and Watts, M. 1996: Liberation ecology: development, sustainability, and environment in an age of market triumphalism. In Peet, R. and Watts, M. (eds), *Liberation ecologies: environment, development, social movements.* London: Routledge, 1–45.

Perkins, J.J. and Thomas, D.S.G. 1993: Spreading deserts or spatially confined environmental impacts? Land degradation and cattle ranching in the Kalahari desert of Botswana. *Land Degradation and Rehabilitation* **4**, 179–94.

Prigogine, I. 1989: The philosophy of instability. *Futures* August, 396–400.

Quan, J., Barton, D. and Conroy, C. 1994: *A preliminary assessment of the economic impact of desertification in Namibia.* Research Discussion Paper **3**. Windhoek: Directorate of Environmental Affairs, Ministry of Environment and Tourism.

Republic of Namibia 1991: *The Nambian Constitution.* Windhoek: Government of the Republic of Namibia.

Rethman, N.F.G., Beukes, B.H. and Malherbe, C.E. 1971: Influence on a north-eastern sandy highveld sward of winter utilization by sheep. *Proceedings of the Grassland Society of Southern Africa* **6**: 55–62.

Richards, P. 1985: *Indigenous agricultural revolution: ecology and food production in West Africa.* London: Unwin Hyman.

Richards, P. 1995: Farmer knowledge and plant genetic resource management. In Engels, J.N.N. (ed.),

In situ conservation and sustainable use of plant genetic resources for food and agriculture in developing countries: report of a DSE/ATSAF/IPGRI workshop 2–4 May 1995, Bonn Röttgen, Germany. Rome and Feldafing: IPGRI and DES, 52–8.

Roe, E. 1995: Except-Africa: postscript to a special section on development narratives. *World Development* **23**(6), 1065–70.

Rohde, R.F. 1993: *Afternoons in Damaralands: Common land and common sense in one of Namibia's former 'Homelands'*. Occasional Paper 41. Edinburgh University: Centre of African Studies.

Rohde, R.F. 1997a: Looking into the past: interpretations of vegetation change in Western Namibia based on matched photography. *Dinteria* **25**, 121–49.

Rohde, R.F. 1997b: Nature, cattle thieves and various other midnight robbers: images of people, place and landscape in Damaraland, Namibia. Unpublished PhD thesis, University of Edinburgh.

Rutherford, M.C. 1980: Annual plant production–precipitation relations in arid and semi-arid regions. *South African Journal of Science* **76**: 53–6.

Sandford, S. 1983: *Management of pastoral development in the third world*. Chichester: John Wiley and Sons.

Scoones, I. 1995: *Living with uncertainty: new directions in pastoral development in Africa*. London: International Institute of Environment and Development.

Scoones, I. 1996: Range management science and policy: politics, polemics and pasture in southern Africa. In Leach, M. and Mearns, R. (eds), *The lie of the land: challenging received wisdom on the African environment*. London, Oxford and Portsmouth: The International African Institute, James Currey and Heinemann, 34–53.

Scoones, I. 1997: The dynamics of soil fertility change: historical perspectives on environmental transformation from Zimbabwe. *The Geographical Journal* **163**(2), 161–9.

Seely, M.K. 1978: The Namib dune desert: an unusual ecosystem. *Journal of Arid Environments* **1**: 117–28.

Seely, M.K. 1998: Can science and community action connect to combat desertification? *Journal of Arid Environments* **39**, 267–77.

Seely, M.K., Hines, C. and Marsh, A.C. 1995: Effects of human activities on the Namibian environment as a factor in drought susceptibility. In Moorsom, R., Franz, J. and Mupotola, M. *Coping with aridity: drought impacts and preparedness in Namibia*. Frankfurt: Brandes and Apsel Verlag/NEPRU, 51–61.

Seely, M.K. and Jacobson, K.M. 1994: Guest Editorial. Desertification and Namibia: a perspective. *Journal of African Zoology* **108**, 21–36.

Seely, M.K. and Louw, G.N. 1980: First approximation of the effects of rainfall on the ecology and energetics of a Namib dune ecosystem. *Journal of Arid Environments* **3**: 25–54.

Shapin, S. and Schaffer, S. 1985: *Leviathan and the air-pump: Hobbes, Boyle and the experimental life*. Princeton, NJ: Princeton, University Press.

Sokal, A. and Bricmont, J. 1998: *Intellectual impostures*. London: Profile.

Solbrig, O. 1991: Savanna modelling for global change. *Biological International* Special Issue **24**, 1–47.

Soroses, A., Lubbock, A., Nangolo, V. and Enjala, L. 1994: Social and gender issues in agricultural and livestock production systems: a case study, Onepandaulo village, Uukwangula ward, Oshana Region, Northern communal areas, Namibia. Unpublished draft report for FAO (Project TCP/NAM/4451), Windhoek.

Stott, P. 1997: Dynamic tropical forestry in an unstable world. *Commonwealth Forestry Review* **76**(3), 207–9.

Stott, P. 1998: Biogeography and ecology in crisis: the urgent need for a new metalanguage. *Journal of Biogeography* **25**, 1–2.

Sullivan, S. 1996a: *The 'communalization' of former commercial farmland: perspectives from Damaraland and implications for land reform*. SSD Research Report **25**. Windhoek: Social Sciences Division, Multi-Disciplinary Research Centre, University of Namibia.

Sullivan, S. 1996b: Towards a non-equilibrium ecology: perspectives from an arid land. *Journal of Biogeography* **23**, 1–5.

Sullivan, S. 1998: People, plants and practice in drylands: socio-political and ecological dimensions of resource-use by Damara farmers in north-west Namibia. Unpublished PhD thesis, Dept. Anthropology, University College London.

Sullivan, S. 1999a: Folk and formal, local and national: Damara knowledge and community-based conservation in southern Kunene, Namibia. *Cimbebasia* **15**, 1–28.

Sullivan, S. 1999b. The impacts of people and livestock on topographically diverse open wood- and shrub-lands in arid north-west Namibia. *Global Ecology and Biogeography Letters, Special Issue on degradation of open woodlands* **8**: 257–77.

Sullivan, S. in press a: Perfume and pastoralism: Damara women as users and managers of natural resources in arid north-west Namibia. In Hodgson, D. *Rethinking pastoralism: gender, culture and the myth of the patriarchal pastoralist.*

Sullivan, S. in press b: How sustainable is the communalising discourse of 'new' conservation? The masking of difference, inequality and aspiration in the fledgling 'conservancies' of north-west Namibia. In Chatty, D. (ed.) *Displacement, forced settlement and conservation.* Oxford: Berghan Press.

Sullivan, S. and Ganuses, W.S. in preparation: Faces of Damaraland: life and landscape in a former Namibian 'homeland' (working title). *Cimbebasia* Memoir Series.

Sullivan, S. and Konstant, T.L. 1997: Human impacts on woody vegetation, and multivariate analysis: a case study based on data from Khowarib settlement, Kunene Region. *Dinteria* **25**, 87–120.

Sullivan, S. and Rohde, R.F. submitted: A response to Illius and O'Connor: on non-equilibrium in arid and semi-arid grazing systems.

Sullivan, S. under revision: Nothing is stationary, all is change: collapse or complexity in an African dryland. *Africa.*

Taylor, M. 1999: 'You cannot put a tie on a buffalo and say that is development': differing priorities in community conservation, Botswana. Paper presented at conference on 'African environments – past and present', St. Anthony's College, University of Oxford, 5–8 July 1999.

TGLP Project 1997: *Full report of research activities and results.* Sheffield: Tribal Grazing Lands Project, Sheffield Centre for International Drylands Research, final report to the Economic and Social Research Council.

Thomas, D.S.G. and Middleton, N.J. 1994: *Desertification: exploding the myth.* Chichester: John Wiley and Sons Ltd.

Thompson, M., Warburton, M. and Hatley, T. 1986: *Uncertainty on a Himalayan scale.* London: Milton for Ethnographia Press.

Twyman, C. 1999: Livelihood opportunity and diversity in Kalahari Wildlife Management Areas, Botswana: rethinking community resource management. Paper presented at conference on 'African environments – past and present', St. Anthony's College, University of Oxford, 5–8 July 1999.

Tyson, P.D. 1986: *Climatic change and variability in southern Africa.* Cape Town: Oxford University Press.

UNCOD 1977: Round-up, plan of action and resolutions. Paper presented, UN Conference on desertification, Nairobi, 29 August – 9 September. New York: United Nations.

United Democratic Front 1991: Documentation prepared and presented by the UDF to the National Land Conference on Land Reform and the Land Question, Windhoek.

Van Rooyen, N., Bredenkamp, G.J., Theron, G.K., Bothma, J. du P. and Le Riche, E.A.N. 1994: Vegetational gradients around artificial watering points in the Kalahari Gemsbok National Park. *Journal of Arid Environments* **26**: 349–61.

Van Warmelo, N.J. 1962: Notes on the Kaokoveld (South West Africa and its people). *Ethnological Publications* **26**. Pretoria: Dept. of Bantu Administration.

Walter, H. 1939: Grassland, Savanne und Busch der arideren Teile Afrikas in ihrer ökologischen Bedingtheit. *Jb. Wiss. Bot.* **87**: 750–60.

Ward, D. (ed.) 1997: *Land degradation in the pro-Namib.* Report of the Summer Desertification Project (DRFN) 1996 funded by USAID and SIDA. Windhoek: DRFN.

Ward, D., Ngairorue, B.T., Kathena, J., Samuels, R. and Ofran, Y. 1998: Land degradation is not a necessary outcome of communal pastoralism in arid lands. *Journal of Arid Environments* **40**, 357–71.

Warren, A. and Agnew, C. 1988: *An assessment of desertification and land degradation in arid and semi-arid areas*. Drylands Paper 2. London: Drylands Programme, International Institute for Environment and Development, London.

Westoby, M., Walker, B. and Noy-Meir, I. 1989: Opportunistic management for rangelands not at equilibrium. *Journal of Range Management* **42**, 266–74.

Wiens, J. 1984: On understanding a nonequilibrium world: myth and reality in community patterns and processes. In Strong, D.R., Simberloff, D., Abele, L.G. and Thistle, A.B. (eds), *Ecological communities: conceptual issues and the evidence*. Princeton, N.J: Princeton University Press, 439–57.

Wilmsen, E.N. 1989: *Land filled with flies: a political economy of the Kalahari*. Chicago: Chicago University Press.

Wolters, S. (ed.) 1994: *Proceedings of Namibia's national workshop to combat desertification*. Windhoek: Desert Research Foundation of Namibia.

2

Environmental myths and narratives

Case studies from Zimbabwe

Deborah Potts

2.1 Introduction

The construction of environmental knowledge is influenced by people's experiences and by their perceived vested interests, and as such is never far from the realm of politics. In a country like Zimbabwe with a long history of white minority settler government followed by a period in which contestation over the means of production (capital, land and labour) has become increasingly heated, the impact of vested interests on environmental discourses is perhaps thrown into particularly sharp relief. This is not to argue that vested political interests are less important in the construction of environmental knowledge elsewhere in Africa or Asia. But in Zimbabwe the identification of some of the interests involved is perhaps easier because race still plays such an important part. Race remains a major determinant of the nature of vested interests because of the entrenched legacy of a state system which gave advantageous access to the means of production to white settlers, and strongly disadvantaged black people. Obviously this is overlaid by other factors such as class, regionalism, ethnicity, education and gender and there is now a degree of blurring between race and class which was not possible under the white minority government.[1] In terms of the main theme of this volume it is discourses about land and natural resources which are under scrutiny. It is worth pointing out, however, that for Zimbabwe one could also analyse the construction of knowledges about the use and distribution of capital or the nature of the labour force and employment issues: these are equally contested.[2]

Zimbabwe is fortunate in having a very rich and diverse literature on environmental and land issues. The aim of this chapter is to draw upon this literature to present an overview of a range of environmental and land-use issues which lend themselves to analysis within the framework of political ecology. In some cases such analysis was already explicit in the original research; in others it was implicit or touched upon; in yet others it was studiously ignored.

The chapter begins with a discussion of the vigorously contested versions of Zimbabwe's land reform programme. It then examines the controversies surrounding irrigated smallholder agriculture on dambos – small wetlands which contain the majority of irrigated land in Zimbabwe. This is followed by an analysis of the nature of soil erosion estimates in

Zimbabwe. Finally there is a brief discussion of a range of other environmental issues for which the results of detailed empirical field research by geographers and others have challenged common assumptions.

2.2 Land reform: constructing failure from victory

The details of Zimbabwe's land reform programme have been described elsewhere (see for example Alexander, 1993; Kinsey, 1982; Palmer, 1990; Zinyama, 1982; Moyo, 1995). Only the bare outlines will be covered here, in order to provide the context for the analysis which follows.

At independence in 1980 Zimbabwe was faced with extreme inequality in land holdings. Excluding areas like national parks, the land was divided roughly half and half between some 800,000 peasant families and some 4,800 white-owned commercial farms (most of them in family ownership). In addition to this extremely inequitable situation the majority of the 'best' agricultural land in agro-ecological terms[3] was allocated as 'white' land. This point is of key significance for the deconstruction of arguments regarding agricultural productivity by sector in Zimbabwe: although it is generally recognised that there was racial inequity in terms of the suitability of land for rainfed agriculture, the overwhelming significance of this factor for explaining the commercial successes of the large-scale white-owned sector in arable farming is not always fully appreciated. Simply put, the majority of marketed arable produce from white-owned land comes from a small proportion of that land: according to Cliffe (1988), about a quarter of the large-scale commercial farms produce most of their output. In 1993, 35 per cent of the land in this sector was located in Zimbabwe's Natural Regions I and II, which are by far the most suited to rainfed arable production, and this land produced 96 per cent of the sector's output of tobacco, 86 per cent of its maize, 76 per cent of its cotton and 92 per cent of its soyabean.[4]

Land was one of the key issues over which the war for independence was fought and inevitably land reform was one of the major planks of government policy after 1980. The nature of the programme was strictly constrained by the conditions of the pre-independence agreement brokered by the British which, *inter alia*, protected private property rights. Broadly speaking, this meant that only land offered for sale at market rates was available[5] – alternative options used elsewhere in the world to finance land reform programmes were forbidden. In addition, the government's realistic expectations of very significant international aid to finance the programme were soon dashed. The UK was (and is) the main donor for land purchases but the Zimbabweans have to match this dollar for dollar. Due to surveying and infrastructural costs the total cost of resettlement land is usually about double the purchase price, which is further held up down the process. The pace of land reform in the 1980s was much slower than the government had hoped for, mainly for these reasons. Critiques of Zimbabwe's land reform make much of the fact that in 1982 the government stated that it aimed to resettle 162,000 households in five years and that it failed to achieve this target. This, however, in many ways is a red herring since it was only the middle one of three revised targets mooted by the government from 1980–85. The final target of 15,000 households per year from 1985–90 was more realistic – this also was not achieved but the gap between plan and reality was much less in this case.

There were four different models discussed for resettlement. Model A was by far the closest to the agricultural systems operating in the communal areas with small family farms. Model B involved producer co-operatives with collective farming. Model C involved master farmers growing cash crops as outgrowers to state farms. Model D (now called the 3-tier model) has seen many modifications but is essentially aimed at those areas where, due to agro-ecological conditions, shortage of grazing land rather than arable land is a constraint on agricultural livelihoods (see Kinsey, 1999; Zinyama, 1982). The vast majority of settlers opted for Model A whereby they were settled in villages with land allocated to individual households – similar to the situation in the communal areas (CAs) whence many settlers had come. In the resettlement areas (RAs), however, the land is under leasehold from the government and there are regulations about the nature of agricultural and livestock production. In the CAs tenure is communal with fewer regulations over its productive use.

By mid-1989 52,000 families (416,000 people) had been resettled. At this point it was generally agreed that the programme was stalled: a much-cited paper by Palmer (1990) mapped out the main parameters of the situation but the key factor was politics – the political elite was losing interest in the issue as more and more of them became land-owners and/or bourgeois themselves (see also Dashwood, 1996). As the 1990s wore on, however, it became clear that the rural electorate could not be so easily dismissed and from 1997 it once again became an extremely live (from an external perspective perhaps *the* most live) national issue. As President Mugabe made wild rhetorical threats[6] about expropriating white land without compensation, the evaluation of the programme by potential donors and other interested parties became increasingly significant.

Nearly all actors involved in Zimbabwe's land reform programme by the end of the 1990s were agreed that land reform was necessary, including the Commercial Farmers Union (CFU) which represents the large-scale farmers who stand to lose. The political necessity of resettlement for future political stability had become self-evident. However, there were and are major disagreements about the success of the resettlement which had occurred. One high-profile anecdote may suffice to illustrate this point: at a major conference on South African rural livelihoods in 1997,[7] Derek Hanekom, the South African Minister for Land Affairs, rubbished the Zimbabwean land reform programme, denouncing it as a failure. Hanekom remained dismissive when it was pointed out that a British Overseas Development Agency (ODA)[8] report in the 1980s had found it to be one of the most successful planned developments in Africa, bringing considerable benefits to the majority of resettled families and yielding an impressive economic return estimated at 21 per cent (Cusworth and Walker, 1988). This was despite support for these figures by Baroness Linda Chalker who was in the audience and who had been in charge of the ODA at the time the report was commissioned.

What was behind Hanekom's reaction? At the time the negative media impact of Mugabe's expropriation threats, which have gravely undermined the programme in terms of 'donor appeal', had not begun. Yet, as I have argued elsewhere, for much of its lifetime the resettlement programme in Zimbabwe has had a 'bad press'. This is partly due to the effectiveness of the various lobbies which had vested interests in retaining the pre-independence pattern of inequality in land holdings. They have been successful in supporting and disseminating various negative myths and narratives about land reform, some of which focus on 'the use, misuse and abuse of environmental and/or agricultural productivity data to criticise the programme' (Potts and Mutambirwa, 1997: 549). Not only have these lobbies been vociferous, they have also been operating in a favourable ideological climate with the ascendancy of market forces as the favoured principle for allocating national and global resources.[9] It is possibly this factor above all which had persuaded Hanekom that Zimbabwe's land reform must be a failure, for there land is given free to the peasant beneficiaries and their tenure is not freehold. South Africa's land reform programme, on the other hand, has been crucially informed and influenced by the World Bank (Williams, 1996). Although the Bank is now wholly convinced of the efficiency of smallholders who are the target of South Africa's programme, it has succeeded in persuading the South African programme to give cash grants to 'enable' households to purchase *freehold* land, rather than the state itself entering the market. It seems, therefore, that Hanekom 'knew' that Zimbabwe's programme must be a failure because its parameters were wrong – it was not market- and private property-oriented. Empirical outcomes were therefore irrelevant.[10]

A significant element of the anti-land reform narratives was the argument that Zimbabwe's agricultural output for domestic and export markets depended on the commercial farming sector. There are also strong linkages between industry (the country's leading sector in 1980) and agriculture, so it was argued that any damage to the latter sector would undermine the entire economy. Not only the CFU, but critics from the agricultural research sector and 'objective' academics voiced these concerns. The arguments rested on the fact that the CAs produced hardly any of the country's commercial agricultural produce at independence and the *assumption* that Zimbabwean peasant smallholders were inherently incapable of significant commercial production – thus converting commercial farms to peasant smallholdings was tantamount to converting them to subsistence production. This narrative was tremendously influential in the 1980s (and is still common today). Paradoxically one of the key academics who published research which was widely used to support it (Kinsey, 1983) has now produced the most telling data supporting exactly the opposite conclusion (Kinsey, 1999). Kinsey was demonised by many in the pro-land reform camp in the 1980s but in fact his key paper did not argue against land reform on the grounds that it *would* impact negatively on national agricultural production. Instead he argued that *if* certain production assumptions were correct (as it turned out, most were not), then land reform *might* have that effect and this needed to be thought about. Evidently there is an objective difference of emphasis here, yet so powerful is the need to construct environmental narratives in support of particular policy trajectories that both sides seized on this paper and proceeded to misuse it for their own ends.

Before returning to Kinsey's more recent publications and their impact on the land reform narrative, let us return to the ODA report mentioned above. The key question is *why* this research which, despite caveats, came to very positive conclusions about the productivity of the programme (see Cusworth and Walker, 1988; see also Palmer, 1990) thereby undermining the gloomy prognostications of the CFU lobby, has had so little impact on evaluations of land reform. This is particularly interesting given that it was commissioned by the major donor and thus it might have been anticipated that the results would be celebrated as a development success story, thereby increasing the international credibility of ODA! Arguably it was because it supported a development narrative which was counter to the one which the British government of the time expected and desired (Margaret Thatcher – the then British Prime Minister – was a staunch supporter of Zimbabwe's (and South Africa's) white minority). Had the report found that settlers had been impoverished by land reform, were unable to farm their land productively and contribute to the market and that Zimbabwe's agricultural and industrial economy had been damaged by the process, it seems likely that it would have been announced in Parliament, released to the press and swiftly acted upon in public denouncement of the land reform process. Since it came to the opposite conclusions it was quietly shelved; and the British government continued to take every opportunity to support the CFU line that nothing must be done to damage the (large-scale) commercial farmers of Zimbabwe.

Since the early 1980s Kinsey has been running a panel study of about four hundred households resettled at the start of the Zimbabwean programme. In 1997 he included a set of counterpart households drawn from a number of CA villages which had provided the largest number of these settler households. The comparisons between the agricultural incomes and living standards of the two sets of households were illuminating: on average, settler households produced over four and a half times the crop output of CA households and 6.8 times the value of marketed crops. They also had roughly double the value of livestock holdings and earned 3.4 times as much from livestock sales. Settler households were larger[11] than those in the CAs, but only by 39 per cent on average – thus their per capita incomes were still much higher. They had more land to farm, which was of course one of the main purposes of resettlement, and planted 51 per cent more land but their crop sale earnings per hectare planted were also 3.3 times as high. Furthermore, on every output index the distribution between households in the RAs was always more equal than it was in the CAs. Finally, real incomes per household have, at least doubled[12] since they were originally resettled, have become more evenly distributed, and their domestic and agricultural assets, measured by an index, have increased by 52 per cent (Kinsey, 1999).

There are other surveys which show that resettled households also *feel* that their lives have improved (see Berry, 1991; Elliott, 1995; Jacobs, 1991). Positive perceptions of the programme and its impact on settlers' livelihoods also dominated in a survey of recent migrants to Harare (Potts and Mutambirwa, 1997). In that study many respondents demanded that land reform be speeded up, because, as one of them put it, 'people scratching on barren land are still waiting for resettlement'.

Even the numbers now resettled can no longer be dismissed as an irrelevance: Kinsey (1999), citing an official government report, states that over 71,000 families had been resettled by late 1996, and a further 20,000 had been given access to additional grazing lands.[13] Given average household size figures from Kinsey's panel, this translates into something like 775,000 people in RAs plus a further 133,000[14] assisted by the grazing schemes which form part of the programme, i.e. benefiting a total of 908,000 people. The Zimbabwe Farmers Union's (ZFU) data from the Central Statistical Office are even more impressive. They report 871,000 people involved in farming in the RAs in 1994 (including 9,500 employees) (ZFU, 1998) which, when added to the grazing scheme totals, suggests that over a million people had by then been directly involved in the government's land reform programme. By comparison there were 5.3 million people in the communal areas in 1992 (Central Statistical Office, 1994).

The empirical evidence then is that Zimbabwe's land reform programme has in many ways been highly successful. The evidence of improving RA agricultural productivity should not, objectively, be a surprise since the rapid expansion of the Zimbabwean peasantry's marketed output (including in the CAs), once independence allowed an enabling framework to be established, has been widely heralded as an 'agricultural revolution' (Eicher and Rukuni, 1994; Zinyama, 1988, 1992; Bratton, 1986, 1987; Thomson, 1988), and resettlement has given RA farmers access to more land than those in the CAs. Unsurprisingly however, given that this is the case with every development initiative, there have been problems. These include corrupt allocation of land to political elites; tensions over the selection criteria for settlers; tenurial insecurity on the schemes; and evidence that the improved living standards in RAs for unknown reasons have not translated into better nutrition for small children (Kinsey, 1999).

Critics of the programme are prone to suggest that the settlers are also causing environmental degradation. Yet again, however, the published evidence is thin and, as will be demonstrated later in this chapter tends not to support this viewpoint. As I have argued elsewhere (Potts and Mutambirwa, 1997), settlers are often criticised for cutting down a lot of the trees in the RAs, but the critics rarely note, perhaps deliberately, that because they are often settled on land that was previously under-utilised and perhaps largely used for grazing, they *have* to cut down trees to make their fields. The underutilisation of significant amounts of previously white-owned land is, of course, one of the major arguments used effectively by the pro-land reform lobby (e.g. see Cliffe, 1988; Weiner *et al.*, 1985). It is inevitable that intensifying the land-use in such cases, especially a dramatic shift from grazing to cultivation, will bring about profound environmental changes and almost certainly speed up soil erosion. However, immediately to term such change 'environmental degradation' without thorough investigation of productivity trends and physical parameters suggests either ignorance[15] or an underlying agenda to denigrate resettlement. The increased productivity of the RAs indicated by Kinsey's work implies that there has been no downward trend in the ability of the areas he studied to produce for agriculture. In other words, the environment has not 'degraded' in terms of its productivity, although it may have changed dramatically.

2.3 The political ecology of dambo cultivation in Zimbabwe

Dambos (*bane* in Shona) are small-scale wetland areas which play a vital role in smallholder agriculture and livelihood security in many CAs in Zimbabwe. They are seasonally waterlogged depressions, usually treeless, which are found at or near the head of a drainage network. Strictly speaking, government legislation, dating back to colonial times, prohibits cultivation on *all* potentially cultivable dambo land. In fact, there is a great deal of variation in the way legal restrictions on dambo cultivation are interpreted and enforced between different CAs (Bell and Hotchkiss, 1991); there is also much variation in senior and field-level officials' attitudes towards the issue (see Bell *et al.*, 1987). Some are convinced that growing crops on dambos will cause irreversible environmental degradation, as argued by the original legislation. The types of degradation alleged to occur were a lowering of the water table and a reduction in dry season streamflow; an increase in soil erosion by both gullying and sheetflow; an increase in siltation in water courses, dams and reservoirs downstream; and 'burning up' of organic matter in sandy dambos, rendering the soil infertile and like building sand (ibid.: 5).

There are 1.28 million hectares of dambos in Zimbabwe, of which only 0.26 million hectares are in the CAs (Whitlow, 1984, cited in Bell *et al.*, 1987: 3). It was estimated in 1987 that some 15,000–20,000 hectares of dambo land were cultivated in the CAs – entirely farmer-initiated. During the dry season this land is irrigated from shallow ground wells and the contribution of such agriculture to national agricultural production is very important (if not always officially recognised), particularly within the smallholder sector. State-supported irrigation in the CAs covers only 7,000 hectares (Owen *et al.*, 1995: vii) but large-scale irrigation in commercial farming areas covers around 150,000 hectares and is of key significance in that sector's output and success.

Historical research has found that dambo cultivation was probably the main arable agriculture practised by the Shona people in the nineteenth century (Wilson, 1986, 1990) and in the early twentieth century Sawer (1909; cited in Mharapara, 1995: p. 3) suggested that rice grown on dambos had been the traditional staple. The use of dambos for crops remains tremendously significant where dambo gardens are still operating, even if in a restricted fashion, for:

> they provide an invaluable source of land for cultivation . . . as well as water for irrigation, livestock and domestic use . . . dambo cultivation is successfully integrated with dryland

farming . . . The additional choice available to the communal farmer who has access to a garden is one of its key advantages . . . there are more options . . . for providing the family with an adequate and varied diet and an increased income. Gardens provide a hedge against starvation in drought years and a surplus for sale in good years. Development costs are minimal, yet higher incomes can be earned from dambo gardens than from conventional irrigation schemes.

(Bell *et al.*, 1987: 141)

Given this situation it is easy to see what a fundamental attack the legislation disallowing cultivation on dambos was on indigenous farming systems, but the policy makers were curiously silent about this. The gardens in the dambos can be tremendously productive and are an important source of marketed vegetables throughout the country (Smith, 1989; Bell and Hotchkiss, 1991). Indeed, some senior officials admit that their education was largely sponsored by dambo vegetable sales (usually by their mother) and some dambo farmers could lay claim to membership of the much prized 'Ten Tonne Club' comprising the few *commercial* farmers who have achieved maize yields of ten tonnes per hectare in any one year – even though such yields on the dambos may have been achieved on small plots of under a hectare (Lambert, personal communication, 1999). Irrigated production from shallow ground wells provides a welcome, if not vital, addition to livelihoods during the dry season when otherwise nothing else can be grown.

The political ecology of the prohibition on dambos is evident from research in the archives. Wilson (1986) discovered that the driving force was almost certainly not *ecological* concerns at all, but the *economic* concerns of white, commercial farmers. For in the 1930s and 1940s these farmers were facing increasing competition in domestic wheat markets from grain grown by the peasantry on the dambos. The archival evidence cited by Wilson shows desperate attempts by various white officials to discover who was behind this entrepreneurial activity by African farmers – that it was their own idea based on logical economic rationale was evidently inconceivable to most colonial officials at the time although this was what had happened. The evidence is also clear that the Natural Resources Board was desperate to find a rationale for stopping the cultivation of wheat and actively pursued the question of whether it was environmentally destructive, but although there were people willing to *assert* that this was the case, no evidence was forthcoming. The best argument they could come up with was that wheat competed with winter grazing – which, fairly obviously, was an insufficient explanation for the tremendously restrictive legislation which was to follow. Tellingly, one Native Commissioner reported that 'extensive growing of wheat on vlei land . . . is the worst thing we have got to deal with' and that '[t]here was an instruction from *the Prime Minister* that the growing of wheat was *not to be encouraged (by the natives)*' (Native Resources Board, 1942, cited in Wilson, 1986: 4, emphasis added). While the Native Commissioner went on to note that the Prime Minister had *not* said that wheat cultivation on the dambos by Africans was to be discouraged, the message was fairly clear. Given that there was also official resistance to a blatant ban on wheat cultivation on African-controlled dambos, the need for an 'excuse' was apparent. Thus when the Streambank Protection Regulation was enacted in 1952, there are good reasons for arguing that the inclusion in this legislation of a prohibition on dambo cultivation was direct use of an environmental argument to 'justify' a policy really aimed at undermining agricultural competition. Furthermore, it was the practices of white farmers which had been particularly damaging to the dambos for they had ploughed up extensive areas (peasant gardens tend to cover only a minority of the dambo), which seems to have caused desiccation, and in many cases their attempts to drain the wetter dambos apparently had accelerated gully erosion (McFarlane, 1995; Beinart, 1984).

However, the narrative does not end there. Evidence of the underlying motivation for the restriction on dambo cultivation emerged at the same time as a major donor-funded project (the Dambo Project), investigating the economic and environmental implications of dambo use (including grazing), was under way. This found that the environmental fears listed above were greatly exaggerated and that the area under dambo gardens could be increased four-fold to 80,000 hectares with minimal impact on downstream flows or soil erosion and fertility (Roberts and Lambert, 1990). The exaggerated fears about dambos derived in part from a basic misunderstanding of the geomorphology and hydrology of the dambos themselves, which had been characterised as 'sponges' gradually releasing water to downstream river systems. This, in fact, is not a very useful model; the 'reality' is far more complicated. In particular, the impact of evapotranspiration rates on dambo gardens on downstream flow seems to have been over-estimated (Faulkner and Lambert, 1991).

Other research has also shown that the regulations concerning dambo gardens are unwarranted. Hydrological analysis by Bullock (1992a) has shown that the idea that dambos (uncropped) can *maintain* dry season stream flows in Zimbabwe is incorrect; nor do any of the studies undertaken elsewhere in the region support this idea (Bullock, 1992b). Research on one of the most visible elements of 'degradation' on dambos – gullies – has found that erosion at the head of gullies *on dambos* is caused mainly by base flow rather than surface flow due to various peculiarities in their geology (i.e. activities on the surface of the dambo, including cultivation and grazing, have little effect) (McFarlane, 1995). Indeed McFarlane suggests that recharging of the interfluves due to replacement of upland woodlands by maize fields, a direct result of official land use planning in colonial Rhodesia, may be one cause of dambo gullying. If this is the case, then government intervention in peasant cropping patterns may have proved to be disastrous in almost every respect.

This latter point about the inappropriateness of government land-use policies in both *ecological and productivity* terms is well illustrated by a recent policy recommendation made by a local researcher, Grant (1995), who has a long history of interest in dambo use in Zimbabwe. The colonial government encouraged or coerced African farmers to alter their settlement patterns, shift their cultivated fields (on which they were very often mainly growing maize) away from drainage lines and onto the watersheds, therefore cutting down the trees there and, as already discussed, prohibited the traditional cultivation of dambo gardens for staple foods. Dambos, however, could be used for grazing – the importance of their role in dry season grazing has already been alluded to (see also Scoones, 1990). Yet after field trials of cultivating and fertilising dambo gardens, including trials *within communal areas*[16] rather than on research stations, Grant (1995: 126) argues that:

> The results indicate that in communal areas summer crops of maize on the dambos could provide the families' requirements of grain with a saleable surplus on a smaller area of land than is needed on the drought prone uplands. This would free marginal upland areas for grazing in summer. Since drought is not the limiting factor in most seasons [on dambos], there is little risk in increasing the fertility inputs, and the dambo lands can be economically cropped without depleting the soils and causing deterioration through destruction of organic matter. In resettlement schemes, dambos which have only been used for grazing could be a most valuable asset for the small-scale farmer.

Grant also reports that the dambos' cropping potential results from the availability of water rather than nutrients, and that maize yields of 7 t/ha could be readily obtained. While Grant herself does not draw any conclusions about the challenge such results present to many decades of past policies, it is evident that the essence of the above quotation is to call for a complete reversion to the land-use patterns which indigenous farmers had previously practised, before the colonial state intervened. It would be hard to find a better example of the need to 'listen' to indigenous knowledge and to consider that 'traditional' practices may well have a useful rationale!

The Dambo Project made clear recommendations that the regulations on dambo gardens should be lifted to allow an increase in the irrigated, cropped area to 80,000 hectares, thereby approximating half the area under large-scale 'commercial' irrigation. This would certainly have a major impact on the volume, value and nature of arable production from the CAs and further transform the relative shares of agricultural production from the communal and commercial sectors. Ecological considerations were not dismissed and there were also recommendations about the nature and pattern of irrigation which should be practised (which would have ruled out whole-scale draining and deep ploughing which had caused the problems on the commercial farms decades before). It placed great emphasis on the social and economic security dambo gardens afforded farmers largely because of their irrigability – a benefit of great significance in an unpredictably varying, i.e. disequilibrial, dryland environment. Earlier research by Theisen (1976, cited in Scoones, 1991: 79) had also established the welfare significance of dambos which were found to be positively correlated with child nutrition, child mortality and educational levels, even arguing that without the dambos: 'first the cattle will die, then the children'. Yet despite concerted efforts[17] to encourage the government to translate the recommendations into institutional practice, so far this has not occurred.

It is impossible to be definitive about why, despite all the evidence discussed, the legislation affecting cropping on dambos has not been amended. Indeed, given the government's determined efforts in resettlement areas to encourage more intensive, commercial agriculture by smallholders it seems somewhat paradoxical that an opportunity perhaps to transform production in those CAs with a high density of dambos has not been seized upon. Sheer inertia probably has much to do with it – changing legislation requires time, commitment and drive and those with the potential power to bring about change are frequently over-burdened. Probably another factor is the continued resistance of some (but by no means all) in the agricultural and ecological research community in Zimbabwe to the idea that dambos can be used safely by communal farmers.[18] This is probably not surprising since old paradigms are notoriously hard to shift in both scientific and policy circles worldwide. In relation to changing actual legislation, it is probable that a doubtful 'scientific' voice in favour of the *status quo* has a very high multiplier effect on the policy inertia already mentioned. While there are also voices arguing *for* legislative change within Zimbabwe (as evidenced by some of the contributions to Owen *et al.*, 1995), I would suggest that changes in the legislation on dambos are only likely to occur and be widely implemented when the *internal* politics are 'right'. In this sense externally funded projects such as the Dambo Project have little part to play in the environmental policy field except inasmuch as they contribute to the knowledge on which local scientists and policy-makers can draw. Political factors play another part for, paradoxically, some peasant farmers have been observed to adhere to dambo restrictions in order to show their support for the post-colonial political order despite recognising that the restrictions are not warranted on environmental grounds (Wilson, 1988).

Another factor discouraging changes in the dambo legislation may be that many of the crops grown on the dambos, such as vegetables and fruit, are 'uncontrolled' in that they do not enter official marketing channels. The negative impact is twofold: there is relatively little government support for these crops (e.g. in research or marketing); and dambo gardeners find it difficult to obtain government-sponsored credit to support their dambo production (fencing is a particular issue) because the government cannot reclaim the debt, as it does with 'official' produce, when it buys the crop. The effect is that dambo production (and productivity) is much more hidden from official eyes than 'dryland' produce. Whether the liberalisation of agricultural trading in Zimbabwe in the 1990s will have an effect on these aspects remains to be seen.

2.4 Soil erosion in Zimbabwe

Do peasants' agricultural practices in Zimbabwe's communal and resettlement areas accelerate soil erosion? The answer is, of course they do – and so do the farming practices of large-scale commercial farmers and dambo gardeners and just about everybody else who disturbs the soil's surface and covering vegetation in order to produce agricultural products useful to the human community. The argument that is sometimes put up against land reform in Zimbabwe (and elsewhere in southern Africa), that peasant farming will create soil erosion, is thus virtually tautological; even the argument that it will cause more erosion than the previous land use is probably largely true, simply because the peasants' use of land is likely to be more intensive and, as already explained, they are so far frequently settled on previously *underutilised* land: the point made by Grant (1995) about dambo use in resettlement schemes is indicative of this, for example. The important question is whether the 'extra' soil erosion matters – is it causing such deterioration in the soil's structure, depth and nutrients that irreversible degradation will eventually occur and productivity be seriously curtailed? This is much more difficult to answer both at the technical level and also because soil fertility management is dynamic over time and often adapts to curtail or manage such negative changes in the soil (see for example, Scoones, 1997).

In Zimbabwe reports of soil erosion occurring at average rates of 50 tonnes per hectare, or more, are common (ibid.). Even President Mugabe has publicly cited such figures in relation to the need to curtail population growth in the 1980s.[19] Yet these figures give a completely false impression of the soil erosion problem in Zimbabwe, since they are derived by falling into all the 'technical' traps of multiplying up from soil erosion plot figures to the larger scale which have recently been so succinctly detailed by Stocking (1996). These technical traps need not detain us here. Of significance instead is the willingness to use and 'believe' such 'data' in Zimbabwe and the causes to which such erosion is attributed.

Biot, Lambert and Perkins (1992) have detailed a number of curious features about the soil erosion spectre in Zimbabwe. There has been a tendency to select the highest recorded erosion figures from tables recording research results, and for these to be used somewhat indiscriminately as though they were the norm for the country as a whole or were, at least, common. Paradoxically, Stocking himself played a part in this mythologising in the 1980s, claiming in a local publication that a field erosion rate of over *one hundred* t/ha/yr was *commonly* exceeded (Stocking, 1984). Yet this was derived from an unpublished research paper by a local soil scientist (Elwell, 1971, cited in Biot *et al.*, 1992: 18) which indicated that while this rate had occurred on one *bare* plot in one research station, a rate of 10.8 t/ha/yr had been measured at another station which was 'perhaps a more typical example of the soil and climatic conditions in the Communal Areas' (ibid. 1992: 18). Furthermore, figures derived from a plot kept artificially bare throughout the year will not translate to CA experience anyway, since fallow or cultivated plots will soon be covered with either weeds or crops which will reduce erosion. Stocking also used 'typical' rates of 75 and 50 t/ha/yr for CA grazing and agricultural land (compared to only 3 and 15 ha/t/yr on 'commercial' farms) from which to derive the financial costs of nutrient loss through soil erosion in an FAO report on Zimbabwe (Stocking, 1986, cited in Biot *et al.*, 1992: 16). The assumption that field soil-loss rates from erosion plots can be multiplied up as averages for the *whole* country (or that you can thereby derive a measure of nutrients *lost*) is a practice he would now criticise, arguing that it can lead to exaggeration of actual sediment loss by a factor of 100 or more (see Stocking, 1996: 150). Unfortunately, however, the damage in policy circles in Zimbabwe had already been done: such figures have been seized on by the commercial farmers' lobby and some ecologists and soil scientists (both official and unofficial) and translated into a tremendously successful element of the arguments against land reform. Thus, for example, the argument put in *The Farmer*, a publication directed at Zimbabwe's commercial farmers, in 1991:

> In no way can the problems of years of neglect and mismanagement in the existing communal lands be solved by sacrificing further large areas of prime agricultural land to a repetition of this historic process of destruction. It must be accepted that the plight and poverty of the communal lands are mainly self-inflicted and that they constitute a national disaster.
> (*The Farmer*, 1991: 23, cited in Biot *et al.*, 1992: 17)

Perhaps more influential in independent Zimbabwe than statements clearly coming from a vested interest was an important national soil erosion survey completed in the 1980s by Whitlow (1988a) which feeds directly into policy initiatives in Zimbabwe. On the very first page it is stated that the '*average*' erosion rates in the communal lands are the 50 and 75 t/ha/yr which, as already discussed, are completely erroneous; it is thus that such data creep into the policy consciousness. The survey itself was based on interpretation of aerial photographs from which a national map showing *the presence* of erosion was derived. The map indicates the *proportion* of land in any particular grid which was found to have erosion features, e.g. there was visible evidence of sheet erosion or gully erosion. In the report the areas where more than 16 per cent of the surface area displayed such signs were denoted as having 'very severe' erosion. There is considerable potential for confusion here since this can all too easily be translated into meaning high *rates* in terms of t/ha/yr, especially in the contexts of a survey which cites such high rates of erosion as the 'norm' in communal lands. Instead, the areas with 'very severe' erosion may not have been experiencing high average rates, despite the observation that soil movement was occurring over a large area. As Biot, Lambert and Perkins (op. cit.: 19) note 'no evidence is presented on the relationship between the occurrence of erosion as observed on aerial photgraphs and that experienced by farmers in terms of lost production for different soil conditions'. Similarly, dryland areas would anyway experience dramatic movement of topsoil in years with significant rainfall events, and this presumably would occur with or without 'disturbance' by farming. Yet this survey has undoubtedly played a key part in the view that land reform should be opposed on *environmental* (rather than just economic) grounds.

We need not labour the convenience for those with vested interests in obstructing land reform of interpreting this erosion study as indicating dramatic environmental degradation in the communal areas compared to the commercial farming areas. The author of the report went on to argue against land reform on just these grounds elsewhere, stating that:

> The erosion survey suggests that resettlement of peasant farmers on *expropriated* commercial farms is likely to promote degradation in areas hitherto little affected by erosion . . . it is likely

that these schemes will simply extend the *severe problems of degradation* currently restricted to Communal Lands.

(Whitlow and Campbell, 1989: 27, cited in Biot *et al.*, 1992: 17, emphasis added)

There are a number of points about the political ecology of this statement which can be made. First, no resettlement land had been expropriated for land reform at the time; it had been purchased on a willing seller–willing buyer basis at market rates. Second, severe degradation in terms of serious output loss to indigenous farmers over time was belied by the facts of the 1980s. During that decade communal farmers in the more favourable agro-ecological regions (i.e. essentially those with more reliable and higher rains) had hugely increased their marketed output, particularly of cotton and maize, and by 1989 dominated the market in those two products – their contribution at independence having been negligible (see Cliffe, 1988; Zinyama, 1988; Eicher and Rukuni, 1994). Furthermore, such data as are available on yields indicate an upward trend for the communal areas in the 1980s, with rainfall the critical factor. An average maize yield of around 695 kg/ha for the communal areas was in use by a number of analysts in the period just after independence (see Weiner, 1988: 67), but data for the latter part of the decade and early 1990s suggest an average yield of 1,370 kg/ha (ZFU, 1997; see also Biot *et al.*, 1992: 21; Elliott, 1995).[20] Commercial farming maize yields, on the other hand, had not increased at all over the period, staying at around 4,700 kg/ha (and using ten times the amount of fertiliser per hectare as the CAs). Whatever the reasons for the increase in the CAs in the 1980s, the 'fact' that more communal land than commercial land is experiencing 'severe degradation' due to soil erosion, as reported in the quotation above, is evidently debatable. This is especially so in the light of recent literature on meaningful definitions of environmental degradation (see for example, Scoones, 1996; Biot, 1991; Blaikie, 1985; Abel and Blaikie, 1990). Third, published research by Whitlow (1988b) has shown that the key variable correlating to soil erosion in the communal lands is *population density* and the role of the colonial legacy of land alienation in this is acknowledged. One possible logical implication of this would be to *reduce* that population density, or at the very least ameliorate the rate at which it increases. This is what the land reform programme in part aims to do – to try and alleviate some of the pressure on the communal lands – since it is accepted that the rate of population increase in the CAs is too high for a manageable programme to reduce the absolute CA population. Evidently the population density/soil erosion correlation suggests that the much lower densities in resettlement areas will *not* be translated into the soil erosion levels (whatever they are) of the CAs. Finally Whitlow (1980) has produced a very useful analysis of the disproportionate incidence of major physical constraints on successful agriculture in the CAs compared to the commercial farming areas, which shows that not only do about 80 per cent of these areas lie outside the officially recognized limits for dryland cropping in Zimbabwe but also that extensive areas are covered with granite outcrops. Arable agriculture in such circumstances is particularly risky and difficult and the potential for soil erosion is heightened. Again, the logical environmental (and economic) conclusion might be to move as many peasants as possible away from such areas to more favoured agro-ecological areas where they might be able to repeat the success of those who have contributed to the 'agricultural revolution'. Yet the conclusions drawn by the author of the influential national erosion report, who also produced the analyses just discussed, were the exact opposite.

There are other reasons to suspect that the soil erosion problem in the communal areas has been exaggerated. Lambert, using estimates of river sediment yields for Zimbabwe and the cited 'average' rates of erosion in the national soil erosion survey, shows that hardly any of this 'supposed' erosion can be ending up in the rivers (despite an acknowledged problem of siltation in many water courses and dams in the country) (cf. Biot *et al.*, 1992). Nor is there obvious deposition in the landscape to make up the balance – in which case, either much less erosion is occurring and/or most of the soil being moved is being spread to other areas which may well be benefiting from the import. This conclusion tallies with Stocking's recent analyses and interpretations of soil erosion in Africa (Stocking, 1996) and quite clearly puts a very different light on the soil erosion 'picture' in the CAs in Zimbabwe.

Detailed research by Elliott (1989) has also shown, in complete contrast to the usually accepted scenario, that in one communal land where there had been large increases in the human and cattle population, the area affected by erosion had stabilised decades ago; even the gullies were stable. The research on dambos by Bell *et al.* (1987) and Grant (1995) already cited also calls into question the rates of erosion commonly assumed in the communal lands. Grant reports that in only one of the 29 dambo sites studied in her field trials was erosion present. While this is somewhat unlikely, since a degree of erosion is pretty well ubiquitous, presumably this can be interpreted to mean that no accelerated, noticeable erosion was present. The Dambo Project used soil erosion plots on different types of land-use on dambos and dry fields in the communal areas to measure erosion. Although this methodology has its limitations (Stocking, 1996), great efforts were made to avoid the most obvious measurement problems. For example, *all* the soil accumulating in the soil tanks was weighed – instead of estimating up from a sample after stirring the water in the tank – and particle size analysis was run from which it could be concluded that there had not been any significant loss of fines. The researchers were confident that the soil losses measured were in the 'right order of magnitude' (Bell *et al.*, 1987: 83). Yet for every land-use type the soil loss was under 1 t/ha/yr which is less than the assumed rate of soil formation on dryland soils (Elwell, 1984, cited in Bell *et al.*, 1987: 81). Furthermore, and as shown in Table 2.1, the soil losses were much lower than those estimated by the predictive model used most commonly in the southern Africa region. The Dambo Project researchers acknowledged that the comparison was problematic in that SLEMSA[21] was designed to predict long-term soil loss and their data covered only one year. Nevertheless this was a wet year, when soil erosion would be expected to be higher than usual, and yet the soil erosion measured was on average 5 to 13 times lower than forecast by SLEMSA (Biot *et al.*, 1992: 18). It was also *70 times less* for dryland arable crops and *270 times less* for dryland grazing than the average figures cited in the politically sensitive national soil erosion survey. The particularly large mismatch

Table 2.1 Comparison of dambo project soil erosion results with SLEMSA predictions

Land use and Slope (%)	Soil loss t/ha/yr	Measured soil loss as % of SLEMSA prediction*
Dambo grazing (1.9%)	0.14	23%–46%
Dambo grazing (2.3%)	0.05	8%–17%
Dambo weed fallow (1.5%)	0.18	7%–18%
Dambo maize (2.3%)	0.36	3%–18%
Dryland scrub grazing (1.8%)	0.27	68%
Dryland maize (1.8%)	0.71	6%–9%

Note: *SLEMSA usually produces a range of possible erosion rates so this shows measured soil loss as a percentage of both the minimum and maximum rate predicted.

Source: derived from data in Bell *et al.*, 1992.

between SLEMSA-predicted and measured rates for smallholder dryland maize is important because this is the main arable land-use type in the CAs and RAs. There can be little doubt that these results challenge the nature of the soil erosion narrative in Zimbabwe. Eschewing the political ramifications of their findings, however, the Dambo Project merely pointed out that it was clear that more field research on actual erosion under dryland maize in the CAs was required.

One final element to the soil erosion narrative for Zimbabwe's communal lands is the role of technical interventions which were supposed to reduce environmental degradation. The changes in land-use and settlement patterns enforced by the colonial state have already been alluded to as problematic in relation to the use of dambos. Wilson (1988) has also shown that in Mazvihwa in southern Zimbabwe many communal farmers themselves are of the opinion that this re-organisation actually increased soil erosion rates because farming the topland dry fields, instead of the lowlands nearer drainage lines, meant that natural watershed vegetation had been removed and water running off the arable fields had further to go before reaching the rivers and therefore increased its erosive power. Farmers also argued that contour ridges which were enforced throughout the southern African region in the 1950s and sometimes earlier had made soil erosion worse, with the siltation of the river progressing geographically along with the erosion 'control' works. The reasons why these measures may have exacerbated the problem were various but included poor design and engineering partly because of cost restrictions. Showers (1989) and Showers and Malahlaha (1992) provide a detailed discussion of these issues with reference to soil erosion measures in Lesotho. It is worth noting that Wilson's farmer informants tended to recognise that contour ridges had great potential for soil erosion control and were not against them *per se*; their criticisms were of the specific nature of the ridges built and the coercive politics involved.

Wilson's findings have also been published in a special issue of *Environment and History* (1995) on Zimbabwe, where several other studies are found in which the usual environmental narratives or technical understandings of environmental issues in Zimbabwe's communal lands are seriously challenged by new field or historical research. Other important publications in this area include Wilson (1989) on indigenous understandings of the roles of trees in fields in the communal areas and the impact of 'scientific' interventions to destump, Scoones (1990) and Scoones and Cousins (1991) on indigenous pastoralist practices and McGregor (1991) on deforestation in the communal areas. The historical perspective taken in these studies lends itself to uncovering the political implications and motivations for the old narratives.

Recent field research by Elliott (1995; 1998) in the RAs on environmental issues is also overturning shibboleths. The tendency to berate settlers in the RAs for causing environmental degradation has already been discussed and criticised above. Rather remarkably, however, there has been very little field research on this issue. As Elliott (1998): observes, 'the debate has been limited by the general lack of objective data or systematic monitoring concerning the environmental impacts of land resettlement'. Her own research on woodland resources in two Model A RAs, therefore, is something of an exception. The research combines detailed interviews with beneficiaries with interpretation of aerial photographs. She found that the decrease in woodland areas since resettlement in the two areas was generally very small: −0.7 per cent and −1.6 per cent, respectively (Elliott, 1995). More detailed GIS analysis of one village in one RA which had started with good woodland cover found that the *total* woodland area had actually increased by 5 per cent (ibid.). Changes in land-use over time were very complex in all the areas studied, with shifts back and forth between cultivated, wooded and grassed areas. Broadly speaking, however, the significant changes have been increases in the cultivated areas and decreases in grassland areas. Elliott cites another RA study (Grundy *et al.*, 1993) which found a much greater 25 per cent decline in the wooded area with resettlement although this was regarded as sustainable as long as the cultivated area did not expand further. In regard to the arguments already made in this chapter, i.e. that resettlement is *bound* to extend the cultivated areas because of prior under-utilisation of many commercial farms, it is worth noting the extent of arable farming before resettlement in the areas studied by Grundy and Elliott: on average less than 5 per cent in Mutamba RA, 12 per cent in Wenimbi-Macheke RA and 4.1 per cent in Tokwe RA, increasing over the time under study to 35 per cent, 20 per cent and 13.7 per cent respectively. Specific resettlement villages may be located in areas on resettlement schemes where there had been *no* previous cultivation at all, as in Devon Ranch in Tokwe (Elliott, 1998) where the resettled smallholders had converted 13 per cent of the land to arable agriculture by 1985. If Kinsey's RA household production and income data pertain to these areas, and there is no reason why they should not, then the national economic gain resulting from these land-use changes must have been significant.

2.5 Conclusion

Zimbabwe's environmental problems have deep historical roots. In contrast to most other African colonies where the colonial enterprise largely rested on peasant agriculture, the white settler state in Zimbabwe strove to diminish competition from this sector and increase the supply of circulating migrant labour; it was therefore in its interests to create pressure on land within the so-called native reserves. Although this took time and its geographical impact was varied across the many different reserves, land shortage did eventually become a major factor in rural people's livelihoods in much of the country. The state then tried to alleviate some of the environmental outcomes of this pressure, when they became so pressing that it was realised that they were undermining the reserves' role as the provider of subsistence livelihoods for the families of the workers incorporated (preferably temporarily) into the 'white' economy. The state, however, was unwilling to accept permanent urbanisation or extend to the African peasantry the agricultural infrastructure, subsidies and credit lines which had allowed and fostered successful European commercial agriculture. For these reasons measures which could have had a really substantial impact on the environmental pressure building up in the reserves were eschewed and coercive, and often misconceived land-use manipulations were implemented in an attempt to balance the resource equation in the reserves – an attempt that largely failed. Thus political factors lay behind the environmental problems and narratives of colonial Rhodesia. The evidence presented above also makes clear that political considerations remain a very important factor in understanding the nature of contemporary environmental narratives in independent Zimbabwe.

Political influence on environmental policies tends to stem from economic interests which are able to translate their needs into political outcomes. The poor are less able to achieve this 'translation'. Yet it must be remembered that political ecology is not always predictable, nor is it the whole story in relation to the environment. This can be illustrated by re-visiting the issue of dambo cultivation. Are there vested commercial interests involved in the lack of institutional change with regard to dambo cultivation today? While this would round off the 'political ecology' narrative, no evidence is known of such influence (although it should be remembered that it was a long time before the vested commercial interests behind the original prohibition became known). Furthermore, the Dambo Project, which resulted in the recommendations to encourage dambo cultivation, was initiated by a local university lecturer in irrigation engineering, who has since gone on to become one of Zimbabwe's really large-scale commercial producers of tomatoes and other vegetables – in other words he is in direct competition with the dambo gardeners; yet he remains a supporter of their initiative and enterprise. Nor is there, today, an absolutely clear division in Zimbabwe in attitudes towards dambo gardens along racial lines. The significance of these points is that it should always be recognised that, while 'the facts' do not always support the 'environmental degradation' story, they may also sometimes stand in the way of a good 'political ecology' story.

Acknowledgements

This chapter has grown in part out of my teaching on the politics and technocracy behind environmental conservation measures in Zimbabwe to Masters students on the MA in Environment and Development at SOAS, and I am grateful to the input and stimulation provided by those students over the years. My thanks also go the Dambo Project team; to Richard Owen and Alan Windram for wonderful hospitality, field trips (and tick-bite fever) and stimulating arguments; and in particular to Bobby Lambert.

Notes

1 For example by the end of the 1980s is was estimated that there were about 800 black members of the formerly white-dominated Commercial Farmers Union, including several cabinet ministers (Palmer, 1990).
2 Thus one of the major issues in contemporary Zimbabwe is the continued control of commercial and industrial enterprises by (usually white) foreigners and white Zimbabweans. Naturally enough the perspectives of the key proponents of more black Zimbabwean ownership, the indigenous businessmen's lobby, are at odds with those of most existing capitalists and those of the driving economic ethos of structural adjustment with its accompanying prioritization of more foreign direct investment.
3 Most significantly this means land with better and more reliable rainfall, the critical factor for successful rainfed commercial production. Other factors such as soil erosivity, soil type, and the presence of granitic domes which are characteristic of many parts of Zimbabwe, also play a part in agro-ecological suitability.
4 These figures are derived from tables in Zimbabwe Farmers Union (1998).
5 This amounted to an initial, but soon exhausted, bonanza of land abandoned by white farmers, many of whom went south to South Africa.
6 These threats were followed through to the point of sending out acquisition letters at the end of 1998, but the following year conditionality imposed by donors appeared to prevent land from actually being taken over.
7 Conference on Rural Reform in South Africa, Poverty Research Unit, Institute of Development Studies, University of Sussex, 1997.
8 Now the Department for International Development (DfID).
9 This ideological issue is relevant in another sense because negative views of the programme may have been engendered to an unwarranted degree by research which found that the Model B schemes of collective co-operatives were generally a failure. Clearly such a model was at ideological odds with the prevailing market ideology and it was not unusual to find observers in the 1980s who were under the impression that Zimbabwe's resettlement was primarily a (failed) socialist, *collectivist* experiment. In fact the amount of published research and interest in these Models (e.g. Akwabi-Ameyaw, 1990, 1997; Mumbengegwi, 1984; Davies, 1990) was somewhat

out of proportion to its impact since by late 1996 fewer than 6 per cent of all settlers were actually on such schemes (see Kinsey, 1999: 171). By comparison, very little research had been published on the Model A schemes with 93 per cent of settlers.

10 See, for example, Masilela and Weiner (1996: 39) who comment that 'an inadequate and ideologically driven assessment of Zimbabwe's resettlement programme is being used to legitimise a neo-liberal rural planning environment in South Africa'.

11 This might be both a cause and an effect of their greater wealth, as they had both more labour available for cultivating and because extended family members would be attracted to that relative wealth.

12 Kinsey quite rightly points out that annual incomes vary so greatly from year to year because of variable rains that meaningful comparisons should try to compare incomes accrued in similar 'rainfall' years. On this basis he compares real mean incomes in 1982/83 with those in 1994/95 which gives a 2.3 fold increase in incomes; the data for the wet year of 1995/96 gives a 5.7 fold increase.

13 This is the old Model D, now called the 3-tier model, which is an attempt to address the fact that the agricultural systems of people in the driest parts of Zimbabwe, which are (and should be) largely based on livestock, do not necessarily require that *people* should be moved but that their livestock often need access to additional grazing resources, preferably on adjacent land obtained by the government.

14 On the assumption that the CA household figure of 6.63 is the relevant multiplier for the 3-tier households.

15 For although many environmental myths are politically inspired, it must not be forgotten that this will rarely be the sole cause.

16 Such trials have been very rare and have the major advantage of testing the cropping patterns actually used by communal farmers in their own environments, making the results more meaningful.

17 For example there were workshops to which key policy-makers were invited and visits to key officials.

18 A good example is a paper in the collection by Owen *et al.* (1995) by Mharapara, a researcher at the Lowveld Research Stations in Chiredzi, Zimbabwe, where it is argued that a 'basic factor' about dambos is that 'the dambo must have the capacity to receive both catchment and incident rain water without being eroded, hold the excess water and release it slowly into the streams' (Mharapara, 1995: 5). Yet in the same collection Bullock (1995) has a paper which shows quite clearly that this view of dambos' role in hydrological systems in southern Africa is erroneous. Mharapara in fact does not oppose cultivation on the dambos *per se*, but argues that the systems used by local smallholders are not adequate and should be replaced by a broad bed–broad furrow system (which would be very labour-intensive).

19 Mugabe cited these figures when opening the Zimbabwe Conservation Conference in November 1985, arguing that Zimbabwe's 'soaring population growth should be controlled and its people taught careful use of natural resources'.

20 Amazingly enough, such commercial successes in turn have been used to argue against land reform, on the grounds that it shows that there is no pressing need for the peasants to get more land as they are doing quite well with what they have! This is clearly a case of heads we win (your systems are unproductive and so must not spread to other areas); tails you lose (your systems are, after all, quite productive so you do not need any more land).

21 SLEMSA: Soil Loss Estimation Model for Southern Africa.

References

Abel, N. 1992: *What's in a number? The carrying capacity controversy on the communal rangelands of southern Africa*. Norwich: University of East Anglia.

Abel, N. and Blaikie, P. 1990: *Land degradation, stocking rates and conservation policies in the communal rangelands of Botswana and Zimbabwe*. London: Overseas Development Institute; Norwich: John Wiley.

Akwabi-Ameyaw, K. 1990: The political economy of agricultural resettlement and rural development in Zimbabwe: the performance of family farms and producer cooperatives. *Human Organization* **49**(4), 320–38.

Akwabi-Ameyaw, K. 1997: Producer cooperative resettlement projects in Zimbabwe: lessons from a failed agricultural development strategy. *World Development* **25**(3), 437–56.

Alexander, J. 1993: State, peasantry and resettlement in Zimbabwe. *Review of African Political Economy* **61**, 325–45.

Beinart, W. 1984: Soil erosion, conservationism and ideas about development: a Southern African exploration, 1900–1960. *Journal of Southern African Studies* **11**(1), 52–83.

Bell, M. *et al.* 1987: *The use of dambos in rural development with reference to Zimbabwe*. Final Report of ODA Project R3869, Loughborough: Loughborough University.

Bell, M. and Hotchkiss, P. 1989: Political intervention in environmental resource use. *Land Use Policy* October, 313–23.

Bell, M. and Hotchkiss P. 1991: Garden cultivation and household strategies in Zimbabwe. *Africa* **61**(2), 202–21.

Berry, B.B. 1991: The impact of agricultural resettlement in Zimbabwe: the Soti Source Model A intensive resettlement scheme. Unpublished MA thesis, Johannesburg, University of Witwatersrand.

Biot, Y. 1991: How long can livestock production be sustained in the Hardveld of Botswana? *Pedologie* **41**(2), 133–47.

Biot, Y., Blaikie, P., Jackson, C. and Palmer-Jones, R. 1995: Rangeland degradation in Zimbabwe. In Biot, Y., Blaikie, P., Jackson, C. and Palmer-Jones, R. (eds), *Rethinking research on land degradation in developing countries*. Washington, DC: World Bank, 113–19.

Biot, Y., Lambert, R. and Perkins, S. 1992: What's the problem? An essay on land degradation, science and development in sub-Saharan Africa. Discussion paper no. 222. Norwich, School of Development Studies, University of East Anglia.

Blaikie, P. 1985: *The political economy of soil erosion in developing countries*. Harlow: Longman.

Bratton, M. 1986: Farmer organizations and food production in Zimbabwe. *World Development* **14**(3), 367–84.

Bratton, M. 1987: The comrades and the countryside: the politics of agricultural policy in Zimbabwe. *World Politics* **398**(2), 174–202.

Bullock, A. 1992a: The role of dambos in determining river flow regimes in Zimbabwe. *Journal of Hydrology* **134**, 349–72.

Bullock, A. 1992b: Dambo hydrology in southern Africa – review and reassessment. *Journal of Hydrology* **134**, 373–96.

Bullock, A. 1995: Hydrological studies for policy formulation in Zimbabwe's communal lands. In Owen, R. *et al.* (eds), *Dambo farming in Zimbabwe: water management, cropping and soil potentials for smallholder farming in the wetlands*. Harare: University of Zimbabwe Publications, 69–82.

Central Statistical Office 1994: *Census 1992: Zimbabwe national report*. Harare: CSO.

Cliffe, L. 1988: Zimbabwe's agricultural 'success' and food security in Southern Africa. *Review of African Political Economy* **43**, 4–25.

Cusworth, J. and Walker, J. 1988: *Land resettlement in Zimbabwe: a preliminary evaluation*. London, ODA (Evaluation Report EV 434).

Dashwood, H. 1996: The relevance of class to the evolution of Zimbabwe's development strategy, 1980–1991. *Journal of Southern African Studies* **22**(1), 47.

Davies, D.H. 1990: Zimbabwe's experience in rural development. *Development Southern Africa* **7**, 166–82.

Drinkwater, M. 1991: *The state and agrarian change in Zimbabwe's communal areas*. London: Macmillan.

Eicher, C. and Rukuni, M. (eds) 1994: *Zimbabwe's agricultural revolution*. Harare: University of Zimbabwe Publications.

Elliott, J. 1989: Soil erosion and conservation in Zimbabwe: political economy and environment. Unpublished PhD thesis, University of Loughborough.

Elliott, J. 1995: Processes of interaction across resettlement/communal area boundaries in Zimbabwe. *Geographical Journal of Zimbabwe* **26**, 1–16.

Elliott, J. 1998: Resource implications of land resettlement in Zimbabwe – insights from woodland change. Paper presented at the conference on 'Zimbabwe Land Reform – The Way Forward', Centre of African Studies, University of London at School of Oriental and African Studies, 11 March 1998.

Elwell, H. 1971: *Erosion research programmes, Rhodesia*. Salisbury: Department of Conservation and Extension.

Environment and History 1995: Special Issue: Zimbabwe, **1**(3), edited by R. Grove and J. McGregor.

Faulkner, R. and Lambert R. 1991: The effect of irrigation on dambo hydrology: a case study. *Journal of Hydrology*, **123**, 147–81.

Grant, P. 1995: The fertility of dambo sils and the related response of maize to fertilizers and manure. In Owen, R. *et al.* (eds). *Dambo farming in Zimbabwe: water management, cropping and soil potentials for smallholder farming in the wetlands*. Harare: University of Zimbabwe Publications.

Grundy, I. *et al.* 1993: Availability and use of trees in Mutanda Resettlement Area, Zimbabwe. *Forest Ecology and Management* **56**, 243–66.

Jacobs, S. 1991: Changing gender relations in Zimbabwe: the case of individual family resettlement areas. In Elson, D. (ed.), *Male bias in the development process*. Manchester: Manchester University Press.

Kinsey, B.H. 1982: forever gained: resettlement and land policy in the context of national development in Zimbabwe. *Africa* **52**(3), 92–113.

Kinsey, B.H., 1983: Emerging policy issues in Zimbabwe's land resettlement programme. *Development Policy Review* **1**(2), 163–96.

Kinsey, B.H. 1999: Land reform, growth and equity: emerging evidence from Zimbabwe's resettlement programme. *Journal of Southern African Studies* **25**(2), 169–92.

Lambert, R. 1999: Personal communication.

McFarlane, M. 1995: Dambo gullying in parts of Zimbabwe and Malawi: a reassessment of the causes. In Owen, R. *et al.* (eds), *Dambo farming in Zimbabwe: water management, cropping and soil potentials for smallholder farming in the wetlands*. Harare: University of Zimbabwe Publications.

MacGregor, J. 1991: Woodland resources, ecology, policy and ideology: an historical case study of woodland use in Shurugwi communal area, Zimbabwe. Unpublished PhD thesis, University of Loughborough.

Masilela, C. and Weiner, D. 1996: Resettlement planning in Zimbabwe and South Africa's rural land reform discourse. *Third World Planning Review* **18**(1), 23–43.

Mharapara, I.M. 1995: A fundamental approach to dambo utilization. In Owen, R. *et al.* (eds), *Dambo farming in Zimbabwe: water management, cropping and soil potentials for smallholder farming in the wetlands*. Harare: University of Zimbabwe Publications.

Moyo, S. 1995: *The land question in Zimbabwe*. Harare: SAPES.

Mumbengegwi, C. 1984: Agricultural producer cooperatives and agrarian transformation in Zimbabwe: policy, strategy and implementation. *Zimbabwe Journal of Economics* **1**, 47–75.

Native Resources Board 1942: Native Enquiry, oral evidence, 1942 (National Archives of Zimbabwe, S988).

Owen R. *et al.* (eds) 1995: *Dambo farming in Zimbabwe: water management, cropping and soil potentials for smallholder farming in the wetlands*. Harare; University of Zimbabwe Publications.

Palmer, R. 1990: Land reform in Zimbabwe: 1980–90. *African Affairs*, **89**(355), 163–81.

Potts, D. and Mutambirwa, C.C. 1997: 'The government must not dictate . . .': rural–urban migrants' perceptions of Zimbabwe's land resettlement programme. *Review of African Political Economy* **24**(74), 549–66.

Roberts, N. and Lambert, R. 1990: Degradation of dambo soils and peasant agriculture in Zimbabwe. In Boardman, J. *et al.* (eds), *Soil erosion on agricultural land*. Chichester: John Wiley.

Sawer, E. 1909: *Cedara memoirs in South African agriculture*, 190–3, quoted in Mharapara, 1995.

Scoones, I. 1990: Livestock populations and household economics: a case study from southern Zimbabwe. Unpublished PhD thesis, Imperial College, University of London.

Scoones, I. 1991: *Wetlands in drylands: the agroecology of savanna systems in Africa. Part 1: Overview – ecological, economic and social issues*. London: IIED, Drylands Programme.

Scoones, I. 1996: Range management science and policy: politics, polemics and pastures in southern Africa. In Leach, M. and Mearns, R. (eds), *The lie of the land: challenging received wisdom on the African environment*. London: International African Institute in association with James Currey.

Scoones, I. 1997: Landscapes, fields and soils: understanding the history of soil fertility management in southern Zimbabwe. *Journal of Southern African Studies* **23**(4), 615–34.

Scoones, I. and Cousins, B. 1991: *Wetlands in drylands: the agroecology of savanna systems in Africa. Part 3f: Key resources for agriculture and grazing: the struggle for control over dambo resources in Zimbabwe*. London: IIED.

Showers, K. 1989: Soil erosion in the Kingdom of Lesotho: origins and colonial response 1830s–1950. *Journal of Southern African Studies* (Special issue on the politics of conservation in Southern Africa) **15**(2), 263–86.

Showers, K. and Malahlaha, G. 1992: Oral evidence in historical environmental impact assessment: soil conservation in Lesotho in the 1930s and 1940s. *Journal of Southern African Studies* **18**(2), 276–96.

Smith, J. 1989: The transport and marketing of horticultural crops by communal farmers into Harare. *Geographical Journal of Zimbabwe* **20**, 1–13.

Stocking, M. 1984: Soil conservation policy in colonial Africa. *Agricultural History* **59**(2), 148–61.

Stocking, M. 1986: *Effects of soil erosion on soil nutrients in Zimbabwe*. Final Report. FAO Consultant Working Paper no. 3, Rome: FAO.

Stocking, M. 1996: Soil erosion: breaking new ground. In Leach, M. and Mearns, R. (eds), *The lie of the land: challenging received wisdom on the African environment*. London: International African Institute in association with James Currey.

Theisen, R. 1976: Development in rural communities. *Zambezia* **4**, 93–8.

Thomson, A. 1988: Zimbabwe. In Harvey, C. (ed.), *Agricultural pricing policy for Africa: four country case studies*. Basingstoke: Macmillan, 186–219.

Weiner, D. 1988: Land and agricultural development. In Stoneman, C. (ed.), *Zimbabwe's prospects*. London: Macmillan, 63–89.

Weiner, D., Moyo, S., O'Keefe, P. and Munslow, B. 1985: Land use and agricultural productivity in Zimbabwe. *Journal of Modern African Studies* **23**(2), 251–85.

Whitlow, R. 1980: Environmental constraints and population pressures on the tribal areas of Zimbabwe. *Zimbabwe Agricultural Journal* **77**(4), 173–81.

Whitlow, R. 1984: A survey of dambos in Zimbabwe. *Zimbabwe Agricultural Journal* **81**, 129–38.

Whitlow, R. 1988a: *Land degradation in Zimbabwe: a geographical study. Report prepared on behalf of the Department of Natural Resources*. Harare: Geography Department, University of Zimbabwe.

Whitlow, R. 1988b: Soil erosion and conservation policy in Zimbabwe: past, present and future. *Land Use Policy* October, 419–33.

Whitlow, R. and Campbell, B. 1989: Factors influencing erosion in Zimbabwe: a statistical analysis. *Journal of Environmental Management* **29**, 17–29.

Williams, G. 1996: Setting the agenda: a critique of the World Bank's rural restructuring programme for South Africa. *Journal of Southern African Studies* Special issue on State and Development **22**(1), 139–66.

Wilson, K. 1986: Aspects of the history of vlei cultivation in southern Zimbabwe. Paper presented to the Dambo Research Project 'Use of Dambos' Workshop, University of Zimbabwe, August 1986.

Wilson, K. 1988: Indigenous conservation in Zimbabwe: soil erosion, land-use planning and rural life. Paper presented to the panel session 'Conservation and Rural People', African Studies Association UK Conference, Cambridge, 14 September 1988.

Wilson, K. 1989: Trees in fields in Southern Zimbabwe. *Journal of Southern African Studies* **15**(2), 1–15.

Wilson, K. 1990: Ecological dynamics and human welfare in Southern Zimbabwe. Unpublished PhD thesis, University College London.

Wilson, K. 1995: 'Water used to be scattered in the landscape': local understandings of soil erosion and land use planning in southern Zimbabwe. *Environment and History* Special issue on Zimbabwe **1**(3), 281–96.

Zimbabwe Farmers Union 1997: Vice-president Emmerson Zhou, personal communication citing Central Statistical Office and AGRITEX Early Warning Unit data (Zimbabwe).

Zimbabwe Farmers Union 1998: Smallholder farmers' viewpoints on land acquisition and distribution. Paper presented at the conference on 'Zimbabwe Land Reform – The Way Forward', Centre of African Studies, University of London at School of Oriental and African Studies, 11 March 1998.

Zinyama, L. 1982: Post-independence land resettlement in Zimbabwe. *Geography* **67**(2), 149–52.

Zinyama, L. 1988. Commercialisation of small-scale agriculture in Zimbabwe: some emerging patterns of spatial differentiation. *Singapore Journal of Tropical Geography* **9**(2), 151–62.

Zinyama, L. 1992: Technology adoption and post independence transformation of the small scale farming sector in Zimbabwe. In Drakakis-Smith, D. (ed.), *Urban and regional change in Southern Africa*. London: Routledge, 180–202.

3

Sea-level rise, subsidence and submergence

The political ecology of environmental change in the Bengal delta

Robert W. Bradnock and Patricia L. Saunders

3.1 Introduction

In the 28 years since its independence many observers have accepted uncritically Henry Kissinger's description of Bangladesh as a 'basket case'. In a world where economic strength is widely seen as the basis of political power, Bangladesh is among the weakest of the world's economies. Its poverty is widely presented as being both the result of and contributing to an extreme form of ecological vulnerability, a vulnerability attributed not only to the characteristics of its physical environment but to its powerlessness in the regional and global power structure. From the malign influence of the Farakka Barrage or the damage done by deforestation in the Himalaya through to rising sea-levels, Bangladesh is portrayed as having one of the world's most fragile environments which is suffering both actual and potential change, with unimaginably damaging human consequences, as a direct result of human activity beyond its borders.

Such environmental damage is frequently portrayed as self-evident. Flooding and cyclone damage are the most widely publicised outside Bangladesh, but a range of other ills, including desertification, salinisation, soil impoverishment, and arsenical contamination of extensive groundwater supplies have all been presented in academic literature and the media as serious and worsening problems. The forecast implications of such changes in what is now by far the world's most densely populated country have included an increasing scale of deaths by malnutrition, starvation and catastrophic events through to the migration of millions of people in search of a more secure future (see Saunders, Chapter 10, this volume).

Each of these environmental challenges has major political implications from the local through to the global level. Political interests may thus be expected to act as a powerful lens through which possible environmental changes are both seen and presented. A growing body of writing in political ecology would suggest that such environmental changes can only be interpreted with reference to the political context in which they are set, and that the 'science' of environmental change is inherently subservient to such a political context. This chapter explores the explanatory power of this view with respect to the debates over sea-level rise, subsidence and submergence in Bangladesh.

3.2 The political ecology of environmental change

Political ecology suggests that 'putting politics first' adds explanatory power to other possible interpretations of environmental change. Indeed, to some, environmental change can only be understood from a political ecology perspective. Not that 'politics' can itself be seen as either self-explanatory or uncontested. There are as many 'politics' as there are institutions and social groups – states, agencies, NGOS, corporations, pressure groups and lobbyists; élites, peasants and the landless, to name only a few. Politics pervades the activities of each group as well as relations between groups.

The title of this chapter might suggest a topic rooted in hard science and far removed from politics. Subsidence, submergence and sea-level rise would all appear to be objectively verifiable phenomena of the physical environment. The extent to which any of them are occurring can be, and often is, presented as a question for scientists from an appropriate disciplinary background to measure, experiment and model, with the intention of analysing how this relatively small component of the world's environmental system works.

Yet in so far as the purpose and the results of such enquiries serve policy objectives rather than the pursuit of pure knowledge, it is important to ask why questions of subsidence, submergence and sea-level rise in Bangladesh have recently become prominent in scientific literature ranging from climatology to geology, hydrology, and oceanography. If political concerns determine the questions, then the questions asked also help to shape the answers obtained. In this chapter we wish to explore whether and in what ways the current 'science' of environmental change in Bangladesh can be explained within a political ecology framework.

Some political ecologists have advanced the view that the environment itself can only be understood as a political construct, that all attempts at measurement, observation and hypothesis testing through the methodology of 'objective science' are doomed by the value-laden and politically informed subjectivity of each observer. Conflict over resources can only be adequately understood, according to this analysis, by reference to systems of economic and political control elaborated in the colonial era.

Bryant (1998), drawing on earlier models of dependency and world systems theory, has argued that in political ecology, 'the role of unequal power relations in constituting a politicised environment is a central theme. Particular attention is given to ways in which conflict over access to environmental resources is linked to systems of political and economic control first elaborated during the colonial era.' Within that framework he has argued that such systems of control could only be properly understood with reference to forces operating at the global level. Political ecology is thus attempting to turn the intellectual spotlight away from the idiographic to the ideological and from the particular to the general, and in some senses runs parallel with the current concern with globalisation (Giddens, 1990).

This change in intellectual stance towards the relationship between global politics and the realities of uneven development coincided with other vitally important changes in the development and environmental agendas which marked the late 1960s. In the environmental field there has been a philosophical shift in perceptions of nature and the environment which may be characterised as a shift from a 'man at the mercy of nature' to a 'nature at the mercy of man' perspective, a view which has proved particularly far-reaching in ideas of 'global warming'. The capriciousness of nature to which people in extreme environments were once seen as being forced to adapt is now commonly interpreted as themselves the result of human activity. Monbiot, writing in *The Guardian*, has expressed this view as starkly as any:

> Climate change is perhaps the gravest calamity our species has ever encountered. Its impact dwarfs that of any war, any plague, any famine we have confronted so far. It makes genocide and ethnic cleansing look like sideshows at the circus of human suffering. A car is now more dangerous than a gun; flying across the Atlantic is as unacceptable, in terms of its impact on human well-being, as child abuse. The rich are at play in the world's killing fields.
>
> (Monbiot, 1999).

Such rhetoric denies environmental complexity and proclaims in prophetic voice an astonishingly broad-brush answer to every feature of environmental change. The certainty of the rhetoric of the 'popular environmental science' hypothesis that global warming is the universal explanation for environmental change carries with it the unstated assumption that every form of 'change' can be explained by the hypothesis. Above all, it claims the ability to determine trends from a multiplicity of individual and unrelated events, without taking into account any of the other variables in the complex system of which they are a part. At the same time a neo-determinism has raised its head in that 'natural resources', notably water, are interpreted in environmentally deterministic ways long since abandoned in the discipline where questions concerning their use and availability were first seriously raised, i.e. geography. In particular, the 'limits to growth' arguments of the late 1960s and 1970s (Meadows *et al.*, 1972), realist schools of international relations, and contemporary resource economics have shown far too little awareness of the nuances and subtleties of defining both 'resources' and 'natural environment', with serious scientific and political implications.

While global theory – economic, political and environmental – has driven much environmental research, regional issues themselves have played a significant part in prioritising individual elements of emerging environmental agendas. In this, scientific and political perceptions of Bangladesh's environment have developed through the interplay of the mutating global environmental agenda and regional and local concerns, a point potently illustrated by the fate of attempts to achieve multilateral agreement over water resource development between India, Nepal and Bangladesh. In a world of increasing global economic interaction through both trade and aid, commercial interests also have a powerful potential stake in the policy implications of alternative scientific interpretations of environmental change. This is the case for the World Bank-sponsored Flood Action Plan for Bangladesh which, as we shall see, draws legitimacy from the problems of flooding in relation to particular narratives of sea-level rise.

In this chapter we explore first the origins of the contemporary environmental agendas in Bangladesh and trace their evolution since the 1950s. We will then discuss a number of ideas about environmental change in Bangladesh, ranging from international concern over global warming to regional and local processes of sedimentation and subsidence. These currently support contrasting environmental agendas and, as such, have policy implications from global to local levels. In conclusion, the chapter examines the strategic significance of alternative environmental scenarios for each of the major political actors.

3.3 Bangladesh's perceived environments: the picture today

A wide range of different agencies have shown an interest in the present state of Bangladesh's environment and of likely trends of change. From the World Bank and other national and international development agencies based in the North, through a series of international and national development and environmental NGOs, there has been a strong focus on stimulating development and preventing threatened disaster.

Despite widely differing origins and concerns among such agencies, there is much common ground between them in their perception of Bangladesh's situation. From its birth in 1971 Bangladesh was taken in the world's eyes to typify a worst-case scenario of environmental catastrophe. Humanitarian concern had already been aroused in December 1970 by a cyclone which according to some estimates killed over 250,000 people (Houghton, 1997: 113) and caused untold damage along the coastal flats and islands of the delta. That disaster drew attention to the Bengal delta at a critical moment in the political history of the region, and the combination of events which followed helped to crystallise a stereotype of Bangladesh which has remained powerful ever since. Floods in 1987, 1988 and 1998 reinforced a view of Bangladesh as permanently at risk of catastrophe. Interestingly, explanations of the 1970 cyclone concentrated on the 'natural' control mechanisms of cyclone origins, development and movement, with their accompanying effects. In contrast, by the 1980s explanation of Bangladesh's 'natural' disasters had shifted radically to human-induced causes, notably deforestation and soil erosion in the Himalaya, of which flooding was perceived to be the predominant effect.

The stereotype of Bangladesh which persisted throughout the changing explanations of environmental instability of the country was rooted in the country's extreme poverty. It is significant that while poverty was almost as great in 1971 as in 1947, it had been at least partially concealed in the overall statistics of economic growth recorded by Pakistan as a whole: just as the 'black hole' of Bihar's poverty and maladministration is concealed from the outside world by the relative dynamism and sheer size of India. Ironically, therefore, Bangladesh's poverty was exposed particularly sharply to the world's eye just at the moment when the country gained independence from Pakistan, thus becoming a crucial factor in the way that the country was seen in terms of its place and influence in regional politics.

Thus Henry Kissinger's widely quoted description of Bangladesh as a 'basket case' was intended less as an economic fact than as a political statement about the importance of its poverty. It was designed to draw attention to the implications of a political demand which in American eyes would seriously threaten US regional security interests, by permanently weakening Pakistan and leaving Bangladesh dependent on a Soviet-leaning India (Bradnock, 1990). The Nixon administration, having started its about-turn in foreign policy with respect to improving relations with China, reacted fiercely to the sudden threat of the break-up of its chief South Asian client ally, i.e. Pakistan. Kissinger similarly saw the break-up as challenging the rather precarious regional balance of power, giving what to the United States was the always unpredictable India a regional dominance which a united Pakistan had previously ensured could not emerge. The July 1971 Indo-Soviet Friendship Treaty further threatened the fragile ring of containment about Mackinder's Heartland,[1] in which Pakistan had offered the United States an apparently stable ally (Mackinder, 1904; Spykman, 1943). Pakistan's sudden disintegration, encouraged by India in a series of strategically shrewd manoeuvres, represented a major geopolitical challenge.

But what were the implications for Bangladesh? From being a part of a middle ranking and economically growing developing country it was to find itself relegated to near the bottom of almost all the international league tables – GDP per capita, domestic food security, level of industrialisation, and investible resources for development. Economic immiseration was accompanied by an almost total lack of military power and a consequent dependence on Indian and international goodwill. Its geostrategic position, almost completely surrounded on its landward borders by India, exacerbated that dependence, for 90 per cent of the catchment area of the giant and capricious Ganges and Brahmaputra Rivers lay outside its borders. At a point when the world development community was focusing on 'dependency', Bangladesh thus achieved its 'independence' as one of the world's most *dependent*, peripheral states. It also became, unlike many other exceptionally poor regions of the world including parts of neighbouring India, a globally recognisable unit in the eyes of the world's media with an accessible and visually demonstrable set of problems relating to poverty and environment. It was in this context that the world community – its agencies and 'experts' – first began to examine Bangladesh's environment.

The challenges posed by that environment seemed particularly severe, and Bangladesh was widely perceived as already in the grip of a Malthusian disaster. In 1995 Myers gave what would be widely recognised as a 'standard' world view of Bangladesh today:

> 'Bangladesh [today is] one of the most impoverished countries on Earth. Its per capita GNP is only $220 or one quarter of the average for all developing countries. A full 84 percent of people are considered to subsist in absolute poverty. Of the rural populace of almost 100 million people in 1988, 21 percent were absolutely landless and 47 percent were functionally landless (with less than 0.2 of a hectare for a household). The average farm in 1990 comprised 0.8 of a hectare. Per capita arable land totalled only one tenth of a hectare. Two-fifths of the labour force were underemployed or simply workless . . . Worst of all, Bangladeshis are becoming increasingly hungry. The average calorie intake is only 94 percent of what is reckoned to be a minimum for active life, and per capita food production has declined to 96 percent of what it was in 1981 . . . It is generally thought (Government of Bangladesh, 1991; Mahtab and Karim, 1992) that the country will become ever less able to feed itself.
>
> (Myers, 1995: 115)

In the early 1970s the widely drawn lesson from such a bleak picture was that rising population pressure and finite resources combined to demand radical social change and a major review of global economic strategy. For Myers writing in 1995, however, the chief lesson was radically different, having changed to what the picture had to say about environmental constraints and global climate change. As he wrote: 'by the time that global warming is likely to be well-established, Bangladesh may well have a population density five times that of the densest developed country, Netherlands, where nine out of ten people live in urban areas' (Myers, 1995: 115). The shift in the dominant paradigms which have helped to shape global environmental agendas is thus a key element in understanding approaches to Bangladesh's own 'environmental crisis'. It is these to which we now turn, focusing particularly on the ideas of the 'limits to growth' and of 'global warming' dominant in the 1970s and 1990s, respectively. We set them within their historical circumstances and review alternative narratives which tend to be excluded from the debate.

3.4 Global environmental agendas

3.4.1 The 1970s: the 'limits to growth' and some alternatives

At the global level Bangladesh's disaster scenario fitted in well with a transformation in US thinking in the 1960s, set in train by the neo-Malthusian environmentalists in the 1960s and given a major stimulus by the 'limits to growth' debate of the early 1970s (Meadows *et al.*, 1972; see Saunders, Chapter 10, this volume). Nowhere illustrated better the perceived absolute limits to resources than a country in which land, the most basic 'resource' was in critically short supply, and where water, the second vital resource, was more demonstrably uncontrollable. Bangladesh achieved independent statehood as this radical shift in US-led thinking was taking place. The inevitable questions were: can Bangladesh survive? Can it protect and feed its people? Can it control its frequently devastating environment? The questions attracted both humanitarian and geopolitical interest.

In the late 1960s the development agenda in the wider South Asian region had been challenged by successive monsoon failures in 1965–66. Catastrophic harvest failures had widespread economic and political effects, and led many observers to believe that with rapidly rising populations the South Asian countries were at risk of the greatest catastrophe of world famine ever experienced. In the short term India recovered rapidly, and the Green Revolution offered an apparently quick fix. But a growing body of writing on the Himalaya began to suggest that optimism was premature. Eckholm (1976) argued passionately that the Himalayan environment was at risk from a series of interlocking environmental changes, each of which formed part of a positive feedback loop accentuating the destabilising features of the other components and sending the whole system into a vicious spiral. As a direct result of human action, starting with population growth and extending through deforestation and the extensification and intensification of farming, to slope collapse, soil erosion and climatic change, stability was being replaced by increasingly massive systemic instability.

This model of Himalayan crisis (Ives and Messerli, 1989) focused on the Himalaya, but as Chapman (1995) has shown, its downstream implications were transparently obvious. Destabilisation of the upstream environment must logically have an impact, possibly an amplified impact, downstream, notably in what by the 1970s was the most densely populated region in the world, the Bangladesh plains. Hence questions of environmental management of the delta came to the fore.

The simplicity and apparent internal cohesion of the 'Model of Himalayan crisis' were its greatest strength, especially as a propaganda tool. However, subsequent research has increasingly cast doubt on its empirical foundations. Each of the links in the postulated chain of causation is either far weaker than suggested or non-existent. The complexity of forces affecting environmental change and the range of scales over which they operate have been shown to defy holistic explanations. In this sense the Himalayan crisis model, seriously wounded by Ives and Messerli in 1989 and conclusively buried by a succession of writers (cf. Thompson *et al.*, 1986; Chapman, 1995), has suffered the fate of other apparently convincing holistic models of destructive environmental change such as desertification (Thomas 1995; see Sullivan, Chapter 1, this volume) or tropical deforestation (Grainger, 1996; Fairhead and Leach, 1996), although like these it continues to be an influential belief, even in the absence of empirical support (see below).

Despite their widely different regional contexts (West Africa, South America, South Asia) each of these models – desertification, tropical deforestation, Himalayan crisis – had several features in common. First, they all took as their starting point a view of nature as inherently stable and resilient, a resilience which was being suddenly and damagingly disturbed by human activity. This human activity, portrayed by some as the inevitable result of a capitalist mode of production in which exploitation – first of the poor, but later of 'the environment' – built on the apparently obvious resources crunch of the early 1970s which itself had reinforced the limits to growth debate. Second, they were all presumed to be the result of global forces – environmental, economic and political. Increasingly frequently, the characteristics of specific regions were significant only in so far as they illustrated global processes.

Perhaps the most surprising feature of the application of the limits to growth scenario to Bangladesh was the ignorance it showed of extensive research on Bangladesh's environment extending back over two hundred years. That Bangladesh's environment was subject to dramatic, catastrophic and unpredictable physical events, sometimes life-threatening on a unique scale, for example, would have come as no surprise to James Rennell writing in the eighteenth century. As the earliest surveyor of Bengal, he observed and measured with meticulous care the surface features of the Bengal landscape, noting its destructive and creative dynamism and through his extraordinarily accurate survey laying the groundwork for subsequent analysis of patterns of change in the courses of the rivers (Rennell, 1781, 1792). Geographers writing subsequently about the Bengal delta drew attention to the dangerous disequilibrium between the attractions of some of the most agriculturally fertile soils in India and the periodic hazard of widespread destruction. Eighty years on, Fergusson (1863) paid particular attention to the interpretation of the observed changes in the delta which were already highly visible from the river landscapes surveyed by Rennell. He drew attention to an apparent lack of change in long stretches of the Sundarban coastline, while also pointing to the infilling which marked much of the swampy territory inland. The scale of sedimentation resulting from the annual flooding astonished both observers.

Similarly Geddes (1925), Bagchi (1944), Spate (1954), Spate and Learmonth (1968), Ahmad (1968) and Johnson (1979) all highlighted the diversity of physical environments and the range of successful human adaptations to them. Geddes, writing in 1933, observed how 'the forest and mangrove swamps of the Sundarbans are being pushed back by cultivators whose fields lie below high tide and are protected by embankments'. Further north in the Barind, a region widely described in the post-Farakka period since 1975 as being 'desertified', Geddes observed that having been 'cultivated and thriving in its early history ... during Muslim rule it gradually lapsed to jungle and waste' (Geddes, 1982: 191), i.e. making clear the influence of political and historical contexts in constraining land-use.

It is particularly striking that to Geddes, and other more recent scholars, the flooding of Bengal was framed as its annual blessing, not its curse. In particular, there was an interest in the huge diversity of soils, the wide range of different cropping patterns practised through three seasons of highly varying productivity, and the subtlety of human adaptation, especially in cropping patterns, to the 'predictably unpredictable' environment. Brammer developed this theme with a meticulously researched analysis of the most recent of Bangladesh's floods (1990a,b). As he argued: 'the physical and the socio-economic environments are complex; they are also dynamic ... these factors make it extremely difficult to isolate or assess the specific consequences of any particular trend or intervention' (Brammer, 1993: 246). At least equal attention was paid to the political history of the region which through the colonial period had seen a once rich agrarian and industrial economy transformed into one of the poorest regions of India. Before the 1970s explanations for this decline were sought not in environmental hazard but in the policies of a colonial system which sought to extract maximum short-term profit.

Given extensive knowledge of the diverse environments of the Bengal delta before the formation of Bangladesh in 1971, it seems pertinent to ask how the environmental agenda came to be so rapidly re-written without any direct reference to, let alone refutation of, earlier field-research based scholarship. It seems that 'scientific' attention was drawn away from explanation of the physical characteristics of the environments and the admiration for the complexity of human adjustment, to speculation revolving around a much more limited range of questions.

3.4.2 The 1990s: 'global warming'

The 'limits to growth' discourse set a global agenda. Awareness of the integrated nature of the world's environment further encouraged a search for universal and global causes of 'environmental change'. In the late 1980s and 1990s by far the most significant of such models in forming a dominant paradigm has been global warming.

Since the publication of the first Intergovernmental Panel on Climate Change (IPCC) report (1990), the global warming agenda has come to dominate perceptions of environmental change and has fuelled the biggest global environmental research effort ever witnessed. It has been the popular explanation of first – and often last – resort for a remarkable range of environmental phenomena, and has been the focus in particular of the model building and forecasting process designed to inform policy decisions at the international level. A good example is a three-page description of 'global warming' in the Arctic published by the UK *Observer* newspaper on 25 July 1999, in which the effects of global warming were held to include not only rapid thinning of Arctic ice but the disappearance of fish stocks, the pending disappearance of species from the walrus to the polar bear, and the eradication of 'Eskimo' [*sic*] communities.

The agenda for the Rio and Kyoto conferences of 1992 and 1997 was constructed around the implications of increased atmospheric CO^2 and its corollaries. These were held to include:

- eustatic sea-level rise, with potentially devastating effects on coastal lowlands;
- increased flooding;
- increased storm risk, especially in the cyclone prone areas of the Tropics;
- desertification;
- salinisation.

Examples of each of these phenomena are now reported regularly in the European and North Anerican press, almost always in the context of global warming. The scale of the perceived threat to the earth's ecosystem is driving both research budgets and policy from a national to a global scale. Yet far from being proven, each link of this 'model' is in effect an hypothesis waiting to be tested, as the reports of the IPCC and the scientific writings of many researchers demonstrate. Of particular significance is the recognition that Atmosphere Ocean Global Change Models (AOGCM) are characterised by 'inherent uncertainty' and that regional climate change models have such pronounced additional uncertainty built in to them that, in the words of Mitchell and Hulme, regional climate prediction is 'a cascade of uncertainty' (1999: 57).

Given this context it is perhaps unsurprising that recent analysis of climate change in the Quaternary is beginning to find evidence that climate, far from being relatively stable over long periods (on the human rather than the geologic time scale), may have been subject to sudden and major transitions. Adams *et al.* (1999), for example, have suggested that 'the past few million years have been punctuated by many rapid climate changes, most of them on timescales of centuries to decades'. They conclude that 'all evidence indicates that long-term climate change occurs in sudden jumps rather than incremental changes' (ibid.: 1–2). They also comment that it is difficult to fix responsibility for sudden climate change in the past on variations in the CO^2 levels because changes in CO^2 follow a time scale of millennia as opposed to climate changes which are known to take only decades (ibid.: 2).

So the science of climate change remains full of uncertainties at quite fundamental levels, yet the political need for clarity and confidence nearly always outstrips the scientific ability to provide it. The extent to which regional factors may also be affected by political agendas has been illustrated by Kandlikar and Sagar (1999). They show that the Bush administration's call before the Rio summit for comprehensive abatement of all greenhouse gases generated intense concern in 'the south', as while CO^2 sources are largely derived from northern industrial economies, methane is derived from inundated rice paddies (grown largely in 'the south') and is also a major and probably more important greenhouse gas. The US Environment Agency estimated that emissions of methane from Indian sources of rice paddy were 37.8 Tg/yr ($1Tg = 10^{12}kg$), over a third of the world's total. The Indian Government suspected that the American decision to press for a cap on *all* greenhouse gases was designed to prevent the setting of overly restrictive limits on greenhouse gases emanating from 'the north'. Interestingly, subsequent Indian methane research suggested that the figure of Indian methane emission from paddy was as low as 4 Tg/yr (Kandlikar and Sagar, 1999: 123).

Despite the inherent and enormous difficulty of predicting global and regional climate change the world has been scoured for regional examples of the damaging 'effects' of global warming, in an effort to reinforce the political message that global level policy changes are essential to avert catastrophe.[2] Bangladesh has served as a powerful tool in such a scenario. In a worst-case scenario Milliman *et al.* (1989) envisaged a change in relative sea-level of 4.5 metres by 2100. Houghton (1997: 111) instead suggests that sea-level rise in the next century will be in the region

> [of] about 1 meter by 2050 (compounded of 70 cm due to subsidence because of land movements and removal of groundwater and 30 cm because of global warming) and nearly 2 m by 2100 (1.2 m due to subsidence and 70 cm from global warming) – although there is large uncertainty in these estimates.

Given his assertion that 'about 7 per cent of the country's habitable land (with about 6 million population) is less than 1 meter above sea-level and about 25 per cent (with about 30 million population) is below the 3 metre contour' (Houghton, 1997: 111) the consequences of these predictions are self-evident. Interestingly, Houghton's observations raise the important point that global warming may account for only a part of the total relative sea-level change, with a larger part coming from subsidence. Again, however, we need to ask questions about what is the origin of the subsidence 'threat', and what is the evidence for it? The links between the two hypotheses are explored in section 3.6 below.

Apart from the direct catastrophic effects for those living in potentially submerged areas of the Bengal delta, global warming scientists have pointed to other damaging side-effects of the putative rise in sea-level. Writing on the possible enforced migration which may result from global warming, Myers (1995: 116–17) argued that already in 1971 'more than 10 million land-hungry and food-short people crossed the border into India'. Myers went on to argue that Bangladesh's low-lying terrain, high population density, susceptibility to storm surges and perennial flooding, with 'over half the country only five metres above sea-level' made the country 'more vulnerable than almost any other country to sea-level rise' (ibid. 116–17): the contribution of Bangladesh's devastating civil war to figures for so-called 'environmental refugees' (see Saunders, Chapter 10, this volume) was not even considered in this narrative.

3.5 A politics of the regional environmental agenda

Environmental issues in Bangladesh and India have had a rather different focus from that suggested by the global concerns outlined above. Although the Bengal delta is one physiographic unit, there has also been a profound difference in the perceptions of environmental hazard and change between West Bengal (India) and Bangladesh. It might be thought that such differences would reflect contrasts between the moribund delta of the west compared with the active delta of the east, with their different patterns of coastal erosion and deposition, sedimentation and salinisation, and seasonal flooding. Instead the completion of the Farakka Barrage in 1975 to prevent flooding, and its subsequent operation until the Indo-Bangladesh agreement of December 1996, illustrates the extent to which contrasting views of environmental change have more to do with a politics of the environment than with its physical geography.

In West Bengal, for example, there has been concern in Calcutta for nearly one hundred years at the progressive silting of the River Hooghly, a distributary of the Ganges and formerly a major outlet to the sea. Proposals to alleviate the problems of Calcutta Port go back to the nineteenth century, and culminated in the building of a diversionary barrage at Farakka to channel water during the dry season away from the main course of the river down the Hooghly. It was argued in India that this would help restrict high tide saline intrusions past Calcutta and also keep silt flushed out from the port. However, as Crow *et al.* (1995) have shown, the decision to build was also motivated by the need for the Congress Central Government to demonstrate support for its own party in the State of West Bengal at a time when it was under severe challenge from the Communist Party of India (Marxist) CPI(M). On the other hand, the construction of the Farakka Barrage, completed four years after Bangladesh's independence, caused anxiety in Bangladesh in relation to control over environment and water resources. From the first dry season of its operation it was attacked as responsible for severe environmental damage. For the next 21 years the Farakka barrage figured strongly in Bangladesh's relations with India, and was held responsible for a wide range of environmental degradation, including increased flooding, increased sedimentation, desertification of extensive regions of western Bangladesh, and salinisation of extensive agricultural land. It encouraged the Bangladesh government and its supporters to press the claim that restrictions to dry season flow were the major constraint on agricultural development and the dominant influence on environmental degradation. In 1994 a special issue of the Bangladesh monthly *The Guardian* drew attention to many of these concerns under the title 'Ganges Water Natural Right of Bangladesh'. Abul Hashem, interviewing the then Secretary for Bangladesh's Irrigation, Water Development and Flood Control, drew immediate attention to this regional context while linking it to global interpretations of environmental change. For example, he asserted that:

'Commissioning of Farakka Barrage has adversely affected the echo-system [*sic*] as well as the underlying economic, political and even strategic factors of our country as, in the echo-system, nation-states are inextricably linked beyond political boundaries. And according to experts the horrible flood of 1987–88 was due to the effect of the commissioning of Farakka'.

(Hashem, 1994: 9–10)

In response to his request to the Secretary to comment it is perhaps unsurprising that the Secretary was in full agreement with these assertions.

These opinions led to a long period of concentrated political effort to achieve politically acceptable ways of both augmenting river flows into Bangladesh during the dry season and of restricting flooding during the wet season. Bangladesh sought to achieve this through a variety of means, including tri-lateral negotiation with India and Nepal, and seeking external aid support for large engineering schemes for river diversion and protection. Global debates provided a very favourable environment for Bangladesh to make the most of its geopolitical weakness. That very weakness, and Bangladesh's total dependence on external resources for development assistance, have also created a major opportunity for commercial interests from the North to stake a claim for development projects.

It is striking that while in West Bengal very little political attention was paid to either the limits to growth debate or the subsequent global climate change arguments, the reverse was true in Bangladesh. This chapter does not have space to explore the reasons for this disparity in detail, but it can be noted that the rural priorities of the West Bengal Communist Party Marxist government over the last twenty years have been focused on land reform, and subsequently on the provision of agricultural infrastructure, and the Farraka Barrage, with its influence on water flow, has played an important role in this. For Bangladesh, Farakka highlighted the sense of powerless dependency the country felt as a result of its strategic encirclement by India, and its lack of control over water both in surplus and in deficit. The environment, on which it could claim such a pronounced dependency, offered a strong platform for internationalising its problems, and the coincidental timing of a rise in international concern with environmental issues gave it one of the very few cards it could play at the international table. For West Bengal Farakka instead played a marginal economic and environmental role. It was considered a single purpose scheme, with no irrigation potential, and extremely limited navigational or other benefits. It was restricted to operating during the dry season. Until late 1996 both for the Indian and West Bengal governments Farakka was regarded as an irritant in relations with Bangladesh but of limited ecological significance. Only when the CPI(M) government of Jyoti Basu re-examined the arguments did the West Bengal Government calculate that the benefits Calcutta was gaining from Farakka were negligible in relation to the political damage in the relationship with Bangladesh, and moved to establish a full agreement. According to unpublished government sources the negative effects of the agreement on the River Hooghly and on Calcutta Port have been slight. Such contrasts in the regional political perspectives of the respective national and state governments of Bangladesh, India and West Bengal deserve closer study in themselves. This is beyond the scope of this chapter, however, and instead we turn now to the 'science' of regional environmental change with specific reference to sea-level rise, subsidence and submergence to explore the 'evidence' driving and supporting particular environmental policy and political narratives.

3.6 The evidence for environmental change: sea-level rise, subsidence and submergence

3.6.1 Going up, going down, or going nowhere?: Sea-level rise

For all delta environments a change in relative sea-level would be expected to have severe implications for human settlement. For Bangladesh, the most densely populated region of the world, it would also have critical importance for the management of water resources. A clearer understanding of the extent and patterns of sea-level rise, however, has theoretical as well as immediately practical significance as it could also shed more light on the processes of global, regional and local environmental change.

The first hypothesis of a relationship between global warming and environmental change in the Bangladesh delta comes from predictions of a rise in sea-level attributable in part to thermohaline expansions of the oceans and in part to melting of ice, particularly in the Antarctic, which is overwhelmingly the largest global store of fresh water. While we do not explore here the scientific basis for this hypothesis in global terms, we note that successive reports from the IPCC recently have reduced the anticipated degree of eustatic sea-level rise. The precise relationship between warming and sea-level rise is seen increasingly as difficult to model with precision, and there is a wide range of variables whose parameters appear still to be largely unknown. None the less, the putative rise in sea-level during the next century continues to attract strong interest.

The implications of such a rise in sea-level have been assumed in much of the literature to be self-evident, that is that there will be a direct rise in local relative sea-levels. In low-lying areas this is assumed to increase the risk of floods and of permanent inundation. In the delta of Bangladesh it was assumed in the early 1990s that it would be possible to calculate from existing maps the area of land which would be inundated given specific alternative rates of sea-level rise. A widely quoted example of such a calculation is given by Houghton (1997, see above). According to this hypothesis, the causes of these supposed changes are attributable entirely to extra-regional human-induced changes in the atmosphere (i.e. 'global warming'), and therefore have immediate direct policy implications for the north. However, if such sea-level changes are indeed starting to occur there are also major policy implications for the Bengal delta.

The strongest proponents of this hypothesis have been members of the 'global environmental community', coupled with governments of countries most 'at risk' from such changes, and regional governments in putatively affected areas have used the global warming scenario to argue support for regional programmes of assistance to tackle 'the problem'. However, the hypothesis has also received wide cover – often in the form of reported 'scientific fact' – from environmental lobby groups such as Greenpeace and Friends of the Earth, aid agencies such as Oxfam, and from journalists such as *The Guardian* environment correspondents Paul Brown and George Monbiot and *The Independent* columnist Geoffrey Lean. As such, it has achieved widespread currency and legitimacy.

3.6.2 But is sea-level rising?

Eustatic sea-level rise is only relevant with respect to Bangladesh in so far as it relates to local level changes. With present data and analytical tools it is impossible to establish eustatic sea-level changes or to distinguish them from local level changes. This is particularly true in Bangladesh, where key features of the hydrology of the enormously complex delta estuarial system and of the underlying geology remain little understood.

Some sources suggest that the delta coast of Bangladesh is currently experiencing a sea-level rise of 1 mm per annum, but this figure is simply an extrapolation of IPCC estimates of eustatic sea-level rise (Spencer and Viles, 1995). In 1990 Brammer argued that as yet there was no evidence of sea-level rise. Quoting Rogers *et al.* (1989) who showed that there had been no systematic changes in rainfall at Calcutta through the 150 years during which records had been kept, and the Bangladesh Flood Plan (1988) which states that there had been no discernible trend in flood frequency in the Jamuna, Padma and Meghna, Brammer questioned the extent to which the evidence currently supported any of the claims for systematic environmental change in Bangladesh.

One reason for uncertainty as to relative sea level change is the absence of reliable measurements. Bangladesh has no fixed and accurately surveyed sea-level measuring gauges. Those that exist have been shown to be attached to structures such as wooden piers that may themselves be subject to significant movement. Contrasts between the findings at individual tidal gauge measuring stations also suggest an extremely wide margin of error, far in excess of any possible change in sea-level itself. In other words, the convincing statements of rising sea-levels reported above mask substantial inaccuracies and measurement problems in the data on which such assertions are based.

3.6.3 Delta subsidence: an alternative threat

Two articles in the UK *Guardian* newspaper in late 1998, which draw on a paper commissioned by the World Bank (Haq, 1994), suggested the opening of a division of scientific opinion between geologists and climate scientists over the causes, significance and future implications of changing relative sea-levels in Bangladesh and its effects on flooding: namely, the importance of land subsidence under the weight of sedimentation versus global warming in causing sea-level rise around Bangladesh.

Haq, writing for the World Bank, maintains that due *primarily* to subsidence:

> There will be an increase in relative sea-level of 1.8 metres by the middle of the Twenty-first Century. By the *end* of the century this figure rises to 3 metres which would mean that Bangladesh could lose 23% of its land, supporting 25% of its population and 25% of its GDP.

He suggests that sea-level rises would increase further if the effects of global warming are included in these estimates. Haq's report, entitled 'Sea-level rise and coastal subsidence: rates and threats', was based on 1992 projections for eustatic sea-level rise (IPCC, 1992). Estimates for subsidence and the consequences for the population and economy of Bangladesh come from an influential article by Milliman, Broadus and Gable (1989) and a later summary by Milliman (1992). These authors – a geologist, an economist and a geographer – were then all with the Woods Hole Oceanographic Institute in Maryland, USA. The emphasis in all three of these papers is that accelerated subsidence could be many times greater than the projected sea-level rise due to global warming. Several factors are claimed to have contributed to delta subsidence including the continuous loading of sediment from the rivers, excessive tapping for hydrocarbons or groundwater, and compaction or shrinkage with drying. With regard to the withdrawal of groundwater in coastal lowlands, for example, Baeteman (1994) suggests that this 'causes nearly instantaneous local land subsidence due to sediment compaction', particularly in fine sediments such as silts and clays. Haq (1994: 19) thus asserts that subsidence has increased due to the extraction of freshwater from the delta for irrigation and drinking water. Citing Milliman (1992) he states that subsidence uncompensated by new sediments 'has been estimated at as much as 2.5 cm per year in someparts (*sic*) of the delta'. 'Findings' of subsidence have been popularised in the liberal media of 'the north' informing articles with the dramatic titles 'Weight and Sea' (Maslin, 1998) and 'Sinking into Poverty' (Crace, 1998), the latter of which emphasised the 'catalogue of human error, thoughtlessness and corruption which has made the situation worse than it otherwise might have been.'

Again, however, on close examination a number of key elements in the subsidence model require substantial qualification, and in some cases can be shown to be wholly irrelevant or misleading when applied to Bangladesh. In the next section we review the 'evidence' for both sedimentation and for subsidence.

3.6.4 How much sediment?

It is widely recognised that flooding and the deposition of silt have long been a common and valued occurrence which benefits agriculture and enables Bangladesh to support a large population. It is commonly stated, however, that excessive flooding is now a severe problem (Maslin, 1998), particularly in relation to a regional Himalayan crisis of deforestation. Myers, for example, claimed in 1995 (p. 115) (without reference to a source) that 'in the Brahmaputra watershed, the rate of deforestation-derived soil erosion in the Himalayas is five times that of the geologic past. This sediment is often considered a prime factor in downstream flooding.' Myers does not explain the basis of the evidence for the comparison between present-day rates and 'the geologic past'. Furthermore, simplistic interpretations of the variations in sedimentation in the delta had already been ruled out by Brammer, among others, who in 1993 had pointed to the enormous effects of the 1950 Assam earthquake on the Brahmaputra's sediment loads (Brammer, 1993; Kingdon-Ward, 1955) 'raising river bed levels by about 3 m (United Nations, 1957)'. Yet Myers' view continues to be commonly repeated. In 1997, for example, Brown claimed that 'upstream of Bangladesh, once heavily wooded mountain slopes have been stripped bare. This means that the trees that once held back the melting snow and the rains no longer do so . . . [and] . . . that the water can rush down all at once and cause even worse floods than before' (Brown, 1998: 100).

Haq (1994) states that 'under normal conditions the delta should receive more than 1 billion tons of sediment and 1,000 cubic km of freshwater'. He argues that this sediment load normally balances the subsidence which occurs both naturally and as a result of human activity. But, if the concomitant popular assertion that the amount of sediment deposited has been reduced in recent years because the diversion of the Ganges River at Farakka were true, it would mean that *less* sediment was entering the country, and less of that was being deposited on the land because of embankments designed to prevent flooding (Maslin, 1998).

We can discern several problems, however, with the quoted estimates. As Alam has argued, 'there are no accurate estimates for sediment discharge to the Ganges–Brahmaputra delta' (Alam 1996a: 179). Haq (1994), for example, states that each year the delta *receives* over 1 billion tons of sediment and 971 m³ of freshwater. Milliman (1992) instead suggests that the same quantities are *transported* by the combined river system, and Milliman *et al.* (1989) suggest that the identical quantities are *transported to the Bay of Bengal* (and represent 6 per cent of total fluvial sediment reaching the world's oceans). In fact, these varying estimates are all versions of the *same* original estimate, made by Milliman and Meade (1983). Potentially they each mean wholly different things, for while in the last scenario all sediment is assumed to be transported to the Bay of Bengal (and therefore none deposited over the delta itself), in the first an unknown proportion, but potentially 100 per cent could be deposited before reaching the Bay of Bengal. Milliman and Meade (1983) say that 1.67 billion tons of suspended sediment are discharged annually through the Ganges–Brahmaputra rivers and the BWDB (Bangladesh Water Development Board) estimate 1.27 billion tons through six rivers (post-Farakka conditions). The BWDB total includes the figures for annual suspended sediment discharge for seven positions on the Ganges, Brahmaputra, Pabna, Daleswari, Old Brahmaputra, and two on Gorai and totals them to get 1.27 billion (BWDB, Table 2: 179; see Alam, 1996a). It should be pointed out that neither figure considers bed load sediments which Coleman (1969) thought might account for 50 per cent of total sediment load.

Still further different estimates have been provided recently. Allison *et al.* (1998), conducting a survey of sedimentation in the Brahmaputra, state that 'the Brahmaputra in

Bangladesh has an average annual water discharge of 19 600 m³/s with a tremendous seasonal range from 2820 m³/s in mid-dry season to an estimated 100 000 m³/s during the 1988 flood' (Environment and Geographic Information Support Project, 1997). Interannual variability is reflected in the range of estimates (387–608 t/yr) of average sediment discharge (Coleman, 1969; Government of Bangladesh, 1987). From their study of sedimentation rates along a 110-km reach of the Brahmaputra (Jamuna) they conclude that sedimentation rates can be as high as 4 cm yr⁻¹, but having stated that their study area has among 'the highest sequestration rates of the Bangladesh flood plain', they proceed to estimate total sediment deposits for the whole basin from their limited, and clearly unrepresentative sample (Allison *et al.*, 1998). Nevertheless, this research on the mouths of the Ganges–Meghna–Brahmaputra system sheds new and challenging light on processes of silt deposition in the Bay of Bengal and on changes to the sea front of the delta over the last two hundred years. In contrast to the long-held view that Bengal's sea front has changed very little since the earliest Rennell mapping reported in 1792, for example, careful analysis of recent maps and of contemporary satellite imagery shows a net progradation, i.e. expansion, of 7.0 km²/yr between 1792 and 1984 (Allison, 1998). Further complicating the picture are important differences between the western and the eastern parts of the delta in that, while the eastern delta is actively prograding, the western delta has been eroding significantly, with seaward-facing shorelines in the west retreating by 3 to 4 kilometres since 1792. Allison (1998) believes this is a function of eustatic sea-level rise and erosion by oceanographic processes, exacerbated by regional subsidence. We should probably add to that explanation the decline as carriers of both water and silt of the western distributaries of the Ganges as the main course of the Ganges has pushed eastwards, which may well have starved the delta front of the silt necessary for its maintenance. In addition, the net progradation since 1792 appears to have been significantly lower since 1840 (4.4 km²/yr since 1840) compared with 7.0 km²/yr between 1792 and 1840 (Allison, 1998). Allison calculates that the prograding of the islands and eastern shoreline accounts for a total of 1–2 per cent of overall river sediment, while 21 per cent of the sediment budget supplies material contributing to the aggradation and progradation of the topset depocentre immediately offshore in the Bay of Bengal.

As well as confusion surrounding estimates of sedimentation, further problems arise because the figures generally provide no indication of the considerable variability characterising sediment load of these rivers both seasonably and annually,[3] as well as in association with tectonic events in the catchment area. As Hofer (1998: 32) points out, measurement of these rates on river systems as large as those of Bangladesh is inherently problematic. He writes:

> The discharge measurement of the big rivers in Bangladesh is a difficult task. The Brahmaputra at Bahadurabad is a river system of approx. 13 km width, divided into about 8 distinct channels which are always changing their course. The Padma at Baghyakul is one stream with a cross-section of 4 km. During our field work in Bangladesh in spring 1993 we visited these two measuring sites and assisted the team of the Bangladesh Water Development Board during the measurements. At Bahadurabad two teams work simultaneously for 5 hours from both sides of the river. The measurements are done from a catamaran, which, for each vertical, is positioned according to angle measurements with regard to flags on the river bank. The flow velocity is measured with a current meter at 20% and 80% depth of each vertical. Through these visits we gained confidence in the discharge data as measurements are done with the highest accuracy possible given the conditions at the measuring sites.

Yet scale and complexity are not the complete answer. Hydrological data are among the most politically sensitive data in South Asia, and it is often impossible to get access to official data sets. Again, as Hofer says:

> [i]t is evident that the discharge data set available for the study is compiled from a variety of sources and, is seemingly, a puzzle of information. This situation very clearly illustrates the restrictions on obtaining hydrological information, especially prominent in India. There is no overall hydrological data base which is officially accessible.

Implicit in these observations is that the way in which figures such as those above are quoted and used with an aura of certainty is wholly inappropriate.

3.6.5 What is the evidence for subsidence?

The chief burden of Haq's argument concerns the likelihood of accelerated subsidence in delta environments. In a review of delta subsidence he suggests that, '[i]n many parts of the world, human activities in the coastal areas have so significantly increased natural subsidence that it may now pose a bigger threat than the projected acceleration in sea-level rise caused by global warming' (Haq, 1994: 16). He goes on to argue that except in northern higher latitudes, all coastal areas are subsiding at various rates and in his first map Bangladesh is shown as predominantly subsiding.

Significantly, however, Haq's paper (1994) includes no direct evidence from Bangladesh, drawing instead on analogy from other deltas such as the Nile and the Mississippi. Milliman *et al.* (1989: 218) make more explicit reference to Bangladesh. In discussing subsidence in major world deltas they suggest that some low-lying deltas have natural subsidence rates as great as 1 to 10 cm yr^{-1}, that is *10 to 100 times the rate of present sea-level rise*. Bangladesh is shown as subsiding at 1 cm yr^{-1}, i.e. at a rate greater than the Nile (3.5 mm yr^{-1}) and less than the Mississippi (1.5 cm yr^{-1}), New Orleans (2 cm yr^{-1}) and Bangkok (much higher, but no figure given). The source for the Bangladesh figures, however, is not provided. Further, and as Baeteman (1994: 71) stresses, data used to measure subsidence vertical sequencing of borehole data 'only represent a summary of the very local setting; they are in no way representative of the entire depositional body'.

This warning is apposite and extends to the whole manner in which the 'evidence' for increasing subsidence has been constructed. For example, the extent to which the Bengal delta is directly comparable in any key respects with those of the Mississippi or the Nile is open to question. Coleman (1969) makes it clear that even tropical rivers contrast sharply in their character by suggesting that 80 per cent of the Ganges–Brahmaputra sediment comprises silt and sand, compared with 70 per cent clay for the Amazon and Fly Rivers. Among other differences are the much higher sediment loads of the major rivers, the contrasting tectonic activity of their relevant basins, the profoundly different characteristics of population and land use in the middle and lower sections of their catchments, and their wholly different climatic regimes. On top of these is the fact that groundwater abstraction in the Bengal delta is still a seasonal phenomenon, with 100 per cent monsoon season replacement of groundwater used during the dry season. This replenishment of the water table would be expected to reduce, possibly to zero, subsidence due to extraction. All these points suggest that comparisons should be treated with the greatest possible caution in the absence of satisfactory locally based empirical research.

In particular, none of the above sources quote field research in Bangladesh in support of conclusions about subsidence. Rather, they draw by analogy on the experience of other deltas. One figure, however, recurs through key papers dealing with this theme. Haq states that, 'Subsidence [uncompensated by new sediment] has been estimated at as much as 2.5 cm yr^{-1} in some parts of the delta.' Quoting Milliman (1992) he suggests that these high rates may be at least partly due to the rapid withdrawal of groundwater from the delta itself. Importantly, the 'evidence' for this conclusion can be traced *to a single well* at Hazipur (Lat. 24° 31′25″, Long. 89° 59′ 04″, drilled while exploring for natural gas). As Alam (1996a: 179) argues:

> The rate of subsidence can be measured indirectly from well logs. There are numerous water wells, but records do not show the stratigraphy or the age of the sediment. Although there are a number of oil and gas exploration wells, most are located in the mobile belt or on the shelf [see below], and almost no stratigraphic analyses have been carried out in the quaternary section of these wells. However at the Hazipur well the Holocene-Pleistocene boundary is shown at 244 m. Taking the base of the Holocene as 10,000 B.P., the rate of subsidence in the area around Hazipur would be about 2.2 cm/year. The Hazipur well is not located in the middle of any known trough, and consequently may not represent the highest rate of subsidence in the basin. Clearly more basin-wide data on Holocene-Pleistocene boundary and C^{14} dates are needed.

In this paper Alam (1996a: 179) asserts that subsidence has occurred at a rate of 2.2 cm yr^{-1} 'in the area around Hazipur', although later (1996b) he says 2.4 cm yr^{-1}. Further, in 'assuming that about 30% of the basin is subsiding at the rate of subsidence at Hazipur' (Alam and Samad, 1996: 179), he extrapolates widely from these figures. Milliman (1992) gives a similar figure of 2.5 cm yr^{-1}. A second well, the Hizla-Maladi well (Lat. 22° 55′ 20″, Long. 90° 28′ 29″)[4] has also been reported by Alam. Here the boundary is 199 metres down and represents a subsidence rate of 2.0 cm yr^{-1}, although he concludes that '[c]learly more basin-wide data are needed' before these figures can be extrapolated widely and with any degree of certainty. Writing a few years previously, Milliman *et al.* (1989) uphold a figure of 1 cm yr^{-1}, citing Morgan and McIntyre (1959: 342) who calculated this average after applying radiometric dating of buried wood in the delta. They caution, however, that 'the data base is so poor that local rates could vary by a factor of 5 or more'.

Some vitally important questions about the sedimentary and solid geology of Bangladesh are demonstrated by the remarkable contrast in findings from the Hazipur well (Alam and Samad, 1996) and a third area, Tangail. In Tangail, Umitsu (1987) has analysed bores down to the Pleistocene–Holocene divide, and here the boundary was found to be about 35 metres down. The difference between Hazipur's 244 metres and Tangail's 35 metres again suggests that it is impossible, even ludicrous, to attempt to establish general rates of subsidence across Bangladesh from two wells alone, or even from a series of wells. Although, and as Alam has pointed out, there is now a wide range of gas drilling wells from which cores could be obtained, to the best of our knowledge there has been remarkably little published work to analyse the information these cores contain with respect to patterns of subsidence.

Even with a good sample of cores it is also problematic to assume a constant rate of subsidence throughout the Holocene from which an annual rate can be calculated. Still less is it possible to argue that very short-term trends in the recent past necessarily conform in any way to the long-term geological history of either subsidence or rise. For example, it must be stressed that the cause of any long-term subsidence indicated by the depth of the Pleistocene–Holocene boundary cannot be the result of a modern process of delta subsidence such as groundwater or natural gas removal, neither of which has been taking place on any significant scale for more than two decades. This also applies to surface processes such as shrinkage. Further, it should also be noted that since the end of the Pleistocene there has been a eustatic sea-level rise of between 110 and 120 metres, and that sedimentation of that order must have been necessary simply to keep pace with post-Ice Age sea-level rise. At the same time, the rivers of the delta were apparently more deeply incised during the Pleistocene, meaning that there may be far greater depths of alluvium near old river beds than elsewhere across the delta surface. An individual sample well may pick up such effects.

In short, while there is abundant evidence of subsidence from various parts of Bangladesh almost throughout the geological record, its origins, scale and timing appear to vary widely. It is clearly wholly inappropriate to present a general pattern on the basis of exceptionally restricted data. Despite a very extensive search of published research, no evidence has been found of recent and accelerated subsidence. Interestingly, Bilal ul Haq (April 1999, pers. comm.) has recently confirmed this, saying that 'as far as I know, there are no real subsidence numbers based on extant data, only guesstimates from the Pleistocene–Holocene history'.

3.6.6 An alternative? The role of plate tectonics

Morgan and MacIntyre's work (1959), and the subsequent work of Umitsu (1987) using radiometric dating of buried wood in the delta as well as fossils and shells at different depths, point to an entirely different hypothesis to account for subsidence, i.e. that of tectonic warping. Morgan and McIntyre were writing before the discovery of plate tectonics, which has revolutionised the study of geology. Nevertheless, it has since become clear that the movement of the Indian plate following the break-up of Gondwanaland, and its collision with Eurasia and the Burma platelet, have been the key formative processes of the entire Bengal foredeep. Thus the dynamic instability of the underlying geological structures of the Ganges–Brahmaputra floodplain is now known to be the result of its location on the subduction zone of the Indian plate under the Asian plate. Since the beginnings of the Himalayan orogeny or uplift about 45Myr ago, this has resulted in a long period of downwarping, continuing into the present, which allowed the basal rocks of the plate's surface to be covered by ever-increasing depths of sediment washed down from the Himalayas. The overall rate of change in the level of the basement controls the general pattern of subsidence of the sediment laid down on it, while relative sea-level is dictated by the rates of sedimentation from the Himalayas and associated ranges.

The rapid developments in plate tectonics which are helping to unravel the geological history of the Bengal basin cannot be explored in detail here. The broad outlines of this process appear well understood, although many crucial elements remain to be pieced together. For example, Uddin and Lundberg (1998a) comment that

'[t]he collision between India and Eurasia did not take place simultaneously along the entire Himalayan belt . . . From 45 Ma to the present India has rotated 33° counterclockwise, the motion relative to Asia having changed from predominantly northeast to more northerly, accompanied by a 50% reduction in velocity'.

The Bengal foredeep has been formed on the subduction zone between the stable but northwards moving peninsular shelf and the building ranges of the Indo-Burman ranges to the east and the Himalaya to the north and northwest (Uddin and Lundberg, 1998b) suggest that sedimentary and meta-sedimentary rocks beneath the shelf are as much as 22 km thick. From the Eocene onwards detritus was washed down to the Indian Ocean, originally to the east of the present Bengal basin. The complexity of these movements need not detain us. It is noteworthy, however, that the delta began to receive substantial deposits of coarse ('clastic') non-marine and shallow marine deposits from the Upper Cretaceous. In the middle Eocene basinwide subsidence produced a marine transgression, creating the Sylhet limestone. From the Miocene a major delta complex was built up by deposits from the north east and a series of minor deltas by deposits from the northwest. All these deposits were river-borne and deltaic on the landward side and submarine delta fans on the seaward side (Uddin and Lundberg, 1998b).

Uddin and Lundberg maintain that during the Miocene a major river, the palaeo-Brahmaputra, flowed south carrying much of the detritus from Assam into the Bay of Bengal. Only much later, with the counter-clockwise rotation of the Indian Peninsula and the consequent closing of the remnant ocean basin from west to east, did large sediment loads reach the delta from the north west. Several studies have demonstrated the astonishing sedimentation rates over the period. While dating remains tentative (cf. Worm *et al.*, 1998: 487), one inferred sedimentation rate from the Surma basin is 1.2 mm/yr – 'one of the highest sedimentation rates in Earth history that was sustained for millions of years'.

Thus the whole Bengal delta is still astride one of the earth's most dynamic tectonic regions. Earth movements continue to generate major earthquakes and differential pressures beneath the surface are producing contrasting regions of uplift and subsidence. Sub-surface troughs, the hinge line of the subduction zone, and the fast-subsiding Sylhet trough (Acharyya, 1998) are just a few elements of Bangladesh's highly dynamic geology which may be considered to override the relatively ephmeral impact of sedimentation putatively caused by the removal of trees in the upstream Himalaya.

3.7 The political ecology of environmental change

This brief review of different components of environmental instability in Bangladesh illustrates the great, and still far from completely understood, complexity and dynamism of its physical environment. It has shown that hypotheses of relative sea-level change have to explain a balance of interacting processes, none of which can be simply measured. Still less can even a wide series of measurements be used to generalise across the delta as a whole, for despite its superficial topographic simplicity Bangladesh's surface features conceal a wealth of diversity.

Given such uncertainty we consider it impossible to either verify global hypotheses regarding global warming based on the Bangladeshi material, or to justify specific policy recommendations which address the possible significance for Bangladesh of a eustatic sea-level rise. As Broadus (1992: 101) suggests, given the large quantities of sediment carried by the delta's rivers a mean sea-level rise of 6 mm per annum would probably not be discernible while Brammer (1989, 1992) believes that the primary impact of a global rise in mean sea-level on Bangladesh will be an increase in flooding in the depressed basins upstream rather than at the coast or within tidal limits. Predictions depend critically on local conditions of accretion and erosion.

The lack of evidence to date for significant relative sea-level change completely contradicts the images of sedimentation, subsidence and submergence put forward by those engaging in the global warming debate. From the above analysis it should be clear that this is not because subsidence is not taking place. Instead it is because when looked at in its overall complexity the best conclusion that can be drawn is that, while local subsidence and local emergence are probably taking place, there is no reliable evidence of widespread subsidence relative to sea-level across Bangladesh. It is also clear that the total land area of Bangladesh has increased steadily, both over the geological time scale and in recorded history, despite a pace of subsidence which would have consigned Bangladesh to an ocean bottom depth of up to 20 kilometres had not deposition more than kept pace with it. As far as we can determine no evidence has yet been published to demonstrate that the rate of deposition has significantly slowed in the present day.

What are the implications of these contrasting scenarios for the different policy-interested groups who have focused on Bangladesh's environment over the last decade? It is clear that alternative explanations of subsidence have a major influence on the predictions of short- and medium-term change. First, it would seem that the use of Bangladesh as an example to bolster claims of environmental damage flowing from global warming are completely without contemporary empirical foundation. If there were a sudden increase in relative sea-level at the maximum predicted levels, major damage would result, but there is as yet no evidence of such a change. Instead, the material discussed suggests that in so far as subsidence is taking place it is perhaps largely the result of long-term tectonic activity in the Bengal catchment area rather than a reflection of human impacts on environment and climate. This is not to say that future use of the delta may not have an environmental impact, but there has been no published evidence, based on field research in Bangladesh, to show that it is taking place. In contrast, long-term subsidence within the geological time span is well documented and increasingly understood.

For lobbies and political interests wishing to use Bangladesh as an argument in a policy programme such a message may be unwelcome. As we have shown above, the sudden increase in interest in assessing Bangladesh's risk of imminent submergence owes everything to a global climatic concern and very little to understanding the processes of dynamic instability in Bangladesh itself. As Chapman has argued with specific respect to environmental change in the Bengal delta, the propagation of simplified myths will not help anyone (Chapman, 1995). In the contemporary world of social science intense interest in the search for universal laws and global processes has often reduced the level of interest in the specific and the regional. Yet it is in the complex interlocking of variables within particular places with their own unique combinations of environmental and human systems that the real world of environmental change is being played out. As Robert Kappel (1997) has argued, 'Empirical findings and deductions show that . . . globalisation does not do away with location. There is no end of Geography.' In other words, what we are concerned to stress is the importance of trying to come to terms with a diversity of environments and with human innovation in relation to this varied and dynamic context. Far from being a 'basket-case', these mark Bangladesh out as a country in which human initiative continues to be put to astonishing effect in coping with environmental uncertainties.

Notes

1 Mackinder was the leading political geographer of the early part of the twentieth century and founder of university geography in Britain. In his Heartland concept he advanced the idea that global power in the new 'closed' world system of states that had emerged by the end of the nineteenth century was directly related to location with respect to key resources and channels of communication. He argued that in the core region of world power geographically lay in what he termed the Heartland, that region of east central Europe which stretched from the Arctic Ocean to

the Black Sea and from eastern Germany to the Urals, and famously asserted that 'Who rules the Heartland rules the world island, who rules the world island rules the world.' In other words, it was a geostrategic concept which underpinned US and Western government strategies of containment throughout the Cold War, i.e. a contest not just between ideologies but in strategic terms as between land (the Soviet Union) and sea (US and Western Europe, i.e. NATO) power. The central geographical location of Pakistan and India thus made them crucial in strategic terms.

2   For a web site that explores these themes from a critical angle see The Tropical Ecology Web Site:http://www.ecotrop.org

3   One study which has gone some way towards incorporating aspects of variability in sediment loads is that by Mahtab *et al.* (1991, citing BWDB 1989) which estimates sediment load for various return periods (from 1/50 dry to 1/50 wet). The range is from 353 mMt (millions of metric tons) to 1482 mMt. Only wet years of 1/10 exceed 1000 mMt.

4   It should be noted that this well appears either to be inaccurately positioned on the map or that the co-ordinates are incorrect.

References

Adams, J., Maslin, M. and Thomas, E. 1999: Sudden climate transitions during the Quaternary. *Progress in Physical Geography,* **23** (1) 1–36.

Ahmad, E. 1972: *Coastal geomorphology of India.* New Delhi: Orient Longman.

Ahmad, K.S. 1968: *The economic geography of East Pakistan.* Oxford: Oxford University Press.

Alam, M. 1987: Bangladesh. In Fairbridge, R.W. (ed.), *The encyclopaedia of world regional geology,* vol. II. Stroudsbourg, PA: van Nostrand Reinhold.

Alam, M. 1989: Geotectonics and subsidence of the Ganges/Brahmaputra Delta of Bangladesh and accompanied drainage, sedimentation and salinity problems. In Milliman, J.D. and Sabhasri, S. (eds), *Sea-level rise and coastal subsidence: problems and strategies.*

Alam, M. 1996a: Geotectonics and subsidence of the Ganges/Brahmaputra Delta of Bangladesh and accompanied drainage, sedimentation and salinity problems. In Milliman, J.D. and Haq, B.U. (eds), *Sea-level rise and coastal subsidence: problems and strategies.* Dordrecht, Boston, London: Kluwer Academic Publishers, 169–92.

Alam, M. 1996b: Geomorphological features of the Hatia and Sandwip Islands of the Bay of Bengal. *The Journal of Noami* **13** (1 and 2), 61–72.

Alam, M and Samad, A. 1996: Subsidence of the Ganges–Brahmaputra delta and impact of possible sea-level rise on the coastal area of Bangladesh. *Dhaka University Journal of Science* **44**(2), 179–91.

Ali, A. 1995: A numerical investigation into the backwater effect on flood water in the Meghna River in Bangladesh due to the south-west monsoon. *Estuaries, Coastal and Shelf Science* **41**, 689–704.

Allison, M.A. 1998: Historical changes in the Ganges–Brahmaputra delta. *Journal of Coastal Research* **14**(4), 1269–75.

Allison, M.A., Kuehl, S.A., Martin, T.C. and Hassain, A. 1998: Importance of flood-plain sedimentation for river sediment budgets and terrigenous input to the oceans: insights from the Brahmaputra–Jamuna River. *Geology* **26**(2), 175–8.

Arlidge, J. 1999: On the edge of the Arctic Ice Pack, living proof of global warming. *The Observer,* Sunday, 25 July.

Baeteman, C. 1994: Subsidence in coastal lowlands due to groundwater withdrawal: the geological approach. *Journal of Coastal research* Special Issue **12**, 61–75.

Bagchi, K. 1944: *The Ganges delta.* Calcutta.

Bangladesh Water Development Board (BWDB) 1989: *Pre-feasibility study for study for flood control in Bangladesh, Vol. 2, Present conditions.* Dhaka: Government of Bangladesh.

Bradnock, R.W. 1990: *India's Foreign Policy since 1971.* London: Pinter/Royal Institute of International Affairs.

Brammer, H. 1990a: Floods in Bangladesh 1: geographical background to the 1987 and 1988 floods. *The Geographical Journal* **156**(1), March, 12–22.

Brammer, H. 1990b: Floods in Bangladesh 2: flood mitigation and environmental aspects, *The Geographical Journal* **156**(2), July, 158–65.

Brammer, H. 1993: Geographical complexities of detailed impact assessments for the Ganges–Brahmaputra–Meghna delta of Bangladesh. In Warrick, R.A., Barrow, E.M. and Wigley, T.M.L. *Climate and sea-level change*. Cambridge: Cambridge University Press, 246–62.

Brammer, H. 1996: *The geography of the soils of Bangladesh*. Dhaka: University Press Limited.

Brammer, H., Asaduzzaman, M. and Sultana, P. 1996: Effects of climate and sea-level changes on the natural resources of Bangladesh. In Warrick, R.A. and Ahmad, Q.K. *The implications of climate and sea-level change for Bangladesh*. Dordrecht: Kluwer Academic Publishers, Chapter 4.

Broadus, J.M. 1993: Possible impacts of, and adjustments to, sea-level rise: the cases of Bangladesh and Egypt. In Warrick, R.A., Barrow, E.M. and Wigley, T.M.L. *Climate and sea-level change*. Cambridge: Cambridge University Press.

Brown, A.E. 1996: *Geomorphology and groundwater*. New York: Wiley.

Brown, P. 1998: *Global warming*. Delhi: Universities Press.

Bryant, R. 1998: *Political ecology*. Unpublished seminar paper, SOAS.

Carter, R.W.G. and Woodroffe, C.D. (eds) 1994: *Coastal evolution: late Quaternary shoreline morphodynamics*. Cambridge: Cambridge University Press.

Chapman, G.P. 1995: Environmental myth as international politics: the problems of the Bengal Delta. In Chapman, G.P. and Thompson, M. *Water and the quest for sustainable development in the Ganges Valley*. London: Mansell, 163–96.

Chen, W. and Molner, P. 1990: Source parameters of earthquakes and intraplate deformation beneath the Shillong Plateau and the northern Indoburmese ranges. *Journal of Physical Research* **95**(B8), 12527–52.

Choudhury, M.I. 1974: Shape of Bangladesh through the ages. *Journal of Bangladesh National Geographical Association* **2**(1 and 2), 1–12.

Coleman, J.M. 1969: Brahmaputra river: channel processes and sedimentation. *Sedimentary Geology* **3**, 129–239.

Crace, J. 1998: Sinking into poverty. *The Guardian* 29 September, E10–E11.

Crow, B., Lindquist, A. and Wilson, D. 1995: *Sharing the Ganges: the politics and technology of river development*. New Delhi: Sage.

Eckholm, E.P. 1976: *Losing ground: environmental stress and world food prospects*. New York: Norton for World Watch Institute.

Environment and Geographic Information Support for Water Sector Planning 1997: *Morphological dynamics of the Brahmaputra–Jamuna River*. Dhaka: Environmental and GIS for Water Sector Planning.

Eysink, W.D. 1983: Basic considerations of the morphology and land accretion potentials in the estuary of the lower Meghna River. *Bangladesh Water Development Board Land Reclamation Project*. Technical Report 15, Chittagong: BWDB.

Fairhead, J. and Leach, M. 1996: *Misreading the African landscape: society and ecology in a forest-savanna mosaic*. Cambridge: Cambridge University Press.

Fergusson, J. 1863: Recent changes in the Delta of the Ganges. *Proceedings of the Geological Society* London, 322–54.

Geddes, A. 1925: *Au Pays de Tagore: La civilisation rurale de Bengale occidentale et ses facteurs geographiques*. Paris: Colin.

Geddes, A. 1982: *Man and land in South Asia*. New Delhi: Concept.

Geddes, A. 1960: The alluvial morphology of the Indo-Gangetic plain: its mapping and geographical significance. *Transactions and Papers of Institute of British Geographers* **28**, 253–76.

Giddens, A. 1990: *The consequences of modernity*. Cambridge: Polity Press.

Government of Bangladesh 1987: *Geology of Bangladesh, technical report no 4*. Master Plan Organisation, Ministry of Irrigation, Water Development and Flood Control, Dhaka: Government of Bangladesh, 4–17.

Government of Bangladesh 1991: *National conservation strategy of Bangladesh: towards sustainable development*. Dhaka: Ministry of Environment and Forests, Government of Bangladesh.

Government of Bangladesh Ministry of Environment and Forests, Department of Environment 1993: Assessment of the vulnerability of coastal areas to sea-level rise and other effects of global climate change. Pilot study Bangladesh Report prepared for the World Coast Conference 1993, Dhaka, November 1993.

Grainger A. 1993: Rates of deforestation in the humid tropics: estimates and measurements. *Geographical Journal*, **159**, 33–44.

Grainger, A. 1996: An evaluation of FAO Tropical Resource Assessment 1990, *Geographical Journal* **162**(1), 73–9.

Gulston, E. 1763: A Persian writer, Hirst, William (1763). *Transactions of the Royal Society of London*, **51**, 251–69.

Haq, B.U. 1994: *Sea level rise and coastal subsidence: rates and threats*. Washington: The World Bank.

Hashem, A. 1994: Ganges water natural right of Bangladesh. *The Guardian*, **IV**(1), 9–10.

Hicken, E. 199?: *River geomorphology*. New York: Wiley.

Hofer, T. 1998: *Floods in Bangladesh: a highland–lowland interaction*. Bern: Geographia Bernensia for University of Bern.

Hofer, T. and Messerli, B. (eds) 1998: *Floods in Bangladesh: history, processes and impacts*. Bern: Geographia Bernensia for University of Bern.

Hoque, M. and Alam, M. 1999: Land subsidence in Bangladesh. Copies of overhead projection slides used at the International Seminar on Sea-level Rise and Sustainable Coastal Management, Dhaka, 18–20 March 1999.

Houghton, J.T. 1997: 2nd edn *Global warming: the complete briefing*. Cambridge: Cambridge University Press.

Houghton, J.T., Callander, B.A. and Varney, S.K. 1992: *Climate change 1992: the supplementary report to the IPCC scientific assessment*. Cambridge: Cambridge University Press.

Intergovernmental Panel on Climate Change 1990: *Climate change – the IPCC scientific assessment*. Cambridge: Cambridge University Press.

Intergovernmental Panel on Climate Change 1992: *Global climate change and the rising challenge of the sea*. The Hague: Coastal Zone Management Subgroup of the IPCC Response Strategies Working Group.

Islam, T. 1994: *Vulnerability of Bangladesh to climate change and sea-level rise: concepts and tools for calculating risk in integrated coastal zone management*. Dhaka: Bangladesh Centre for Advanced Study (BDAS), Resource Analysis (RA) and Approtech Consultants Limited.

Ives, J.D. and Messerli, B. 1989: *The Himalayan dilemma: reconciling development and conservation*. London and New York, Routledge.

Johnson, B.L.C. 1982: 2nd edn *Bangladesh*. London: Heinemann.

Johnson, M.R.W. 1994: Volume balance of erosional loss and sediment deposition related to Himalayan uplifts. *Journal of the Geological Society of London* **151**, 217–20.

Johnson, S. and Alam, A.M.N. 1991: Sedimentation and tectonics of the Sylhet Trough, Bangladesh. *Bulletin of the Geological Society of America* **103**, 1513–27.

Kandlikar, M. and Sagar, A. 1999: Climate change research and analysis in India: an integrated assessment of a South–North divide. *Global Environmental Change* **9**, 119–38.

Kappel, R. 1997: *Centre and periphery in the global order. Theoretical aspects of asymmetries and symmetries in the globalisation process*. University of Leipzig Papers on Africa, Politics and Economics Series No 07.

Khan, F.H. 1991: *Geology of Bangladesh*. New Delhi: Wiley Eastern Ltd.

Kingdon-Ward, F. 1955: Aftermath of the great Assam earthquake of 1950. *Geographical Journal*, **121**, 290–303.

Leach, M. and Mearns, R. (eds) 1996: *The lie of the land: challenging received wisdom on the African environment*. London, Oxford and Portsmouth: The International African Institute, James Curry and Heinemann.

Lepkowski, W. 1998: Arsenic crisis in Bangladesh. *Chemistry and Engineering Newsletter*. American Chemical Society.

Lindsay, J.F., Holliday, D.W. and Hulbert, A.G. 1991: Sequence stratigraphy and the evolution of the Ganges–Brahmaputra delta complex. *American Association of Petroleum Geologists Bulletin* **75**, 1233–54.

Mackinder, H.J. 1904: Geography as the pivot of history. *Geographical Journal* **23**.

Mafizuddin, M. and Hossain, M.S. 1990: Spatio-temporal variation of groundwater level in Dhaka city. *Oriental Geographer* **34**(1 and 2), (printed in 1992).

Mahtab, F.U. (ed.) 1991: *Report of the task force on Bangladesh development strategies for the 1990s, Volume 4, environmental policy*. Dhaka: University Press Limited.

Mahtab, F.U. 1992: The delta regions and global warming: impact and response strategies for Bangladesh. In Schmandt, J. and Clarkson, J. *The regions and global warming: impacts and response strategies*. New York and Oxford: Oxford University Press.

Mahtab, F.U. and Karim, Z. 1992: Population and agricultural land-use – towards a sustainable food production system in Bangladesh. Bangladesh Agricultural Research Council. *Ambio* **21**(1), p. 50–5.

Maslin, M. 1998: Weight and sea. *The Guardian* 23 September, S4–S5.

Meadows, D.H., Meadows, D.L., Randres, J. and Behrens, W. 1972: *The limits to growth*. London: Pan.

Milliman, J.D. 1992: Management of the coastal zone: impact of offshore activities on the coastal environment. In Hsu, K.J. and Thiede, J. (eds), *Use and misuse of the seafloor*. Chichester: Wiley.

Milliman, J.D., Broadus, J.M. and Gable, F. 1989: Environmental and economic implications of rising sea-level and subsiding deltas: the Nile and Bengal examples. *Ambio* **18**(6), 340–5.

Milliman J.D. and Haq, B.U. (eds) 1996: *Sea-level rise and coastal subsidence: causes, consequences and strategies*. Dordrecht: Kluwer Academic Publishers.

Milliman, J.D. and Meade, R.H. 1983: World-wide delivery of river sediment to the oceans. *Journal of Geology*, **91**, 1–21.

Milliman, J.D. and Syvitski, P.M. 1992: Geomorphic/tectonic control of sediment discharge to the ocean: the importance of small mountainous rivers. *Journal of Geology* **100**, 525–44.

Mirza, M. and Monirul, Q. 1996: Diversion of the Ganges water at Farakka and its effects on salinity in Bangladesh. *Environmental Management* **22**(5), 711–22.

Mitchell, T.D. and Hulme, M. 1999: Predicting regional climate change: living with uncertainty. *Progress in Physical Geography* **23**(1) 57–78.

Mollah, M.A. 1993: Geotechnical conditions of the deltaic alluvial plains of Bangladesh and associated problems. *Engineering Geology* **36**, 125–40.

Monbiot, G. 1999: Apocalypse now. *The Guardian* 29 July.

Moore, W.S. 1997: High fluxes of radium and barium from the mouth of the Ganges–Brahmaputra River during low river discharge suggest a large groundwater source. *Earth and Planetary Science Letters* **150**, 141–50.

Morgan, J.P. and McIntyre, W.G. 1959: Quaternary geology of the Bengal Basin, East Pakistan and India. *Bulletin of the Geological Society of America* **70**, 319–42.

Murthy, T.S. and Flather, R.A. 1994: Impact of storm surges in the Bay of Bengal. *Journal of Coastal Research* Special Issue **12**, 149–61.

Myers, N. with Kent, J. 1995: *Environmental exodus: an emergent crisis in the global arena*. Washington: The Climate Institute.

Nicholls, R.J. and Leatherman, S.P. 1995: Sea-level rise and coastal management. In Morgan, D.F.M. and Thompson. D.A. (eds), *Geomorphology and land management in a changing environment*. New York: Wiley, 229–44.

Rennell, James 1781: An account of the Ganges and Burrampooter Rivers. *Philosophical Transactions* **71**, 87–114. (Subsequently added as an appendix to successive edition of the Memoir.)

Rennell, J. 1792, 2nd edn: *Memoir of a map of Hindoostan, or the Mogul Empire*. London, Nichol and Richardson.

Rogers, P.P. 1997: *Measuring environmental quality in Asia*. Cambridge, MA: Harvard University Press.

Rogers, P.P. 1998: Water and development in Bangladesh: a retrospective on the Flood Action Plan. Unpublished seminar paper, Cambridge MA.

Rogers, P., Lydon, P. and Secker, D. 1989: *Eastern waters study: strategies to manage flood and drought in the Brahamputra basin*. Washington, DC: ISPAN, USAID.

Spate, O.H.K. 1954: *India and Pakistan*. London: Methuen.

Spate, O.H.K. and Learmonth, A.T.A. 1968, 2nd edn: *India and Pakistan* London: Methuen.

Spykman, N.J. 1944: *The Geography of Peace*. New York: Harcourt Brace and Co.

Thomas, D.S. 1993: Sandstorm in a teacup? Understanding desertification. *Geographical Journal* **159**, 3: 318–31.

Thomas, D.S.G. 1994: *Desertification: exploding the myth*. London: Wiley.

Thompson, M., Warburton, M. and Hatley, T. 1986: *Uncertainty on a Himalayan scale*. London: Ethnographica.

Uddin, A. and Lundberg, N. 1998a: Cenozoic history of the Himalayan–Bengal system: sand composition in the Bengal Basin, Bangladesh. *GSA Bulletin* **110**(4), 497–511.

Uddin, A. and Lundberg, N. 1998b: Unroofing history of the eastern Himalaya and the Indo-Burman ranges: heavy mineral study of Cenozoic sediments from the Bengal Basin, Bangladesh. *Journal of Sedimentary Research* **68**(3), 465–72.

Umitsu M. 1985: Natural levees and landform evolutions in the Bengal lowland. *Geographical Review of Japan* Series B **58**(2), 149–64.

Umitsu, M. 1987: Late Quaternary sedimentary environment and landform evolution in the Bengal lowland. *Geographical Review of Japan* Series B, (2), 164–78.

Umitsu, M. 1993: Late Quaternary sedimentary environment and landforms in the Ganges Delta Sedimentary. *Geology* **83**, 177–86.

United Nations 1957: *Water and power development in East Pakistan*. UN Tech. Assist. Prog. Rpt, TAA/PAK/15 (the Krug Mission Report). New York: UN.

Viles, H. and Spencer, T. 1995: *Coastal Problems: geomorphology, ecology and society at the coast*. London: Edward Arnold.

Ward, R.C. and Robinson, M. 1990: *Principles of hydrology*. London: McGraw-Hill.

Warrick, R.A. 1993: Projections of future sea-level rise: an update. In McLean, R. and Mimura, N. (eds), *Vulnerability assessment to sea-level rise and coastal zone management. Proceedings of the IPCC Eastern Hemisphere Workshop*, Tsukuba, Japan, 3–6 August 1993. Tokyo: Secretariat of the Eastern Hemisphere Workshop.

Warrick, R.A. 1993: Sea-level rise. *Earthquest* Spring, Science capsule, Boulder, CO: Office of Interdisciplinary Earth Studies.

Warrick, R.A. and Ahmad, Q.K. 1996: *The implications of climate and sea-level change for Bangladesh*. Dordrecht: Kluwer Academic Publishers.

Warrick, R.A., Barrow, E.M. and Wigley, T.M.L. 1993: *Climate and sea-level change*. Cambridge: Cambridge University Press, 263–75.

Warrick, R.A. and Rahman, Atiq 1992: Future sea-level rise: environmental and socio-political Considerations. In Mintzer, Irving M. (eds), *Confronting climate change: risks, implications and responses*. Cambridge: Cambridge University Press, 97–112.

Worm, H.-U., Ahmed, A.M.M., Ahmed, N.U., Islam, H.O.O., Haq, M.M., Hamback, H.U. and Lietz, J. 1998: Large sedimentation rate in the Bengal Delta: magnetostratigraphic dating of Cenozoic sediments from northeastern Bangladesh. *Geology* June, **26**(6), 487–90.

World wide web source

Bangladesh Environment Network 'Memorandum submitted to the Honourable Finance Minister of Bangladesh', October 3 1998 Internet at bangladeshenv@makelist.com

The Tropical Ecology Web Site: URL:http://www.ecotrop.org

4

A political ecology of forest management

Gender and silvicultural knowledge in the Jharkhand, India

Sarah Jewitt and Sanjay Kumar

4.1 Introduction

In addition to emphasising the need for more 'bottom-up' or 'participatory' approaches to development in recent years, many development planners and donor agencies have become increasingly aware of the gender-specific nature of environmental degradation. In contrast to the 1950s and 1960s when traditional top-down, male-dominated development discourses left little space for either gender or environmental concerns, current emphases on 'sustainable development' have placed both issues at the forefront of the development agenda. Two important factors responsible for this 'sea change' in development thinking have been the growing popularity of the environmental movement from the late 1960s and the establishment of 'women in development' (WID) approaches during the early 1970s. While the environmental movement drew attention to global energy shortages and the Third World's 'fuel wood crisis' (Eckholm, 1984; Agarwal, 1986; Dankelman and Davidson, 1988), WID research highlighted major gender inequalities in divisions of labour, access to natural resources (notably land), wage rates, participation in decision-making, mobility outside the home and access to basic requirements such as food, health care and education (Boserup, 1970; Harriss and Watson, 1987; Moser, 1993; Braidotti et al., 1994; Wieringa, 1994; Agarwal, 1992; 1997a). It also focused attention on inequalities in gender divisions of labour which give women a double and often triple work burden consisting of reproductive work (child care and housework) plus subsistence production (notably the collection of environmental resources such as fuel wood and water) and, for many women, wage labour (Boserup, 1970; Agarwal, 1992; 1997a; Jackson, 1993a; 1993b; Mies and Shiva, 1993; Moser, 1993; Braidotti et al., 1994).

By the mid-1980s, environmentalist concerns coupled with popular media images of 'poor women from the South, burdened by heavy loads of fuel, fodder and water, against a backdrop of barren landscapes' (Braidotti et al., 1994: 87) had focused attention on the idea that women, as the main victims of environmental degradation, would be the most appropriate contributors to environmental protection (Dankelman and Davidson, 1988; Agarwal, 1992; Braidotti *et al.*, 1994; Joekes *et al.*, 1994; Jackson, 1993a). In support of this idea, a number of researchers pointed to the important role that many Third World women play in community-based resource management and emphasised the need for development planners to secure their input into such schemes (Foley and Barnard, 1984; 1985; Shepherd, 1985; 1989; Cecelski, 1992; Mishra, 1994).

At the same time, eco-feminist ideas about an innate women–nature link started to stimulate interest in women's role as environmental custodians. The Indian eco-feminist, Vandana Shiva, has been particularly influential in promoting the view that women's 'closeness to nature' has enabled them to develop comprehensive agro-ecological knowledges and environmental management practices (Shiva, 1988). She argues that many agricultural innovations from all over the world were made by women and gives numerous examples of the ways in which women act as 'intellectual gene pools' through their role as 'selectors and preservers of seed' and their emphasis on the conservation of bio-diversity.

These images of women's closeness to and willingness to protect nature were important stimulants in the emergence of a 'women, environment and development' (WED) perspective which emphasised a 'special' relationship between women and the environment (Braidotti *et al.*, 1994; Joekes *et al.*, 1994; Leach *et al.*, 1995). In the 1985 Nairobi Forum, a special workshop was held on 'women and the environmental crisis' and thereafter WED emphases on women as environmental managers and key contributors to sustainable development became important themes in mainstream development discourse (Braidotti *et al.*, 1994).

In more radical and alternative development fora, meanwhile, the idea of a special women–environment link gained support among certain neo-populist and eco-feminist writers seeking a more appropriate and environmentally sensitive route to development (Shiva, 1988; Marglin, 1990; Parajuli, 1991; Banuri and Apffel Marglin, 1993; Escobar, 1992; 1995). Vandana Shiva, in particular, has been very vocal in her critique of the 'patriarchal model of progress' which, she argues, has traditionally favoured mono-culture, uniformity and homogeneity at the expense of a loss of biodiversity and the marginalisation of women who depend upon nature for sustenance. For Shiva, men's domination of and mastery over nature has been associated with new patterns of domination and mastery over women which have excluded them from participating as partners in both science and development. She further argues that Indian women, as victims of this violence, are rising to protect the environment as a means of preserving their survival and sustenance.

Shiva draws support for these views from her observation of women's role in the use and management of forest-based resources in Northern India. In particular, she cites the Chipko movement in Uttarakhand as evidence for women's environmentalist concern and willingness to put themselves at risk in order to protect forest resources.[1] Coinciding as it has with the interest of mainstream development policy-makers in both participatory and WED approaches, the wide following that Shiva has achieved both in India and abroad has helped to place gender concerns firmly on India's environment and development agendas. Since the publication of the National Forest Policy (1988) which emphasised the involvement of local people in the planning process, for example, the need to involve women in forestry development projects has become a major feature of Indian forest policy rhetoric.

Among a number of academics working in the development field, however, the idea of a 'special' women–environment link has been greeted with much scepticism because of its misleading simplicity, essentialism and political naïveté (Agarwal, 1992; Jackson, 1993a;

Braidotti *et al.*, 1994; Leach *et al.*, 1995). Of particular concern are WED's treatment of women as a unitary category undifferentiated by class, caste, region, ethnicity, age or marital status and its failure to distinguish between (frequently female-dominated) environmental work and (usually male-dominated) environmental management (Jackson, 1993a; 1993b; Agarwal, 1997a; 1997b; 1998; Locke, 1999).

To encourage a closer examination of gender–environment relationships, proponents of 'gender analysis' (Jackson, 1993a; 1993b; 1994) and 'feminist environmentalism' (Agarwal, 1992) perspectives have called for the replacement of WED by more robust 'gender and development' (GAD)[2] and 'gender, environment and development' (GED) perspectives. Although rarely explicitly acknowledged as such, much of this work is characterised by a strong political ecology core; notably in its attempts to deconstruct the idea of an innate women–nature link by examining the wider socio-cultural factors that have traditionally placed women in close contact with the natural environment. A major argument has been that to further understandings of gender-specific responses to environmental problems it is necessary to look beyond the idea of a 'special link' with nature towards an examination of wider inequalities in gender divisions of labour, property and power.

Bina Agarwal's work in India, for example, suggests that 'women's and men's relationship with nature needs to be understood as rooted in their material reality, in their specific forms of interaction with the environment' (Agarwal, 1992: 126). Agarwal has also highlighted how the ability of many Indian women to both act on their environmental concerns and put their ecological knowledge into practice is often severely restricted by their limited land rights coupled with cultural restrictions on their mobility and participation in public decision-making fora (Agarwal, 1994a; 1994b, 1997a; 1997b; 1998). In most parts of South Asia, for example, inheritance systems are patrilineal, residence patterns are patrilocal and the management of private land as well as common property resources is usually strongly male dominated. In addition, the concept of female seclusion (*purdah*) is important in certain areas and amongst certain socio-economic and religious groups[3] and can influence women's interaction with men and therefore their access to public spaces and decision-making processes (Agarwal, 1994a; 1997a; 1997b). Agarwal points out that for women to 'speak out in group meetings, especially in the presence of men but also in the presence of other women, requires overcoming learned behaviour patterns that emphasise the virtue of women's silence and soft-spokenness' (Agarwal, 1994a: 110).

In a similar vein, Cecile Jackson argues that 'there cannot be a special relationship between women and environments because women are not a unitary category, and their environmental relations reflect not only divisions among women but also gender relations and the dynamics of political economies and agroecosystems' (Jackson, 1993b: 1950). She also draws attention to the fact that although there are many examples of women's involvement in environmental protection, there are also instances of women having little interest in environmental issues or even being involved in environmental degradation (Jackson, 1993a; 1993b). Indeed, there is growing evidence to show that women are frequently disadvantaged by development programmes that promote environmental protection or assume that women want to be involved in it (Jackson, 1993a; 1993b; Sarin, 1995; Shah and Shah, 1995; Agarwal, 1997a; 1997b; 1998; Locke, 1999). At the same time, there are numerous cases of men bearing the brunt of environmental decline and/or being actively involved in environmental protection initiatives (Shah and Shah, 1995; Leach *et al.*, 1995; Agarwal, 1998; Mawdsley, 1998; Locke, 1999).

In the light of these findings, there has been significant recent theoretical debate amongst academics about the dangers of translating simplistic WED/eco-feminist emphases on a 'special' women–environment link into development policy-making. WED has also been criticised for treating women as an undifferentiated category while at the same time 'invisibilising' men, their environmental knowledge systems and the problems that they face as a result of environmental degradation (Braidotti *et al.*, 1994; Shah and Shah, 1995; Leach *et al.*, 1995; Agarwal, 1998; Mawdsley, 1998; Locke, 1999). With the exception of the work carried out on conjugal contracts in Zimbabwe (Jackson, 1995), resource management in the West African forest zone (Leach, 1991) and participatory forest management in South Asia (Sarin, 1993; 1995; Agarwal, 1994a; Shah and Shah, 1995; Hobley, 1996; Locke, 1999), relatively little detailed empirical work has been carried out to date on the practical implications of 'tokenistic' and undifferentiated gender policy-making. Using a gender-sensitive political ecology perspective, this chapter seeks to close the gap somewhat by drawing upon empirical data on community-based and official 'joint' forest management systems in two contrasting tribal (*adivasi*) dominated districts in the Jharkhand region of south Bihar. Sections 4.2 and 4.3 will provide a brief account of Indian forest policy, its attempts to take on board gender issues and the problems with its rather narrow conceptualisation of gender and community. Section 4.4 will provide a brief introduction to the Jharkhand region and to the research area, focusing particularly on gender relationships and inter-community variations in socio-cultural outlooks and land tenure systems. Section 4.6 provides the empirical core of the chapter and draws particular attention to (inter- and intra-) community- and gender-based differences in local forest use and management practices and the implications that these have for forest development planning. Particular stress is placed on the need for policy-makers to replace their broad-brush, undifferentiated and often superficial emphases on local participation with more nuanced investigations into local culture and development priorities. Section 4.8 provides a conclusion to the chapter.

4.2 Forest decline and India's forest policy

Deforestation is considered to be one of India's most serious environmental problems with annual forest losses reaching around 1.5 million hectares in the early 1980s and then slowing to around 47,300 hectares per year in the early 1990s (Palit, 1993). This is a major problem for many rural villagers who depend heavily upon forests for fuel wood, timber for house construction and agricultural implements, cattle fodder, potential agricultural land, food, medicinal herbs and many other (often economically quite valuable) non-timber forest products (NTFPs). It is also a serious problem for India's economy which relies heavily on forests as providers of important raw materials for industry.

In an effort to satisfy these often conflicting demands on forest resources while at the same time working towards an environmental goal of achieving 33 per cent forest cover for India as a whole (Indurkar, 1992; Palit, 1993; Pathak, 1994), the Indian government has placed increasing emphasis on the establishment of 'joint forest management' (JFM) initiatives. The aim of these programmes is to provide local people with an incentive to undertake long-term forest management and protection by enabling them to claim a share of the profits gained from any timber that they grow in designated (usually the less commercially valuable Protected Forest) areas.

One of the first States to initiate a JFM programme was West Bengal which in July 1989 made provisions for 25 per cent of the value of the timber grown in protected areas to be handed over to the forest protection committee after harvesting. In June 1990, the Government of India took the initiative on board in a resolution which stated that if local communities 'successfully protect the forest, they may be given a portion of the proceeds from the sale of the trees when they mature' (Government of India, 1990: 3). At present, 20 out of the 26 Indian State Governments have issued orders for the implementation of JFM in their States.

4.3 Gender policy in Indian forest policy

Since the publication of the National Forest Policy (1988), the Indian government has endorsed the need to involve local people in forest-related planning. Further support for this trend has been made possible by the initiation of externally aided large-scale 'Forestry Projects' in different States[4] by donors which maintain a strong participatory and (in theory at least) gender-sensitive emphasis:[5] a position that has been strengthened by early criticism of the failure of many JFM programmes to encourage women's membership on forest protection committees (Sarin, 1995; 1998; Shah and Shah, 1995). The World Bank-aided Forestry Project in West Bengal, for example, now boasts a separate 'women in development' cell within the State Forest Department and has extended the provisions for JFM committee membership to two household members instead of one. The project also includes a number of mechanisms for ensuring women's interest and participation including the development of a women's sub-committee, the establishment of planning teams that include women on a preferential basis and the employment of a co-ordinator for women's activities to assist the project.

This interest in gender concerns has been a major factor in prompting Indian forest policy makers to integrate women at every level of the new JFM strategy, although the exact form that this integration takes varies from State to State (see Table 4.1).[6] The 'Bihar State Government resolution on Joint Forest Management', for example, stipulates that there must be a minimum of three and a maximum of five women members on the executive committee of the village forest protection and management committee whereas in Haryana, JFM committee membership is open to all adults.

In spite of this increased awareness of gender issues among forest policy-makers and planners, however, it cannot yet be said that women's issues are being properly addressed. In most cases, the newly-formed forest management strategies are only superficially gender sensitive as they are formulated with little reference to the concerns and realities of women at the grassroots level (Correa, 1997; Sarin, 1995; 1998; Agarwal, 1997b; Jahan, 1998). Bina Agarwal, for example, is concerned that attempts to develop new institutional arrangements may create a 'system of property rights in communal land which, like existing rights in privatized land, are strongly male centred' (Agarwal, 1997b: 1) with the result that membership rather than citizenship becomes the defining criterion for access to forest resources.

Another danger is that many forest-related projects are infused with essentialist notions about a special women–environment link which discourages sensitivity to class, caste, age, religious and regional differentiation and often leads development planners to treat women as an homogeneous entity. To make matters worse, it is quite common for little or no socio-economic research to be conducted prior to the implementation of forestry projects with the result that the project's impacts on different segments of the village female population is often poorly documented (Correa, 1997; Sarin, 1996; 1998; Locke, 1999). Despite its rhetoric about the importance of gender equality, for example, the World Bank undertakes little or no empirical research to confirm that its 'gender-sensitive' policies are being implemented successfully on the ground (Jahan, 1998; Locke, 1999).

With respect to JFM programmes more specifically, many States display a strong element

Table 4.1 Women's representation in Village Forest Committees and entitlement to benefit in JFM resolutions

State	General body membership	Minimum representation of women in the managing committee	Benefit-sharing entitlement
Andhra Pradesh	1 female and 1 male per household	3 out of 9–13 members	Unspecified
Bihar	1 representative per household	3–5 out of 15–18 members	Management committee to decide
Haryana	All adults	2 women but the whole committee could be women	Equal access to loans for men and women
Himachal Pradesh	1 female and 1 male per household	2–3 out of 9–12 members	For all villagers
Jammu and Kashmir	1 female and 1 male per household	2 out of 11 members	Institution to decide
Karnataka	1 representative per household	2 out of 15 members	Among beneficiaries
Madhya Pradesh	1 representative per household	Not specified	Equally among members
Maharashtra	Unspecified	2 out of 11 members	Equally among members
Orissa	1 female and 1 male per household	3 out of 11–13 members	Equally between households
Punjab	No general body	1 woman	Equally between households
Rajasthan	Unspecified	Unspecified	Equal shares for members
Tripura	1 representative per household	Unspecified	Distributed among members
West Bengal	Joint membership of husband and wife	Not specified	Either husband or wife
Tamil Nadu	1 female and 1 male per household	50% of women	Unclear

Source: Sarin (1998)

of tokenism in their provisions for the participation of women. Locke's research on an ODA-funded participatory forest project in southern India, for example, led her to conclude that the desire to pay lip-service to gender issues within JFM programmes

> has been translated into a preoccupation with formal provisions for women's participation in local forest management institutions and with the necessity of identifying women's preferences for forest resources and, to a lesser degree, their knowledge and values about forest resources.
> (Locke, 1999: 270)

Unfortunately, however, the systems for checking if these formal provisions work satisfactorily in practice (or whether women's participation actually results in any degree of control over forest resources) have in practice often been conspicuous by their absence.

A similar situation is apparent in the Bihar JFM programme, which provides no justification for why it limits the maximum number of female executive committee members to five. Similarly, although almost all State government orders prescribe a certain minimum number of women representatives in the managing council of the village forest protection committees, there is often no similar minimum number in the 'general body' committee: a potentially problematic scenario given that the power of women in the executive committee is likely to be seriously constrained by the lack of a significant female presence on the 'general body' committee.

There is also an implicit emphasis in many programmes on the role of women as 'conservationists' or 'bearers of ecological knowledge' which has encouraged policy-makers to secure women's participation in forestry projects. While this can in many ways be viewed as a very positive step, few JFM programmes actually specify which rights are secured for which class of women and how women's participation in JFM committees is likely to vary in different regions or amongst different community and religious groups. Within patrilineal inheritance systems, income from (as well as control over) landed property usually remains in the hands of male household members. So, as Agarwal points out, there is a danger that the shift from usufruct (citizenship) to membership rights over environmental resources could further increase women's economic vulnerability and dependence on men (Agarwal, 1997b). Such issues are important considerations for programmes that seek to effectively empower women (and local communities more generally) to manage forest resources on principles of equity and sustainability.

Similarly, there is little scope within most JFM programmes to adapt to the particular decision-making and environmental management traditions that characterise different regions or communities. Just within the Jharkhand region, for example, substantial variations can be found in the decision-making institutions of different tribal and non-tribal communities and this can have a significant impact on the ease with which they can adapt to fit into Bihar's particular JFM model (Jewitt, 1995; 1996). Another important regional and socio-cultural variable that can have a critical impact on the success or failure of forest management strategies is that of land tenure. While a particular property regime or system of tenure may be quite compatible at one level with the conservation of forest resources, it may foster major negative consequences at another level. Alternatively, systems of forest management that are beneficial to men or better off villagers may bring few benefits to women or the poor (Sarin, 1995; 1996). Given such differences in cultural traditions and socio-economic circumstances, it is sometimes difficult for local communities to accept the imposition of what may be community and/or gender-insensitive systems of property management.

4.4 Background to the Jharkhand Region

Although not recognised as an 'official' administrative unit by the Indian state, the Jharkhand region is considered to comprise of the Chota Nagpur plateau and parts of upland Santhal Parganas in South Bihar plus neighbouring districts in Madhya Pradesh, West Bengal and Orissa (see Figure 4.1). There are over 30 different Scheduled Tribes in the region, the most numerically dominant of which are the Munda, Oraon, Santhal, and Ho. But despite the fact that the Jharkhand is often thought of as a 'tribal' region, its social structure has undergone tremendous change over the last century and particularly during the last 40 to 50 years. In many areas (especially Ranchi, Hazaribagh and Palamu districts), the ethnic make-up of the population has become substantially less *adivasi*-dominated and the region

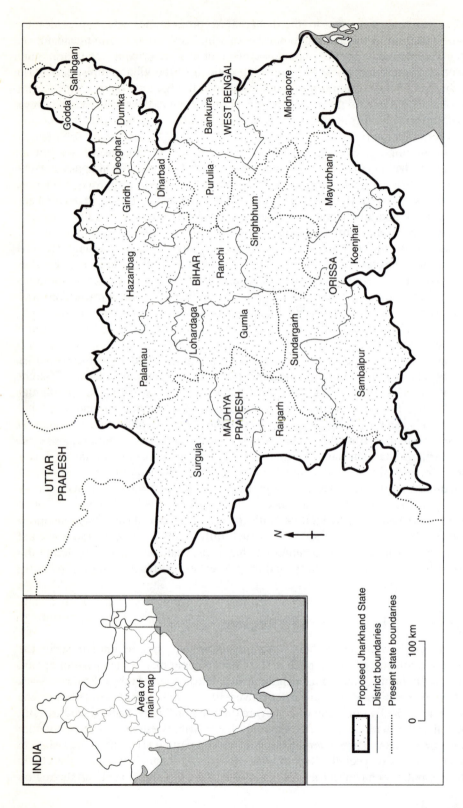

Figure 4.1 The research area. *Source:* Jewitt (1996)

as a whole now has a tribal population of around 30 per cent. The *adivasis* share a common cultural (and often religious) outlook with a variety of 'artisan castes' or *sadans* who make up around 50 per cent of the region's population and are classified variously as Scheduled Tribes, Scheduled Castes and Backward Castes (Nathan, 1988; Kelkar and Nathan, 1991). As a result, few villages nowadays conform well to Weiner's (1978) model of a 'single tribe' settlement and most have at least a few caste Hindu, Scheduled Caste, Backward Caste or Moslem villagers in addition to a cluster of *sadan* households.

The main religion for *adivasi* people in the Jharkhand is a semi-Animist faith known widely as *Sarna* although a number of Scheduled Tribe *sadans* are Hindus and *Sarna* itself is being increasingly influenced by Hinduism (Roy, 1970; 1984; 1985; Sachidananda, 1979; Rosner, undated). Hinduism followed by Islam are the most important religions for non-*adivasi* Jharkhandis, although the region also has a significant population of both tribal and non-tribal Christians. Socio-culturally, too, there are some important differences between the Jharkhand tribes and also between *adivasi* and non-*adivasi* society.

Agriculture forms the main source of subsistence for most Jharkhandis, although there are important variations between the different tribal groups.[7] On average, land holdings are small (usually under 5 acres), soil quality is often rather poor, and the lack of scope for large-scale irrigation facilities has limited the widespread adoption of 'green revolution' high yielding varieties of rice and wheat. Consequently, most households supplement what they grow with edible forest produce such as fruit, flowers, nuts, leaves, mushrooms and game. Forests are also a very important source of firewood, timber for house construction and agricultural implement making, fodder, grazing and a variety of products vital for everyday life. In many areas, however, forest decline has limited the availability of these items and many tribal communities must now supplement their traditional subsistence strategies with activities such as seasonal migration, mining, agricultural labour, cash cropping and the sale of forest produce (Sachidananda, 1979; Munda, 1988; Corbridge, 1986; Pathak, 1994). In particular, the harvesting and sale of forest products from frontier (forest–agriculture interface) areas offer easy economic gains to many Jharkhandis. As a result, increasing numbers of women are cutting fuel wood for sale to urban populations, although responses to this phenomenon are filtered through the local customs of the area and of the community to which the women belong.

As in many other hill and tribal communities (Agarwal, 1997b), gender relations in the Jharkhand are relatively egalitarian with women enjoying quite a high social status and 'economic value' compared to their non-tribal counterparts. An important illustration of this is the tradition of 'bride price' being given to the girl's parents (instead of a dowry to the boy's parents) to compensate them for the loss of their daughter's labour (Harriss and Watson, 1987; Kelkar and Nathan, 1991). In addition, extreme discrimination against women such as female infanticide or selective female abortion is very uncommon amongst *adivasis*.

Similarly, despite the fact that land inheritance patterns in the Jharkhand are patrilineal, the importance of sons is not as great as in many other societies as it is common for parents with no sons to get a daughter married in the *ghar-jamai* tradition whereby the new son-in-law takes over the family farm and hopefully provides an heir to inherit the property (Roy, 1984). In addition, *adivasi* society recognises the responsibility of women in managing agriculture in the absence of male family members (Roy, 1985; Kelkar and Nathan, 1991): a system which provides Jharkhandi women with some opportunities to put their ecological knowledges and decision-making skills into practice.

With the steady influx of plains Hindu ideas in the region, however, these traditions are changing quite quickly. Indeed, the practice of giving bride price is declining among the Oraon tribe in the south-western part of the Jharkhand (although it is still common amongst the Munda, Ho and Santhal tribes in the south and south-east) and the region's female:male sex ratio has been declining continuously throughout the century (Kelkar and Nathan, 1991). In Ranchi district, for example, the female:male sex ratio fell from 1022 : 1000 in 1881 to 927 : 1000 in 1991 (Government of India, 1881; 1981; 1991). In addition, although female seclusion is not practised by *adivasi* and *sadan* women (who are often heavily involved in marketing, agriculture and the gathering of forest produce), the participation of women in traditionally male-dominated village-level decision-making institutions has nevertheless traditionally been rather limited. According to Agarwal, such constraints can be linked to wider issues of 'gender ideology, viz. the social constructions of acceptable female behaviour, notions about male and female spaces, and assumptions about men's and women's capabilities and appropriate roles in society' (Agarwal, 1997b: 26).

In addition to these wider social constraints, there are some important political ecology issues underlying local divisions of labour which influence gendered aspects of villagers' ecological knowledges and environmental responses. In many cases, prevailing gender divisions of labour are reinforced by taboos which restrict women's (and, very rarely men's) behaviour (Kelkar and Nathan, 1991) and help to prevent women from expanding their knowledge base, sharpening their decision-making skills and improving their economic status more generally. The most universal taboo amongst the Jharkhand tribes is the common South Asian taboo against women ploughing (Blaikie, 1985; Henshall Momsen, 1991; Sontheimer, 1991; Agrawal, 1995) a situation that can be interpreted as a means of justifying men's control over the production process (Kelkar and Nathan, 1991). In a similar vein, there are also taboos against women hunting, roof-making and (less obviously) carrying items on their shoulders (which is done by men only) rather than on their heads (Roy, 1984; 1985). Indeed, the method by which *adivasis* carry items is so sex specific that one way of asking about the sex of a new baby is 'to ask whether the child will carry on the head or the shoulder' (Kelkar and Nathan, 1991: 58).

At the regional and national levels, factors such as socio-economic status, religious affiliation and ethnic background can act as important influences on how gender roles are organised and re-negotiated over time whereas at the local (intra- and inter-household) level, issues like age and marital status can be very important (Jackson, 1995; Agarwal, 1997b; Locke, 1999). Although the tendency for women to withdraw from market and forest-based labour as their socio-economic status improves (Agarwal, 1997a) is less pronounced in the Jharkhand and tribal areas, wider regional, religious, class, community and seniority-related influences can nevertheless act as important differentiating factors among women. In terms of forest management, for example, significant differences exist between tribal communities and most areas are characterised by important variations amongst and between *adivasi* or *sadan* women and those from Moslem, caste Hindu and even Backward Caste households (Jewitt, 1996).

4.5 The fieldwork areas

The fieldwork has taken place over a period of ten years and draws upon Kumar's extensive experience in the Indian Forest Service plus Jewitt's PhD research in two Oraon-dominated villages in Bero Block, Ranchi district. Kumar's work as a Divisional Forest Officer in Daltonganj North Division and Ranchi East Division has enabled him to gain extensive knowledge about the forest management systems characteristic to different tribal groups. In addition, he has worked as a Divisional Forest Officer in Research and Evaluation and also as a member of the Gender and Equity Group of the National Support Group of Joint Forest Management which was established by the Society for Promotion of Wastelands Development, New Delhi.

The field research was conducted primarily in Munda-dominated villages in Singhbhum district and Oraon-dominated villages in Ranchi district; the main reason for this choice being a desire to compare villages with different land tenure arrangements. Most of the forests in Ranchi district came under state ownership with the introduction of the Bihar Land Reforms Act in 1950 and were thereafter declared and managed as Protected Forests under Chapter IV of the Indian Forest Act. In the Munda-dominated areas of Singhbhum district, on the other hand, many villages are still governed under the Mundari '*Khuntkatti*' system[8] whereby Mundari villagers have dual status as landlords and right holders over local forests.[9] In other words, most of the forests in Oraon-dominated areas are government property whereas in Munda areas, they are family (village) property. Our assumption was that this distinction in forest tenure would have an important bearing both on community-based forest management systems and, relatedly, on the different roles of village women in the use and management of local forests. There are also significant agricultural differences between the two areas which influence gender division of labour and the financial importance of forests to local communities. Generally speaking, Ranchi district is agriculturally more dynamic than Singhbhum, being characterised by a shift towards more lucrative vegetable cultivation and a higher degree of women's involvement in farming.

4.6 Inter- and intra-village variations

4.6.1 Inter- and intra-village variations in forest labour

Contrary to WED/eco-feminist stereotypes of fuel wood collection and other forest-based gathering as 'women's work', it is common throughout the Jharkhand for men to participate in this activity (Kelkar and Nathan, 1991) although 'the modalities by which they do so may differ and reflect other social patterns of disadvantage to women' (Joekes *et al.*, 1994: 139). It is common, for example, for men to cut large pieces of fallen or dry firewood and take them home using items of transport such as cycles and bullock carts that women rarely have access to.

In both Ranchi and Singhbhum districts, the fuel wood collection season starts in late October, when the main agricultural season is over, and finishes by the start of the monsoon in June. During this time, women go frequently to the jungle to collect dry branches and cut small saplings. Echoing Agarwal's (1997a; 1997b) findings elsewhere in India, age and marital status are important factors influencing intra-household work allocation and where there is more than one adult female in a household, the task of fuel wood collection is usually delegated to the younger women. In addition, girl children over the age of about seven are often expected to help out whenever they are available. Men, by contrast, tend to make fewer trips to the forest and often go in all-male groups to combine the collection of fuel wood with more social activities such as hunting for game.

When focusing on gender divisions of labour, however, it is important not to ignore the existence of variations between households from different community, socio-economic and religious groups. The most obvious are between *adivasi/sadan* villagers – which are characterised by quite a high level of gender equality and female mobility – and relatively well-off Moslem, caste Hindu and some Backward Caste households which tend to aspire to the ideal (if not the practice) of female seclusion (*purdah*) and try to discourage women from undertaking forest-based labour or marketing activities. In most cases, the extra-household mobility experienced by individual women is influenced strongly by the economic status and perceived socio-cultural standing of their households. Those that can afford to replace women's labour with that of male household members or hired labourers often choose to do so, regardless of which community they belong to. Thus, even amongst *adivasis* and *sadans*, it is common for relatively well off households to buy in fuel wood to relieve female household members from the drudgery of going to the forest to collect it. Conversely, it is not unusual for women from poor Moslem and caste Hindu households to be heavily involved in fuel wood collection. Generally speaking, however, it is more common for men from better off Moslem, caste Hindu and (to a lesser extent) Backward Caste households to play a greater role in the collection of fuel wood than is the case in *adivasi* and *sadan* families who can delegate such tasks to their female members.

These socio-cultural variations are echoed with respect to the cutting of fuel wood for sale purposes which, in contrast to WED/eco-feminist discourses about women as environmental custodians, is viewed primarily as women's work in the Jharkhand. Generally speaking, it is concentrated amongst the poorer socio-economic groups who cannot afford to heed traditional cultural restrictions on the cutting of green (living) trees for sale and has tended in the past to be more common in Oraon areas than in Munda areas; primarily because of the stronger socio-cultural restrictions placed on the cutting of forest trees for non-domestic use by the *Khuntkatti* system. Nowadays, however, a significant number of Munda households in the Bandgaon area of West Singhbhum district have taken to stealing timber from government as well as *Khuntkatti* forests for sale in urban areas as door frames or planks for doors and windows. Reflecting the dangerous nature of such activities and the relatively high economic value of the timber, the marketing of such products is usually carried out by Munda men rather than women.

With respect to the collection of large timber, gender divisions of labour are rather more pronounced in Munda villages where only men go to the forests to bring wood for the construction and repair of buildings and agricultural implements. Reflecting wider taboos which restrict women's control over the production process (Kelkar and Nathan, 1991), it is common in Singhbhum for *adivasi* and *sadan* women to be allowed to collect large timber only when male household members are either indisposed or away and even then they can only bring limited numbers of small diameter poles. Non-*adivasi/sadan* women from relatively well off households, meanwhile, rely much more heavily on male household members for the collection of such items. When no male household members are available and large timber is required, meanwhile, women from all community groups have to rely upon the *madad* system[10] whereby male villagers (usually from the same community) provide labour in exchange for a specified amount of food and rice beer per person per day. In some Mundari-*Khuntkatti* areas, where the *gram-sabha* (village council) hires watch men to protect the village forest, it has become common for female-headed households to pay these watchmen to fetch a certain agreed number of poles. In Oraon areas, by contrast, there are significantly fewer cultural restrictions on women collecting large timber from forest areas, although this is an activity that few of the better-off Moslem, caste Hindu or (to a lesser extent) Backward Caste women participate in. The main exception to this pattern is the collection of the timber used for Madwa (the thatched stage where marriage rituals are performed) which in both Munda and Oraon areas is invariably brought only by men.

Another aspect of forest-based work in the Jharkhand which contrasts with prevailing

WED/eco-feminist emphases on gathering as 'women's work' is the collection of non-timber forest products (NTFPs) which, with a few important exceptions, is usually quite evenly divided amongst women and men. For locally used large tree-based NTFPs, for example, it is common for men to shake the trees and then join the women and children in picking up the forest products from the ground. Other jointly conducted activities include the inoculation, cutting and scraping of lac (for making shellac), cultivation of tassar cocoons, collection of honey, wax, gum, resin, *datun* (sticks for brushing teeth) and *gungu* (*Bauhenia vahlii*) leaves for making raincoats and umbrellas.

Reflecting the fact that wider forms of socio-economic discrimination against women exist even in areas with quite high levels of female autonomy and 'economic value' (Kelkar and Nathan, 1991; Agarwal, 1997b), however, the most male-dominated 'gathering' tasks are the collection of economically valuable NTFPs and medicinal herbs.[11] NTFPs that are used primarily for domestic purposes such as *sal* (*Shorea robusta*) leaves, *datun*, mushrooms and leafy forest vegetables are collected by women in both areas, although women in the better-off (especially Moslem and caste Hindu) households often try to avoid such work. Loose restrictions on women's mobility are also indicated by the fact that cattle grazing, which involves working away from the home (usually in or near the forest) for significant periods of time, is also strongly male-dominated, although in Oraon areas young (pre-teenage) girls often share this task with male relatives.

Similarly, when it comes to the barter or sale of NTFPs, it is usually men who are responsible for taking the more valuable NTFPs such as *sal*, *mahua* (*Madhuca indica*) and *piyar* (*Buchanania latifolia*) seeds or *lac* to market and if women do go, they are usually accompanied by a male family member. When surplus domestic stocks of less valuable NTFPs like *datun* or leafy vegetables are sold, by contrast, women often go alone to market. Significantly, the cash incomes gained from NTFP sales are generally kept by the person who makes the sale; a situation which naturally tends to favour men who deal primarily with the most valuable products.

4.6.2 Inter- and intra-village variations in silvicultural knowledge

To a large extent, these gender, community, socio-economic, age, religious and regional variations in divisions of responsibilities are influential in the formation of environmental knowledges. In contrast to WED/eco-feminist discourses on women's 'holistic and ecological knowledge of nature's processes' (Shiva, 1988: 24), however, evidence from the Jharkhand points to the dangers of 'invisibilising' men's ecological knowledge, on the one hand, and ignoring important *intra*-gender variations in environmental knowledge possession, on the other.

One of the most fundamental factors affecting the extent to which villagers can develop and extend their silvicultural knowledge systems stems from a basic familiarity with neighbouring forest areas. Given the predominance of patrilocal residence patterns in the Jharkhand, as elsewhere in India (Agarwal, 1997a), obtaining detailed silvicultural knowledges is a much simpler task for men than it is for women who usually see the village forest for the first time when they marry and move to their husband's villages. As a result, they have to spend time finding out things like where the forest boundary lies and which are the best places to gather fuel wood and items like *datun*, mushrooms and leafy vegetables. The task is even more difficult for women who did not grow up in rural areas and find themselves having to learn about forest-based gathering work from scratch. Similarly, non-*adivasi/sadan* women who marry into households with less economic or socio-cultural standing can be expected to suddenly start performing forest-based work that would have been socially unacceptable in their parents' homes.

Nevertheless, the existence of prevailing gender divisions of labour that give many Jharkhandi women the primary (if not exclusive) responsibility for fuel wood collection should, following the logic of WED/eco-feminist discourse, make this the task in which they display the most holistic silvicultural knowledges. Indeed, one of the main arguments used by proponents of the 'women-as-environmental-custodians' view is that they prefer to use dead wood for fuel rather than cutting living tree branches or young saplings (Fortmann, 1986). Evidence from the Jharkhand, however, provides strong support for Cecile Jackson's (1993b) claim that weight and burnability are just as important to firewood collectors as environmental protection factors. Although women in both districts stated a preference for the relative dryness and lightness of dead and fallen timber, they estimated that supplies of such wood would run out less than a month after the start of the firewood collection season and villagers would be forced thereafter to start cutting green wood for fuel.

In addition to environmental 'damage' caused by the felling of saplings and living branches from mature trees, evidence from both Munda and Oraon villages pointed to the often careless way in which tree cutting is carried out by female fuel wood collectors: a situation that rather makes a mockery of WED/eco-feminist discourses about women possessing an 'holistic and ecological knowledge of nature's processes' (Shiva, 1988: 24). Even amongst women who make regular trips to collect firewood, for example, few cut trees in a way that encourages re-growth.

In part, this may be because the tools that women use to fell trees (usually a small axe or sickle shaped '*daoli*') do not give them a wide enough reach to hit the bottom of the sapling without bending for long hours and risking damage to their backs. A more significant factor, however, seems to relate to inter- and intra-gender differences in silvicultural knowledges and attitudes towards forest protection. Indeed, throughout the research area there appears to be rather limited knowledge among women about how to prepare cut tree stumps in ways that enhance the growth of coppice shoots. In addition, young, usually unmarried, girls tend to have quite different attitudes towards fuel wood cutting compared to older women from the same community and village. Whereas young female fuel collectors not only cut saplings with abandon but are also often quite reckless in their failure to distinguish between good and inferior timber species, many of their older relatives scold them and try to persuade them to collect *jhari-jhunti* (bushes of inferior species) for their fuel. In many cases, their advice goes unheeded until the girls in question have families of their own and start to take a more long-term view about the need for forest protection. Even then, the double or even triple work burden of women with families puts severe time constraints on their forest-based activities. The girls, meanwhile, often respond to such criticism by stating that the forest has declined significantly since these older women used to undertake fuel wood collection (i.e. before they started delegating such work to their daughters and daughters-in-law), so they can't understand what a time-consuming activity it is nowadays. They also stress the dangers of working alone in the forest[12] plus the increased risk of being caught by the forest guard and charged for (real or otherwise) illegal tree felling if they linger there unnecessarily.

In contrast to the failure of many women to try to stimulate tree regeneration, quite a number of men from all communities are very knowledgeable in the art of coppicing. In part, this is an artefact of the heavier, long-handled axes that men use for fuel-wood cutting which enable them to fell trees at the base and achieve a slanting cut that helps to stimulate coppice regeneration. An additional, age-related reason stems from the fact that between 1965 and

1972, many of the older generation of village men were employed by forest contractors to undertake forest felling operations and have therefore been taught how to coppice trees in a 'scientific' manner.[13] This involves manipulating the cambium layer (which remains adhered to the bark of tree stumps) to reduce the number of coppice shoots produced and thereby minimise competition for limited nutrients. When trees are cut by women, by contrast, the un-manipulated stumps tend to sprout too many new shoots which die off quickly due to low nutrient availability and high levels of competition from other shoots.

4.6.3 Inter- and intra-village variations in silvicultural management

These disparities in local environmental knowledges, coupled with the fluidity and constant re-negotiation of divisions of labour have an important influence on local systems of forest management. Analyses of these variations from a gender-sensitive political ecology perspective suggest, on the one hand, that in contrast to prevailing WED/eco-feminist discourses about a special women–environment link, the 'job of [forest] management is essentially a male one' (Kelkar and Nathan, 1991: 116). This is because it is usually men who are in the best position to gain environmental knowledge and utilise it when participating in male-dominated resource management institutions. On the other hand, such analyses draw attention to significant inter- and intra-gender variations in silvicultural knowledge systems that warn against too narrow a focus on gender alone.

The implications of these issues for practical policy-making are obviously quite significant, yet it is only relatively recently that they have received attention in the development literature. Bina Agarwal's work has been an important stimulus in highlighting how the access of Indian women to public places and decision-making processes has traditionally been limited by the concept of *purdah* coupled with more general socio-cultural restrictions on women's mobility and autonomy (Agarwal, 1994a; 1997a; 1997b). More specifically, recent work on JFM in India (Sarin, 1995; Shah and Shah, 1995; Agarwal, 1997a; 1997b; Locke, 1999) has shown how women are often discouraged from attending forest protection committee meetings because they feel shy about expressing their views in public. Other common factors that can work against women's participation in forest protection committee meetings include the lack of a 'critical mass' of women, a fear that their views will not be taken seriously and the scheduling of meetings at times when women are too busy to attend (Shah and Shah, 1995; Agarwal, 1997b; Locke, 1999).

Although there are some important exceptions within the Jharkhand region, these trends are certainly very representative of the situation in many of the villages that we studied in Ranchi and Singhbhum districts. In Munda villages where forest management systems are in operation, for example, the decision to ban the cutting of a particular species is usually taken by the *gram sabha* (village council) which is an exclusively male domain. Indeed, it is quite common for the *gram sabha* to inform village women that they will incur a fine if they fell trees on the prohibited species list: a situation that reflects wider concerns about the burden of forest protection falling primarily upon women (Sarin, 1995; Shah and Shah, 1995; Agarwal, 1997b; 1998; Locke, 1999). In Oraon areas, meanwhile, most decisions about forest management are taken by strongly male-dominated institutions such as *Parhas* or *Panchayats*,[14] although decisions to prohibit the cutting of particular species are often more open to women than in Munda areas. Indeed, there have been some Oraon-dominated villages in which women have initiated the establishment of either mixed or exclusively female forest protection committees and, in most cases, men respect the decisions taken by such committees. In the Oraon-dominated villages of Barwe in Ormanjhi block and

Jahanabaj in Bero block, exclusive women's committees have been functioning satisfactorily since 1992 and 1994, respectively.

One possible reason why female-dominated forest protection committees are more common in Oraon areas stems from the greater participation of Oraon women in agriculture which makes them more aware of forest and village boundaries than their Munda counterparts. Indeed, Oraon women are often just as active as Oraon men in guarding their forests from intruders (especially women) from adjacent villages whereas Munda women often transgress their village forest boundaries without fear of being obstructed by neighbouring villagers. The greater fluidity of access to neighbouring forests in Munda areas results from the fact that Mundas have better developed trans-village clan affiliations than Oraons who are more village or hamlet oriented and therefore more aware of village territories. The traditional concept of a *Parha* has also remained better developed in the Oraon region whereas in Munda areas the *khunt* (clan group descended from an original *khuntkattidar* or settler) is often more important than the village *per se* (Roy, 1970; 1984; 1985).

While community- and gender-based variations in forest management can be very important, too narrow a focus on these factors, however, can conceal important intra-village and gender-based differences. The common tendency for Jharkhandi villages to be made up of a mixture of Scheduled Tribe, Scheduled Caste, caste Hindu, Backward Caste and Moslem villagers means that the decision to protect a forest area is usually influenced by a whole series of wider socio-cultural factors. Significantly, a number of forest protection committees in the Jharkhand have been initiated by young caste Hindu, Moslem and Backward Caste men who play a greater role in the collection of fuel wood than most of their *adivasi/sadan* counterparts who can rely more on their womenfolk to undertake this task. Many of the forest protection initiatives set up by *adivasi* and *sadan* men, meanwhile, were established to address shortages of building timber (which is collected mainly by men) rather than fuel wood.

Similarly, when it comes to villagers' participation in forest protection committee meetings, some of the most vocal discussants are often those men who are most involved in fuel collection and who are looking to solutions to the fuel wood problem. In villages where women are actually allowed to participate in forest management committees, however, it is usually *adivasi/sadan* women who lead the discussions while women from better-off Moslem, caste Hindu and some Backward Caste households who play no role in forest-based gathering activities either remain absent or say little. In many cases, these patterns are further mediated by age, marital status (in the case of women) and socio-economic standing within the community. Despite the fact that burdensome activities like fuel collection tend to be delegated to younger household members, discussions about forest protection are often dominated by older villagers (of both sexes and all communities) whose seniority ensures them a significant hearing in such fora.

When it comes to formulating practical management strategies, intra-village and intra-gender variations often become even more important and the dangers of taking an undifferentiated view become very obvious. A good illustration of this is the recent conflict that has taken place between Moslem and *adivasi/sadan* women in the village of Maheshpur in Angharha block where an all-female forest protection committee was established in 1991 (Roy and Mukherjee, 1991). The main reason behind the conflict relates to the fact that many of Maheshpur's better-off Moslem women use kerosene or gas instead of wood as a cooking fuel and do not rely on the collection and sale of NTFPs as a source of income. As a result, they view forests primarily as a future source of timber revenue. The village's *adivasi* and *sadan* women, by contrast, have a strong subsistence-related dependence on forests and prefer a management option that maximises fuel wood and NTFP yield. The failure of women from different community groups to agree on a management strategy that suits everyone has resulted in the break-up of the committee.

4.7 Effects on the implementation of JFM

Given the existence of such differences between women of different communities from within the same village, let alone between different regions, it is not hard to see the potential dangers of using an undifferentiated WED/eco-feminist approach as the basis for the implementation of JFM programmes in India. As with many development projects which have a strong emphasis on women as environmental custodians, there is a danger that JFM will increase the drudgery of women's fuel wood collection work without helping them significantly to overcome traditional restrictions on their participation in forest-based decision-making. Locke's findings, for example, suggest that typically the 'closure of forest areas for regeneration occurs without any consideration for how women who previously used the forest are to meet their obligations regarding the collection of forest resources' (Locke, 1999: 275). In a similar vein, Agarwal's work shows how women risk becoming marginalised by the failure of many JFM initiatives to give them a 'formal independent rights in the new resource and not merely indirect benefits mediated through male members' (Agarwal, 1997b: 23). Most programmes also fail to take advantage of opportunities to empower women and encourage them to develop their self-confidence by formalising their participation in public decision-making fora (Agarwal, 1997b).

In the Jharkhand, it is certainly the case that the establishment of fuel wood cutting bans in protected forest areas has caused inter-gender and community conflict as firewood collectors have to go much further afield to collect their daily fuel requirements. In areas where forest protection is widespread, it is often necessary for collectors to undertake much more arduous work such as the gathering of dry fallen leaves or small twigs from thorny bushes like *putus* (*Lantana camera*). Significantly, therefore, while most JFM programmes recognise women's role as the primary fuel-wood collectors, few acknowledge or take measures to ease their work burden when forest protection restricts their gathering activities in local forests. Similarly, and as findings from elsewhere in India suggest (Sarin, 1995; Shah and Shah, 1995; Agarwal, 1997b; Locke, 1999), although many JFM programmes have made attempts on paper to allow women to play a role in forest management, few actually recognise the constraints (and wider issues of gender ideology – Agarwal, 1997b) that women face in taking up such opportunities in practice.

Probably the biggest potential source of future conflict, however, is the mechanism by which the benefits from JFM are to be shared among participating villagers (Sarin, 1995; Shah and Shah, 1995; Agarwal, 1997b). The provisions of the Bihar JFM programme, for example, state that the benefits (cash or kind) from JFM forests are to be given to JFM committee members of which there is one per household. In practice, of course, this regulation effectively filters the material and cash benefits of JFM to men as they are much more likely than women to become the designated committee member. Extensive interviews conducted by Sanjay Kumar suggested that in many villages, this situation has caused resentment among women who feel committee membership should be made more accessible to enable them to receive a separate share of the benefits accruing from JFM. A number of women solidified their demand for a separate share of JFM benefits by arguing that in addition to having primary responsibility for the sustenance of their households, they suffered the most from the closure of forests by JFM committees as it affected their fuelwood collecting activities. And as there are substantial inter-community variations in the extent to which women and men suffer from forest closures, it is not hard to foresee further conflict over benefit sharing between and within genders, communities and socio-economic groups.

4.8 Conclusion

Although the WED/eco-feminist idea of a 'special link' between women and nature has been very significant in raising awareness of gender–environment issues, there is a real danger that it may actually divert attention away from the establishment of nuanced understandings about people and place. Despite the fact that most development projects now boast a 'gender' component, this is rarely translated into in-depth analyses of local political ecology or gender relations and often amounts to little more than tokenism. As Locke discovered in her study of JFM in Southern India, the general view on women in national level policy-making is as 'an undifferentiated and marginalised category whose inclusion in JFM merits a clause' (Locke, 1999: 270).

Clearly, simply getting women a place on the policy-making agenda is not enough; especially if it comes at the cost of promoting a very simplistic and often wildly-inaccurate picture of gender–environment relations. The material discussed here illustrates from a variety of angles how shaky a foundation undifferentiated WED/eco-feminist approaches can provide for the formation of locally appropriate forest management programmes. The continuing tendency of such approaches to romanticise women's relationships with nature often occlude, not to mention drastically simplify, the tremendous variations that can occur between regions, communities, genders and age groups. Moreover, their failure to recognise the constant re-negotiation of environmental responsibilities within households in response to factors such as environmental degradation or opportunities for seasonal migration has serious implications for the drafting of locally appropriate and acceptable development programmes.

Perhaps even more problematic, however, is the fact that WED/eco-feminist assumptions about women's roles as environmental custodians have often caused an increase in their drudgery by creating potentially false expectations about their desire or ability to participate in environmental conservation or management programmes. JFM programmes, for instance, frequently create significant increases in the work burden of firewood collectors when local forests are closed for regeneration and fuel has to be collected from much further afield. In most cases, this burden falls primarily upon women. As the Jharkhand case studies show, however, this is not always the case but local complexities are likely to be missed without a deeper understanding of the political ecology and socio-cultural realities influencing resource use and management strategies. Even attempts to use participatory rural appraisal techniques to add a gender analysis dimension to environmentally-oriented development projects often fail as their snapshot nature is insufficient to reveal wider socio-political factors that can influence resource use and management (Mosse, 1994; Mayoux, 1995; Locke, 1999).

What is urgently needed, therefore, is a shift away from an undifferentiated and largely instrumental 'add women and stir' WED approach (Braidotti *et al.*, 1994), towards a deeper, more place- and people-sensitive form of gender analysis that can take on board the highly political yet ever changing socially constructed nature of people–environment interactions. Evidence from the Jharkhand confirms Jackson's view that women (and men) 'act as agents in both environmentally positive and negative ways' (Jackson, 1993: 413) and highlights the need to focus in on the 'material realities' (Agarwal, 1992) of men's as well as women's environmental relations. More significantly, however, it demonstrates how important a gender-sensitive political ecology approach can be for facilitating more in-depth understandings of the regional, community, religious, age and other differences *within* gender groups as well as of the wider socio-cultural and political-economy contexts within which environmental problems occur and environmental responsibilities are negotiated. Without this, there is a likelihood that little more will be achieved than the replacement of traditional, male-dominated development paradigms with equally narrow and theoretically simplistic female-oriented ones.

Acknowledgments

Much of Jewitt's initial fieldwork in Ambatoli was carried out in conjunction with Stuart Corbridge and all of her doctoral research was greatly assisted by two female research assistants: Pyari Lakra and (from October to December 1993) Subani Kujur.

Notes

1 The Chipko movement grew out of a long tradition of peasant protest against commercial forestry operations which restricted local people's traditionally free access to forests, thus depriving them of important subsistence resources (Guha, 1989; 1993; Pathak, 1994; Rangan, 1996). In the early 1970s, local people showed their opposition to commercial timber auctions by embracing the trees that were due to be cut down. The name Chipko stems from the imperative of the Hindi verb *chipakna* which means to adhere or embrace.

2 Unlike WED, which considers wider gender inequalities as beyond its remit, GAD rejects the idea of a special, unvarying women–environment link on the basis either of biology or the nature of women's work. Instead, emphasis on the environment, where it is considered, is 'seen merely as part of general entitlements and capabilities ascribed to individuals by social relations of gender, class and so on' (Joekes *et al.*, 1994: 139). Particular attention is focused on intra-household inequalities in access to resources and the importance of bargaining between women (as well as between men and women) over divisions of responsibilities.

3 These practices tend to be strongest in northern India amongst upper-caste Hindu communities and Muslim groups and weaker in South India and amongst lower caste and tribal communities (Agarwal, 1997a; 1997b). Nevertheless, these regional, religious and socio-cultural variations are usually cross-cut by broader rural/urban and class/caste divisions which influence the extent to which women will observe *purdah* and participate in household decision-making. A common generalisation is that poorer women, because they cannot afford *not* to work and (are therefore unable to observe *purdah*), have greater mobility outside the household and greater autonomy within it. They also have less to lose in socio-economic terms than 'middle' position peasant women who have their family status to think of (Agarwal, 1994).

4 Fifteen externally aided forestry projects are underway in 11 states of India at a total cost of Rs. 27,300 billion (Government of India, Ministry of Environment and Forests, 1997).

5 In the World Bank-assisted forestry projects operating in the Indian states of West Bengal, Andhra Pradesh, Uttar Pradesh, Kerala and Maharashtra, the participation of local people, particularly women, is seen as both a critical criterion for the success of official programmes and a key to forest regeneration and development (World Bank, 1992; 1995a; 1995b; 1998).

6 As State governments receive almost 70 per cent of the resources for JFM programmes from either central government or external donor agencies, they are supposed to follow the JFM prescriptions set by these agencies which are uniform for all States and do not take into account the social and geographical variability between or within States: a situation that can result in inflexible (and therefore potentially unsustainable) JFM structures.

7 The Munda, Santhal, Ho and Oraon tribes, for example, practise settled agriculture and have gained an important niche in the service sector whereas the Birhor, Paharia and Asur tribes have maintained a strong tradition of hunting and gathering. In between these extremes, shifting cultivators like the Sauria Paharia and artisan tribes like the Mahali, Lohara and Chic-Baraik remain caught up between highly precarious forest-based economies and the agricultural labour market.

8 The term *khuntkattidar* refers both to the original settlers of a village and to their male descendants of the same clan who are the only people entitled to inherit *khuntkattidari* land.

9 For example, 121 out of 222 forests in Tamar Thana and 119 out of 282 forests in Khunti Thana are Mundari *Khuntkatti* forests. These forests have the status of Private Protected Forests under the Bihar Private Forest Act (which is the same Act that governed most private forests before the 1950s' land reforms).

10 '*Madad*' literally means help or assistance.

11 Most forms of medicinal knowledge are strongly male-dominated and controlled by a few 'experts'; notably male herbal therapists, *Ojhas* (witch doctors) or *Pahans* (village priests).

12 In both areas, villagers fear professional 'head-cutters' (*otangas*) who hide in jungle areas and hunt people for sacrifice (Jewitt, 1996).

13 The contractor system was in vogue between 1965 and 1982, although after 1972 poor timber stocks brought a general decline in the number of workable annual harvesting coupes and corresponding contractor activities.

14 The *Parha* system is a traditional form of village administration which has jurisdiction over a group of villages and is run by village elders. After 1949, village-level administration changed somewhat with the introduction of the *Gram Panchayat* system of local governance throughout India. The superimposition of this new local form of 'representative democracy' on top of the *Parha* system, plus the fact that the *Gram Panchayat* had direct access to local development funds, resulted in the breakdown of most *Parhas*.

References

Agarwal, A. 1995: Dismantling the divide between indigenous and scientific. *Development and Change* **26**, 413–39.

Agarwal, B. 1986: *Cold hearths and barren slopes: the woodfuel crisis in the Third World*. New Delhi: Allied.

Agarwal, B. 1992: The gender and environment debate: lessons from India. *Feminist Studies* **18**(1), 119–58.

Agarwal, B. 1994a: Gender, resistance and land: interlinked struggles over resources and meanings in South Asia. *The Journal of Peasant Studies* **22**(1), 81–125.

Agarwal, B. 1994b: *A field of one's own: gender and land rights in South Asia*. Cambridge: Cambridge University Press.

Agarwal, B. 1997a: Gender, environment, and poverty interlinks: regional variations and temporal shifts in rural India. *World Development* **25**(1), 23–52.

Agarwal, B. 1997b: Environmental action, gender equity and women's participation. *Development and Change* **28**, 1–44.

Agarwal, B. 1998: Environmental management, equity and ecofeminism: debating India's experience. *The Journal of Peasant Studies* **25**(4), 55–95.

Banuri, T. and Apffel Marglin, F. (eds) 1993: *Who will save the forests? Knowledge, power and environmental destruction*. London: Zed Books.

Blaikie, P.M. 1985: *The political economy of soil erosion in developing countries*. New York: Longman Scientific and Technical.

Boserup, E. 1970: *Women's role in economic development*. New York: St Martin's Press.

Braidotti, R., Charkiewicz, E., Hausler S. and Wieringa, S. 1994: *Women, the environment and sustainable development: towards a theoretical synthesis*. London: Zed Books.

Cecelski, E. 1992: *Women, energy and environment: new directions for policy research.* Toronto: International Federation of Institutes for Advanced Study.

Corbridge, S.E. 1986: State, tribe and religion: policy and politics in India's Jharkhand, 1900–1980. PhD dissertation, University of Cambridge.

Correa, M. 1997: *Gender and joint forest planning and management: a research study in Uttar Kannada district, Karnataka.* New Delhi: India Development Services, Bangalore and Society for Promotion of Wasteland Development.

Dankelman, I. and Davidson, J. 1988: *Women and environment in the Third World: alliance for the future.* London: Earthscan.

Eckholm, E. 1984: *Fuelwood: the energy crisis that won't go away.* London: Earthscan.

Escobar, A. 1992: Reflections on 'development'. *Futures* **24**, 411–36.

Escobar, A. 1995: *Encountering development: the making and unmaking of the Third World.* Princeton NJ: Princeton University Press.

Foley, G. and Barnard, G. 1984: *Farm and community forestry.* Earthscan technical report no. 3, London: International Institute for Environment and Development.

Foley, G. and Barnard, G. 1985: *Farm and community forestry.* ODI Social Forestry Network. Paper 1b, London: ODI.

Fortmann, L. 1986: Women in subsistence forestry. *Journal of Forestry* **84**(7), 39–42.

Government of India 1881: *Census of India, 1881.* New Delhi: Government of India.

Government of India 1981: *Census of India, 1981.* New Delhi: Government of India.

Government of India 1990: Resolution (1 June) on 'involvement of village communities and voluntary agencies for regeneration of degraded forest land'. New Delhi: Government of India.

Government of India 1991: *Census of India, 1991.* New Delhi: Government of India.

Government of India, Ministry of Environment and Forests 1997: *Annual report 1996–7.* New Delhi. Government of India.

Guha, R. 1989: *The unquiet woods: ecological change and peasant resistance in the Himalaya.* Delhi: Oxford University Press.

Guha, R. 1993: The malign encounter: the Chipko movement and competing visions of nature. In Banuri, T. and Apffel Marglin, F. (eds), *Who will save the forests? Knowledge, power and environmental destruction.* London: Zed Books, 80–113.

Harriss, B. and Watson E. 1987: The sex ratio in South Asia. In Momsen, J. and Townshend J. (eds), *The geography of gender in the Third World.* London: Hutchinson, 85–115.

Henshall Momsen, J. 1991: *Women and development in the third world.* London: Routledge.

Hobley, M. 1996: *Participatory forestry: the process of change in India and Nepal.* ODI Rural Development Forestry Study Guide 3. London: ODI.

Indurkar, P. 1992: *Forestry, environment and economic development.* New Delhi: Ashish Publishing House.

Jackson, C. 1993a: Women/nature or gender/history? A critique of ecofeminist 'development'. *The Journal of Peasant Studies* **20**(3), 389–419.

Jackson, C. 1993b: Doing what comes naturally? Women and environment in development. *World Development* **21**(12), 1947–63.

Jackson, C. 1994: Gender analysis and environmentalisms. In Redclift, M. and Benton, T. (eds), *Social theory and global environment.* London: Routledge.

Jackson, C. 1995: From conjugal contracts to environmental relations: some thoughts on labour and technology. *IDS Bulletin* **26**(1), 33–46.

Jahan, R. 1998: Gender and international institutions. In World Bank *Proceedings of the gender and development workshop.* Washington, DC: World Bank.

Jewitt, S. 1995: Voluntary and 'official' forest protection committees in Bihar: solutions to India's deforestation? *Journal of Biogeography* **22**, 1003–21.

Jewitt, S. 1996: Agro-ecological knowledges and forest management in the Jharkhand, India: tribal development or populist Impasse? Unpublished PhD dissertation, University of Cambridge.

Jewitt, S. 2000: Mothering Earth? Gender and environmental protection in the Jharkhand, India. *The Journal of Peasant Studies* **22**(2), 94–131.

Joekes, S. with Heyzer, N. Oniang'o, R. and Salles, V. 1994: Gender environment and population. *Development and Change* **25**, 137–65.

Kelkar, G. and Nathan, D. 1991: *Gender and tribe: women, land and forests in Jharkhand*. New Delhi: Kali for Women.

Leach, M. 1991: Engendered environments: understanding natural resource management in the West African Forest Zone. *IDS Working Paper* **16**. Sussex: IDS.

Leach, M., Joekes, S. and Green C. 1995: Editorial: gender relations and environmental change. *IDS Bulletin* **26**(1), 1–8.

Locke, C. 1999: Constructing a gender policy for joint forest management in India. *Development and Change* **30**, 265–85.

Marglin, S.A. 1990: Towards the decolonization of the mind. In Apffel Marglin, F. and Marglin, S.A. (eds), *Dominating knowledge: development, culture and resistance*. Oxford: Clarendon Press, 1–28.

Mawdsley, E. 1998: After Chipko: from environment to region in Uttaranchal. *The Journal of Peasant Studies* **25**(4), 36–54.

Mayoux, L. 1995: Beyond naivety: women, gender inequality and participatory development. *Development and Change* **26**, 235–58.

Mies, M. and Shiva, V. 1993: *Ecofeminism*. New Delhi: Kali for Women.

Mishra, S. 1994: Women's indigenous knowledge of forest management in Orissa. *Indigenous Knowledges and Development Monitor* **2**(3), 3–5.

Mosse, D. 1994: Authority, gender and knowledge: theoretical reflections on the practice of participatory rural appraisal. *Development and Change* **25**, 497–526.

Moser, C. 1993: *Gender, planning and development: theory, practice and training*. London: Routledge.

Munda, R.D. 1988: The Jharkhand movement: retrospect and prospect. *Social Change* **18**(2), 28–42.

Nathan, D. 1988: Factors in the Jharkhand movement. *Economic and Political Weekly*, 30 January, 185–7.

Palit, S. 1993: *The future of Indian forest management: into the twenty-first century*. Joint Forest Management Working Paper 14. New Delhi: National Support Group for Joint Forest Management, Society for Promotion of Wastelands Development and Ford Foundation.

Parajuli, P. 1991: Power and knowledge in development discourse. *International Social Science Journal* **127**, 173–90.

Parajuli, P. 1996: Personal communication during second conference on the reconstruction of Jharkhand, August 1996, Cambridge.

Pathak, A. 1994: *Contested domains: the state, peasants and forests in contemporary India*. New Delhi: Sage.

Rangan, H. 1996: From Chipko to Uttaranchal: development, environment and social protest in the Garhwal Himalayas, India. In Peet, R. and Watts, M.J. *Liberation ecologies: environment, development, social movements*. London: Routledge, 205–26.

Rosner, V. undated: *The flying horse of Dharmes*. Ranchi: Satya Bharati Publications.

Roy, S.B. and Mukherjee, R. 1991: Status of forest protection committees in West Bengal. In Singh, R. (ed.), *Managing the village commons. (Proceedings of the national workshop on managing common lands for sustainable development of our villages: a search for participatory management models.)* 15–16 December 1991, Bhubaneshwar. Bhopal: Indian Institute of Forest Management, 113–16.

Roy, S.C. 1970: *The Mundas and their country*. London. Asia Publishing House.

Roy, S.C. 1984: *The Oraons of Chota Nagpur: their history, economic life and social organisation*. Ranchi: Man in India Office.

Roy, S.C. 1985: *Oraons, religion and customs*. Delhi: Gian Publishing House.

Sachidananda, S. 1979: *The changing Munda*. New Delhi: Concept Publishing Company.

Sarin, M. 1993: *From conflict to collaboration: local institutions in joint forest management*. New Delhi: National Support Group for Joint Forest Management, Society for Promotion of Wastelands Development and Ford Foundation, Joint Forest Management Working Paper 14.

Sarin, M. 1995: Regenerating India's forests: reconciling gender equity with joint forest management. *IDS Bulletin* **26**(1), 83–91.

Sarin, M. 1996: Actions of the voiceless: the challenges of addressing subterranean conflicts related to marginalised groups and women in community forestry. Theme paper for FAO Conference on 'Addressing Natural Resource Conflicts Through Community Forestry', January–April 1996.

Sarin, M. 1998: *Who is gaining? Who is losing? Gender and equity concerns in joint forest management*. New Delhi: Society for the Promotion of Wasteland Development.

Saxena, N.C. 1998: Extract from *The saga of participatory forest management in India*: Chapter Three 'Locally inspired collective action'. *Wastelands News* **XIII**(2), 30–9.

Shah, M.K. and Shah, P. 1995: Gender, environment and livelihood security: an alternative viewpoint from India. *IDS Bulletin* **26**(1), 75–82.

Shepherd, G. 1985: *Social forestry in 1985: lessons to be learned and topics to be addressed*. ODI Social Forestry Network. Paper 1a, London: ODI.

Shepherd, G. 1989: *Putting trees into the farming system: land adjudication and agro-forestry on the lower slopes of Mount Kenya*. ODI Social Forestry Network Paper 8a, Summer 1989, London: ODI.

Shiva, V. 1988: *Staying alive: women, ecology and survival in India*. New Delhi: Kali for Women.

Sontheimer, S. (ed.) 1991: *Women and the environment: a reader*. London: Earthscan.

Weiner, M. 1978: *Sons of the soil*. Princeton, NJ: Princeton University Press.

Wieringa, S. 1994: Women's interests and empowerment: gender planning reconsidered. *Development and Change* **25**(4), 829–48.

World Bank 1992: *India forest sector review*. World Bank Report No. 10965 IN 1992. Washington, DC: World Bank.

World Bank 1995a: *Towards gender equality*. Washington, DC: World Bank.

World Bank 1995b: *Staff appraisal report: Madhya Pradesh forest project*. Washington, DC: World Bank.

World Bank 1998: *Implementation completion report: West Bengal forestry project*. Washington, DC: World Bank.

Part 2

Water and 'Virtual Water'

5

Contending environmental knowledge on water in the Middle East

Global, regional and national contexts

J. Anthony Allan

5.1 Introduction

> Water flows uphill to money and power.
> (Reisner, 1984)

The purpose of the following discussion is to shed light on processes of contention associated with the development of water allocation and management policies in water stressed regions. The main focus will be the Middle East and North African (MENA) region (Fig. 5.1) because it is this region that is in the midst of diffusion of 'new' approaches to water allocation and management. In addition, the MENA case is internationally significant because the MENA region is the first to enter a period of progressively worsening water stress (Falkenmark, 1986; Allan, 1998). The year 1970 marked approximately the point when the region overall went into water deficit. Many minor MENA economies, measured as minor in terms of their population, had been experiencing water stress for over a decade before the 1970s.

Defining water stress requires the adoption of heroic assumptions. Human communities need water to drink and prepare food, to keep themselves and their homes healthy and to sustain livelihoods. They may also choose to devote water to maintaining an agreeable urban environment via a municipal system of water provision. This last can be a demanding sector in arid countries. In very general terms, an individual needs one cubic metre of water to drink each year, about 100 cubic metres for domestic purposes and about 1000 cubic metres to raise the food consumed annually. Livelihoods may be extremely water-intensive if they are based on agriculture; by comparison, individuals dependent on modern urban livelihoods, software design, for example, have negligible water requirements.

Those contributing to water policy discourses, and particularly to advocating and contending approaches different from those in place, frequently have different assumptions in mind when analysing policy options. If water self-sufficiency means access to enough water for all needs, the minimum quantity needed per person per year will be about 1000

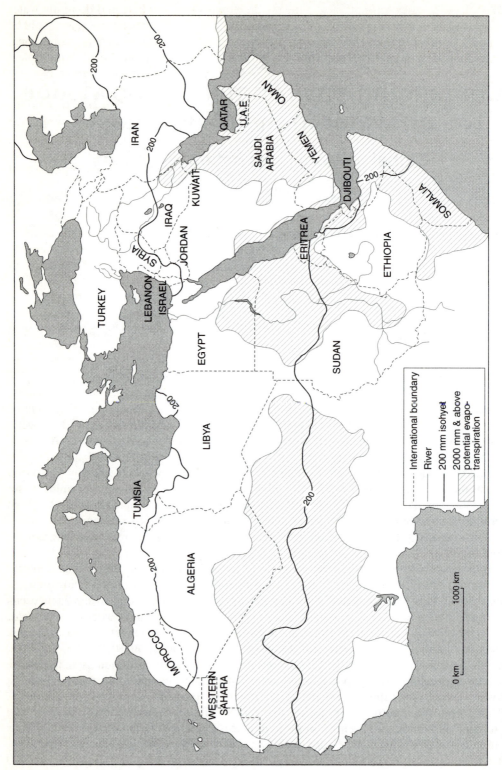

Figure 5.1 The MENA region (Middle East and North Africa)

cubic metres. If water self-sufficiency means the provision of drinking and domestic water and a further quantity to support livelihoods, 200 cubic metres per person per year should be sufficient. An economy with the capacity to generate livelihoods and engage in international trade enables its communities – urban and rural – to purchase food. Local hydrological systems are part of regional and global environmental systems and, more importantly as we shall see, global economic systems.

The other principle over which there is contention in managing water relates to water as an environmental issue. The peoples and governments of the MENA region regard water as an economic resource which contributes to the improvement of the standard of living of its peoples rather than as an essential element in maintaining the quality of current and future lives and environments. Water policy in the region is not inspired by the principles of environmentalism (Eckersley, 1992; Redclift, 1987).

The MENA region provides an ideal case for review of ways in which knowledge concerning water is constructed. In particular, this relates to a rapid shift from millennia of satisfactory water availability and its allocation in economic systems which were water self-sufficient, to the arrival of a regional water deficit in the 1970s. This was related to population increase and was simultaneous with the peak of the environmentalist debates in the 'north' which so influenced President Carter. Early in his 1976–79 presidency he confronted Congress over economically and environmentally unsound water projects.

President Carter's politically damaging contention with Congress and with the entrenched bureaucracies of the US Bureau of Reclamation and the Corps of Engineers have been effectively and compellingly chronicled in Mark Reisner's (1984) novel *Cadillac Desert*. In essence, Carter's new environmentalism conflicted with an 'old-school' approach to environmental resource development epitomised by the New Deal public works politics of the 1930s. By the 1970s these had become the foundation of a classic 'pork barrel' mechanism channelling federal funds to meet the expectations, seen as entitlements, of Members of Congress and their constituents. The US government agencies, i.e. the Bureau and the Corps, in ensuring their own continued existence reinforced the system rather than reaching for the principles of sound economics and environmental sustainability which would have threatened their survival. If water politics are unprincipled and not benign in 'the north' in the face of environmentally inspired innovation, we should not expect them to be conflict-free or amenable to new approaches in the relatively poor countries of 'the south'.

From an environmental perspective the Carter approach was right but ill-timed. The US political economy had the capacity to assimilate the ideas and policy reforms which he advocated, inspired by the two decades of the environmentalist movement of the 1960s and the 1970s. While good for both water and wider environments, as well as the US economy, however, Carter's approach was very bad for his presidency because of institutional resistance within the government bureaucracies. All the measures he recommended, and especially the restructuring of the Bureau and the Corps, were implemented by his successor.

The most important feature of this brief reference to the construction of a new US water knowledge is that it was so recent. Following the political theorist Eckersley (1992: 7), his proposed reforms were the beginning of a US 'survivalist' phase in which central government intervened to promote sustainability and the rehabilitation of water resources and water environments, to counter the fear that the negative impact of economy on ecology would eventually come full circle and undermine the US economy. Otherwise, the idea that parts of the US, especially the arid south-west of the country, could be seriously impairing its long-term environmental, and therefore its economic viability, was not a significant element in the political discourse until the 1980s.

The MENA region, however, is much less well endowed in terms of water resources than the United States. The MENA economies are economically weak and poorly developed even if they enjoy the privileges of the rentier when oil prices are high. The institutional capacity of their national government agencies is weak and thus the MENA region is characterised by 'strong societies and weak states' (cf. Migdal, 1988). This has serious consequences when 'new knowledge' pointing to the need for water policy reform encounters the deeply held 'beliefs' of water-using communities which are both numerous and well connected with officials and politicians associated with water allocation and management. The national water bureaucracies of the region are often ancient, and where they are not, they are deeply entrenched in old, rather than new approaches to these issues.

5.2 An evaluation of the MENA region's water endowment

The MENA region's water resources and its water policies have been well documented for the past 50 years. The water resources are considered to be sufficiently important that they were the first to be reviewed and published by the Land and Water Division of the FAO (1997a and 1997b). A number of hydrological and economic factors impact on the discourse on water policy reform. First, imprecision in measuring water availability and water use at a national level is significant as the contending entities advocating and resisting water policy reform can dispute whether there is a water deficit at all. Second, there can be disagreement on whether national economic security is a sufficient strategic goal. No community apparently enjoys the prospect of being non-water-self-sufficient in the sense of being unable to raise its own food needs. Drawing attention to a new and historically unprecedented national deficit is too politically hazardous an initiative for most politicians. Third, there are a number of social and political processes involving water-using communities and political leaderships which will be shown to be a form of 'sanctioned discourse' (Tripp, 1996). These determine the extent to which water policy-makers can impose unpopular water policy reforms on users of large volumes of water in sectors with a long tradition of heavy water use.

The major indicator of the scale of the water deficit of an economy is the level of its food imports. The reason food imports are such a strong indicator of water deficit is that the water required to raise food is what an economist would refer to as the dominant consumptive use of water. The use is dominant whether viewed from the point of view of the individual citizen or the national economy. Water used in the agricultural sector exceeds by ten times the water used by the industrial and municipal sectors combined.

In the arid and semi-arid Middle East the dominance of the agricultural water demand is stark. There is little or no naturally occurring soil water even in the winter when parts of the region do receive rainfall. By contrast, for economies located in temperate latitudes, Europe and the humid tracts of North America for example, the issue of the relative demands of the agricultural and the industrial (including service) sectors is scarcely evident. In temperate latitudes crop production is almost totally based on soil water which occurs naturally. In these contexts soil water tends to be taken for granted such that the huge volumes of water utilised by agriculture are not counted as part of the national water budget. Water, in effect, is a free good.

Water discourse founded on the experience of the temperate North is likely to miss much that is fundamental in the environmental endowment of the arid and semi-arid MENA region. While water is treated as a free good in temperate humid regions, in the semi-arid and arid Middle East and North Africa agricultural water is expensively won through the costs of storage and distribution. Storage is needed to ensure timely availability and to reduce the loss of water needed by the economic system. Mobilising such water, in addition, can be politically stressful both nationally – through environmental impacts – and internationally – through riparian conflict. The comparative economic disadvantage of the Middle East and North Africa with respect to water is an extreme and classic case.

Soil water and the economic efficiency of water use, however, are vital issues in any review of MENA water. The reasons, though not immediately apparent, are powerful. First, it is *global soil water* which balances the water budgets of all the economies of the Middle East and North Africa, with the arguable exception of Turkey. Second, the *effective allocation of water* between economic sectors, i.e. between agriculture and industry, is fundamental to economic and political stability because it influences both returns from economic activity and levels of employment. The environmental significance of water and water quality will not be addressed here. This is not because these are unimportant, but I will argue that understanding the global availability of water (i.e. soil water) and the economically sound allocation of water are the major current water policy and management issues being contended for wherever is effectively the first region to run out of water.

The first issue, global soil water, is an idea being promoted by the scientific community, particularly that at SOAS (cf. Allan, 1994; 1995; 1996a). It has also been taken up by international agencies such as the World Bank (McCalla, 1997) and by regionally significant international bodies such as the European Union (Brusset, 1998). The millennial initiative of the World Water Council to provide a global vision for water for the next century has identified trade in commodities acting as 'virtual water' as the key factor which will ameliorate the impact of increasing regional international and intra-national water deficits (World Water Council, 1999).

5.3 Old beliefs, new knowledge on water allocation and management: contending constructions

More crop per drop (IIMI, 1997); more jobs per drop; more care per drop; more stake per drop.
(Allan, 1998)

We had reached 'a superb agreement' based on complete misunderstanding.
(Valery d'Estaing [The French President]
at the Tokyo Summit, quoted in Carter, 1982: 113)

Perceptions of the value of water are as paradoxically enduring and changeable as any other perceptions. Water is a relatively concrete entity enabling and affecting the lives of all humankind, but for most people water, like air, comes free or at neglible cost. An individual human can exist on 10 litres per day. This small volume can, with some effort, be conveyed by unaided human labour from a number of kilometres away to its point of use. The 200–300 litres per day consumption of the individual in the political economies of 'the North' cannot be accessed without elaborate pumping and conveyance technology. But the costs of such infrastructures and of treating, pumping and conveying water are negligible to the northern consumer.

According to World Bank guidelines the costs of water should not be higher than 2 per cent of family GDP in any economy. Five per cent is regarded as an unreasonable level

(Serageldin, 1994). Poor families in the North would have water bills approaching this level if water was charged at its delivery cost. Most poor households in the North are protected from 'unreasonable levels' of water charges by stepped tariffs or other devices of varying sophistication. An initial volume of water, sufficient for basic health, may be provided free or at a very low cost. Further volumes may be charged at higher levels or at progressively higher levels to deter excessive use. In some cases, as in the United Kingdom, the whole water bill of families receiving social security benefits may be covered by the state. During the water crisis in Yorkshire, UK in 1995 it was revealed that about 25 per cent of the company's customers were having their bills paid by the state (Kinnersley, 1997).

While perceptions of the value of water differ from community to community there is an underlying sense that water is elemental and should be freely available. For example:

> Throughout the whole of religious tradition rivers have been gods. Water has been the soul. And water is the ultimate life. Maybe that's what we brought out of the African deserts – the notion that water is life. I think that's a staple, that spring sources and flowing water are the spirit . . . are life. In *Revelation*, it issues from under the throne of God, pure as crystal. The divine influx. Somehow we make that connection.
>
> (Hughes, 1965: 1)

Reflecting this elemental quality, those who inspired the principles of the world's religions conveyed a regard for water and the environment in general, emphasising the blessings and pleasures which they bring and the obligations they are due. Muslims, for example, have been urged for thirteen centuries to pursue what is identified as a 'sustainable' approach to environmental resources, as in the following quote: 'Cultivate your world as if you would live for ever and prepare for your hereafter as if you would die tomorrow', ('The Hadith' cited by Mubarak, 1891). Such is water's fundamental place in sustaining life and livelihoods that human societies have devoted political energy and substantial economic resources to ensuring secure supplies, albeit without ensuring equitable access or freedom from the risk of water resource shortages for everyone. From the late nineteenth century until the 1970s, what we might call the first phase of (industrial) modernity, water resource discourse and water resource politics and management were dominated by the vision and politics of what has been termed the *hydraulic mission* (Swyngedouw, 1999a; 1999b; Reisner, 1984), i.e. focusing primarily on the technological aspects of water provision. This mission was first and most fully implemented in the United States (Reisner, 1984) and emulated in a very different polity, the former Soviet Union (Brezhnev, 1978). A similar mission was integral to the rhetoric and resource allocation politics of many other political economies such as post-imperial Spain (Del Moral, 1996; Swyngedouw, 1999b).

The Giddens–Beck notion of 'reflexive modernity' (Beck, 1992; 1995; 1996a; 1996b; Beck *et al.*, 1996; Giddens, 1990) is useful in explaining shifts in approach to public perceptions of environment and related 'risks' in the late phase of 'industrial modernity'. They argue that changes in awareness and perception have occurred as a result of reflexive processes, i.e. internal shifts in subjective understanding. The concept is especially useful in analysis of socio-political approaches to the environment and especially in understanding the way that water resources have been perceived during and since the 1970s. In the Northern economies 30-year discourses characterise the protracted contention over water policy (Beck, 1995; Carter, 1982: 76; Hajer, 1996; Allan, 1996b). President Carter, for example, found participation in the transition to more 'environment-friendly' policies particularly rough. What he thought was a solution appeared to be a problem to the US legislature, as the following extracts from his diary indicate:

> Had a rough meeting with about 35 members of the Congress on water projects. They are raising Cain because we took those items out of their 1978 budget, but I am determined to push this item as much as possible. A lot of these projects would be ill-advised if they didn't cost anything, but the total estimated cost of them at this point is more than $5 billion, and my guess is that the final cost would be more than twice this amount.
>
> (JC Diary, 770310, in Carter, 1982: 78)

> I had several serious disagreements with Congress, but the issue of water projects was the one that caused the deepest breach between me and the Democratic leadership. As a governor and during my campaign, I had repeatedly emphasized the need to eliminate waste and pork-barrel projects in the federal government. Some people had heard and understood what I was saying. The members of Congress had not. They were amazed when I moved to cut out the worst examples of this abuse – unnecessary dams and water projects that would cost billions of dollars and often do more harm than good. The problem was that scores of these plans were in progress, from the original conception to the final construction stage. Some of the more senior members had been waiting many years for their particular proposals to get to the top of the list. The projects represented major political plums for each district, tangible symbols of the representative's influence in Washington. For ten or fifteen years, in every congressional campaign, the promise of a new lake or canal was put forward to create temporary construction jobs, satisfy local pride, and win votes.
>
> I understood the importance of these long awaited projects to the legislators, but during the years since their initial conception, circumstances had changed, environmental considerations had increased in importance, costs and interest charges had skyrocketed, other priorities had become much more urgent, and any original justification for some of the construction had been lost forever. *Still the inexorable forces toward legislative approval moved on. Other recent Presidents, graduates of the congressional system, had looked on the procedure as inviolate. I did not.*
>
> (JC Diary, 770310, in Carter, 1982: 78–80)

Explanations of the transition, from water policies dominated by the 'old water knowledge' inspired by notions of the hydraulic mission, to the 'new water knowledge' – some aspects of which are captured in President Carter's words above – are diverse. A number of disciplines have contributed to explanations concerning why, how and when transformation in water policy and water management practice occurred.

Economists have made an important contribution by identifying a temporal sequence in approach by natural resource-using communities. Karshenas (1994) has suggested that emphasis shifts from natural resource use with attendant degradation in an early phase of socio-economic development, to resource use without degradation and finally to reconstruction of the natural resource. Economists claim that the lengths of these phases and the pace of change from degradation, to sustainable use and to reconstruction depend on the levels of 'socio-economic' development achieved by a political economy (Karshenas, 1994; Allan and Karshenas, 1996). The Karshenas concept is much strengthened if it is associated with social theory emphasising the importance of the 'social adaptive capacity' of 'communities' and national economies in enabling water policy reform and the adoption of measures to improve water use efficiency (Ohlsson, 1998; Turton, 1999).

The major contribution of economists, however, has been to explain why water policies are as they are in the most extreme water-stressed region, the Middle East and North Africa, and the non-intuitive question of why water scarcity has not been a serious problem in these areas. Economic history and economic geography show that natural resource contexts do not determine economic outcomes. Economic policy options available to natural resource-using communities can be numerous and they are especially numerous in diverse and strong economies. Strong and diverse and even oil-enriched economies have the option to achieve 'factor equalisation', by substituting capital for labour or for natural resources. Thus, in the decades since the MENA region ran out of water in about 1970, the oil-enriched economies with about half of the region's population have been able to mobilise water from other regions via trade in commodities which are water-intensive in production. A major example is grain. The MENA region was accessing about 25 per cent of its water in this way by the late 1990s. The MENA region includes both the oil-enriched economies and many countries strengthened, at least in the 1970s and 1980s, by the remittances of professionals and workers working in the Gulf. More water was entering the region as 'virtual water' embedded in grain imports annually than flowed in the Nile each year into Egypt's agricultural sector (Allan, 1997). The Nile is the MENA region's major water resource.

Political scientists have made their contribution to explanation for why change occurs by showing that policy reform usually only occurs when there has been an attention-grabbing shock (Kingdon, 1984) such as a drought (Allan, 1995b and 1996a). Extreme natural events tend to achieve an exceptional convergence of awareness on the part of major and minor water users, as well as on the part of policy-makers, legislators and influential agents, such as the media. Political scientists also point out that the pace of policy reform is subject to a range of political influences and circumstances. 'Weak states' find it very difficult indeed to implement the institutional reforms necessary to achieve water use efficiency and well-regulated water use. This is especially the case where there is a strong society. This phenomenon has been analysed and confirmed in the water-stressed Middle East (Migdal, 1988; Allan, 1996b).

Another political science concept, that of the 'interests' of the community or nation in ensuring beneficial outcomes for them of any water management intervention, has proved to be very useful. Finally the concept of discursive analysis (cf. McHoul and Grace, 1993) is useful in illustrating how users of water contend with those advocating water policy reform. The process of contention and the achievement of 'consensus' take time and outcomes never accord exactly with the goals of any of the contending parties; certainly not those of the alien scientist and consultant. A particularly relevant version of discursive analysis in the MENA region involves the notion of 'sanctioned discourse' (Tripp, 1996), i.e. the discourse which is permissible where the beliefs of society are deeply entrenched. In MENA polities beliefs regarding the availability of water can have been almost continuous over six millennia, and fundamental for the evolution of water policy is the consideration that the water resource will be sufficient for all the economic needs of all users and all strategic needs. No Middle Eastern politician will deploy alien 'new knowledge' about the lack of sufficiency of water to confront deeply held communal beliefs about water. The lock which such discourse puts on water sector policy is especially evident in political economies which have a very long tradition of water management, for example, Egypt.

The contribution of social theorists and anthropologists to explaining water has only very recently been recognised within the broader decision-making and policy arena. Social theory helps explain why the ideas of alien hydrologists, drought specialists and economists have little impact on the national policies of the governments of water scarce political economies. Notions of 'belief systems', 'information gaps' and 'mutual knowledge' (Giddens, 1984: 334–43) provide profound insights into the processes which alien innovators and local politicians and communities encounter when new knowledge is being recommended by outside professionals and scientists. 'Belief systems' in this case seem *not* to reflect the experience of five millennia of occasional drought given that the systematic permanent deficit is deliberately de-emphasised.

After 1950 many political economies in the Middle East and the Mediterranean, including Spain, entered a period of progressively more serious national water deficits – defined as insufficient water to meet all needs including that for self-sufficient food production. The communities experiencing this transition into water deficit were not equipped to deal with the new circumstances. Their ideas were based on perceptions that 'water could be analysed as a resource that embraces both "material" as well as "symbolic" interests' (Bourdieu, 1977: 182). The idea of 'mutual knowledge' (Giddens, 1984) is also very useful in analysing the way alien knowledge enters and gains prominence in water-short communities. Giddens' notion captures very well the resistance to inputs and recommendations encountered by the consulting community and scientists working on water and the physical environment and on related science and resource economics. Thus the assumption held by 'outside experts' that water is only a 'material' resource runs counter to local knowledges which identify water as a 'symbolic' resource. Ideas purveyed by 'alien' scientists may be understood, and become, 'mutual knowledge' for part of the population, usually an élite acquainted with 'northern' science. That a phase of mutual knowledge has been reached, however, does not mean that water policy can at that point be easily reformed. The process of reform is subject to the protracted discourse mentioned above which is in turn subject to the interests of stakeholders other than those approaching problems of water management as solely technical issues. Attenuation of the adoption of ideas and their incorporation into policy can take 30 years, an example being the Israeli adoption of the concept of allocative efficiency for water (Allan, 1996b). Here the importance of high returns to water outside the agricultural sector was recognised in 1962 (Palmer, 1962), but it was not until 1986 that policies reallocating water were implemented by the Israeli legislature. In less well-founded economies without the economic capacity (Karshenas, 1994) or social adaptive capacity (Ohlsson, 1998) of countries such as Israel, the process could take much longer.

In 'the South' contention over water policy, such as that engaged in by President Carter in the United States and by US environmental activists, scarcely occurs. Evidence of the equivalent reflexive process in the MENA region to date, with the exception of Israel (Lonergan and Brooks, 1993; Feitelson, 1996), have only found expression and involvement in Northern international agencies and in the writings of outside environmental scientists and economists addressing water policy reform (Brooks, 1994; Allan, 1996b: 100; Serageldin, 1995; World Bank, 1994, 1995, 1997a, 1997b). This 'alien' construction of knowledge has been accelerating in the post-Cold War circumstances of the 1990s. But with respect to water in the MENA region, it is only technical élites who have taken up principles of 'new water knowledge' as communicated by 'alien' advocates. As described above, the situation remains one of coexistent or 'mutual', and contested, knowledges with regard to water management.

In some countries of the region, i.e. Jordan, Tunisia, Morocco and Cyprus, policies are being shaped by this 'new knowledge' (Feitelson, 1996). Water pricing of municipal water has been adopted, for example, and in Tunisia, Morocco and Cyprus schemes to charge for irrigation water are being discussed and introduced (World Bank, 1998: 8–9). Further diffusion and uptake of new ideas in the near future can be expected as the international prominence of a new 'vision' for water is amplified through an orchestrated global effort by agencies and governments to make water a millennial priority (Global Water Partnership, 1999: 1).

5.4 Global factors ameliorating contention

The preceding section takes an historical approach in analysing changes in the management of water resources. Equally helpful insights can be gained from taking a geographical approach and examining issues at the global, regional and local levels. The geographical segmentation can be hydrological or political. Years of immersion by the author in the integrated river basin management literature and working in the company of professionals in that field reinforced an inclination to believe that hydrological and environmental principles are crucial in reaching sound conclusions on how to manage water resources. This impression has been further strengthened by the apparent adoption of watershed principles by groups convened to seek cooperation over water resource management in major river basins such as the Nile. The series of annual conferences convened since 1993 under the title of Nile 2002 is such an initiative (Nile 2002, 1993–99). International lawyers labouring under conventions coordinated by the International Law Association and by the International Law Commission (ILC) of the United Nations similarly have had to take on board hydrological principles. This has been a particular emphasis of their initial analysis of the non-navigational uses of international waterways (Khassawneh, 1995; McCaffrey, 1995; McCaffrey and Sinjela, 1998).

In the protracted three-decade contention over legal principle and definition, however, it became evident that hydropolitics rather than hydrology were fundamental in determining water management (McCaffrey and Sinjela, 1998). The pattern of adoption of the 1997 ILC Convention on the Non-navigational Uses of International Waterways by the nations of the global community will further emphasise the political nature of shared water resources. It is likely that upstream riparians will be slow to sign up to the 1997 Convention, however, and countries such as Turkey, which are in the midst of major civil works affecting river flows, will be especially slow.

In part this is because the river basin remains a conceptual icon of immense material and symbolic value to environmental scientists. In cleaving too closely to the concept environmental scientists prevent themselves from contributing effectively to the interdisciplinary discourse in which the explanation of water policy lies. In practice, the 'closed' environmental system of the river basin is often a relatively minor influence on water management policy in both Northern and Southern political economies. Paradoxically this can be especially the case when an economy runs out of water. The reason is that the communities and nations that live in the river basins operate in 'open' economic systems. Thus when politicians with communal and national responsibilities encounter water stress in their 'closed' hydrological systems, or in those parts to which they have legitimate or practical access, they will seek solutions *outside* their accessible watersheds. This enables them to find readily available and stress-free solutions in 'problemsheds' via whatever operational system is to hand. They reach beyond local constraints to regional and global markets. Usually it is the global trading system which provides the most effective alternative resources. Regional systems are less likely to provide solutions, at least for basic commodity shortages, because all the national units in the region tend to endure similar natural resource endowments. But somewhere in the global system there will be providers enjoying comparatively advantageous circumstances. Global players, especially in the food industries, can provide solutions to local water resource deficits via the water, food and trade nexus (McCalla, 1997).

Such alternative water resources are often unconventional. For example, the water embedded in grain imports is massive because it requires at least 1000 tonnes (cubic metres) of water to produce a tonne of grain. Each tonne of grain has over 1000 tonnes of water 'virtual water' embedded in it (Allan, 1998).

Virtual water has many political blessings for politicians managing weak political economies with poor social adaptive capacities. For countries of the MENA region it is a solution from outside which, for once, is not a political problem in that the 'North' has made available adequate volumes of 'virtual water' to meet local water deficits at remarkably low prices since the early 1970s. The actual value of 'virtual water' is probably incalculable. Is it the free water which infiltrates the soil profiles of temperate latitudes in the industrialised north? Or is it the marginal cost of providing such water in the economy into which the 'virtual water' is imported? If we were to assume the water were to be valued at one, ten or one hundred US cents per cubic metre the respective values of the water in a tonne of grain would be $10, $100 and $1000. In practice, the tonne of grain is currently imported for about $140 per tonne, about half its production cost in the US or Europe. USDA and European Union subsidies on wheat, for example, make for a very heady economic advantage to the grain importer.

The political advantages of 'virtual water' are substantially greater than their economic ones. The reason is that the importation of 'virtual water' is not a political problem provided that attention is not drawn to the water, food and trade nexus. 'Virtual water' has the immense advantage of being non-stressful provided it remains as politically invisible in the political system as it is economically invisible in national and international economic systems. Water reform policies, on the other hand, such as regulatory regimes, water markets and care for the environment, inspired by economic principles and by principles of environmental sustainability, confront overstretched Southern politicians with (political) problems with high associated political prices. The reason that such secure and easily available 'virtual water' is significant to water-short economies is that the politicians in these economies can defer dealing with the impacts of their accumulating water deficits because these reserves of accessible 'water' exist. The existence of virtual water dampens the widespread awareness of the extent of national water deficits. The impact of the existence of 'virtual water' on the pace of water policy reform is immense if incalculable.

The volumes of water transferred across the world via trade, embedded in water-intensive commodities such as grain, are massive in terms of the occasional and accumulating water deficits experienced in water-stressed regions. Such strategic water is relatively easily mobilised; very easily mobilised compared with the problems that engineers would face in shifting such high water volumes.

5.5 Conclusion

The first part of this study emphasised that the last three decades of the twentieth century in the North have been a period when perceptions of water resources have been transformed as part of a reflexive response to awareness that water environments were at risk (Pearce, 1992; McCulley, 1996) from policies underpinned by the assumptions of the 'hydraulic mission'. In the period 1960–80 environmental activists and activist scientists influenced communities, constituencies and politicians to operationalise a different evaluation of water environments. The reflexive response of Northern water science and the communities and polities which manage water has not been taken up by an equivalent suite of activists, activist scientists and persuadable officials and politicians everywhere in the South.

Circumstances in the MENA region are paradoxical. The MENA region is the first region to encounter what has been argued should be strategically and economically damaging water deficits. However, the anticipated MENA water deficit hazard has not materialised. This chapter argues that a complex interplay of unrecognised economic solutions, belief systems and political processes contributes to the persistence of as yet inflexible approaches to water use and allocation. In particular, while operationally effective global trading systems exist which ameliorate the regional water deficit, awareness of them is of such destabilising potential that the social and political systems are trapped in a 'sanctioned discourse' of non-awareness.

I have also reviewed water and water policy in the MENA region as an example of how a significantly water-stressed part of the South has reacted, in terms of perception and water policy reform, to ideas generated in the transition from industrial to reflexive modernity in the North. Risk society theory is helpful in providing an overarching interdisciplinary framework contributing relevant analytical categories for the technical and social aspects of knowledge and impact. The water-stressed MENA communities and political economies have most reason of all in the Southern regions to move from water policies of industrial modernity to those of reflexive modernity. In practice, the era of industrial modernity is being extended by the manipulation of awareness of risk by politicians' natural inclination to remain in harmony with the belief systems of their peoples. In this context, belief systems about the fundamental place of water in livelihoods are best left uncontested.

The MENA region is possibly an exceptional example of how the perception of risk, in this case the risk of water shortages, can be manipulated if socio-political circumstances are enabling. MENA water resources are perceived as much by cultivated non-knowledge as by knowledge. Silent solutions to the water resource risk are de-emphasised. As a result the disjuncture between knowledge and impact is extreme. There are 'specific rules, institutions and capacities that structure the identification and assessment of risk in a specific cultural context. They are 'the legal, epistemological and cultural power-matrix in which risk politics is conducted' (Beck, 1999: 83).

Risk society theory has potential utility in policy-making. Risks have causes. Risks have beneficiaries as well as victims. Are these actors the only ones with liability or should public agencies also be involved? What type of politics mediates knowledge and non-knowledge of risk and are there means of 'proving' these knowledges? What compensation measures administered by what political institutions can be mobilised to compensate those affected by unmitigated extreme events?

The MENA region is a risk society in waiting. It has the major risk of water shortages hanging over it but it does not yet deploy the capacity to interrogate the problem. Even more than risk societies in the North the MENA political economies are

> trapped in a vocabulary that benefits the risks and hazards interrogated by the . . . definition[s] of first industrial modernity. They are singularly inappropriate not only for modern (screening) catastrophes, but also for the challenges of manufactured insecurities. Consequently we face the paradox that at the very time when threats and hazards are seen to become more dangerous and more obvious, they simultaneously slip through the net of proofs, attributions and compensation with which the legal and political systems attempt to capture them.
>
> (Beck, 1999: 83)

Policy-makers and those who advise them at local to global levels can be informed by risk society theory. Some axioms of application relevance encountered in the theory and discussed here in relation to the MENA region and its water resources are that perceptions are local while the industrial way of life is spatially and temporarily open to extend across the globe. Risk may be socially visible or invisible. Bringing risk to consciousness so that it becomes an actual threat is a demanding social and political process with possible associated political prices. The points where risks impact are not obviously tied to points where the risk origins are measurable; thus there is a disjunction between knowledge and impact.

The MENA case study is especially powerful in exemplifying how risk, in this case water shortages, can be socially invisible in relation to a region's status regarding economic development and environmental resource management practices. In this I maintain that consciousness of risk requires both 'scientific' argument and engagement with cultural contexts leading to contestation. As Goldblatt (1996) argues, 'the politics of risk is intrinsically a *politics of knowledge*, expertise and counter-expertise'.

Acknowledgements

This chapter could not have been written without the generous sharing of insight and knowledge by numerous scientists and professionals over half a lifetime. The major stimulus to look at the politics of water policy came from David Kinnersley and the direction has been much reinforced recently by Ivan Cheret: two very cerebral water professionals. Conviction that the direction was relevant has also been much encouraged by formal and informal discussions with staff of the international agencies – David Grey, Andrew Macoun and Christopher Ward (The World Bank). Colleagues and researchers in the SOAS Water Issues Group have been immensely stimulating especially in the past year when Tony Turton (University of Pretoria) was with us and so many are completing their graduate research projects. Relevant or not, the decision to research water issues has always received the support of colleagues at SOAS and its administrative infrastructures.

References

Allan, J.A. 1994: Overall perspectives on countries and regions. In Rogers, P. and Lydon, P. (eds), *Water in the Arab world: perspectives and prognoses.* Cambridge, MA: Harvard University Press, 65–100.

Allan, J.A. 1995a: Water in the Middle East and in Israel-Palestine: some local and global resource issues. In Haddad, M. and Feitelson, E. (eds), *Joint management of shared aquifers: second workshop.* Jerusalem: Palestine Consultancy Group, Jerusalem and the Harry S. Truman Institute for the Advancement of Peace, 31–42.

Allan, J.A. 1995b: The role of drought in determining the reserve water sector in Israel. *Drought Network News*, International Drought Information Center, 17(3), October 1995, 21–3.

Allan, J.A. 1996a: Drought as a concept and drought as an instrument of policy. In Haddad, M. and Feitelson, E. (eds), *Management of shared aquifers.* Third Workshop, Jerusalem: Palestinian Consultancy Group and the Truman Institute for the Advancement of Peace.

Allan, J.A. 1996b: The political economy of water in the Jordan Basin. In Allan, J. A. (ed.), *Water, peace and the Middle East, negotiating water in the Jordan Basin.* London: Tauris Academic Studies, 75–119.

Allan, J.A. 1998: Moving water to satisfy uneven global needs: 'trading' water as an alternative to engineering it. *ICID Journal*, **47**(2), 1–8.

Allan, J.A. 1999: Virtual water. UNESCO *Courier* Paris: UNESCO, March 1999, 29–31.

Allan, J.A. 2000: *The Middle East water problem: hydropolitics and the global economy.* London: Tauris Academic Publications.

Allan, J.A. and Karshenas, M. 1996: Managing environmental capital. In Allan, J.A. (ed.), *Water, peace and the Middle East: negotiating resources in the Jordan Basin.* London: Tauris Academic Publications, 121–35.

Beck, U. 1992: From industrial to risk society. *Theory, Culture and Society*, **9**, 97–123.

Beck, U. 1995: *Ecological politics in an age of risk*. Cambridge: Polity Press.

Beck, U. 1996a: *The reinvention of politics*. Cambridge: Polity Press.

Beck, U. 1996b: The sociology of risk. In Goldblatt, D. *Social theory and environment*. Cambridge: Polity Press.

Beck, U. 1999: What is a 'risk (society)'? *Prometheus*, **1(1)**, Winter 1999, 75–9.

Beck, U., Giddens, A. and Lash, S. 1996: *Reflexive modernization*. Cambridge: Polity Press.

Bourdieu, P. 1977: *Outline of a theory of practice*. Cambridge Studies of Social Anthropology, Cambridge: Cambridge University Press.

Brezhnev, L. 1978: *The Virgin Lands*. Translated by R. Daglish, second printing 1979, Moscow: Progress Publishers.

Brooks, D.B. 1994: Economic, ecology and equity: lessons from the energy crisis in managing water shared by Israelis and Palestinians. In Isaac, J. and Shuval, H. (eds), *Water and peace in the Middle East*. Amsterdam: Elsevier, 441–50.

Brusset, B. 1998: Comment at the World Bank MENA Water Initiative Conference, Cairo, June 1998.

Carter, J. 1982: *Keeping faith: memories of a president*. New York: Bantam Books.

Del Moral, L. 1996: The debate on the financial and economic regulation of water in contemporary hydrological planning in Spain. In Allan, J.A. and Radwan, L. (eds), *Perceptions of the values of water and water environments*. Proceedings of the European Community Erasmus Seminar, London: Departments of Geography of SOAS and Middlesex Universities, 37–45.

Eckersley, R. 1992, 1997 edn: *Environmentalism and political theory: towards an ecocentric approach*. London: UCL Press and New York: State University of New York.

FAO 1997a: *Water resources of the Near East region: a review*. Rome: FAO, Land and Water Development Division, Aquistat Programme.

FAO 1997b: *Irrigation in the Near East region in figures*. Water Reports No. 9, Rome: FAO, Land and Water Development Division, Aquistat Programme.

Feitelson, E. 1996: Economic and political dimensions in changing perceptions of water in the Middle East. In Allan, J.A. and Radwan, L. *Perceptions of the value of water and water environments*. Proceedings of the Erasmus Seminar held at the University of Middlesex, London, 1996.

Giddens, A. 1984: *The constitution of society*. Cambridge: Polity Press.

Giddens, A. 1990: *The consequences of modernity*. Cambridge: Polity Press.

Global Water Partnership 1999: *Water – a millennial priority*. Framework for Action: achieving the vision activity, Framework for Action of the Global Water Partnership, Wallingford: HR Wallingford.

Goldblatt, D. 1996: *Social theory and the environment*. Cambridge: Polity Press.

Hajer, M. 1996: *The politics of environmental discourse: ecological modernization and the policy process*. Oxford: Clarendon Press.

Hughes, E. 1965: quoted in Thomas Pero, 1999, Poet, pike and a pitiful grouse, in *The Guardian* [Saturday Review], Saturday, 9 January 1999, p. 1.

IIMI [International Institute for Irrigation and Management] 1997: Achieving more crop per drop is the Mission of IIMI.

Karshenas, M. 1994: Environment, technology and employment. *Development and Change* **25**(4), 723–57.

Khassawneh, A. 1995: The International Law Commission and Middle East Waters. In Allan, J.A. and Mallat, C. *Water in the Middle East: legal, political and commercial implications*. London: Tauris Academic Studies, 21–8.

Kingdon, J. 1984: *Agendas, alternatives and public policies*. New York: HarperCollins.

Kinnersley, D. 1997: personal communication.

Lonergran, S. and Brooks, D. 1993: *The economic, ecological and geopolitical dimensions of water in Israel*. Centre for Sustainable Regional Development, Victoria, British Colombia: University of Victoria.

McCaffrey, S. 1995: The International Law Commission adopts draft articles on international watercourses. *American Journal of International Law* **89**, 395ff.

McCaffrey, S. 1998: Legal issues in the United Nations Convention on International Watercourses: propsects and pitfalls. Paper delivered at World Bank Seminar on international watercourses, Washington, DC: World Bank, November 1997.

McCaffrey, S. and Sinjela, M. 1998: The United Nations Convention on International Watercourses. *American Journal of International Law*, **92**, 97ff.

McCalla, A. 1997: Water, food and trade. Paper delivered at the World Bank Mediterranean Development Forum in Marrakech, May 1997.

McCulley, P. 1996: *Silenced rivers: the ecology and politics of large dams*. London: Zed Books.

McHoul, A. and Grace, W. 1993: *A Foucault primer: discourse, power and the subject*. London: UCL Press.

Meadows, D.H., Meadows, D.L., Randers J. and Behrens, W.W. 1972: *Limits to Growth*. New York: Universe Books.

Migdal, J. 1988: *Strong societies and weak states: state-society relations and state capabilities in the Third World*. Princeton, NJ: Princeton University Press.

Mubarak, A. (administrator and engineer in Egyptian governments between 1848 and 1892) 1891: *al-Azhar*, **4**(10), May 1891, 309–15.

Ohlsson, L. 1998: *Environment, scarcity and conflict: a study of Malthusian concerns*. Göteborg: Department of Peace and Development Research.

Palmer, S.E. 1963: Comments of Stephen E. Palmer, Jr., at the American Embassy, Tel Aviv, on the Jordan Waters Contingency Planning sent to the Department of State, 23 October 1963. Ref POL 33–1 ISA-Jordan.

Pearce, F. 1992: *The dammed: rivers, dams, and the coming world water crisis*. London: The Bodley Head.

Redclift, M. 1987: *Sustainable development: exploring the contradictions*. London: Methuen.

Reisner, M. 1984: *Cadillac desert*, New York: Penguin Books.

Serageldin, I. 1994: *Water supply, sanitation, and environmental sustainability*. Washington DC: The World Bank.

Serageldin, I. 1995: *Toward sustainable management of water resources*. Washington, DC: The World Bank.

Swyngedouw, E. 1999a: Modernity and hybridity: the production of nature: water and modernisation in Spain. Paper presented to the SOAS Water Issues Study Group, University of London, 25 January 1999.

Swyngedouw, E. 1999b: Hybrid waters: on water, nature and society. In Swyngedouw, E. (ed.), *Sustainability, risk and nature: the political ecology of water in advanced countries*. Proceedings of a workshop convened in the University of Oxford, 15–17 April 1999. Available from the Geography Department, University of Oxford.

Tripp, C.H. 1996: personal communication.

Turton, A.R. 1999: *Water scarcity and social adaptive capacity: towards an understanding of the social dynamics of managing water scarcity in developing countries*. MEWREW Occasional Paper 9, London: SOAS Water Issues Group, March 1999.

World Bank 1994: *A strategy for managing water in the Middle East and North Africa*. Washington, DC: The World Bank.

World Bank 1995, reprinted 1997: *From scarcity to security: averting a water crisis in the Middle East and North Africa*. Washington, DC: The World Bank.

World Bank 1997a: *Water pricing experiences: an international perspective*. World Bank Technical Paper No. 386, Washington, DC: The World Bank.

World Bank 1997b: *Water markets in the Americas*. Washington, DC: The World Bank.

World Bank 1998: *MENA/MED Water Initiative*. Proceedings of the First Regional Seminar on Water Policy Reform, Cairo, 1–3 June 1998. Volume 1 – Summary. World Bank, European Union, European Investment Bank, Washington, DC: The World Bank.

World Water Council 1999: *World Water Vision*. Second Draft, Paris: World Water Vision c/o UNESCO.

6

Precipitation, people, pipelines and power in southern Africa

Towards a 'virtual water'-based political ecology discourse

A.R. Turton

6.1 Introduction

A discourse is currently taking shape within the broader social science community at the level of metatheory. This discourse, termed 'political ecology', challenges the very notions on which various aspects of the scientific endeavour can be called 'science' at all; if by 'science' we adhere to the ideals of objectivity, neutrality, and replicability. Political ecologists question the relationship between people and environment in a manner which challenges the basis of individual social sciences as separate disciplines, while creating an overarching framework within which interdisciplinary research can take place in a meaningful way. This chapter attempts to place what the author considers to be a key developmental problem for southern Africa – namely the spatial and temporal maldistribution of water and its relationship with the spatial distribution of the human population – within this broader political ecology discourse. As a point of departure, I summarise and critique the thinking of selected political ecology theorists, focusing particularly on Atkinson (1991) and Eckersley (1997). This is followed by an attempt to identify and isolate what the author considers to be key variables within the context of the southern African water sector. A theoretical model is built based on different relationships between these variables, in the hope that this will contribute to debate on what the political ecology discourse for water in southern Africa can hope to achieve in terms of multidisciplinarity. The chapter concludes with a suggested research agenda for the future.

6.2 Philosophical background

Political ecology, as espoused by Atkinson (1991), is an ideology as much as a methodology. For Atkinson, it is a paradigm with strong political undertones that is based on the philosophical roots emerging from the Enlightenment and subsequent Marxist ideology. As such, it has a strongly normative dimension. The philosophical basis for Atkinson's formulation is vested in the notion of 'alienation'; in essence, that people have become alienated from 'nature'. For Atkinson, political ecology thus is concerned with the need to make fundamental changes in the social and political machinery that structure our daily lives in order to overcome this alienation.[1] To this end, and as Atkinson argues, the ultimate reconfiguration of these social dynamics will have to square with the sustainable self-reproduction of nature. This implies that there are definite choices about how we live our lives in relation to 'nature' and how we utilise the wider environment. The ultimate social choice is encapsulated, therefore, in the question: '[w]ill the choices currently being made by our society satisfy our material and spiritual needs and avoid ecological destruction?' (Atkinson, 1991: 171). In other words, political decision-making lies at the heart of the debate and as such can be construed as being one of the 'problems' contributing to alienation.

One necessary precondition for the ultimate achievement of a consciously self-regulating society is the requirement to simplify and render more transparent the operations of society and our relationship with nature (Atkinson, 1991: 180–1). In other words, there is a growing desire among the population of a given political entity to be allowed to question the decisions made by political decision-makers about the environment. As institutions which play something of a populist role in environment and development, Non-Government Organisations (NGOs) and charities have become increasingly relevant in this regard. Another necessary precondition voiced by Atkinson is the need to diffuse social tensions arising from the unequal social relations and divisions of labour which characterise capitalist society (Atkinson, 1991: 181), and which in some cases are underpinned by explicitly discriminatory ideology and legislation (cf. the apartheid administrations of South Africa and Namibia). In other words, the mechanisms by which resource allocations are made[2] are likely to become the locus of conflict in their own right.

The hallmark of capitalist consumerism – the incessant urge to accumulate – is seen by Atkinson as the fundamental cause of an assumed and impending ecological catastrophe. But to destroy nature is in essence to destroy oneself. For this reason, it is necessary to destroy the impetus of what seems now as a culturally entrenched economic logic, whilst simultaneously building new structures that will enable our descendants to live 'in a sustainable relationship with the rest of Creation' (Atkinson, 1991: 187). To this end, political ecology is constructed by Atkinson as advocating a confrontation of capitalism amounting to nothing less than its universal overthrowal. As such, he considers that a viable future will rest upon the philosophical premises of the realisation of the promise encapsulated in the 'ecological paradigm' (ibid.: 194). In other words, because the consumerism of the North is seen as being at the heart of the problem,[3] this opens the way for political ecology thinking to become part of an emerging North–South agenda.[4] Extending this ecological paradigm back in time, Atkinson (ibid.: 195) notes that modern 'organicist philosophy' can be traced to the conceptions of Hegel and Marx with respect to the terms of reference of an adequate secular philosophy. Stated simply, Hegel's 'philosophical system' is interpreted by Atkinson as presenting the active human consciousness on the one hand and nature on the other; as dialectical moments unified through the cultural and political process. Marx translated Hegel's second dialectical moment – nature – into the way in which society exploits nature through 'modes of production'. Nature-in-itself was lost by this translation. The excuse for ignoring 'nature' as such by Marx is highly relevant in the quest to re-establish the balance of the Hegelian dialectic. Seen from this perspective, Marxist philosophy is not a 'dialectic materialism' at all, but rather a 'dialectic humanism' or 'dialectic socialism' (ibid.: 196). Instead, the philosophy of a viable ecological future is a true 'dialectic materialism': its main concern is confronting the fundamental material natural process with a human consciousness 'resolved in an appropriate cultural, social and political framework that is capable of operationalizing human needs in nature on an everyday basis and into the long-term' (ibid.: 196). In other words, political ecology as viewed by Atkinson is more than just environmental politics. It represents instead a whole new philosophy that questions the relationship between humans and the environment in a fundamental manner, raising a whole new spectrum of social and political ramifications.[5] The answer to the fundamental problem of 'alienation' in practical terms is seen as emerging by means of a philosophy of ecological consciousness otherwise known as 'sustainability'

Political ecology as espoused by Atkinson (1997) can be regarded as being somewhat reactionary. This may well mean that the current water sector decision-makers in southern Africa, as well as by decision-makers elsewhere in the developing contexts of 'the South', are likely to view the whole discourse as being radical, politicised and possibly even too far-fetched to be taken seriously. This clearly has implications for academic work which draws on a political ecology approach, specifically regarding the possible use of that research by decision-makers. Significantly, while a more recent generation of political ecologists are highly critical of the merits of the 'northern' idea of 'sustainable development' (cf. Bryant and Bailey, 1997: 4), they have yet to develop an alternative to this mainstream concept.

It is illuminating, therefore, to examine political ecology from another perspective, so as to gain deeper insight into the possible value of the discourse. According to Eckersley (1997), there are three clearly discernible phases of writing that can be attributed to political ecologists. Each of these phases can be linked to distinct ecological themes or preoccupations (ibid.: 7) described as the 'participation', 'survival' and 'emancipation' phases of the political ecology thinking and regarded in Hegelian terms as respectively the thesis, antithesis and synthesis of political ecology thinking (see Figure 6.1 for a diagrammatic summary of the evolution of these positions).

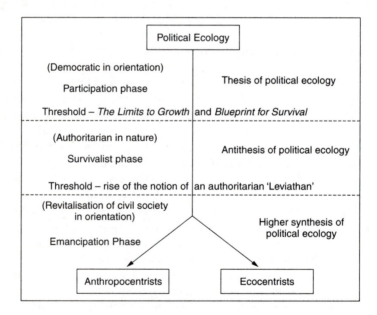

Figure 6.1 Schematic representation of the various phases in the development of political ecology philosophy

Eckersley (1997) maintains that the 'participation' phase of political ecology thinking was triggered by widespread public concern over environmental degradation in the developed countries during the 1960s. After years of persistent agitation, this movement generated recognition of the existence of something of a global environmental crisis. An important milestone in this endeavour was the Earth Day celebration in 1970 which can be viewed as widespread public acknowledgement that environment mattered. Emerging from this was the notion that there may be ecological limits to 'economic growth' that cannot be overcome by human technological ingenuity (Eckersley, 1997: 8). This amounts to the emergence of two mutually exclusive ideas. On the one hand, 'economic growth' was considered to have taken place only at the expense of ecological 'integrity'. On the other, 'ecological sustainability' was viewed as distinctly separate from 'economic growth', and thereby unattainable if 'economic growth' was the desired condition. The predominant form of political thinking during this phase was centred in part around what was seen as a crisis of participation, whereby excluded groups sought to ensure a more equitable distribution of environmental 'goods' (ibid.: 9).

While this debate focused on notions of limits to what the environment could provide, it also tended to reinforce, rather than challenge, the prevailing view of the environment as being just another resource there for human consumption. Running concurrently with this thinking was a period of revision of socialist theory in general, spearheaded by the rise of the New Left. The ideas that emanated were readily absorbed into the counter-culture and 'back to nature' movements of the 1960s (Eckersley, 1997: 10). This incorporated notions of grassroots democracy and social justice, which are two pillars on which modern Green parties rest today (ibid.: 11).

The second 'survivalist' phase of political ecology thinking grew from the first, with the threshold between them being the publication of two prominent early 1970s documents: the Club of Rome's *The Limits to Growth* and *The Ecologist* magazine's *Blueprint for Survival* (Eckersley, 1997: 11–12). This marked a shift in intellectual thinking away from seeing the problem merely as one of participation, to one of actual survival. Fuelling this concern were the first NASA images of 'spaceship earth', floating as if it were an 'oasis in the desert of infinite space' (ibid.: 12). In other words, gone was the notion of an ever-expanding boundary for economic growth, akin to the expansionist excesses of the Wild West frontier. In its place was the realisation that a new normative framework was in order, based on assumptions of relative efficiencies and recycling.[6] Significantly, this added a global dimension to the ideas of environmental degradation, manifest in notions of environmental collapse as the common fate of humanity. Emerging from this was the first European Green Party, the British People's Party, which subsequently changed its name to the Ecology Party in 1975 and later to the British Green Party in 1985 (Eckersley, 1997: 12). The belief that economic growth was limited by ecological constraints necessitated solutions: a managerial ethic promoting the development of appropriate technology and the instituting of pricing policies to constraint demand and impacts.

Despite a number of methodological problems inherent to the *Limits to Growth* arguments, particularly that it does not incorporate sufficiently the possibilities for innovation or for changing consumer behaviour, these seem not to have detracted to any appreciable extent from their core message. For example, the message was iterated in the Club of Rome's 1974 report, issued in response to reactions to the original 1972 *The Limits to Growth*. An extract of this reads as follows:

> For the first time in man's (*sic*) life on earth, he is being asked to refrain from doing what he can do; he is being asked to refrain his economic and technical advancement, or at least to direct it

differently from before; he is being asked by all future generations of the earth to share his good fortune with the unfortunate – not in a spirit of charity, but in a spirit of survival.

(quoted in Eckersley, 1997: 13)

Importantly, this argument is highly politicised as it apparently supports the rigid freezing of the economic inequalities that exist between North and South, to the obvious benefit of the North. In effect, the argument is relevant for states which are securely located in a post-industrialisation phase of development, when large parts of the developing world are almost pre-industrial in terms of their own economic development.

The landmark essay, 'The tragedy of the commons' by Garrett Hardin (1968) also emerged from this 'survivalist' period in environmental thinking. Hardin's now famous parable of the medieval herdsmen overstocking the commons demonstrates the dynamic that prevails when people are motivated solely by the objective of maximising individual economic gains in the short term. Hardin's answer to this tragedy was 'mutual coercion, mutually agreed upon by the majority of the people effected'. This was indicative of the survivalists' key concern for finding a solution to assumed impending ecological disaster, by discovering a minimally acceptable way of life rather than continuing to search for the 'good life' at the expense of 'the environment' (Eckersley, 1997: 14). Other writing from this time echoes these sentiments. For example, Richard Barnet (1980) wrote that:

[t]he specter of the hungry mob supports Hobbesian politics, a world of struggle over inadequate resources that cries out for Leviathan, the authoritarian state that can keep minimal order. The Malthusian fantasy offers an alternative to the Leviathan state. There is no need for a civil authority to regulate scarce goods, because Nature, cruel only to be kind, periodically thins the surplus population by famine.

Another example of the literature from this period was that of Robert Heilbroner's (1974) sombre inquiry. This portrayed as the only hope for the survival of humankind the obedient rallying behind a centralised authoritarian state, thought to be the only form of institution that would be capable of extracting the types of sacrifices needed to regulate distribution and redirect the economic sectoral outputs of agriculture and industry along more ecologically sustainable lines (Eckersley, 1997: 14). It must be added, however, that while Heilbroner saw the centrally planned, authoritarian state as being a necessary transitional scenario for the post-industrial economy, it is clear that this is not what he personally would have wished for. Instead, he supported the notion of a state that was diminished in scale from the dangerous level of gigantic nation–states, towards a form of decentralised *polis* along the lines of ancient Greece (Eckersley, 1997: 15).

William Ophuls (1973) is also representative of this school of thought. In this author's view the world is confronted with a limited choice between either 'Leviathan or oblivion'. Significantly, both Heilbroner's and Ophul's view of human society parallel the herdsmen found in Hardin's 'The tragedy of the commons', i.e. people are constructed as selfish hedonists who rationally only seek private gain. This establishes a direct philosophical link to the self-interested human who roamed in both Hobbe's and Locke's *State of Nature* (Eckersley, 1997: 15). For Hobbes, they are seen as being in perpetual conflict with the interest of the larger social community, whereas for Locke, they are in intermittent conflict with these broader interests (Eckersley, 1997: 16). Thus the survivalist school can be understood in terms of being a form of new eco-social contract theorists. The new 'ecological contract' is based in terms of the Hobbesian premise of scarcity and would therefore require an all-powerful Leviathan to enforce it. In other words, if citizens did not voluntarily surrender certain freedoms, then restrictions would have to be externally imposed by a sovereign power.

The survivalist school essentially asked whether socialism was ecologically salvageable or not, thereby contributing two distinct intellectual aspects to the political ecology debate (Eckersley, 1997: 17). First, they have drawn attention to the seriousness of the overall ecological crisis that exists. Second, the authoritarian solutions which emerged as the result of *The Limits to Growth* debate encouraged a search for a deeper cultural transformation along with alternative, non-authoritarian institutions that would foster a more co-operative response to the environmental crisis.

The third 'emancipation' phase of political ecology thinking resulted from the criticism of the authoritarian solutions that were being offered by the survivalists. The response was to push the limits of the eco-political debate beyond the realm of the physical limits to growth, to the point where the very notion of material progress was being questioned (Eckersley, 1997: 17). In terms of this thinking, there were a number of social and psychological costs that were associated with the dominance of instrumental rationality, including alienation, loss of meaning, the coexistence of extremes of wealth and poverty, dependence on welfare, dislocation of tribal cultures and the growth of an international urban monoculture with a resultant loss of cultural diversity (ibid.: 18). For example, William Leiss (1974) wrote:

> [n]o elaborate argument should be necessary to establish that there are some limits to economic and population growth. But everything depends on whether we regard such limits as a bitter disappointment or as a welcome opportunity to turn from quantitative to qualitative improvement in the course of creating a conserver society.

Other authors such as Rudolf Bahro (1982; 1984; 1986) wrote that the environmental crisis had arisen as a direct result of the 'quintessential crisis of capitalism', which had now forced society to re-examine fruitfully not only the psychological costs of competition, but also the expansionary ethos of our materialist culture and imperialist attitude to other living species (Eckersley, 1997: 19). Yet another author, Christopher Stone (1974), used the opportunity to enquire whether the environmental crisis had not offered an opportunity for the metaphysical reconstruction and moral development of humankind. To this end, Stone (1974) wrote:

> whether we will be able to bring about the requisite institutional and population growth changes depends upon effecting a radical shift in our feeling about 'our' place in the rest of nature . . . A radical new conception of man's (*sic*) relationship to the rest of nature would not only be a step towards solving the material planetary problems; there are strong reasons for such a changed consciousness from the point of making us far better human beings.

Following Eckersley (1997: 19–20), the significance of the emancipatory school to the overall debate on political ecology is threefold. First, the environmental crisis is now regarded as being a crisis of culture in the broadest sense of the meaning. Second, emancipatory ecopolitical theory may be understood as challenging the then prevailing political ecology discourse and widening its agenda on three distinctly separate but interrelated levels, i.e. human needs, technology and self-image. Significant to this, for example, is the debate over the appropriateness of technology. Third, they have directed considerable attention towards the revitalisation of civil society rather than, or in addition to, the state. As such they are focused on integrating the concerns of the ecology movement with other emerging activist groupings such as those dealing with feminism, peace and the 'Third World' aid and development.

This summary of trends in political ecology thinking has been articulated to provide an enabling framework for the case material explored in the rest of this chapter. Against this philosophical background I now turn to an analysis of the problems facing decision-makers with regard to the provisioning of a crucial natural resource, namely water. My regional context is southern Africa where water allocation is affected by the spatial and temporal maldistribution of the resource and its relationship to an uneven spatial distribution of resource users. My primary aim is to explore how power relations influence the use, management and allocation of a natural resource under these constraining circumstances.

6.3 The provision of water in southern Africa

6.3.1 Isolating the variables

For southern Africa, the distribution of precipitation and people, and the interaction between these two variables, underpin the developmental dilemma of the region. Regarding precipitation[7] there are four distinct aspects which are important. First, there is a marked spatial maldistribution of water, with a distinct latitudinal and longitudinal trend, i.e. there are generally higher precipitation levels in the north and east, decreasing progressively to the south and dramatically to the west. Second, there is a temporal dimension to this maldistribution of water. This means that rainfall tends to be distinctly seasonal in pattern. Third, the amount of precipitation that falls is subject to a high degree of inter-annual variability, which increases in magnitude with increasing aridity. These three elements combine to introduce a high level of stochasticity in the overall precipitation patterns, particularly in more arid areas. This has significant implications for crop planning, surface run-off, soil erosion and river flows. In terms of water management they mean that large storage reservoirs[8] have to be planned and built, because the reliability and predictability of precipitation patterns are of a low order of magnitude. Fourth, but less important for the purposes of this chapter, is water quality, which generally is of a reasonably high standard except in specific areas where acidic rain falls and where point source pollution exists. Similarly, eutrophication and salinisation do occur in impoundments due to return flows of effluent and evaporative losses but these have little relevance for the current discussion, however.

Regarding people, and for the purposes of this discussion, three issues are important. First, the spatial distribution of people in southern Africa is generally at variance with the availability of water. In other words, population distribution in general tends to be concentrated in areas that are far from supplies of water. Second, there is a significant temporal aspect to the population base in the sense that the whole of southern Africa has a very high population growth rate. Third, migration greatly affects the distribution of people, such that there is high in-migration to urban areas. This is an artefact of colonial and apartheid policies which, through taxation and other legislation, instituted dependence among the African population on white-controlled urban industry, particularly mining, in order to procure cash incomes. Significantly, the larger urban and industrial areas tend to be focused on places with water shortages such as the Gauteng area of South Africa (on a high plateau, far from water supplies and facing a significant water shortage as a result), Gaborone in Botswana, and Harare and Bulawayo in Zimbabwe (all on watersheds and with unique water supply problems of their own). Migration push-factors include loss of livelihoods due to overpopulation, poverty, declining levels of land per capita (i.e. crucial in areas with largely subsistence farming economies) and drought. Figure 6.2 shows the poor relationship between water use and water availability in South Africa while Figure 6.3 provides a breakdown of water uses. Note that the industrial heartlands of South Africa (Gauteng and Mpumalanga Province, in north-east of the country) have no available water. The survival of these areas depends on inter-basin transfers from a number of other catchments such as the Upper Thukela River in Kwazulu-Natal to the south-east. Note also that water utilisation is way in excess of available resources in parts of the Cape, i.e. in the west of the country. In Figure 6.3 note the large proportion of the water budget that was allocated nationally to irrigation and afforestation.

These mismatches lead to the crux of the problem: that is, if water is concentrated in areas that are spatially distant from the population centres, then what is required is the transportation of water to the people (or vice versa). This is where the heart of the political ecology dilemma

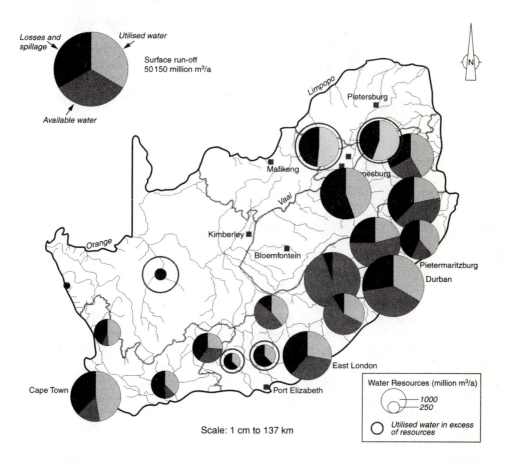

Figure 6.2 Map of South Africa showing the spatial distribution between water use and availability in 1996. *Source:* Basson *et al.*, 1997: 51. *Note:* The industrial heartlands of South Africa (Gauteng and Mpumalanga Province, in north-east of the country) have no available water and the survival of these areas depends on inter-basin transfers from a number of other catchments such as the Upper Thukela River in Kwazulu-Natal to the south-east. Water utilisation is way in excess of available resources in parts of the Cape, i.e. in the west of the country

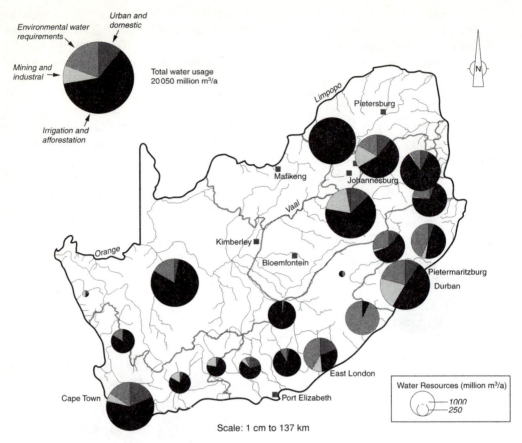

Figure 6.3 Map of South Africa giving a breakdown of the dominant uses of water during 1996. *Source:* Basson *et al.*, 1997: 11

lies. In order to move water over long distances, pipelines[9] are employed. Because pipelines bring life-giving and job-creating water to areas where the demand for water is high, they perform a function that can be regarded in its broadest sense as being 'allocative'. In short, pipelines allocate a given volume of water to a specific spatial entity. It is precisely this allocative aspect of pipelines that introduces the dimension of power into the situation and it is through this that pipelines contribute to a lively political ecology debate. In its crudest form, power is derived from the privilege or the relative advantage that the receiving entity derives from having been favoured over the non-receiving entity (cf. Bryant, 1998; Mollinga and van Straaten, 1996; Bryant and Bailey, 1997: 38–47). Seen in this way, pipelines become conduits of power because they allocate water from an area of relative abundance to an area of relative scarcity. Further, the water so allocated has an economic cost (whether or not this aspect is actually reflected in the final price that is charged for the water). Thus the allocation creates situations of relative advantage and disadvantage between human populations.

Having isolated these four fundamental variables – precipitation (Pr), people (Pe), pipelines (Pi) and power (Po) – it is possible to construct a model (or series of models) that reflect the different relationships that each has depending on the configuration of the other. This enables a distinct water political ecology discourse to emerge.

6.3.2 Analysis of the relationships between the variables

As a point of departure, let us accept that a fundamental developmental problem in southern Africa at a strategic level is the need to reconcile the spatial differences that exist between the availability of water (Pr) and the human population (Pe). In addition to this, we have stated that there are two other fundamental variables: the engineering system which is used to bridge the spatial gap existing between Pr and Pe, i.e. the pipelines (Pi); and second, the plethora of power relationships that the decision-making structures in society have *vis-à-vis* the other variables (Po).

Having identified these four variables, we can examine relationships which might exist in their different configurations. As a point of departure, it becomes evident that if a disparity exists between Pr and Pe, then tension exists between these two variables. This tension can be operationalised by using the concept of 'water scarcity', and is illustrated diagrammatically in Figure 6.4a. The tension created in Figure 6.4a as the result of this 'water scarcity' is because they are not coincident spatially, and it has a number of ramifications. For simplicity, let us assume that the existence of a 'water scarcity' will have a negative effect on the livelihoods and economic potential of the social group that occupies the spatial entity experiencing the scarcity. In Figure 6.4b a power (Po) relationship is apparent, coming directly from this tension called 'water scarcity'. This is derived from either the existence of an engineering solution (Pi) or absence thereof. The existence of a pipeline will alleviate the tension (that is derived from 'water scarcity') and will thus increase the relative advantage of the spatial entity that receives the new additional flow of water. The converse is also true. The pipeline in Figure 6.4b reduces the tension by alleviating 'water scarcity' but sets up the complex power (Po) relationship due to the provisioning of a resource-poor area by a resource-rich area.

In a positive sense, a pipeline can be an advantage to the group of people who receive the water, raising relative economic prosperity, health and wealth. As Bryant and Bailey (1997: 39) note, when unequal access to a valued resource occurs, the stimulus can exist to monopolise the resource, so as to ensure that the economic benefits associated with it accrue to the actor (or the constituency) concerned. In a negative sense, the absence of a pipeline can disadvantage the group of people who occupy the spatial entity experiencing 'water scarcity'. This might be manifest, for example, in large amounts of time and energy spent fetching and carrying water (frequently by women and children), impoverishment, disease and the absence of economic development opportunities. The marginalisation of a politically weaker group of people can leave them vulnerable to other environmental changes of an episodic nature, thereby exposing them disproportionately to the risks that are incurred by the powerful actors' attempts to monopolise the benefits associated with a resource (ibid.: 40). Thus the lack of water is a barrier to sustainable socio-economic development; while a

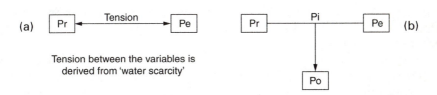

Figure 6.4 The relationship between the two variables, precipitation (Pr) and people (Pe)

lack of development is a barrier to solving water problems (Lundqvist and Gleick, 1997: viii). The latter is seen to be a form of 'social resource scarcity' (Ohlsson, 1999: 161).

The act of deciding to develop a pipeline, therefore, has profound political ramifications, which can be used by a political élite to advantage themselves. Within an overall setting of general resource scarcity, a powerful élite can entrench their dominant position by deciding to build pipelines that advantage specific sectors of society, and disadvantage others. This is called a process of 'resource capture'[10] and was pursued as a deliberate strategy by the apartheid government of South Africa to institute 'social resource scarcity' among the economically weaker majority by bringing in to existence major engineering solutions which advantaged the white minority at the expense of the black majority. In specific terms, this favoured one economic sector – commercial agriculture[11] – because this was a political constituency that was important for the maintenance of the apartheid regime at that moment in time. As well as ensuring the provisioning of this sector it maintained subsidised rates for its consumers, thereby retaining 'the support of the white farmers who owned most of the land in the country' (Abrams, 1996). This has culminated in water being seriously undervalued within the commercial agriculture sector in southern Africa, accompanied by a general lack of conservation awareness. In other words, water pipelines, together with unrealistic pricing mechanisms, 'bought' support for an illegitimate regime. Conversely, the agenda of the new democratically elected African National Congress (ANC) Government, has dictated that water will now be given to the previously disadvantaged areas and is supported by the new South African National Water Act (36/98). One of the significant components of the Reconstruction and Development Programme (RDP) is directly linked to the development of pipelines to take water into previously marginalised spatial entities. Given the background of a 'finite' and unequally distributed water resource, this is likely to continue to have both political and economic ramifications. The notion of a finite water resource is somewhat restrictive, however, because it dictates that no other water is available. It will be shown later in the chapter that this is not true and that alternative sources of water do exist, provided that the decision-making élite adopts a new water paradigm.

Let us examine these variables in a little more detail by constructing a hypothetical model. In this model, the notion of power can be explored in greater detail by showing how it is derived, or where it impacts, in relation to the overall configuration. Let us assume that a spatial entity has conditions of water scarcity in general. Within this spatial entity, there are two social groupings of people, which for explanatory purposes will be denoted as Pe1 and Pe2.

Against the background of water scarcity, the decision-making entity could choose to alleviate the water shortages within one specific community (Pe1) and not in another (Pe2). This in turn will advantage the former community (Pe1) both economically and socially. In return for this 'privilege', there is likely to be an increase in support for the decision-making entity that 'flows' from the constituency in what can be understood as 'positive power'. This 'positive power' can be in the form of votes, taxes, patronage and goodwill. In response to this support, the decision-making entity can use this power in a negative sense to continue the marginalisation of the second community (Pe2). This circle of self-supporting relationships is shown in Figure 6.5.

In political science terms, 'negative power' can be maintained in two distinct ways. First, a subtle power[12] can be understood as existing as long as the water scarcity is perpetuated. This will undermine the economic and social potential of the given spatial entity or constituency, and can be used as an instrument for marginalisation and disempowerment, which in turn translates into a form of control. This is where I consider the work of Ohlsson

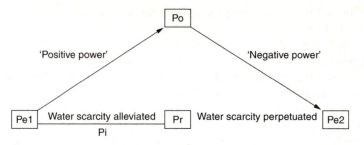

Figure 6.5 Schematic representation of two forms of power relationships that can result from the politics of pipelines

(1998, 1999; discussed further in Turton, 1999b) to be valuable. It is based on the concept of 'social resource scarcity' which, by explaining the spiral of disempowerment that comes into play within a community that is living under conditions of constant water scarcity, is more subtle than the situation of physical 'water scarcity' alone. Ohlsson's work fits neatly into a political ecology discourse and, in particular, adds to its usefulness for developing country contexts where access to 'natural resources' is often crucial in determining economic opportunities. Second, a more brutal form of power[13] might be exerted over a specific spatial entity or constituency in the form of government supported harassment. It can be argued in this context that funding for such directly repressive activity is derived from flows of power to the state in the form of political support from the constituency that has been advantaged, at least in part, by its preferential access to a critical resource (in this case water). This links the notions of 'resource capture' and the resultant economic disempowerment to 'ecological marginalisation' (cf. Homer-Dixon and Percival, 1996) in a causal way.

The above conceptualisation can clearly be used to explain patterns in resource provisioning and the distribution of power in South Africa prior to the 1994 democratic elections,[14] specifically with regard to the agricultural sector. The following statistics are revealing in this regard (Turton, 1998a: 143). In 1980, 54 per cent of the total water consumed in South Africa went to the agricultural sector, which in turn contributed a mere 6 per cent to the GDP. In contrast, the industrial sector consumed 11 per cent but contributed 45 per cent for the same year. During 1990, agriculture consumed 52 per cent of the total water and contributed 6 per cent to the GDP, whereas industry consumed 13 per cent while contributing 31 per cent to the economy during the same year. During 1995, agriculture consumed 72 per cent of all of the water while still only contributing 6 per cent to the economy, whereas industry consumed only 11 per cent while contributing 30 per cent to the GDP for the same year. The conclusion that can be drawn from this data series is that agriculture is inefficient at converting scarce water into a contribution to the overall South African economy (Turton, 1998b). Further, that the primarily white farmers of the commercial agricultural sector were privileged as a result of this favourable allocation.

As is well known, the black majority of South Africa were increasingly marginalised under the Nationalist Party minority government, often restricted to less productive parts of the country which were established the 'Bantustans' or 'Homelands' (cf. Percival and Homer-Dixon, 1995: 8) which contributed to structural scarcity. Land rights and water rights were linked, however, so scarcity of one also meant scarcity of the other. For example, during 1994, a survey conducted in rural KwaZulu-Natal revealed that 76.2 per cent of the population in the survey area only had access to water from springs and streams, none had taps in their homes, 15 per cent made use of communal standpipes, 1.6 per cent had access to reservoirs and 7.1 per cent had no access to safe potable water at all (Percival and Homer-Dixon, 1995: 12).

No wonder then that a major shift has taken place within the South African water sector since the democratic elections of 1994. Given that the pre-1994 minority government was, in political science terminology, oligarchic, i.e. illegitimate, unpopular and consequently facing an endless barrage of challenges (cf. Turton and Bernhardt, 1998), it depended on 'buying' support because, by definition, it only had a minority support-base. This was done, at least in part, by allocating natural resources, including water, in such a way as to advantage a given constituency and to disadvantage another. Because resource allocation is driven by political reasons it entails inefficiencies, but these inefficiencies are regarded as expedient because this is the price the regime has to pay for political security and support. Because water demand management (e.g. through pricing mechanisms), while improving efficiency, will be unpopular among the constituents with power, it runs counter to the underlying logic inherent within the paradigm of minority political rule. Thus, and as mentioned above, one implication of the ownership of water through riparian rights is the fact that water tended to be misallocated in the economy. Conversely, it can be argued that a legitimate government with broad-based, popular support, can in fact introduce water demand management schemes, as the regime under these conditions is not under constant threat. In other words, water demand management cannot be the sole responsibility of economists or engineers. It is a social and political issue too (Turton 1999b). Political ecology as a discourse allows these separate specialist disciplines to come together.

It can be said, therefore, that just as water is needed by people to sustain life, engineering solutions like pipelines are needed to sustain governments under conditions of water scarcity. The metaphor can be extended further. Just as water flows down a pipeline, power flows too – the latter is just a little more difficult to detect and quantify. But are pipelines the only solution in hydropolitical terms? It is to explore this question that we now turn our attention.

6.4 'Virtual water': an alternative paradigm

The time is ripe for consideration of an alternative water sector policy. Indeed, a number of states are currently involved in so-called water sector reforms, indicating that existing policies are no longer appropriate. Here I draw on the concept of 'virtual water' as introduced by Tony Allan in analysis of the ways in which the Middle East and North African (MENA) states balance their water budgets (cf. Allan, 1996b; 1999b; see also Chapter 5, this volume) and assess its applicability for the allocation of water in southern Africa.

'Virtual water' is the volume of water needed to produce a commodity or service (Allan, 1996a). Typically it takes around 1,000 tonnes of water to grow one tonne of grain. This represents the 'virtual water' value of grain. 'Virtual water' is also present in hydroelectric power and constitutes the volume of water needed to produce a given unit of electricity. The important point about 'virtual water' is that it manages to harness the most valuable portion of the water endowment of any given state – the soil moisture – which normally cannot be quantified or valued. The logic for a 'virtual water' paradigm can be developed as follows. Whereas there are many examples of water scarcity at local or regional levels, water scarcity does not exist in global terms. This is because vast quantities of surplus water exist in certain parts of the world, present, for example, as the soil moisture of grain-exporting states. Significantly, these states have an abundance of natural precipitation, and the governments concerned often subsidise the farmers to grow for the export market. This means that relatively cheap water can be imported to states with relative water scarcity in the form of grain. As such, it is easier, and less ecologically destructive, to import one tonne of grain than to pipe in 1,000 tonnes of water.

At the same time, there has been a global shift away from the notion of national food self-sufficiency to one of national food self-reliance. The ultimate goal is to grow sufficient food to meet the world's needs, and to deliver that food to wherever it is needed (Lundqvist and Gleick, 1997: 22). If the government of a semi-arid region decides to adopt a policy of national self-sufficiency in food, then it means that large quantities of water will be needed for the agricultural sector. This could be called the 'more crop per drop at whatever cost' option. Associated with this approach are costs in political, economic and environmental terms. For example, the ecological impacts of such a strategy might be viewed negatively by the powerful states of the North, possibly affecting trade negotiations, foreign aid packages and the withdrawal of financial support. Conversely, if the same government opts for a policy of national self-reliance in food, then it does not need to mobilise water for agriculture in the physical sense. Rather, it can use its existing water for less water-intensive industrial purposes, for which it will have a higher rate of return (Turton, 1998a; 1999b), will create 'more jobs per drop at a reasonable cost', freeing up the country's water budget and could be considered to be more environmentally sustainable. In these contexts, pipelines and their associated engineering support systems can be understood to be satisfying requirements for food self-sufficiency at the expense of unsustainability, whereas 'virtual water' can be seen as satisfying requirements for food self-reliance, supporting economic growth while observing a need for environmental sustainability. Let us explore the ramifications of this in a southern African context.

Currently, a number of water transfer schemes are underway in southern Africa. They are becoming increasingly complex and costly as the only available water becomes ever more distant. In fact, in strategic terms the only significant water that remains available for exploitation is found in the Zambezi and Zaire basins. Some of the major projects that are currently under way include the following:

1   The Lesotho Highlands Water Project (LHWP) captures the headwaters of the Orange River in Lesotho and re-directs it to the industrial heartland of South Africa via the Vaal River sub-basin. The return flow is back into the Orange Basin. The first water has started to flow already and additional phases of construction are being considered that will almost double the volume of supply.
2   The North–South Carrier (NSC) in Botswana is nearing completion. Most of the pipes have been laid and smaller aspects such as pump stations and valve chambers are being finished off. The overall length is in the order of 350 kilometres and it will harness the water from the Moutloutse, and later the Shashe River, in the Limpopo Basin, taking it down to Gaborone. The source of supply is the Letsibogo Dam that has been completed and is currently filling up, albeit slower than was anticipated.
3   The Eastern National Water Carrier (ENWC) in Namibia takes water from a number of sources including ground and surface water found in the north east of the country, down to Windhoek in the centre.

In addition to these projects, there are a number of new projects being planned. Many are, or are likely to become, subject to highly emotive debate particularly as sophisticated international special-interest groups, such as environmental NGOs, put increasing pressure onto foreign donors not to support the projects. These projects include the following:

1   The Matabele–Zambezi Water Project (MZWP) is being planned to take water from the Zambezi River just below Victoria Falls. It is likely to be very expensive due to the high operating head and resultant energy costs needed to pump the water. As a result, its logic is being linked to the development of the Batoka Gorge Dam that will reduce the head while providing the energy needed for the pumping. This in turn means that Zambia is going to be drawn into a debt situation for a dam that they have no need for, and that will actually divert water away from themselves and therefore be to their own detriment. Zambia is in fact deriving foreign currency from ecotourism that is based on the white water rafting below Victoria Falls, which is of a world-class standard. This will be lost if the dam is built. The author is currently doing some research aimed at determining if this pipeline will be linked to the NSC in Botswana, as they are spatially very close together. If this happens, the throughput will be higher, making the economics different and possibly more attractive. This is an extremely complex issue in hydropolitical terms, and one that is likely to become very emotive. Research is difficult because no respondent is prepared to be quoted due to the sensitivities surrounding the project.

2   The Namibian government has announced its attention of developing a pipeline from the Okavango River (Turton, 1999b; Ramberg, 1997). In addition to this it is mooting the possibility of developing a hydroelectric scheme at Popa Falls on the Okavango River. This is causing some unease in Botswana and is likely to be vociferously opposed by environmental groups. There is already a coalition of such NGOs working under the name of the Okavango Liaison Group.

3   There are some unconfirmed reports that planning is underway to develop a major pipeline from the Zaire Basin down to Namibia.

4   The Namibian government is in an advanced planning stage for the development of a dam on the western reaches of the Kunene River which separates Namibia from Angola. Two sites are being considered – the Baynes and Epupa Falls sites. There are complex political dynamics around this whole project that are beyond the scope of this chapter. One specific angle is linked to the inundation of traditional ancestral burial sites and grazing land of the Himba people (cf. Bollig, 1997). A second refers to the ecological implications of the development for an area important as an attraction for high-income and low-impact eco-tourism.

Pipelines and their associated politics represent what can be described as the *realpolitik* of water. 'Virtual water', and its associated politics, represent a softer option to the problem of the spatial maldistribution of water and people, that is based on a consensual and accommodative style of political decision-making, using the notion of 'some, for all, forever'.[15] If serious research is done within the framework of political ecology thinking, it may be found that the above-mentioned projects may not even be needed, if the rationale of a 'virtual water' based development strategy is considered as a viable alternative. Researchers will need support, however – this is the underlying rationale for this chapter – as this endeavour is likely to take them into areas where the sanctioned discourse (also referred to as 'public transcript' (cf. Bryant and Bailey, 1997: 42)) would have us believe that the water sector is not the domain of the social scientist, but rather the engineer and the hydrologist.[16]

Returning to the political ecology discourse, the two concepts, 'ecological sustainability' and 'economic growth' can be understood as linked in a dialectic that emerged from the 'sustainable development' debate of the 1980s. The thesis of the dialectic is being driven from the developed world, which is calling for 'ecological sustainability'. This impacts in a direct political sense on the developing world because it does nothing more than entrench existing unequal relationships between the North and South. Regarding environment it allows international donor agencies to exert what might be termed 'green conditionalities' (cf. Leach and Mearns, 1996: 23) whereby environmental goals are used as a form of leverage over national governments of 'the South'. In this context the antithesis as characterised from the perspective of the developing world is 'economic development'.

It has been argued here that in the context of the water sector the concept of 'virtual water' allows a synthesis of these two positions, in that it both frees the natural resource allowing it to contribute to development in other sectors and, by lessening the impacts of both water extraction and the engineering works that are associated with this, it contributes to the sustainability of use of this resource (see Figure 6.6). The framework of 'virtual water' rests critically, however, on the ability of water-scarce states to import 'virtual water' in the form of grain and/or other necessary commodities. In this the oil-rich MENA states have a healthy advantage (cf. Chapter 5 by Tony Allan). Without a shifting of donor funding from the engineering works associated with water provisioning in water-scarce contexts to assisting with the import of 'virtual water' in its various forms, it is debatable as to whether the concept will prove of practical value to the states of southern Africa.

The following argument to support this view is offered for consideration by the scientific and policy-making community in southern Africa. First, the debate between 'ecological sustainability' and 'economic growth' is being driven by the developed states of the North. Second, at the heart of the debate lies a search for the post-industrial society. This is at direct odds with the needs of the developing world, which is hampered in many cases by the existence of forms of pre-industrialisation. Third, the debate is likely to be perceived by decision-makers and activists as being to the exclusive benefit of the North, at the direct expense of the South. The issue is thus likely to be placed on the North–South agenda in a more vociferous way in future. Thus, if taken to its logical conclusion, this might result in a

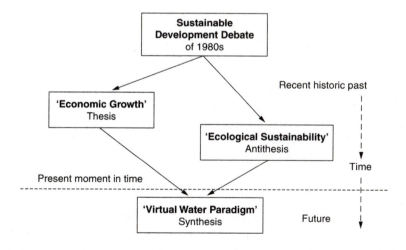

Figure 6.6 Schematic representation of an emerging dialectic in the context of water, showing the thesis and antithesis of 'economic growth' and 'environmental sustainability', with 'virtual water' suggested as a viable alternative

sharp polarisation into two distinct groups – those calling for 'ecological sustainability' and those calling for 'economic development'. In the context of water, a 'virtual water' option might offer a viable alternative by incorporating elements of both 'sustainability' and 'development'. If it is to be adopted as a paradigm for both thinking and policy, however, a serious research agenda needs to be formulated. The following are some suggested areas of interest:

1   The existing definition of 'virtual water' is too crude and abstract. It needs to be made more specific and capable of being operationalised and quantified in economic, social and political terms. Is virtual water based on international trade in water-rich products that are produced by industry, for example? If so, then what of the poorer developing states that lack the capital to harness their water surplus[17] and sell it as 'virtual water', or the foreign currency surplus with which to buy 'virtual water'? Is 'virtual water' based only on the trade of cereals as for the MENA states? If so, then what is the significance of this option in cultural terms? If there is a cultural preference for local grains,[18] how will this impact on the viability of a 'virtual water' policy? Is virtual water based more broadly on the trade of agriculturally derived products that harness the valuable soil moisture? If this is so, then the rationale of existing policy options changes significantly. For example, selling beef from Botswana is tantamount to exporting the valuable soil moisture of the Kalahari in the form of meat to the water-rich European Union, in much the same way that exporting oranges from Israel was. The Israeli policy has subsequently been reviewed[19] in light of a 'virtual water' approach. If the focus is on agricultural products, then what is the economic significance of exporting 'virtual water' in hydroelectricity from the Zambezi River rather than building pipelines?
2   Within the context of southern Africa, what will be needed at the political level to use 'virtual water' to stimulate intra-regional trade, problems which are currently hampering the economic integration of SADC states? For example, could a specific policy be developed that would mobilise the water surplus found in Angola and Zambia, and allow this to be used to supplement the water deficits of states like Namibia, Zimbabwe, Botswana and South Africa?
3   Is a 'virtual water'-based developmental strategy sufficient to allow for a dialectic synthesis between the thesis of 'economic growth' and the antithesis of 'ecological sustainability' in southern Africa?

What is clear is that there is a global dynamic currently shaping the economic future of all developing states. This is operating within the framework of a North-driven notion of 'ecological sustainability'. Now is the opportunity to mobilise the scientific and research community, in an effort to determine the relative advantages and disadvantages inherent within any strategic developmental option that is chosen. We are moving into unknown territory – we are crossing an invisible threshold into a new paradigmatic frame of reference – where existing knowledge can no longer offer us sufficient assurance that the policy choices being considered are the best ones and such choices are based instead on imperfect considerations of relative risk.[20] The overall framework of political ecology provides a fertile research ground for multidisciplinarity. The world is complex and fragmentation into specialised academic disciplines has muddled our understanding of how the world works. Political ecology can be used to reconcile these differences by providing a road map that can steer policy-makers on that difficult to navigate course, balancing precariously between the political complexities of the need for economic growth and the apparent precipice of ecological collapse. Such is the *problematique* of a risk society, which is being thrust upon us as we enter the new millennium, whether we like it or not.

Acknowledgements

The efforts by the author to write this chapter have been the direct result of the support of five key people who are gratefully acknowledged. Professor Tony Allan guided the author over a number of years, specifically regarding a deeper understanding of the concept of 'virtual water'. He also made it possible for the author to work with the SOAS Water Issues Group. It was during this period that the specific chapter was born. Professor Philip Stott of the SOAS Geography Department provided guidance on the political ecology aspects of the chapter. Dr Leif Ohlsson of Göteborg University provided intellectual stimulation and was willing to test out new ideas in the rapidly changing arena of natural resource scarcity. The help of Professor Kader Asmal, the Minister of Water Affairs and Forestry, who has led such a fundamental transformation in the South African water sector, is gratefully acknowledged. Despite his very busy schedule, the Minister still found the time to guide the author (and reprimand him where his words were considered injudicious) in a positive manner. Thanks must also go to Professor Marie Muller of Pretoria University, who initially supported the author's interest in hydropolitics, and who ultimately urged the author to go to London to improve his interdisciplinary skills believing these to be 'the way of the future'. Finally, Dr M.S. Basson of BKS (Pty) Ltd made it possible for me to obtain the maps of water distribution and patterns of use, and I am grateful to both BKS (Pty) Ltd and the department of Water Affairs and Forestry for permission to reproduce these images. In addition to the above, the role of the author's family (Ansie, Rex and Melissa) is also noted, as they have sacrificed a lot in order to sustain him in London at the SOAS Water Issues Group. The London Goodenough Trust has also provided an intellectually rich 'home away from home'. The author will remain indebted to these people and institutions and wishes to thank them sincerely for their support and guidance, but he alone accepts responsibility for the contents of this chapter.

Notes

1 Editors' note: Atkinson here is politicising the thinking which characterises 'deep' or 'transpersonal' ecology, i.e. the positing of a spiritual and in some senses mystical reorientation to 'nature' in the finding of our 'right place' as part of, rather than separate from, the wider biophysical environment, in contrast to the managerial and technical approach to environment supported by the so-called 'shallow' science of ecology (see, for example, Naess, 1973, 1985, 1986, 1987, 1989; Devall and Sessions, 1985; Devall, 1988; Fox, 1990).

2 In this regard, pioneering research by Leif Ohlsson (1999) is of great value. With regard to the allocation of water Ohlsson's framework suggests the existence of both a first and second order set of conflicts. A first order conflict occurs as the result of direct competition for access to water. As water becomes scarcer, a regulative framework will need to be established which results in a second order of conflicts.

3 Barry Buzan (1994) raises the notion of a relationship between the centre–periphery structure of the post-Cold War political economy that gives the centre both the power and the international legitimacy to reimpose a degree of unequal political relations on the periphery. This is placed within the context of water in Turton (1999a) where it is shown that NGOs challenge the

sovereignty of the developing state by monopolising the 'adaptive capacity' that the developing state lacks.

4 The works of authors such as Berel Rodal (1996) are illuminating in this regard. Rodal states for example that the post-Cold War era has ushered in a new, 'truly international agenda' that is dominated by global environmental issues. I discuss this in relation to water in Turton (1999a).

5 Conrad Kottak (1998) alludes to some of these as constituting a challenge to the state.

6 As iterated recently at a working conference on water law in South Africa in the paper presented by Francis Wilson (1998; cf. the website www.uct.ac.za/org/rssa).

7 For the purposes of this chapter, 'precipitation' will mean water in whatever form it is found in the hydrological cycle. This is not strictly in accordance with other definitions of precipitation. Essentially, the water found in the lower Zambezi River that is allocated to the generation of hydro-electric power in Mozambique, is the same water that fell as precipitation (in the strict hydrological sense of the word) over the highlands of Angola.

8 Due to prevailing levels of evapotranspiration, this in itself is a problem. For example, evaporation from Lake Kariba accounts for 20–25 per cent of the annual flow of the Zambezi River at that point (MacDonald and Partners, 1990: 2.7). Evaporation from the Omatako Canal, a component of the Eastern National Water Carrier (ENWC) in Namibia, accounts for 70 per cent of the water carried by this scheme at the point of measurement (Davies *et al.*, 1993: 163). Such engineering solutions, therefore, are extremely wasteful and come at a high environmental cost (cf. Turton, 1998: 67).

9 It must be noted that the term 'pipeline' is being used in the widest possible context. Huge schemes such as the Lesotho Highlands Water Project tend to transfer water from one river basin to another. Strictly speaking, it is incorrect to assume that the water stays in pipelines for the entire distance of the transfer. Normally the water is pumped via pipeline either over a watershed, or through a mountain (by tunnel) until the next river basin has been reached, where the water is discharged into the receiving river. For this chapter, the variable called 'pipeline' will be used to mean any form of water transfer scheme, be it reservoir, canal, tunnel or pipeline.

10 Acknowledgment is given to Thomas Homer-Dixon and the Toronto Group for this concept (Homer-Dixon and Percival, 1996).

11 Conley (1997) gives a detailed explanation of the changes in the South African water law, placing irrigated agriculture in a broader context of political change.

12 The French word for power as *pouvoir* is useful to explain the distinction of subtle power in the form of control.

13 The French word for power as *puissance* is useful to explain the distinction of brutal power in the form of force or might.

14 Refer to Turton (1998b) for more details of the South African case of 'resource capture'.

15 Full acknowledgment is given to Prof. Kader Asmal, the South African Minister of Water Affairs and Forestry, for articulating this so eloquently in Cape Town on 11 November 1998.

16 Turton (1999b) cites an example of the subtle intrusion of political ramifications into the 'normal' domain of engineers and hydrologists. This involves the decision to build a pipeline from the panhandle of the Okavango Delta. Normally it would be the realm of engineers to make such decisions, and certainly within the sovereign competence of the Government of Botswana to do so. Yet suddenly, an upstream riparian decides to build a pipeline and the whole issue becomes one of international politics (refer to Ramberg, 1997). From that moment on, political factors became as relevant as any engineering equation to the development of that pipeline. An invisible but important threshold has been crossed. The politics of pipelines has been thrust upon us. Where are the social science specialists who can provide insight to such complex decision-making? Are they even allowed to sit on International River Basin Commissions where such issues are thrashed out? The answer at this stage is an emphatic no, because the prevailing paradigm is that water is the exclusive domain of engineers, hydrologists and possibly freshwater ecologists. Significantly, political ecology thinking says that this need no longer be the case. The sanctioned discourse or 'public transcript' is being challenged.

17 Zambia, Angola and possibly Mozambique are examples of Southern African states with a water surplus.
18 It has been shown (Lichtenthäler, 1999), for example, that:

> cereals are not only central but absolutely essential to Yemeni cuisine. Importantly, the perceived social and cultural values of some homegrown varieties – of which 25 are known for sorghum alone – and their distinct place and function within Yemeni daily life, explains the strong preference for local grains over foreign imports. Moreover, homegrown cereal foods, especially at lunch, are believed to enhance the daily and socially significant *qat* chewing experience in the afternoon. *Qat* is a narcotic stimulant chewed by the majority of Yemeni men in the company of friends and relatives. The production and consumption of homegrown cereals strengthens social values and notions of identity.

19 Refer to Feitelson (1998) for a detailed study of how a window of opportunity made this politically possible.
20 This is what is being called the 'risk society'. Refer to Beck (1992; 1995; 1996; 1999), Beck *et al.* (1996), Giddens (1984; 1990) and Allan (1999b) for a deeper insight into the significance of this newly emerging discourse.

References

Abrams, L.J. 1996: Policy development in the water sector – the South African experience. In Howsam, P. and Carter, R.C. (eds), *Water policy: allocation and management in practice*. London: E & FN Spon.

Allan, J.A. 1996a: Electronic mail sent to the author dated 16 September 1996.

Allan, J.A. 1996b: Policy responses to the closure of water resources: regional and global issues. In Howsam, P. and Carter, R.C. (eds), *Water policy: allocation and management in practice*. London: E & FN Spon.

Allan, J.A. 1999a: Personal communication with the author on 11 January 1999 at the School of Oriental and African Studies, University of London.

Allan, J.A. 1999b: Water in international systems: a risk society analysis of regional problemsheds and global hydrologies. Paper presented at the conference on 'Sustainability, Risk and Nature: The Political Ecology of Water in Advanced Societies', University of Oxford, 15–17 April 1999.

Atkinson, A. 1991: *Principles of political ecology*. London: Belhaven Press.

Bahro, R. 1982: *Socialism and survival*. London: Heretic Books.

Bahro, R. 1984: *From red to green*. London: Verso.

Bahro, R. 1986: *Building the Green movement*. London: Heretic Books.

Barnet, R.J. 1980: *The lean years: politics in the age of scarcity*. London: Abacus.

Basson, M.S., van Niekerk, P.H. and van Rooyen, J.A. 1997: *Overview of water resources availability and utilization in South Africa*. Pretoria: Department of Water Affairs and Forestry.

Beck, U. 1992: From industrial to risk society. *Theory, culture and society* **9**, 97–123.

Beck, U. 1995: *Ecological politics in an age of risk*. Cambridge: Polity Press.

Beck, U. 1996: The sociology of risk. In Goldblatt, D. (ed.), *Social theory and the environment*. Cambridge: Polity Press.

Beck, U. 1999: What is a risk society? *Prometheus* **1**(1), 75–9.

Beck, U., Giddens, A. and Lash, S. 1996: *Reflexive modernization*. Cambridge: Polity Press.

Bollig, B. 1997: Contested places: graves and graveyards in Himba cultue. *Anthropos* **92**, 35–50.

Bryant, R.L. 1998: Power, knowledge and political ecology in the Third World: a review. *Progress in Physical Geography* **22**, 79–94.

Bryant, R.L. and Bailey, S. 1997: *Third World political ecology*. New York: Routledge.

Buzan, B. 1994: National security in the post Cold War Third World. Paper presented at the conference on National Security in Developing Countries, 26 January 1994 at the Institute for Strategic Studies, University of Pretoria, South Africa.

Conley, A.H. 1997: To be or not to be? South African irrigation at the crossroads. In Kay, M., Franks, T. and Smith, L. (eds), *Water: economics, management and demand*. London: E & FN Spon.

Davies, B.R., O'Keefe, J.H. and Snaddon, C.D. 1993: *A synthesis of the ecological functioning, conservation and management of South African river ecosystems*. Water Research Commission Report No. TT 62/93. Pretoria.

Devall, B. 1988: *Simple in means, rich in ends: practising deep ecology*. Salt Lake City: Peregrine Smith Books.

Devall, B. and Sessions, G. 1985: *Deep ecology: living as if people mattered*. Salt Lake City: Peregrine Smith Books.

Eckersley, R. 1997: *Environmentalism and political theory*. London: UCL Press.

Feitelson, E. 1998: The implications of changes in perceptions of water in Israel for peace negotiations with Jordan and the Palestinians. Jerusalem: Department of Geography, Hebrew University of Jerusalem.

Giddens, A. 1984: *The constitution of society*. Cambridge: Polity Press.

Giddens, A. 1990: *The consequences of modernity*. Cambridge: Polity Press.

Hardin, G. 1968: The tragedy of the commons. *Science* **162**, 1243–8.

Heilbroner, R.L. 1974: *An inquiry into the human prospect*. New York: Norton.

Homer-Dixon, T. and Percival, V. 1996: *Environmental scarcity and violent conflict: briefing book*. Population and Sustainable Development Project, American Association for the Advancement of Science and University of Toronto.

Kottak, C.P. 1998: Challenge to the state. Paper presented at the International Congress of Anthropological and Ethnological Science (ICAES), 26 July 1998 at Williamsburg, Virginia, USA.

Leach, M. and Mearns, R. 1996: Environmental change and policy: challenging received wisdom in Africa. In Leach, M. and Mearns, R. (eds), *The lie of the land: challenging received wisdom on the African continent*. London: Villiers Publications.

Leiss, W. 1974: *The domination of nature*. Boston: Beacon.

Lichtenthäler, G. 1999: Environment, society and economy in the Sa'dah Basin of Yemen: the role of water. Draft copy of a PhD dissertation, Geography Department, School of Oriental and African Studies (SOAS), University of London.

Lundqvist, J. and Gleick, P. 1997: *Comprehensive assessment of the freshwater resources of the world: sustaining our waters into the 21st century*. Stockholm: Stockholm Environment Institute.

MacDonald, M. and Partners 1990: *Sub Saharan Africa hydrological assessment: SADCC countries: regional report*. Cambridge: MacDonald and Partners.

Mollinga, P.P. and van Straaten, C.J.M. 1996: The politics of water distribution. In Howsam, P. and Carter, R.C. (eds), *Water policy: allocation and management in practice*. London: E & FN Spon.

Naess, A. 1973: The shallow and the deep, long range ecology movement: a summary. *Inquiry* **16**: 95–100.

Naess, A. 1985: Identification as a source of deep ecological attitudes. In Tobias, M. *Deep ecology*. San Diego: Avant Books, 256–70.

Naess, A. 1986: The deep ecological movement: some philosophical aspects. *Philosophical Inquiry* **8**, 10–31.

Naess, A. 1987: Self-realization: an ecological approach to being in the world. *The Trumpeter* **43**(3), 35–42.

Naess, A. 1989: *Ecology, community and lifestyle: outline of an ecosophy*. Translated and revised by D. Rothenberg. Cambridge: Cambridge University Press.

Ohlsson, L. 1998: Water and social resource scarcity – an issue paper commissioned by FAO/AGLW. Presented as a discussion paper for the 2nd FAO e-mail conference on Managing Water Scarcity. WATSCAR 2.

Ohlsson, L. 1999: *Environment, scarcity and conflict: a study of Malthusian concerns*. Stockholm: Department of Peace and Development Research. University of Göteborg.

Ophuls, W. 1973: Leviathan or oblivion? In Daly, H.E. (ed.), *Towards a steady state economy*. San Francisco: Freeman.

Percival, V. and Homer-Dixon, T. 1995: *Environmental scarcity and violent conflict: the case of South Africa*. Population and Sustainable Development Project, American Association for the Advancement of Science and University of Toronto.

Ramberg, L. 1997: A pipeline from the Okavango River? *Ambio* **26**(2), 129.

Rodal, B. 1996: *The environment and changing concepts of security: Commentary No. 47*. Ottawa: Canadian Security Intelligence Service Internet Publication.

Stone, C. 1974: *Should trees have standing? Towards legal rights for natural objects*. Los Altos, CA: Kaufmann.

Turton, A.R. 1998a: The hydropolitics of Southern Africa: the case of the Zambezi River basin as an area of potential co-operation based on Allan's concept of 'Virtual Water'. Unpublished MA dissertation, Department of International Politics, University of South Africa, Pretoria.

Turton, A.R. 1998b: The monopolization of access to a critical natural resource: the case of water in South Africa. Paper presented at the Congress of the International Union of Anthropological and Ethnological Sciences (IUAES), Symposium on Resource Management through Indigenous Socio-cultural Practices, 28 July 1998 at Williamsburg, Virginia, USA.

Turton, A.R. 1999a: *Water and state sovereignty: the hydropolitical challenge for states in arid regions*. MEWREW Occasional Paper No. 5. London: SOAS Water Issues Study Group, University of London.

Turton, A.R. 1999b: *Water scarcity and social adaptive capacity: towards an understanding of the social dynamics of water demand management in developing countries*. MEWREW Occasional Paper No. 9. London: SOAS Water Issues Study Group, University of London.

Turton, A.R. 1999c: *Sea of sand, land of water: a synopsis of some strategic developmental issues confronting the Okavango Delta*. MEWREW Occasional Paper No. 6. London: SOAS Water Issues Study Group, University of London.

Turton, A.R. and Bernhardt, W. 1998: Policy-making within an oligarchy: the case of South Africa under apartheid rule. Paper presented at the Congress of the International Union of Anthropological and Ethnological Sciences (IUAES), Symposium on Policy, Power and Governance, 27 July 1998 at Williamsburg, Virginia, USA.

Wilson, F. 1998: The political economy of water in South Africa: a holistic approach. Paper presented at the Working Conference on the Implications of the New Water Policy: Problems and Solutions, 11–13 November 1998 at the Royal Society of South Africa, University of Cape Town.

Part 3

The Relations of Power, Global to Local

7
Ecological possibilities and political constraints

Adjustments of farming to protracted drought by women and men in the Western Division of The Gambia

Kathleen Baker

7.1 Introduction

That African smallholder farmers adapt to changing circumstances is well documented in the literature (Richards, 1985, 1986; Osmeobo, 1987; Goldman, 1992; Netting, 1993; Tiffen *et al.*, 1994; Amanor 1994; Mortimore, 1989, 1998). But why is it that while they are so adaptive, the majority of smallholders do not achieve significant improvements in their living standards? The literature abounds with explanations for the poor performance of African agriculture (cf. Stebbing 1938; Dumont 1962, 1988; Hart, 1982; Blaikie, 1985; Lowe 1986; Gakou, 1987; Hinderink and Sterkenburg, 1987; Amanor, 1994; Mortimore 1989, 1998 among others), but so much depends on the scale of study and on the orientation of the researcher that there is no consensus. With so many hypotheses, the only certainty is that no single set of explanations for the problems of African agriculture has widespread applicability.

Focusing first on the theme of the adaptability of smallholder farmers, this chapter analyses changes that more than 30 years of drought have forced on farming in the Western Division of The Gambia. Although the drought has had many negative effects on farming, skilful changes to their livelihoods have given farmers, both men and women, the opportunity of developing local economies in different directions. Despite this local innovation the question remains as to why the potential for achieving agricultural and rural development has not been realised. The analysis reveals that where adaptations or solutions to the problems of the drought have been based on locally constructed knowledge, there is a greater chance of success than where they have been based on external perceptions of how agriculture should develop. The potential success of indigenous solutions has not been fully realised, however, because policies impinging on the agricultural sector, of which many are externally influenced, have given little scope for the development of agriculture, other than through prescribed channels. Where access to such channels is limited for both men and for women, their capacity to achieve rural development is seriously constrained.

After outlining the methods used in the field research, the characteristics of the drought and the agricultural situation in The Gambia, this chapter turns first to women's farming on the wetlands and then to men's farming on the drylands to examine key features of each and the major constraints under which they operate. Adopting a 'political ecology' frame, I then explore the nature and success of responses made by women and by men to changing circumstances.

I derive material for this chapter from a series of visits to The Gambia in 1981, 1990 and 1991, and in 1999. Between 1981 and 1990, the visual change in the riverine landscapes of the Lower Gambia was considerable: land which yielded paddy in 1981 had become unproductive by 1990 owing to the drought (see below), and remained in this state in 1999. The effects of the drought were not so readily apparent on the drylands, although farming in these areas also proved to have been badly affected. Prompted principally by the situation in the riverine wetlands, fieldwork in 1990 and 1991 investigated the effects of drought on farming and the coping strategies adopted by farmers, both men and women, in seven villages of the Western Division (*see* Figure 7.1). Two of these village – Nyofelleh Medina and Kassa Kunda were re-visited in 1999 to find out whether there had been further changes in farming. Two other villages, Jambanjally and Tujereng, also among the first seven, were visited briefly and discussions were held with local people to confirm whether information derived from the visits to Nyofelleh and Kassa Kunda was correct.

Field information was collected using a range of techniques including Participatory Rural Appraisal (PRA), semi-structured interviews and observation. PRA was conducted with groups of village members, both men and women, in each of the villages. The groups were somewhat fluid as people would join in and leave as work (or perhaps boredom) drew them away. Overall, a total of about 25 people were involved in these meetings in each of the villages. Men usually outnumbered women, though care was taken to ensure that men's views did not dominate over those of women. Wherever possible, groups of women were met to try to ensure that responses had not been prejudiced by the presence of men.

Discussions were also held with key informants at various levels Included among these were village-level extension workers and school teachers, village head men and head men's wives, and aid donors including the World Bank, EU and the Catholic Relief Services, the last being one of the largest NGOs in The Gambia. Discussions were also held with officials at the National Environment Agency (NEA) and at the State Department of Agriculture. Triangulation was used where possible to confirm (and/or to query) findings, and secondary source information yielded further evidence on the effects of drought on farming and on farmers' adaptive strategies. The next section on the drought and Gambia's agricultural economy provides a context for discussion of the field work.

7.2 The Gambia, the drought and the agricultural economy, in brief

Situated at approximately 13° North of the equator, The Gambia is on the borders of the semi-arid Sudan savannas and the moister Guinea savannas. Average annual rainfall for 1992–97 was around 900mm (NADC *et al.*, 1998) although, as Figure 7.2 indicates, means are hardly useful figures as the standard deviation about the mean in each month suggests substantial variability. This is confirmed by Webb (1986) for The Gambia and by Sivakumar (1991) for much of Sahelian West Africa.

With regard to the drought, there are few involved in agriculture who do not perceive increasing desiccation as one of the greatest problems facing the sector. Charting the changes in rainfall over the past 30 years, however, does not show conclusively that rainfall

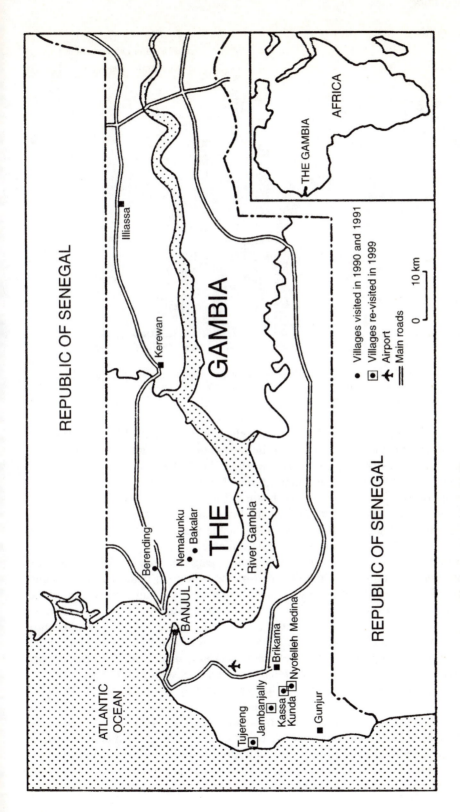

Figure 7.1 The Gambia, showing the location of the research villages

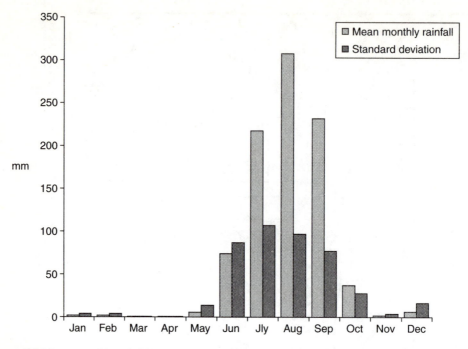

Figure 7.2 Mean monthly rainfall and standard deviation for Banjul, The Gambia (1978–97). *Source:* The Meteorological Office, Bracknell

has declined and perhaps the use of the term drought is not justified. While the National Environment Agency (NEA) (1992) states that the mean annual rainfall in the Gambia has fallen by about 30 per cent since the mid-1970s, work by Webb (1986) demonstrates that the overall record for 18 stations in The Gambia basin shows little more than a tendency towards decreasing annual rainfall over the period of historical records. Moreover, confirming the changes is difficult owing to the paucity of the data. For example, monthly rainfall statistics provided by the Meteorological Office, Bracknell, for the period 1978–97 are frequently incomplete and so a good run of annual totals is unavailable.

Although the rains have not failed every year, in many years since the late 1960s they have been below the average recorded for the first part of the century, a pattern which concurs with that for the Sahel overall (*see* Figure 7.3). Whether or not mean annual rainfall has declined, of major concern for rural dwellers in The Gambia is an apparent increase in the unpredictability of rainfall distribution. In particular, the commencement and conclusion of the rains have been uncertain in recent years (Oladipo and Kyari, 1993). The problems that this can cause are well exemplified by the 1998 rainy season which started well but stopped much earlier than expected, ruining cereal harvests. One observation common among farmers interviewed was that the rainy season had contracted by approximately one month since the drought began. This is of major significance as the rains are confined to a five- to six-month period in the year. Unpredictability in the annual rains has thus led to livelihoods being even more precarious than in the past. Whether or not a drought can be truly said to exist, or whether it is more that the pattern of rainfall distribution has been more erratic, the term is used throughout this chapter because of its frequent use under different rainfall conditions by those who live in the country.

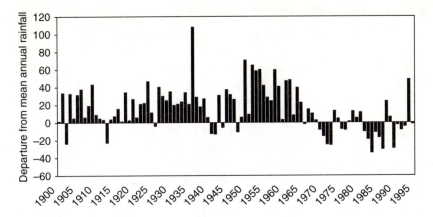

Figure 7.3 Departure from mean annual rainfall in the West African Sahel

Central to the geography of The Gambia is the River Gambia, which rises in Guinea, flows north into Senegal and then west along the length of the country to the coast. Each year, the river is swollen by rainfall and run-off along its course. From July to November the water level rises and the river floods. This is critically important to farming which is divided between wetland cultivation where the water table is either at or near the surface, and the rainfed drylands further away from the river where the water table is several metres below the surface. In Mandinke villages wetland cultivation is usually the domain of the women while dryland farming is the domain of the men. Wetlands consist of riverine areas and also inland depressions where the rising water table during the rainy season brings water either to the surface, or very near to it. These highly prized areas are cultivated mainly with rice during the rainy season and the period when the river is in flood, i.e. May–June to November–December.

Women may also cultivate vegetables on the wetlands during the dry season as the water table is still near the surface and crops can be irrigated from temporary, shallow wells. Some two-thirds of households in the villages visited during fieldwork grew vegetables. This exceeded estimates by the NADC *et al.* (1998: 28) that 47 per cent of households in the Western Division grew vegetables, even though the latter figure is almost 50 per cent greater than estimates of households growing vegetables in The Gambia as a whole. In other words, this gives some indication of the importance of vegetable growing in the area of research.

On drylands, which are entirely dependent on rain for their moisture, the great majority of Mandinke men cultivate staple cereals, primarily millet and sorghum, as well as The Gambia's major cash crop, groundnuts. Other crops such as maize, beans and cassava may be grown, as are fruit trees, particularly oranges and mangoes. Dryland cultivation of field crops is limited to the rainy season, i.e. June to November, although cassava may be left in the soil during the dry season and harvested up to 18 months after the cuttings are planted. Where livestock are kept, they are usually the main responsibility of men. Cattle, goats and sheep are kept by both sedentary farmers and by semi-nomadic pastoralists and their importance for the rural economy is considerable. The focus of this chapter, however, is on field crops, fruit and vegetable cultivation.

7.3 Women's wetland farming: characteristics and constraints

Rice is an important crop of the wetlands and is normally grown by women. Although international statistics do not differentiate between upland and wet rice, they do reveal an overall decline of almost 40 per cent in production between 1966 and 1996 (FAO Production Yearbooks, various) (*see* Figure 7.4). Estimates indicate that 73 per cent of households in the Western Division grow rice (NADC, 1998: 27), a figure which compares closely with the study villages where PRA discussions revealed that approximately three-quarters of households grow rice. As virtually all of this is consumed within the household, a severe reduction in rice production must inevitably have had serious implications for domestic food security, as well as for women's income-generation. Since commencement of the drought, the river level has fallen to such an extent that saline water from the Atlantic has penetrated over 250km from its mouth in the dry season and is found 100km from the estuary mouth even in the wet season (NEA, 1997). Park (1993) has identified a similar pattern of declining flood levels in the River Senegal. Prior to the onset of the drought, when dry season river levels were higher and when the volume of the annual flood was greater, this saline incursion was regularly washed back to sea. In recent years, the floods have been insufficient to cleanse the river and, as a consequence, the flood plain of the Lower Gambia has been inundated with saline water. This has destroyed much riverine wet rice cultivation (Baker, 1995). Official Gambian rice statistics are instructive: while approximately 60 per cent of the rice produced in The Gambia is wet rice (Table 7.1), in the Western Division there is no flood rice recorded at all and 100 per cent of production is derived from upland rice. Field evidence has shown that these statistics are not wholly accurate as wet rice continues to be grown in inland depressions. However, it seems that the extent and productive capacity of these enclaves has also diminished over the past 30 years as the water table has fallen with the drought.

In both the riverine areas and in inland depressions where the water table rises but does not reach the surface, women also grow upland rice. This does not require flooding and is grown in similar fashion to other rainfed cereals, the seeds of which are broadcast. It does, however, require moist soils. The proportion of wet to upland rice depends very much on the local

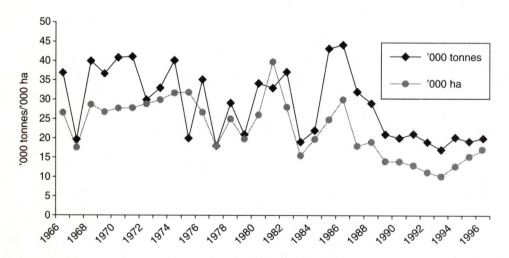

Figure 7.4 Production and area of paddy in The Gambia, 1966–96. *Source:* FAO Production Yearbooks

Table 7.1 Relative importance of swamp and upland rice

	Rice production in The Gambia ('000 tonnes)	Rice production in Western Division ('000 tonnes)
Upland	6.52 (39.07%)	2.73 (100.00%)
Swamp (wet) rice	10.17 (60.93%)	0.00
Total	16.69	2.73

Source: Adapted from NADC *et al.*, 1998: 10

environment. Farmers' preference for wet rice is directly related to yield: although varieties grown on both wetlands and uplands are largely the same, wet rice yields around one-third more than that grown under relatively dry conditions in upland areas. After the first and main harvest, the paddy grows again to a second, smaller harvest because of the abundance of moisture. By contrast, upland rice yields only one crop. Although millet and sorghum are staple cereals, rice is the preferred cereal in much of The Gambia and formerly women produced most of the rice consumed in the village.

From PRA discussions with both women and men in 1990, 1991 and 1999, it emerged that the rice harvest lasted for most of the year in the 1960s because water was so plentiful. In 1990 and 1991, in all the villages visited, the rice harvest lasted only three months or less into the next crop year (Baker, 1992), and by the late 1990s, the rice harvest lasted no more than a few weeks. While the major cause of the shortfall in rice is declining productivity due to the drought, a contributory factor is population increase over this time period. As Table 7.2 shows, the population in each of the villages visited in 1999 reflected a significant increase between the census of 1983 and that of 1993. It is likely that this has also had a negative effect on per capita food production, but discussions with farmers strongly indicated drought and rainfall variability to be the major causes of agricultural problems. In villages such as at Nyofelleh Medina, for example, there was no rice harvest at all in 1999: while the rains started well they stopped both abruptly and very early, before the grains had formed properly. Millet and sorghum fared little better under these conditions and, given that little or no wet rice could be cultivated either because of recent declines in the area of swampland, the food security situation under such conditions can be considered critical.

As well as rainfall, declining soil fertility was cited by women as a significant contributor to reduced rice harvests. Fertiliser was described as beyond the purse of most farmers, particularly since the elimination of subsidies by 1990, and not one woman involved in the PRA meetings in any of the villages used inorganic fertiliser on her cultivable land. Because

Table 7.2 Changes in population in Kassa Kunda and Nyofelleh Medina

	Kassa Kunda Total population (absolute nos.)	% inc. 93/83	Nyofelleh Medina Total population	% inc. 93/83
1983	419		328	
1993	568	+35.56	480	+46.34

Source: Adapted from Population and Housing Census of The Gambia, 1983 and 1993, *Statistics on Settlements*, vols 4 and 10, respectively.

concern about the high price of fertiliser was expressed by every farmer, both female and male, involved in the study, there seemed little reason not to accept that this was a problem. These findings, however, contradict those produced by the NADC *et al.* (1998) which revealed that the percentage area under rice which received fertiliser was significantly higher in 1997 than it had been in 1992 (*see* Table 7.3). Given that imports of fertiliser into The Gambia fell from a total of 22,465 tonnes in 1985 to 1,013 tonnes in 1997, this becomes even more difficult to understand (NADC *et al.*, 1998). One possible explanation for the statistics is that more farmers in the Western Division might have used fertiliser, but far less than the recommended amount per unit area. Official statistics do suggest that farmers frequently, though by no means always, use sub-optimal levels of fertiliser (NADC *et al.*, 1998: 40). It is doubtful whether the 1997 pattern of fertiliser use recorded by NADC *et al.* (1998) will be repeated in 1999 as fertiliser was virtually inaccessible in this year due to the collapse in 1998 of the government distribution system, the Gambia Co-operative Union (GCU).

Besides the addition of fertiliser, alternative methods of increasing the productivity of rice land could be achieved by restoring the fertility of the soil through traditional practices of fallow or increasing the area under cultivation. In Kassa Kunda, for example, land was plentiful but here too women faced problems as they could not clear any larger an area by hand. Access to much needed animal-drawn farm implements was difficult: PRA discussions revealed that the price of these had risen relative to income over the past decade, and farmers' dependence on traditional hand implements had increased (*see* Table 7.4). Where a household had access to animals and animal-drawn implements, women paid the men to clear new land for them. This was now rare, however, owing to the problems of obtaining, and the cost of maintaining, animal drawn implements.

7.3.1 Adjustments made by women to the effects of drought

One response by women to the loss of their rice was to increase non-farm activities, particularly trading. Most who were interviewed bought groundnuts from their husbands and processed them into peanut butter. Much of this was used in the kitchen, though a larger proportion is now sold than in the past. Many sold roasted peanuts or cooked cassava in the market; some worked for their husbands selling fuel wood and some made soap, particularly in the wet season (Baker, 1995). Income-generating alternatives to rice were relatively few for women although several made their limited income go further by money-lending at a very small scale – and always with other women. For one group of three women, for

Table 7.3 Percentage area under swamp and upland rice receiving fertiliser in The Gambia

	Compound fertiliser	Urea
Upland rice		
1992	32	31
1997	54	49
Swamp rice		
1992	00	01
1997	91	22

Source: Adapted from NADC *et al.* (1992) Table 6, p. 10 and (1998) Table 6.3.1, p. 23
Note: Total may exceed 100 per cent as more than one type of fertiliser may be used on the same plot.

Table 7.4 Matrices derived from PRA meetings showing changes related to farming in Kassa Kunda and Nyofelleh Medina

	Kassa Kunda		Nyofelleh Medina	
	Situation 10–15 years ago	*Situation at present*	*Situation 10–15 years ago*	*Situation at present*
Change in rainfall	●●●●●●	●●	●●●●●●●	●●●
Use of fertiliser	●●●●●●●●	● ●	●●●●●●	●●●
Use of organic manure	●●●●●●●●	●	●●●●●●●	●●●
Use of animal-drawn farm implements in village	●●●	●●●●●	●●●●	●●●●●●
Use of animal-drawn farm implements by individual households	●●●●●●●●●●	—	●●●●●	●●
Availability of farm labour	●●●●●●●	●●●	●●●●●	●●●●
Number of urban migrants from village	●	●●●●●●●●	●●●	●●●●●
Dependence on remittances from urban migrants	●●●	●●●●●●	●●	●●●●●●●
Planting of fruit trees	●●●	●●●●●●	●●●	●●●●●●●

Source: Fieldwork by the author, 1999

Note: The groups were each asked about changes in the variables listed in the table. They were given 10 oranges in one case, 10 stones in another and asked to apportion them to indicate the direction and approximate extent of any change involved. Agreement was eventually reached on each issue following extensive discussion among the group example, each would contribute a few *dalasi* to a kitty each week or each month. The total became the property of one of the participants each time and thus increased the spending power of each of the women on a rotational basis.

At the beginning of the 1980s when expatriates were becoming increasingly aware of the effects of the drought, aid donors proposed that an alternative, and in some cases an additional, source of income for women could be derived from vegetable gardening. Traditionally, vegetables were grown in or near the compound mainly in the wet season. With assistance from international donors, communal gardens, often with a permanent water source, increased rapidly through the 1980s, and women were encouraged to grow a much wider range of vegetables through the dry season. Seed was provided by the facilitators of these schemes and attention was paid to ecological aspects of vegetable gardening to ensure that crop production was feasible. Not all women were included in vegetable gardening projects. Some did not wish to participate, or in some cases such as at Nyofelleh, there was not room for everyone. Where demand for vegetable plots exceeded supply on project gardens, communal gardens were sometimes established, based on local initiative. There was one such garden at Nyofelleh. This, together with others similar, were usually located in the riverine areas untouched by problems of soil salinity, or they were located in inland depressions where wet rice was grown in the rainy season. In such locations the water table remains fairly near the surface, even in the dry season, allowing the digging of temporary wells for irrigation of the vegetables. These wells are filled in with the onset of the rains and the change in cropping from vegetables to rice.

Dietary benefits of vegetables were widely acknowledged in the villages, but vegetable gardening has been far from the success expected by those involved in it. First, vegetables are not a substitute for rice. They may provide an income with which rice can be bought, but vegetables are not a replacement for rice in the diet. Second, labour demand for vegetable cultivation is much higher than it is for rice. Rice requires labour mainly during peak periods such as for land clearance, sowing or transplanting, weeding and harvesting. Vegetable cultivation, on the other hand, requires labour every day. Vegetable gardens have to be watered at least twice a day, seed has to be sown in nurseries and transplanted into the gardens, plots have to be manured with dung gathered in and around the village, and weeding is an unending and back-breaking task. Third, protecting the vegetable gardens from attack by animals is time-consuming and can be arduous. Since vegetables are grown mainly in the dry season, there is always the threat that animals will force their way into the gardens attracted by the green vegetation in an otherwise dry landscape.

In much of semi-arid West Africa animals are rarely closely herded in the dry season as during this time there tends to be little for them to destroy. As cultivation systems extend from the wet into the dry season, the impact of animals on vegetable gardens and on cassava (below) has become a major concern in rural areas. Certain Djola groups in the Gambia appear to have addressed this successfully by hiring boys in the dry season to take the village herd away from the settlement and cultivation, and in this way this women's dry season vegetable crops are protected. Where this is not yet the practice, the vegetable gardens had to be guarded from shortly after dawn when the animals begin grazing, to dusk, when they make their way back to the village for the night. Guarding the gardens is thus a major demand on women's time.

It is noteworthy that most women now cultivate vegetables through the dry season and rice through the rainy season. Cultivating and harvesting crops in two seasons represent a major increase in women's workloads, a change which should have been rewarded with increased income. Yet PRA discussions indicated that the two harvests together barely provided the food security that they had had from good harvests of rice in the 1960s. While rice production was much lower than in the past, vegetable production levels were comparatively good. What these patterns meant, however, is that women's livelihoods have changed from predominantly subsistence, where virtually all the rice produced was consumed, to one very heavily dependent on the sale of vegetables. It is with the sale of vegetables that problems appear to have arisen.

Women in Nyofelleh Medina, for example, described the marketing of vegetables as the 'biggest headache they had'. This corroborated complaints made to me by women during early 1990s fieldwork, and suggests that various issues were consistently problematic. Observation and discussions with key informants, for example, indicate that a major concern is that markets are frequently saturated with vegetables. Selling the vegetables directly to consumers was by far the most profitable method. Alternatively, wholesale merchants might wish to buy the vegetables, but their approach often seems to be to harass women into selling at a lower price. If the women refused to sell to a wholesaler early in the day, and were unable to dispose of their produce to private buyers, they had little choice at the end of the day but to sell for a low price to private consumers. Another option might be to return to the wholesaler who might take the produce, though probably for a price even more unattractive than it had been earlier in the day. Agreeing a price was one thing, but the merchants usually refused to pay until they had disposed of the produce themselves. Extracting the money from these buyers could be extremely difficult and it emerged from PRA discussions that women expected to have to make several visits to the market to collect their dues. Other options were to dump the produce near the market, or carry it back to the village where some of it would be consumed and the rest would become food for the goat or compost. While women are more than capable of striking a hard bargain, respondents both in the villages and in the urban areas confirmed that women really did have a major problem disposing of surplus vegetable produce. Accessing markets can also be problematic. Although women near Banjul have a better chance of marketing their vegetables, this is far from true of producers in the more remote rural areas which are those where women have been encouraged by aid donors to develop vegetable gardens. Women in Nyofelleh Medina and Kassa Kunda transport their vegetables to the market at Brikama (*see* Figure 7.1) either by bus, by getting a lift, or on foot. For the aggravation caused by marketing, returns from vegetables rarely compensated for the loss of rice. Nevertheless, women persisted with them as other opportunities for income generation were so few.

Remarkably little attention seems to have been paid to the marketing of produce by the instigators of gardening projects. According to the World Bank office in Banjul in 1990, it was expected that the hotel industry would buy local produce and indeed they do to some extent, although observation revealed that hotels still import a substantial quantity of vegetables, frozen, from Europe. According to key informants from the European Union offices in The Gambia, local producers cannot guarantee supplies and so the hotel industry, or indeed any local processing industry, could not rely on them. In keeping with the country's Structural Adjustment Programme, the government seems little interested in becoming involved with the marketing of vegetables, particularly at the smallholder level. In addition, there is a staunch belief that the private sector will fill the gap. Similar complaints were noted by Campbell and Daniels (1988) in a report of a horticultural marketing mission conducted by the University of Wisconsin and others in association with the then Department of Agriculture. Almost a decade later the situation in the villages visited is as bad if not worse. Dependence on vegetables is now greater as the effects of drought have intensified and rice production is lower than it has been in the living memory of most women involved in the PRA. One possibility could be to encourage large-scale capital-intensive peri-urban farms near Banjul to use smallholders as contract growers, specifying the quality of produce required by the hotel industry or any other large-scale user. There seems little enthusiasm by the government to become involved in such issues. This situation accords with the findings of Bräutigam (1998). She argues that although much of the development work conducted by the mainland Chinese and the Taiwanese in Africa was ecologically sound, it did not lead to tangible economic development, primarily due to a lack of the necessary institutional framework to enhance small-scale, village-level marketing success.

7.3.2 Political ecology and women

In the Western Division of The Gambia it would seem that, while drought has been a major influence on women's land management strategies, political decision-making at local levels and beyond has had a major effect on women's activities. While their access to land, credit, seed, fertiliser, other inputs and to farm machinery is influenced by political decision-making, largely at the local level problems with marketing appear to have arisen because of a lack of awareness, or interest, at higher levels and the failure by those in power to make political decisions which could assist women. This may be because vegetable gardening schemes have been based too heavily on externally constructed perceptions of what would assist women and thus bring about socio-economic development in rural Gambia. While projects have succeeded in ensuring that the production of vegetables is successful owing to sound autecological techniques, instigators have assumed too much in anticipating that problems of marketing would take care of themselves or that mechanisms to aid crop disposal would evolve. Perhaps one of the reasons that an appropriate institutional framework to promote the successful disposal of vegetables has not emerged is because vegetable cultivation was perceived initially by project instigators as a supplement to subsistence production and a means of mitigating losses from rice due to the drought. While the expansion of vegetable production has undoubtedly benefited local diets, gardening has far exceeded subsistence demands by producing a substantial marketable surplus. Although there is now widespread recognition among relevant government departments and aid agencies of the problems of crop disposal, there has been little improvement in the marketing system in the villages visited over the past decade. The issue of marketing has thus been avoided by both those who instigated vegetable gardening projects and by the government, which, by keeping faith with its Structural Adjustment Programme, is reluctant to involve itself in vegetable marketing. Both these attitudes are influenced by externally constructed views on rural development in The Gambia and, because of them, Gambian solutions to Gambian problems are not being sought with sufficient vigour.

7.4 Dryland farming by men: characteristics and constraints

The problems are very different on the drylands. Here, the staple cereals millet and sorghum are cultivated together with groundnuts, the country's chief cash crop. Other crops such as cassava and beans are also grown, but the first three dominate the landscape in the rainy season. In Mandinke villages the drylands are normally the domain of the men, while among other ethnic groups such as the Djola, gender divisions are not quite so clearly demarcated. Dryland farming has also suffered from the drought. Yields for millet, sorghum and groundnuts have declined and are frequently well below one tonne per hectare equivalent. Variability in rainfall is a major problem for dryland crop production and although mean annual rainfall patterns for the Sahel suggest that the rains are increasing, their distribution has not always been conducive to better harvests. In 1998, cereal yields were particularly low because of the early cessation of the rains. Declining or virtually static production of major field crops such as groundnuts and millet over the past 30 years, has forced changes (*see* Figures 7.5 and 7.6): farm families have had to extend the area cultivated to maintain production levels, to increase the level of inputs used to increase yields and hence output, to supplement farm income from either off-farm or non-farm employment, or to resort to a combination of some, or all, of the above. The possibilities and constraints surrounding these options are considered below.

With rural–urban migration reducing the labour available on farms, there has been little scope for many families to extend the area they cultivate or to re-open land which has lain fallow for many years. As migrants are usually younger people and are predominantly men, the result is that those left to cultivate dryland fields are often drawn from the elderly who

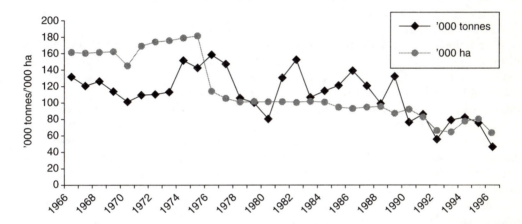

Figure 7.5 Production and area of groundnuts in The Gambia, 1966–96. *Source:* FAO Production Yearbooks

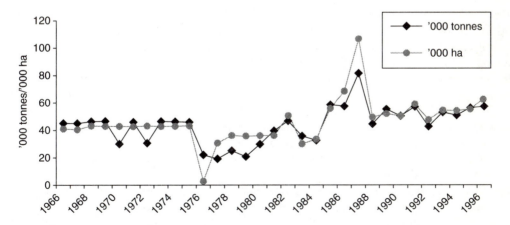

Figure 7.6 Production and area of millet in The Gambia. *Source:* FAO Production Yearbooks

would have retired had the labour force been greater. In contrast to times past, labour is rarely hired now. For a start, there is little money available for payment, and an earlier system of recruiting casual labour from farmers visiting from elsewhere (cf. Swindell, 1978, 1980) has broken down in response to the greater monetary returns available through work in urban areas. In recent years labour shortages have contributed to a tendency to cultivate only fields which are near villages meaning that fallow periods have been reduced to one or two years, or even to nothing (Baker, 1995). Population growth and processes of rural–rural migration also contribute to changes in patterns of farming. In some villages such as Nyofelleh Medina, for example, the village has grown so much that some of the *kabilos*, i.e. groups of households which farmed and controlled land in a sector of the village (ECOS International, 1986), are now comparatively short of land. For farmers in these *kabilos*, even where labour is available, returning to long fallowed land is becoming increasingly difficult. By contrast, in Kassa Kunda, village *kabilos* still have land surplus to current requirements. The changes affecting the length of the fallow period may in part be attributed to the drought but other factors have also played a part, not least population increase. As Table 7.2 indicates, village populations have grown significantly with a doubling of the proportion of children in the population over the previous 20 years (Baker, 1992).

With fallows significantly reduced over the past 20 years (Baker, 1995) and with low levels of inputs, what of the sustainability of dryland cultivation? Dung from animals remains an important input, although access to animal manure is greater for those who either keep animals or who have the resources to hire animals so that they can be tethered on their fields. The presence of animals in the village was of considerable importance. It was evident in Kassa Kunda that fallows were between one and three years, while in Nyofelleh Medina they had largely been eliminated, the reason being that Kassa Kunda had lost most of its animals in recent years due to theft occurring during the dry season when animals wander relatively freely. Nyofelleh has also suffered this problem, although not to as great an extent, probably due to its greater distance from the sizeable urban centre of Brikama. Thus access to animal dung influences the length of the fallow. In Kassa Kunda fields are fallowed for up to three years in order to restore some of its fertility, while in Nyofelleh Medina a greater availability of animal manure enabled farmers to cultivate the land continuously. In both villages dryland farmers rotated groundnuts and either millet or sorghum, reportedly to prevent the decline in nutrients that is seen to accompany cultivation of the same crop year after year. Supporting this view are the observations of a preliminary field investigation in 1991 in Nyofelleh Medina and Kassa Kunda which indicated that where land had been cultivated with the same crop for around ten years, either millet or groundnuts, regeneration of shrubs and trees was very slow. In this study grasses dominated the vegetation even after the land had been left to fallow for five years. Where a rotation had been practised, however, the regeneration of shrubs and young trees was comparatively well developed within a fallow period of five years. Although no scientific attempt was made to control for variations in soil between the observed plots, not surprisingly the findings confirmed farmers' views that where fallows were minimal, rotational cultivation was more beneficial to the soil than cultivation with the same crop year after year.

Although secondary sources suggest that a greater area under rice now receives fertiliser than it did at the start of the decade (*see* Table 7.3), the picture is not so clear for dryland crops. A greater area under maize and groundnuts received fertiliser in 1997 than in 1992 (*see* Table 7.5), but estimates suggest that a smaller proportion of the area under coarse grains now receives fertiliser. PRA discussions suggested that there had been a significant reduction in the use of fertiliser in the study villages for all crops (*see* Table 7.4), the main

Table 7.5 Percentage area under selected dryland crops receiving fertiliser in The Gambia

	Compound fertiliser	Urea
Groundnuts		
1992	43	03
1997	65	01
Maize		
1992	71	13
1997	88	11
Coarse grains		
1992	72	25
1997	54	06

Source: Adapted from NADC *et al.*, (1992) Table 6, p. 10 and (1998) Table 6.3.1, p. 23
Note: Total may exceed 100 per cent as more than one type of fertiliser may be used on the same plot.

reasons being price rises and problems of accessibility. High prices have been a disincentive throughout the decade, but this year, with the liquidation of the GCU, supplies of fertiliser were very difficult to obtain. A major criticism of the GCU, and one of the reasons for its liquidation, was its gross inefficiency with regard to the timely delivery of inputs. A report by the then Ministry of Agriculture (June 1997) reveals that between 10 and 20 per cent of farmers were unable to use fertilisers because of their late delivery. Now, however, the main suppliers of fertiliser are private enterprises most of which are found in Brikama or Serrekunda, and have yet to develop an efficient delivery system to the rural areas. Only small numbers of farmers – fewer than 5 per cent of those who participated in the discussions – currently use inorganic fertiliser. Loss of the GCU also means that access to other inputs, namely new seed, insecticide and pesticide, has become more difficult. Groundnut seed of high quality is being distributed by the EU as part of a programme to promote groundnut production, but this was not available to all, and farmers in neither Kassa Kunda nor Nyofelleh Medina had been touched by the EU programme. The problems of access to insecticide and pesticide were much the same as for fertiliser, with the net result that none of the farmers involved in recent discussions used it at all and its use was deemed to be minimal anywhere in the Western Division.

Similar constraints affected the use of farm machinery. PRA discussions suggested that at village level the number of farm implements had increased by some 50 per cent over the past decade, but this was because the villages had grown so much. Individual families recorded a decline in the number of animal-drawn farm implements which they either owned or to which they had access (*see* Table 7.4). Its inefficiency notwithstanding, the GCU had at least provided both credit and supplies of farm implements and its dissolution has exacerbated existing problems of access to these inputs.

Remittances from migrants to urban areas have been an important lifeline when access to other methods of income generation, particularly with regard to dryland farming, have been limited. When prompted about dependence on remittances, farmers asserted that they could not exist on these without income from the farm. A decade ago, however, remittances simply eased the pressure on life at village level. They were not used for food, but for school fees and equipment, for overseas travel for family members and for health care. Today, remittances are essential for purchasing food in addition to other items. Such conclusions are similar to those of Murton (1999) in Machakos, Kenya, where the prosperity of rural households was directly related to the size of remittances from urban migrants.

7.4.1 Adjustment by men to problems caused by the drought

The day-to-day survival of villagers and their households becomes a critical question given these conditions: of declining yields; of limited access to inputs such as fertiliser; of shortened or eliminated fallows; of the shortage of farm labour and animal-drawn machinery; and of constraints on land following the growth of village populations. While farming remains the major input in terms of household survival a number of trends suggest that substantial adjustments have been made since the time that I began fieldwork in this area. As has been observed, for example, dependence on urban remittances has increased with the number of migrants to urban areas rising over the past decade. While discussions about farming revealed that millet and groundnuts were undeniably important in area terms, it also emerged in 1990 and 1991 that farmers were modifying their cropping patterns and that cash crops other than groundnuts were being introduced.

Cassava in particular had grown significantly in importance by 1990, although its cultivation has recently declined somewhat for reasons explained below. While not new to the area, prior to the drought cassava had been grown primarily for subsistence purposes. As such, it was limited to the compound or to small field plots. Given the drought-induced shortage of food in urban markets, however, and despite a curtailing of the expansion of cassava in the mid-1980s when it was almost eliminated from the Western Division by a mosaic virus, cassava production increased substantially in the rural areas in the early 1990s. The demand for cheap food provided a market for the crop and, because other aspects of farming were so depressed, the area planted to cassava in the Western Division expanded rapidly despite a reluctance among farmers to extend its cultivation too far in case blight struck again. Its popularity has increased for several further reasons. For example, it is tolerant of soils with a comparatively low nutrient status, is relatively drought-tolerant and requires little in the way of labour for land preparation, planting, weeding or harvesting. The demand for cassava by urban markets has led to the development of a marketing system which is successful largely because of relatively informal links between rural and urban areas. The crop is purchased by a contractor who may live in the village where the crop is produced, or who may be a migrant from the village and retain strong links with it. Where the standing crop is bought, the contractor, not the grower, is responsible for organising the harvest. This helps to solve one major problem for farmers, i.e. that of labour, as local youths are hired by the contractor to harvest the crop. The team of harvesters uproot the crop and leave the stems ready for the farmer to cut into short lengths and plant as cuttings as soon as the soil has been hoed. If the cuttings are planted in the rainy season, there is no need for watering and most usually grow.

While labour requirements for cassava production are generally low, if left in the ground for up to 18 months, protection from livestock attracted to its foliage becomes necessary in the dry season. As with vegetable gardens, protecting cassava from animals is both time-consuming and expensive and for this reason the rate of increase in cassava cultivation evident in 1990 has not been sustained. Unlike women, however, who have had little option but to work hard at protecting dry season vegetables from itinerant bovines, men have been able to develop alternative cash crops, particularly fruit.

Even before the drought began in the late 1960s, farmers were planting trees in their compounds and around their plots. This is evident from the age of fruit trees in the villages.

With increasing desiccation in the early 1970s, the planting of oranges increased. These provide shade, are aesthetically pleasing and the fruit is consumed in the village or is marketed in urban centres such as Banjul and Dakar. In the early 1990s there was evidence of a significant increase in fruit tree planting, particularly oranges. A decade later, fruit production is the dryland farmer's major source of income in Kassa Kunda and Nyofelleh Medina, and also in Jambanjally and Tujereng, the two villages where fieldwork was conducted in 1999. In Tujereng, which also benefits from trade in fish owing to its proximity to the sea (*see* Figure 7.1), few farmers plant millet and sorghum any longer. Where income-generating activities are fewer, such as at Kassa Kunda and Nyofelleh Medina, subsistence crops are still important although cash crops dominate the dryland farmer's agenda.

In all of these villages the planting of oranges is now secondary to the planting of mangoes, owing to the far greater capacity of the latter to cope with the drought. By 1990/1991 farmers interviewed were discovering that oranges with their fibrous rooting systems were not as drought-tolerant as had been anticipated, and that mangoes with their long tap roots were more drought-resistant. Even a decade ago farmers were being selective about the types of mango that they were planting; for the most part, it was the quick-growing varieties which were preferred. These came to fruition in approximately five years, far more quickly than older varieties.

Demand for fruit is greatest in the urban areas and once again, local contractors or contractors from the urban areas buy the standing crop, accept the responsibility of harvesting it and pay the farmers for a crop which, once mature, requires the minimum of labour. As with the selling of vegetables by women, however, the process of payment was rarely as straightforward and just as the above picture suggests. For example, farmers were frequently short of cash towards the end of the rainy season and merchants at that time would try to get farmers to agree a price for the next mango or orange crop by persuading them to accept an advance. When the harvest was ready shortly before the next rains, farmers claimed that traders were then reluctant to pay what was still owed, or that they paid less, on the grounds that the crop was of low quality. Thus, and as with the women vegetable gardeners, dryland farmers have problems getting a fair deal for their fruit crops. Traders, on the other hand, claimed that market saturation meant that they received lower than expected prices for their crops and because of this had no alternative but to reduce the price for the fruit, particularly where the quality was deemed to be low.

7.4.2 Internal innovation and external perception: influences on changes in dryland farming

In analysing these changes in dryland farming, a clear division emerges between responses to drought which have been driven by indigenous knowledge and those based on external perceptions of what would benefit dryland farming. Although it is not possible or appropriate completely to separate the two, we begin by considering how indigenous knowledge has been used to respond to the drought and move on to the impact of externally constructed knowledges.

In the face of persistent drought, interviews with both farmers and the traders who buy crops in the villages for sale in the urban markets of Banjul in The Gambia, and Kaloack and Dakar in Senegal, affirm that close bonds between rural and urban areas have been fundamental for innovation of new survival strategies by dryland farmers. Knowledge of the dynamics of urban markets has enabled rural producers to diversify their cropping patterns to supply urban markets suffering from a reduced export of food from the rural areas due to the effects of drought. A further consequence of the drought has been increased rural–urban migration (cf. Table 7.4), which is considered to have put additional pressure on urban food supplies. It is possible that cutbacks associated with Structural Adjustment have also stimulated local markets but traders with whom this was discussed were adamant that the main cause was the reduction in food crops, particularly cereals, as a result of the poor rains. Rural suppliers have discovered urban markets for cassava and fruit, and links between producers and consumers have been facilitated by local traders. Although cassava may help to supplement any shortfall in cereals, the same cannot be said for mangoes and oranges. Nevertheless, there is a major market for them. The production of cassava and fruit makes no heavy demands on scarce inputs such as fertiliser, nor on scarce labour resources (except for the protection of cassava from animals in the dry season). Thus the export of these crops to the urban areas represents an indigenous solution within the constraints characterising the rural areas; a circumvention of problems created by the drought. They have been, and they remain, an important element of dryland farmers' survival strategies, although the profits from these relatively new ventures are not as great as they might have been for reasons discussed below.

The move to mangoes, in particular, makes both ecological and economic sense as the trees are drought-tolerant and can yield a substantial return for low investment of labour. The change, however, does represent a move from subsistence crops to greater dependence on cash crops, which is acceptable as long as a market exists for the produce and access to it can be assured. This is where the problem arises as there seems little awareness by government or aid officials concerned with the agricultural sector that such changes are taking place. As a result, very little is being done to link producers with markets. Farmers and even local traders were extremely frustrated by the failure of government to assist with the marketing process. In the case of oranges and more particularly of mangoes, there does seem to be scope for developing the export market as demand for these increases in the West. Currently, the main exporters are the large capital-intensive peri-urban farms around Banjul but, in spite of the increasing supply of fruit from the rural areas, no official effort was identified which encouraged the establishment of channels for the disposal of domestically produced fruit.

Importantly, the dominance of agricultural policy by The Gambia's Structural Adjustment Programme, which advocates the reduction of government involvement in the economy, is an additional disincentive to the State Department of Agriculture to become involved in marketing. Two things are evident from this: first, policy for the agricultural sector, influenced by an internationally-led Structural Adjustment agenda, is based largely on externally construed 'knowledge' of West African farming and environment, which, in this case, does not appear to be assisting smallholder farmers in their attempt to diversify their agricultural base. However, this negative aspect of the effect of externally constructed perceptions of what is good for The Gambia is to some extent countered by the view that Structural Adjustment (together with the drought) may have played a part in stimulating domestic markets. That it is beneficial that demand for cheap food has increased as the effects of job losses and cutbacks have bitten is a moot point. Second, the reluctance by government to become involved in the problem of crop disposal might also be linked to a general disregard for the importance of smallholder producers.

Aid donors have also had significant influence on farming at the local level. These have set up many schemes designed to help domestic agriculture, but one of the most significant schemes in recent years is that masterminded by the EU to revive groundnut production. The EU has distributed improved seed in several divisions, including the Western Division. With the improved seed comes the necessary inputs – and this is popular with the farmers. The 1999 harvest was a major success with estimated production being well in excess of recent harvests, although it has to be said that discussion with NGOs, the EU office and other donor agencies recognised the good harvest to be only partly due to the input of the EU. At a local level, farmers were adamant that favourable rains were the main cause of a good groundnut harvest. It should also be added that the rains, which had been plentiful early in the season, had stopped suddenly. While this saw the cereal crops virtually ruined, it was adequate for groundnuts. However, the success is unlikely to be recorded in The Gambia's crop production statistics. The Gambia has privatised its groundnut marketing with the blessing of the World Bank. After the entire marketing sector had been sold to a single multi-national, Alimenta, problems began. In November 1998, the Gambian government announced a price of *Dalasi* 2720/tonne for groundnuts over the radio. Shortly after that Alimenta offered The Gambian government just over half that price for the groundnuts, confirming to all that Alimenta was concerned more with turning a profit and less with paying groundnut farmers a reasonable price for their crop. This left The Gambian government seeking funds to make up the shortfall in the price.

Problems also arose between The Gambian government and Alimenta with regard to collection of the groundnut crop. The Gambian government was still responsible for collecting the groundnuts from the farmers via the Gambia Co-operative Union (GCU) and delivering them to the Alimenta Gambia Groundnut Corporation. Owing to severe problems in the management and functioning of the GCU, as explained above, it was liquidated in 1998 with no adequate replacement. The result was that in addition to there being no access to credit or inputs (however inefficient their supply by the GCU), the mechanism for collecting groundnuts had also been abolished. Farmers thus had major problems disposing of their harvest but it would appear that the main concern to the government was the conflict that developed with Alimenta which was widely reported in the press (*Daily Observer*, 3, 4, 10 and 15 June 1999; *Weekend Observer* 5–7 June 1999). Returning to the plight of the farmers, the usual collection points no longer functioned and the announcement of the location of a reduced number of buying points arrived late and was shrouded in confusion. Promissory notes were given and payment was still being made in April 1999 when transactions ought to have been completed several months earlier. Although the government gave assurances that they would pay the price announced in November 1998, farmers interviewed were adamant that they had eventually received less than half that amount. Those farmers who lived nearer the Senegalese border had allegedly done better. When they sold their groundnuts in Senegal the price they received was similar to that announced in November on Gambia Radio.

What emerges yet again is how Gambian farmers are influenced by policies which have been based on external perceptions of what is good for Gambians. The EU, for example, is committed to reviving groundnut production in spite of the need for diversification in the agricultural sector. However, their potential achievements in groundnut production in 1998–99 were thwarted by a conflicting policy, in this case the effect of privatisation of groundnut marketing – encouraged under Structural Adjustment. Whatever the inefficiency and corruption, the problems caused by the GCU appear minimal in comparison with the disruption and financial loss suffered by farmers in Nyofelleh Medina and Kassa Kunda in 1999 due to these externally driven policies.

7.5 Conclusions

The intention of this chapter has been to provide evidence for the ability of farmers to adjust to changing circumstances. It has shown that skilful innovations fail to realise their potential due to inappropriate political decision-making. Political factors, often far removed from village level, exercise considerable control on the local agro-ecology. What emerges is that solutions to the problems of drought have been more successful where they have been inspired by Gambians than by external 'experts'. Policies at higher levels and reflecting external influence have conflicted and constrained the development of both women's and men's livelihoods. Aid agencies have successfully promoted vegetable production, but current policies relating to the rural sector fail to assist with much needed systems for crop disposal, and so greater commercialisation of gardening is constrained. The EU is promoting a revival of groundnut production following years of low productivity due to drought, pests and disease. While the ecological requirements of the crop are being met, conflicting policies at national and international levels have seriously undermined any achievements at field level. Finally, achievements by men in circumventing the effects of drought by diversifying crop production on drylands have not been acknowledged and, as with the need for improved markets for vegetables, markets for fruit also need assistance. In the spirit of Structural Adjustment there is the constant hope that the private sector will move in and invest in production. But currently it is difficult to avoid the conclusion that there is little search for a meeting place between the innovations taking place in indigenous agriculture and agricultural development policy, and that there are few appropriate channels for the latter to provide support for the former.

Acknowledgements

Thanks are due to Omar Ngum, Ismaila Sagnia and Lamin Jarjusey who assisted with the field research in 1990 and 1991. Omar Ngum again helped me in 1999 and made a very significant contribution to the field work in the villages and to all other forms of information collection. Of equal importance are the people in the study villages shown in Figure 7.1. Their generosity of time and information was as great in 1999 as it had been several years earlier and I am deeply grateful for their contribution to the fieldwork and their warmth and hospitality to me. Dominic Thackray provided invaluable assistance in the map drawing for Figure 7.1. Finally, I would like to thank the School of Oriental and African Studies for funding the fieldwork in West Africa.

References

Amanor, K.S. 1994: *The new frontier: farmers' response to land degradation, a West African study.* Geneva: United Nations Research Institute for Social Development (UNRISD) and London and New Jersey: Zed Books.
Baker, K.M. 1992: Traditional farming practices and environmental decline, with special reference to The Gambia. In Hoggart, K. (ed.), *Agricultural change, environment and economy: essays in honour of W.B. Morgan.* London: Mansell, 180–202.
Baker, K.M. 1995: Drought, agriculture and environment: a case study from The Gambia, West Africa. *African Affairs* **94**, 67–86.
Bates, R.H. 1981: *Markets and states in tropical Africa: the political basis of agricultural policies.* Berkeley and Los Angeles, CA: University of California Press.
Blaikie, P. 1985: *The political economy of soil erosion in developing countries.* London and New York: Longman.
Bräutigam, D. 1998: *Chinese aid and African development: exporting green revolution.* London and Basingstoke: Macmillan Press.
Campbell, G.R. and Daniels, L. 1988: Technical report: horticultural marketing mission to The

Gambia. The Gambia Agricultural Research and Diversification Project, AID Project 635–0129. University of Wisconsin with Virginia State University, University of Michigan and Ministry of Agriculture, Ministry of Water Resources, Republic of The Gambia.

Central Statistics Department, Department of State for Finance and Economic Affairs, Republic of The Gambia July 1996: *Population and housing census of The Gambia 1993: statistics on settlement*. Volume 10. Banjul: Republic of The Gambia.

Daily Observer 3 February 1999: GGC premises occupied by armed police. Banjul.

Daily Observer 4 February 1999: Government explains GGC closure. Banjul.

Daily Observer 10 February 1999: GGC did not engage in any money laundering. Banjul.

Daily Observer 15 February 1999: Government's allegations are unfounded. Banjul.

Dumont, R. 1988: *False start in Africa*. Translated by Phyllis Nauts Ott. London: Earthscan. Originally published in French under the title *L'Afrique noire est mal partie*. Paris: Éditions du Seuil.

ECOS International 1986: *Study of land administration and pricing policy in The Gambia*. Report submitted to The Ministry of Local Government and Lands, The Government of The Gambia, Banjul by ECOS International: Charlotte, North Carolina.

Gakou, M.L. 1987: *The crisis in African agriculture*. London: Zed Books and Tokyo: the United Nations University.

Goldman, A. 1992: Population growth and agricultural change in Imo State, Southeastern Nigeria. In Turner, B.L., Hyden, G. and Kates, R.W. (eds), *Population growth and agricultural change in Africa*. Gainesville, FA: University Press of Florida.

Hart, K. 1982: *The political economy of West African Agriculture*. Cambridge: Cambridge University Press.

Hinderink, J. and Sterkenburg, J.J. 1987: *Agricultural commercialization and government policy in Africa*. London and New York: KPI.

Lowe, R.G. 1986: *Agricultural revolution in Africa*. London and Basingstoke: Macmillan.

Ministry of Agriculture June 1997: *Adoption/diffusion evaluation report of crop and livestock extension recommendations to farmers*. Banjul: Republic of The Gambia.

Mortimore, M. 1989: *Adapting to drought: farmers, famines and desertification in West Africa*. Cambridge: Cambridge University Press.

Mortimore, M. 1998: *Roots in the African dust: sustaining the drylands*. Cambridge: Cambridge University Press.

Murton, J. 1999: Population growth and poverty in Machakos District, Kenya. *Geographical Journal* **165**(1), 37–46.

National Agricultural Data Centre (NADC), Department of Planning, Ministry of Agriculture 1992: *Statistical yearbook of The Gambia agriculture: 1992*. Based on 1992–93 National Agricultural Sample Survey (NASS), Banjul: Republic of The Gambia.

National Agricultural Data Centre (NADC), Department of Planning, Department of State for Agriculture 1998: *Statistical yearbook of Gambian agriculture: 1997*. Based on 1997–98 National Agricultural Sample Survey (NASS), Banjul: Republic of The Gambia.

National Environment Agency 1997: *State of the environment report – The Gambia*. Banjul: NEA with the support of the World Bank/IDA.

National Environment Agency 1992: *The Gambia Environmental Action Plan 1992–2001*. Banjul: NEA.

Netting, R. McC. 1993: *Smallholders, householders; farm families and the ecology of intensive, sustainable agriculture*. Stanford, CA: Stanford University Press.

Oladipo, E.O. and Kyari, J.D. 1993: Fluctuations in the onset, termination and length of the growing season in northern Nigeria. *Theoretical and Applied Climatology* **47**(3), 241–50.

Osmeobo, G.J. 1987: The migrant Igbira farmers and food crop production in Bendel State, Nigeria. *Agricultural Systems* **45**, 123–43.

Park, T.K. 1993: Arid lands and the political economy of flood recession in Fuuta Tooro. In Park, T.K. (ed.), *Risk and tenure in arid lands: the political ecology of development in the Senegal River Basin*. Tuscon and London: University of Arizona Press, 1–124.

Raynaut, C. (ed.) 1997: *Societies and nature in the Sahel*. London: Routledge.

Richards, P. 1985: *Indigenous agricultural revolution*. London: Hutchinson.

Richards, P. 1986: *Coping with hunger: hazard and experiment in an African rice-farming system*. London: Allen and Unwin.

Sivakumar, M.V.K. 1991: *Drought spells and drought frequencies in West Africa*. Niamey, Niger: ICRISAT.

Stebbing, E.P. 1938: The man-made desert in Africa: erosion and drought. Supplement to the *Journal of the Royal African Society*, **XXXVII**(CXLVI), 40.

Swindell, K. 1978: Family farms and migrant labour: the strange farmers of The Gambia. *Canadian Journal of African Studies* **12**(1), 3–17.

Swindell, K. 1980: Serawoollies, Tillibunkas and strange farmers: the development of migrant groundnut farming in The Gambia. *The Journal of African History* **21**(1), 93–104.

Tiffen, M., Mortimore, M. and Gichuki, F. 1994: *More people, less erosion: environmental recovery in Kenya*. Chichester: John Wiley and Sons.

Timberlake, L. 1985: *Africa in crisis: the causes, the cures of environmental bankruptcy*. London: Earthscan.

Webb, J.L.A. Jnr. 1986a: *Rainfall and risk in The Gambia River basin: implications for investment planning*. USAID project 625–0012. Technical document No. 1. Banjul: USAID.

Webb, J.L.A. Jnr. 1986b: *The agricultural statistics of The Gambia: a user's guide*. USAID project 625–0012. Technical document No. 2. Banjul: A joint publication of the Gambia River Basin Development Organisation, and The Planning Division.

Webb, J.L.A. Jnr. 1986c: The Gambia in graphs: a summary of the national agricultural statistics. USAID project 625–0012. Technical document No. 3. Banjul: A joint publication of the Gambia River Basin Development Organisation and The Planning Division.

World Bank 1989: *Sub-Saharan Africa: from crisis to sustainable growth*. Washington, DC: The World Bank.

Weekend Observer 5–7 February 1999: GGC GM refutes Government's allegations. Banjul.

8

Rainforest

Biodiversity conservation and the political economy of international financial institutions

Korinna Horta

8.1 Intertwined realities: ecology and politics

In historical geography as interpreted by David Harvey, all ecological projects are simultaneously political-economic projects and vice versa (Harvey, 1996). While international policy-makers have declared environmental protection to be a key priority of development aid, they have not accepted the conceptual framework which relates ecology to political economy. International policy is reflected in the discourse of public international financial institutions which have adapted to the 'environmental mood' in their main donor countries. Both the World Bank and the Global Environment Facility (GEF) have taken up the banner for biodiversity conservation as one of the most pressing issues facing humankind today. Their discourse meshes findings from conservation biology with neo-populist policy statements emphasising the need for bottom-up and highly participatory procedures. Their approach, however, depoliticises the issues and reconstructs them as purely technical problems amenable to technical solutions which they themselves offer to provide (Gasper, 1996a; Bryant, 1997).

This chapter reviews contending approaches to biodiversity ranging from the concerns raised at the global level by the natural science community and shaped by the discourses of conservation biology to what have been identified in development discourses as local level priorities concerning the 'sustainable livelihoods' of farmers, fishermen, pastoralists and other communities throughout 'the South'. It then examines the appropriation of the concept of biodiversity by international financial institutions. While they approach the concept in an apolitical manner, their policies relating to biodiversity are driven by international politics. Furthermore, the actual implementation of their conservation policies is shaped to a large degree by their internal political economy.

8.2 Contending approaches to biodiversity

The term 'biodiversity' is a relatively recent entry in the lexicon of European languages. It began to circulate in the early 1980s and has since 'spread like wildfire' in thousands of publications (Flitner, 1998). In 1992, rising concern about biodiversity loss spawned a legally binding United Nations agreement, the Convention of Biological Diversity (United Nations, 1992). The pivotal event helping to generate all this attention was the National Forum on BioDiversity held in Washington, DC in 1986 under the auspices of the National Academy of Sciences. The proceedings of the forum were published in a volume with the title *Biodiversity*, which was edited by Harvard University biologist Edward O. Wilson (Wilson, 1988) and became perhaps the most influential textbook on the matter. Since then biodiversity has become a hot topic which 'galvanizes the conservation, scientific and funding communities' (Zerner, 1996: 72). Yet, as Zerner continues: 'The idea of a disjunct, autonomously developing natural world easily leads to biodiversity conservation missions in which human groups are marginalized' (ibid.: 72).

Biodiversity has to be understood as a heterogeneous and all-embracing concept which encompasses a complexity of meaning and levels. The identification of the biodiversity problem by the natural sciences provides only a point of departure for necessary in-depth analyses of the institutional, political and socio-economic variables that lie at the heart of biodiversity conservation and erosion (Machlis, 1992; Blaikie and Jeanrenaud, 1997).

8.2.1 A natural science construct of environment

The term biodiversity as used in the Convention on Biological Diversity is defined as 'the variability among living organisms from all sources, *inter alia*, terrestrial, marine and other aquatic ecosystems and the ecological complexes of which they are part; this diversity includes diversity within species, between species and of ecosystems' (United Nations, 1992: Art. 2). When describing biodiversity, biologists usually refer to three hierarchical levels, ranging from whole systems at the landscape or ecosystem levels to single species and genes: genetic diversity is the sum of genetic information contained in the genes of plants, animals and micro-organisms; species diversity refers to the variety of living organisms; and ecosystem diversity relates to the diversity of habitats and the variety of ecological processes (cf. McNeely *et al.*, 1990).

Soulé (1991) adds two layers to this 'biospatial' hierarchy by including 'assemblages', which are biotic communities within a defined ecosystem, and 'populations', which are dynamic assemblages of individuals which maintain genetic information that may ramify and merge. The ecological functions of biodiversity cover the entire spectrum of life-support systems. They range from genetic diversity, often highlighted with reference to global agriculture, food security and future medicines (Brown *et al.*, 1993), to the preservation of soils and water quality and the maintenance of the gaseous composition of atmosphere (Watson and Heywood, 1995).

8.2.1.1 *Moist tropical forest*

Concern over biodiversity loss is linked overwhelmingly to the deforestation of tropical moist forests, and these environments are focused on in some detail here. Tropical moist forests are widely held to be the habitats that are the richest in species (Wilson, 1988; Brown *et al.*, 1993; Groombridge, 1994). With the exceptions of certain groups such as conifers and salamanders, the strongest trend worldwide is the latitudinal diversity gradient which means that group after group reaches its maximum richness in the tropics, most particularly in the tropical rainforests and coral reefs (Ehrlich and Wilson, 1991). As a result, some argue that as much as 50 per cent of the earth's biodiversity is estimated to live in tropical rainforest regions (Myers, 1988). Others estimate that anywhere between 50 and 90 per cent of all species on earth are in these regions (World Resources Institute, 1992). Recent studies have also highlighted that ecotones, the transition zones between rainforest and savanna, are key areas in the generation of biodiversity (Smith, T.B. *et al.*, 1997). A study on Cameroon's little greenbul (*Andropadus virens*), a small forest bird, for example, found that despite interbreeding, species in the rainforest and in the ecotone develop differently because the pressures for survival in the two habitats are very different.

A number of problems flow from this current focus on tropical moist forest biodiversity, however, with implications for the rights of people for whom these and other environments are significant. First, with much attention held by tropical moist forest, the biodiversity of other terrestrial ecosystems, such as temperate coniferous forests, grasslands and Mediterranean shrublands, appears to be underexplored. In particular, the biological diversity of dry tropical forests may often have been underestimated (Groombridge, 1994) and may even match that of tropical moist forests (Stott, 1991). Perhaps more importantly is the observation by Stott (1991, 'Tropical Ecology Website', 3 May 1999) that savannas, as home to the majority of people in tropical countries should be considered the most important terrestrial environment in both ecological and economic terms. Similarly, while oceans, coastal waters, estuaries and wetlands are increasingly at risk from human activities (World Resources Institute *et al.*, 1992), knowledge about marine and freshwater biodiversity remains very limited (Norse, 1993). Thus some biodiversity appears more equal than others: while some land-use systems and agricultural practices enhance biodiversity within managed landscapes, for example (Srivastava *et al.*, 1996), such environments tend not to be high priority in conservation terms.

Second, while there appears to be agreement that tropical moist forests contain the highest concentrations of terrestrial biodiversity, there is disagreement as to what constitutes a forest area. The United Nations Food and Agriculture Organization (FAO), which has carried comprehensive assessments of the situation of tropical forests (United Nations and FAO, 1993), has defined forests as ecological systems with a minimum of 10 per cent crown cover of trees and/or bamboo which are not subject to agricultural practices. This definition is considered by some as too broad, however, because it includes many open vegetation formations which normally would not be regarded as forests (Groombridge, 1994). A more widely accepted definition of what constitutes a forest is that of 'closed canopy forest' described as mostly woody formations with a minimum crown cover of 40 per cent (ibid.).

Third, and given this disagreement over what constitutes forest, there is similar disagreement as to what constitutes 'deforestation' or the loss of forest area. Deforestation has occurred in temperate and tropical regions throughout history (Williams, 1990). However, definitions of deforestation vary from a complete clearing of tree formations and their replacement by non-forest land-uses, to a 'degradation' of forest biodiversity, involving changes in tree species composition, wildlife species and gene pools. This latter definition is advanced commonly by conservation organizations, such as IUCN and WWF (Barraclough and Ghimire, 1995) and reflects the inclusion of biodiversity considerations.

So, how much moist tropical forest is being lost annually? There is no single answer. According to FAO, some 154,000 square kilometres of tropical forest were being lost annually between 1981 and 1990, which corresponds to a 0.8 per cent compound annual rate of deforestation (UNFAO, 1993). A higher estimate is provided by the World Resources Institute, which puts annual loss of tropical forest at 204,000 square kilometres (World Resources Institute *et al.*, 1990). The problem appears to be that measuring and assessing changes to forests depends on the consistent application of categories and definitions throughout, but widely acceptable measures have not been developed (Groombridge, 1994). However, the overall trend of accelerating rates of forest loss in the tropics is not disputed (although see Fairhead and Leach, 1996), and the impacts on biodiversity may be more far-reaching than deforestation statistics indicate.

For example, this is indicated by research on the 'edge effect'. Data on deforestation of Brazil's Amazon region have been the subject of some dispute. Initial measurements by the Brazilian National Institute for Spatial Research, which were widely reported (World Resources Institute *et al.*, 1990), indicated a rate substantially higher than the one revealed by subsequent Landsat satellite images (Skole and Tucker, 1993). The divergent assessments provided arguments for those who felt that the seriousness of forest loss was vastly overstated. Skole and Tucker explained the difference as stemming from a different evaluation in the forest-*cerrado* boundaries used by the different researchers. They concluded that while their research indicated considerably less area deforested, their findings document that the patterns of forest clearing matter as much or possibly more than numbers of forest acres lost, because of what is known as the edge effect. Networks of roads, powerlines and farms increase access into the forest from the edge between tropical forest and deforested areas and lead to increasing 'habitat fragmentation'. The indirect effects of deforestation are estimated to be two to three times greater than the area of deforestation. As a result, Skole and Tucker conclude that although their estimates of deforestation are lower than previous estimates, the effect on biological diversity is greater (Skole and Tucker, 1993).

8.2.1.2 The taxonomists' impossible dream

Speciation and extinction are natural processes which occur continuously. The rate at which humans are now altering the environment and contributing to extinction processes, however, is argued by some to be unprecedented in human history (Watson and Heywood, 1995), although rapid and dramatic extinction events have occurred in the past. An estimate put forward by both the United Nations Environment Programme (UNEP) and by Harvard University biologist E.O. Wilson is that the human-induced rate of extinction is 1000 to 10,000 times the natural background rate (Watson and Heywood, 1995; Wilson, 1988).

The two world bodies charged specifically with environmental protection and conservation, i.e. UNEP and the International Union for the Conservation of Nature (IUCN), have reached similar estimates of species loss in recent studies. IUCN, in the most comprehensive inventory to date, estimates that about 25 per cent of all mammals and 11 per cent of all known bird species are threatened with extinction (Ballie and Groombridge, 1996). UNEP in its Global Biodiversity Assessment concludes that due to projected loss of forest cover over the next 25 years a range of 2 to 25 per cent of the better known groups, i.e. plant and bird species, will be lost (Watson and Heywood, 1995).

Estimates of species in tropical forests range from 3 million to 30 million or more, of which only about 1.4 million species have been named so far (Raven, 1988). Present estimates of how many forms of life exist on earth have to be approached with caution because, as E.O. Wilson puts it, the number of species of organisms is not known even to the nearest order of magnitude (Wilson, 1988). E.O. Wilson's statement is confirmed by a recent study carried out by British taxonomists in a small patch of forest in south-central Cameroon. After collecting data on eight groups, including the flagship taxa of birds and butterflies, the study concluded that the scientific effort required to provide inventories of biodiversity even in this single area of forest would exceed anything attempted so far anywhere in the world. They added that taxonomists and ecologists worldwide do not have the resources to study the wide range of taxa as they are being affected by deforestation in a single region (Lawton *et al.*, 1998).

This lack of taxonomic precision leads critics to charge that the loss of species is being overstated, arguing, for example, that estimates of future extinction rates lack any kind of empirical basis and are therefore unnecessarily alarmist (Simon and Wildavsky, 1993). Charles Mann in an article in *Science* emphasises that the inadequacy of existing taxonomic data raises questions about the possibility of predicting species loss since if species have actually not been discovered, one cannot be sure if they became extinct or never existed in the first place (Mann, 1991).

8.2.1.3 The world is not an island

Predictions of species loss are often based on principles of the 'equilibrium theory of island biogeography' (MacArthur and Wilson, 1967). This has constituted the theoretical underpinnings for the subdiscipline of 'conservation biology' and has been influential in practical terms in guiding the design of conservation areas so as to maximise the numbers of species conserved (cf. Terborgh, 1974; Simberloff and Abele, 1976; Diamond, 1976; Gilbert, 1980). The theory stipulates that the number of species in island systems increases approximately as the fourth root of the land area, depending further on rates of species immigration and extinction as well as the influence of distance from a source of new island colonisers (cf. Wilson and Simberloff, 1969). The theory has been used in the generation of predictions of species losses in terrestrial ecosystems on continents, by positing that the creation of 'habitat islands' as human land-uses encroach on areas around conservation areas is ecologically equivalent to the existence of land bridge islands, i.e. those which were once connected to continental land masses and which have only been isolated since their submergence due to sea level rise (cf. Soulé *et al.*, 1979). In this it is assumed that if the date of isolation, the number of species at time of isolation and the size of the island are known, then both the rate of species extinction since creation of the island, and the 'equilibrium' number of species which can be sustained in relation to the size of the island, can be calculated. Given these assumptions, devastating predictions have been made for the rates of extinction that can be expected for even some of the largest conservation areas, causing great concern among conservationists and conservation institutions.

More recently, Oxford University professors Smith and May and World Conservation Monitoring Centre (WCMC) scientists Pellew, Johnson and Walter, have drawn on documentation of the loss of plant and animal species since 1600 to assess the extinction threat and its relationship to predictions posed by species-area models (Smith, F.D.M. *et al.*, 1993). Even though they focus on data which have been compiled opportunistically and not systematically, and even though their focus is on a few comparatively well-studied groups, i.e. birds and mammals, they have hoped that they can overcome some of the roughness of extinction estimates derived from species-area relations and projected rates of destruction of natural habitats. They conclude that for better known taxa, the estimates of extinction rates are of the same order of magnitude as those derived from species-area relations (Smith, F.D.M. *et al.*, 1993).

Application of the theory within continental settings, however, is deemed by many to be extremely problematic and to have very limited predictive power. For those concerned with the effects of changing land-use practices, for example, it cannot be assumed that the manipulation of environments around conservation areas is equivalent to isolation within a hostile environment, i.e. as with water surrounding an island (Lugo, 1988). The land surrounding conservation areas and 'island habitats' might offer potential new habitats as well as cushioning processes of extinction by increasing the area available to mobile animal populations (Western and Ssemakula, 1981). A further critique is that the 'species-area curve' derived from island biogeographic calculations implies that infinite growth in area corresponds to infinite growth in numbers of species and thereby fails to consider that habitat loss can occur without substantial species loss (Mann, 1991). Similarly, habitats are not equivalent and a more important determinant of species diversity instead might be available energy and not size of available terrain (cf. Wylie and Currie, 1993). The statistical procedures used in many studies have also been severely criticised (cf. Boecklen and Gotelli, 1984) while Whittaker *et al.* (1989) affirm the role of both autecology and abiotic factors in changing habitats through time and in both creating and constraining opportunities for different complements of species. Importantly, this de-emphasises the theoretical constructs of ecological 'equilibrium' and 'climax communities', focusing, perhaps more realistically, on dynamic behaviour, non-deterministic change and factors contributing to 'non-equilibrium' (cf. Wiens, 1984; Sullivan, 1996; Stott, 1998).

8.2.1.4 Biodiversity and climate linkages

Environments and species community patterns have changed constantly in the past, and they will continue to change in the future, particularly under the possible influence of global warming (Graham, 1992). While there are scientific uncertainties about anthropogenic climate change, there are indications that global warming could be occurring at a rapid rate when compared with most palaeoclimatic trends (Schneider *et al.*, 1992). While contested, there are a number of anticipated habitat changes associated with anthropogenic effects. Those posited for forest environments are frequently used in support of an environmentalist agenda and are summarised as follows:

1　**Deforestation and local climate change**
　Rainforests not only need rain to grow, they also produce local rain as much of the moisture on the forest canopy evaporates quickly, forms clouds and produces rainfall further downwind. As a result, deforestation leads frequently to the desiccation of previously humid soils (Barraclough and Ghimire, 1995). Farmers in coastal regions of West Africa have long understood the linkage between the loss of forest cover, changing rainfall patterns and declines in the yields of their crops (Horta, 1991). Scientists are now corroborating the farmers' findings. An orthodoxy that the destruction of West African rainforest during the past two decades has led to droughts has been supported by studies carried out by the Massachusetts Institute of Technology which indicate that further deforestation might lead to the collapse of the West African monsoon (Pearce, 1997). Such ideas are contested, however, with Fairhead and Leach (1996), for example, drawing together a range of data to suggest that forest islands in locations in West Africa have actually increased in area over the last century.

2　**Forests and global climate change**
　Conversion of forests into cropland and pasture is postulated to cause a net flux of carbon to the atmosphere and a corresponding increase in atmospheric carbon dioxide because the concentration of carbon in forests is higher than in the agricultural areas that replace them. During the first phase of deforestation, most occurred in northern countries. In

recent decades loss of tropical forest has been the main contributor. Tropical moist forests are estimated to contain about 200 tons of carbon per hectare, which is substantially more than boreal forests (110 t/ha) or temperate broadleaf forests (*ca.* 100 t/ha) (Graham *et al.*, 1990). It is estimated that tropical forest loss contributed approximately 1.6 gigatonnes of carbon per year to the atmosphere, while fossil fuel combustion released an additional 5.5 gigatonnes (Watson and Heywood, 1995). The numbers indicate that forests may constitute a significant factor in the carbon exchange with the atmosphere.

3   The possible impact of 'global warming' on forests

While it is difficult to forecast precisely what the effects of global warming might be on the earth's biota, natural warming events in the past can serve as a reference. One such event occurred at the Pleistocene–Holocene boundary, approximately 10,000 years ago, when some 35 genera of large terrestrial animals became extinct in North America alone (Graham, 1992). Those adhering to climate change as the primary stimulus for such rapid rates of extinction suggest that species respond to environmental changes individually rather than as communities of species and conclude that the design of biological reserves should facilitate the flexible migration of species instead of focusing on preserving static community patterns (Graham, 1992). A fierce debate exists, however, over the relative contribution of hunting by humans to these rapid rates of megafaunal extinction (cf. Martin *et al.*, 1961; Martin, 1966; Martin, 1973).

Nevertheless, what could be likely impacts of warming events on tropical forest areas? According to Hartshorn (1992), it is unlikely that higher temperatures *per se* would have direct negative impacts on tropical forest communities. For one reason, tropical forest regions are less hot than surrounding regions as high temperatures are modulated by cloud cover. If global warming causes increased cloud cover over tropical forest regions, then average daily temperature increases may not be significant. Seasonal patterns and the distribution of rainfall are more important than temperature in stimulating many biological activities (Hartshorn, 1992). There may, however, be a myriad of indirect impacts, ranging from climate change-induced tropical cyclones that can devastate tropical forests to changes in human settlement patterns as people search for new sources of agricultural land and water as a result of global warming (Harte *et al.*, 1992; Soulé, 1992). We should not forget, however, that climate changes may create opportunities as well as costs, that the complexity of long-term climate phenomena makes any linear predictions for the effects and character of change extremely unpredictable, and that predicted global warming may itself be masked by the effects of unpredictable but quite possible events such as the eruption of a so-called 'super volcano' (e.g. *The Week*, 2000).

8.2.2 Social dimensions of biodiversity

Biodiversity conservation as constructed by the natural sciences is often justified as 'a redemptive act: an attempt to protect bounded zones of the non-human world, described as intact, pristine or undisturbed' (Zerner, 1996: 69). Claims regarding the importance of biodiversity conservation rest upon a broad spectrum of ethical, moral, economic and multi-level arguments (Blaikie, 1995). Urban élites in both the North and the South who are concerned with the need to preserve 'Nature' generally offer two rationales for biodiversity conservation. Either they emphasise the aesthetic and amenity values of wilderness as something that needs to be preserved or they focus on possible commercial uses of biodiversity ranging from tourism ventures to industrial–pharmaceutical uses of chemical compounds found in biodiversity-rich areas (Barraclough and Ghimire, 1995). These objectives often do not represent local priorities and, as a result, global strategies to conserve biodiversity may not easily mesh with local societal dynamics. The marginalisation of local people who inhabit or use these areas, however, can be a consequence flowing from this. Since most of the earth's biodiversity is thought to be geographically located in the South, there is the tendency for a North–South divide between local realities of biodiversity as lived by hundreds of millions of rural and indigenous peoples in southern countries and northern plans to protect natural resources in the South (Colchester, 1994).

Moore, Chaloner and Stott (1996) raise the question at the crux of the matter of *whose* biodiversity are we talking about anyway? Similarly, we might ask *which* biodiversity, as frequently all-encompassing terms such as 'biodiversity' and 'natural resources' mask the reality of a conservation focus on a handful of desirable, spectacular and internationally valuable species (cf. Sullivan, in press a and b). Moore *et al.* (1996: 212) argue that the political ecology of rainforests and/or 'biodiversity' represents the desire of the North to maintain a controlling interest over the resources of the South, an argument which deserves nuanced analysis, particularly as it echoes concerns voiced by developing country governments in international environmental fora, most notably of Brazil, China and Indonesia. It is necessary, however, to emphasise that there is no homogeneous North or South. While '[m]ost biodiversity arguments turn out to be cruel deceptions, hindering competitive development in the South, condemning people to extremely hard lives, and deflecting the ordinary processes of change' (Moore *et al.*, 1996: 213), this is particularly applicable in relation to establishment of protected areas and national parks where this excludes local people from 'their' land and resources. Also important is the question of whose 'competitive development' does this promote? The proximate causes of biodiversity loss are often linked to a variety of external causes such as large-scale industrial logging and mining operations or monocrop plantations, etc. In authoritarian states, where public protests are met by harsh repression, this type of development often wreaks havoc on both environment and local communities, while benefiting southern élites as well as transnational corporations and their shareholders in northern countries.

Recent concern, particularly in social science analyses, emphasises the importance of local social forces in ensuring environmental sustainability. From this perspective, biodiversity protection is a social process that depends on actions at the local level (Davis, 1993). These views increasingly are incorporated in the development discourse of international financial institutions. The World Bank's long-term strategy for Sub-Saharan Africa, for example, promises to 'release the energies to allow ordinary people . . . to take charge of their lives' (World Bank, 1989b: 4). Biodiversity conservation programmes now almost universally emphasise the need for 'people-orientedness' and participation (Jeanrenaud, 1997). Integrating local people in development and conservation, however, means dealing with complex social, economic and ecological realities. This requires a breadth of knowledge and skills that most development and conservation projects find difficult to muster (Bailey, 1996).

For example, local situations can be complex with different classes of producers pursuing different strategies and uses for the environment (Little and Brokensha, 1987). The interests of local élites may diverge from the majority of the rural peasant population. The distinguishing characteristic between dominant groups and local communities is that although the latter are numerically the majority, their political power base is weak and they usually have little or no share in the decision-making processes affecting the land, forests and water resources with which their livelihoods are linked (Ghimire and Pimbert, 1997).

8.2.2.1 Sustainable Livelihoods

Redclift (1987) argues that biodiversity conservation and 'sustainable development' can only become a reality when the livelihoods of the poor are given priority. They are the forest-dwellers, small farmers, fishing communities and pastoralists, whose livelihoods and biodiversity are inextricably linked through a mosaic of activities which meet their needs for food, medicines, construction material, and so on, for whom 'natural resources' embody many of their cultural, aesthetic and spiritual values. The forest and the land are often an inseparable part of the identity of 'communities', thus implicating biodiversity maintenance in the cultural survival of these groups (Bailey, 1996).[1]

Chambers (1986) has developed the concept of 'sustainable livelihood thinking' which establishes causal relationships between development and livelihoods, and environment and livelihoods. While the concept of sustainable livelihoods is increasingly adopted in mainstream development discourse (for example, by the British Department for International Development (DfID) and the London-based International Institute for Environment and Development (IIED), it is unclear to what degree international financial institutions are willing to use the concept as a framework for the analysis of development and conservation projects on which they could base their funding decisions.

Sustainable livelihood thinking creates an indicator to help counter the effects of international development which systematically marginalises the most vulnerable groups (Redclift, 1987). Shiva (1992: 213) argues that when forests, land and water are being 'developed' or 'scientifically managed', or – one might add – protected for biodiversity conservation, then they are appropriated from communities whose lives and livelihoods they have supported for centuries. Unless local communities enjoy strong protection from the state, they can be dispossessed of their resources when these become commercially attractive to others (Barraclough and Ghimire, 1995). With respect to conservation efforts, rural populations and indigenous peoples can suffer adverse effects on their livelihoods and food security as a result of the establishment of protected areas that reduce their access to what had previously been common property resources (Ghimire and Pimbert, 1997; Horta, 1994).

8.2.2.2 Local knowledge

An important dimension of the sustainable livelihoods approach is the acknowledgement and integration of the appropriateness of local knowledge for environmental use and management. This has emerged from research affirming 'indigenous technical knowledge' and 'folk' or 'citizen science'. An example is the description offered by Jacobs about management systems amongst the Maasai with its detailed knowledge of a myriad issues ranging from elaborate grazing sequences to ensure dry-season reserves of hay and water, to the nutritional value of livestock, many grasses, herbs and seeds at the appropriate stage of their growth (Jacobs in Little and Brokensha, 1987). Similarly, Paul Richards (1985) in his study of traditional knowledge systems in West African farming systems found the environmental management of small farmers to be dynamic, innovative and based on experimentation and argues for the support of indigenous science instead of undercutting it with foreign expert advice.

For some this has been translated into a romantic notion that local people possess 'inherited ecological caution' (Lonsdale, 1987: 274) such that they will not cause resource depletion or irreversible destruction. Tradition, however, is a process, i.e. living only while it changes (Vansina, 1990: 251). Recognising the stewardship of local and indigenous peoples over their resources and the value of local knowledge should not mean that resource-use practices are somehow frozen in time. Whether or not indigenous peoples are somehow bearers of a conservationist ethic is a contentious question (Little and Brokensha, 1987; Colchester, 1994). As Little and Brokensha (1987) argue, it is rather limiting to expect some sort of maintenance of, or return to, 'traditional' patterns of resource management. Unfortunately, however, it is often considered that local people can only be allowed to live in or near biodiversity conservation areas if they adhere to 'traditional' practices and resource-use technology. As such, the conditions placed on the involvement of local people, and the appropriateness of their knowledge about the environment can amount to what Goodland has described as 'forced primitivism' (Goodland, 1982: 21; Colchester, 1994), posing questions concerning human rights over self-determination which are as pressing as those associated with displacing people from conservation areas.

8.2.2.3 *Indigenous peoples: cultural ecology, history and local–global linkages in the conservation of biodiversity and the sustainability of livelihoods*

Given the above, i.e. the assertion among international donors that 'sustainable livelihoods' link both environment and development and that local ecological knowledge is an integral part of this, the status of 'indigenous peoples' *vis à vis* conservation areas and 'natural resources' is receiving increasing attention. 'Indigenous peoples' here refers to people who are considered descendants of a population with prior, if not first, claim to a territory. As such they normally have social and cultural characteristics distinct from the dominant culture of the nation–state in which they live. The term is becoming increasingly synonymous with concepts such as tribal peoples and cultural minorities (Gray, 1991). Indigenous peoples are considered to have a unique status which means that they should receive special attention because of their historical claims to the lands of their ancestors and the general disruption of their lives when they enter in contact with the modern world (Sponsel *et al.*, 1996). The World Commission on Environment and Development, for example, warns of 'cultural extinction' (WCED, 1987: 114) when it describes the situation of indigenous and tribal peoples whom it recognises as being the holders of skills which enable them to manage and utilise complex ecological systems. There are an estimated 200 million indigenous or tribal peoples in the world today, or about 4 per cent of the world population (Burger in Gray, 1991; World Bank, 1982).

In order to counter the increasing vulnerability of indigenous peoples to the loss of their traditional lands, WCED recommends that 'the starting point for a humane policy for such groups is the recognition and protection of their traditional rights to land and the other resources that sustain their lives' (WCED, 1987: 115). Similarly, the World Bank's paper on 'Tribal Peoples and Economic Development' recognises that these are people who apparently hold knowledge concerning ways of using resources of tropical forests without degrading or destroying them (see also Chandler, 1991). Based on this recognition the World Bank commits itself not to support projects on tribal lands, or those that will affect tribal lands, unless the tribal society is in agreement with the objectives of the project and the borrowing state has the capacity to ensure no harmful effects to such people from the project (Goodland, 1982). This situation among the donor community has contributed in some senses to a strengthening of the rights of indigenous people. As such, indigenous peoples' organisations are now more able to mobilise in instances where they feel marginalised by global debates about biodiversity (International Alliance of Indigenous-Tribal Peoples of the Tropical Forests and International Work Group for Indigenous Affairs, no date). So, for example, The Charter of the Indigenous-Tribal Peoples of the Tropical Forests, an international coalition of tribal groups which gives a voice to peoples who are often in remote (and the biologically most diverse) regions, states in its Article 42 that:

> The best guarantee of the conservation of biodiversity is that those who promote it should uphold our rights to the use, administration, management and control our territories. We assert that guardianship should be entrusted to us, indigenous peoples, given that we have inhabited them for thousands of years and our very survival depends on them.
> (International Alliance of the Indigenous-Tribal Peoples of the Tropical Forests, 1992)

A principal concern has to do with the emphasis in international agreements on the sovereignty of the state in exploiting the natural resources within its jurisdiction which does little to strengthen ancestral rights to territories if the state chooses to ignore these rights (United Nations, 1992: Article 3). Stemming from this are concerns regarding the intellectual property rights of local communities whose activities may have influenced what are regarded as 'wild species', whose prior knowledge of these species is often overlooked, and who may have enhanced biodiversity in general (cf. Nelson and Serafin, 1992; World Resources Institute *et al.*, 1992; Bailey, 1996; Ghimire and Pimbert, 1997). The international Convention on Biodiversity calls for the equitable sharing of the benefits arising from 'the knowledge, innovations and practices of indigenous and local communities' (United Nations, 1992: Art. 8(j)). Similarly, the Global Biodiversity Assessment of the United Nations Environment Programme declares that the equitable sharing of benefits of biodiversity is a prerequisite for creating the incentives needed to maintain the Earth's biological wealth (Watson and Heywood, 1995).

   In part this recognises the importance of history in relation to 'the natural environment' by emphasising that biodiversity cannot be viewed as separate from and unshaped by the history of human action (Zerner, 1996). This context has been brought out particularly strongly by anthropologists Fairhead and Leach who in comparisons of historical vegetation cover of the Ziama Reserve in the prefecture of Kissidougou, Guinea Bissau, West Africa with present-day forest cover found that forest cover had actually increased substantially over the past 40 years despite assertions of widespread deforestation (Fairhead and Leach, 1993, 1996). Not long before a mission from the World Bank and a leading conservation organisation had concluded that the area had been subject to massive environmental degradation, which resulted in a World Bank forestry loan to the Government of Guinea with the stated goal of halting the alleged destruction (World Bank, 1990b). Fairhead and Leach do not downplay problems stemming from large-scale logging operations, the establishment of plantations or other industrial interventions in the forest area. What they succeed in establishing is that the long-term historical and the socio-political contexts, which link local people to their forest environment, are essential to understanding the dynamics of a changing environment. Little and Brokensha emphasise the same idea when they state that local resource management has to be examined in the context of social and historical change, and that simplistic causal statements about the breakdown in local resource management and associated ecological problems are inappropriate (Little and Brokensha, 1987; see also Sullivan, 1999).

A focus on the close connection between biodiversity and agriculture, and on the ecological knowledges of 'indigenous peoples' also emphasises links between local and global contexts. For example, genetic diversity important at global levels, particularly in agriculture, has frequently been manipulated and selected by farming populations at the geographic source of such species over millennia. Similarly, the few food staple species on which the majority of world population depends can be improved by cross-breeding with either locally selected varieties or their wild relatives thereby facilitating global agriculture and food security (Brown *et al.*, 1993; National Research Council, 1996; Srivastava *et al.*, 1996). A similar connection exists between biodiversity and human health. Traditional medicine directly derived from local biodiversity is the main health care for a majority of people in developing countries. In addition, biodiversity in tropical forests has yielded numerous pharmaceutical compounds which have been synthethised into popular Western drugs and pharmaceutical companies indicate varying degrees of interest in incorporating ethnobotanical research in their research and development programmes (Balick *et al.*, 1996).

Given that the purely technical approach of collecting and storing genetic material is both expensive and unsatisfactory in the long term, as well as frequently accompanied by a loss of cultural information on how to use the varieties in *ex situ* collections (Watson and Heywood, 1995), it seems that supporting 'sustainable livelihoods' in biodiversity-rich regions may be a promising way to serve the biodiversity needs of both local and international communities. In view of rapid social and economic change, however, including the spread of monetarised economies and new aspirations regarding material and other acquisitions, it is less clear if rural populations and indigenous peoples will continue either to want or be able to protect and generate local biodiversity. It is against this background that the rise of a 'global biodiversity agenda' and its institutional context needs to be considered.

8.3 Ascendancy of the global biodiversity agenda

> [W]hen stories of nature and the human community are linked to power and funding, they have important ethical, political and legal consequences.
>
> (Zerner, 1996: 69)

Environmentalism in the North has been successful in building domestic constituencies for biodiversity protection and getting the attention of governments (Fairman, 1996). Norgaard adds that environmentalists and natural scientists have themselves become part of the political and administrative fabric of Western nations (Norgaard, 1994). Once these political constituencies were mobilised, it became a question of donor government self-interest to establish environment friendly policies to guide their development aid and to create environmental aid budgets (Connolly, 1996). Domestic pressure in some of the major donor countries led the World Bank, the world's largest development agency, to adopt a whole set of environment-friendly policies. The establishment in 1991 of the Global Environment Facility (GEF), the world's most important source of grant funding for projects intended to benefit the global environment, was in part driven by the same pressures. In addition, however, it represented a conscious strategy on the part of northern governments to pre-empt the creation of a southern-driven financial mechanism at the United Nations Conference on Environment and Development (UNCED) in 1992, also known as the Rio Earth Summit

(Fairman, 1996). The fact that most of the loss of biodiversity was occurring in southern environments helped direct the burden of adjustment at developing countries to the point where, at least in theory, more rigorous standards for development and conservation activities may be applied to the south than domestically in northern countries (Bell, 1987).

8.3.1 The single largest public financier of development/environment projects

A considerable portion of national aid budgets is channelled through the World Bank, which makes the institution vulnerable to the possibility of having its budgets cut by its main shareholders, i.e. the Group of Seven Industrialised (G7) countries. While the World Bank is 'owned' by all its member states (of which there were 180 as of 1996), its financial strength depends on direct contributions from its wealthiest member countries, or on collateral provided by the same countries. This enables the World Bank to borrow on international capital markets at advantageous interest rates. As a result, the survival of this large multilateral agency depends to a large degree on its ability to sense the mood in the donor countries and to adapt to it (Hancock, 1989). The World Bank has been adapting to the environmental priorities of its principal shareholders ever since the mid 1980s when two highly publicised cases revealed its vulnerability to environmental criticism by establishing the link between World Bank-funded forest colonisation schemes and massive deforestation in northwest Brazil and Indonesia's Outer Islands (Lutzenberger, 1985; Secrett, 1986).

It is within the context of how environmental problems are being perceived in the major donor countries that the ascendancy of the environment as a priority of the World Bank has to be understood. While some of the environmental criticism had aimed at reducing the World Bank's power to intervene in developing countries, the World Bank's role was strengthened by adopting the environmental agenda as its own (Sachs, 1992). The World Bank's participation in 1989 in the publication of a major biodiversity strategy document launched by the world's largest conservation organisations signalled the elevation of biodiversity concerns to the top of the institution's environmental agenda (World Bank, 1990a). This helped lay the groundwork for the World Bank to establish itself as the world's main financier of projects specifically aimed at the environment and biodiversity conservation.

The environment first becomes a heading in the World Bank's annual reports in 1987, which identifies poverty of countries and of people as a major cause of environmental degradation, a situation the Bank seeks to remedy by promoting economic growth with emphasis on improving the incomes of the poor (World Bank, 1987: 33). In the same year, the World Commission on Environment and Development published its report *Our Common Future*, which popularised the concept of 'sustainable development', linking conservation and development. The report also called for a change in development patterns in order to make them compatible with biodiversity conservation by highlighting that the disappearance of tropical forests demonstrated the need to attack the problem at its source (WCED, 1987). Following the publication of the WCED report, the Bank added specificity about its environmental efforts in its annual reports. Perhaps the most significant aspect was the World Bank's implicit acknowledgement of its own role in causing environmental problems, by committing itself to anticipate the environmental consequences of large-scale development projects and to carry out appropriate mitigation measures.

In order to meet the new challenges, the World Bank's small office for environmental affairs became a fully-fledged environmental department in 1988. The environment was further elevated within the Bank's structure in 1993 when the Vice-Presidency for Environmentally Sustainable Development was established with the goal of breaking barriers between disciplines and sectors in order to ensure that all Bank-promoted development activities were environment-friendly and sustainable (World Bank, 1995a) From a single staff person in the mid-1970s, the World Bank's environmental staff grew to 300 environmental experts by 1997 (World Bank, 1997a).

In recent years, the World Bank has refined its mission statement from one of promoting economic growth to promoting sustainable development, in which it considers biodiversity to be of key importance (World Bank, 1992). In the institution's discourse, its twin goals of poverty alleviation and human development depend on environmental sustainability and biodiversity conservation (World Bank, 1995b). The key role accorded biodiversity leads the World Bank to acknowledge that specific targeted investments in biodiversity conservation *per se* (i.e. financing of a nature reserve) only have very limited impacts as long as biodiversity concerns do not figure prominently in overall decision-making. As a result, its discourse and policies commit the institution to incorporate biodiversity concerns in all of its activities, ranging from its policy dialogue with governments and the promotion of policy reforms at the macro-economic level to the design and implementation of individual development projects. Many of the latter are in biodiversity-sensitive sectors such as agriculture and forestry, infrastructure, mining, energy and the like.

In addition, World Bank statements on sustainable development are permeated by a discourse emphasising the need for highly participatory approaches and the participation of local people in decision-making that directly affects their lives (World Bank, 1989b). In the area of biodiversity conservation in particular, World Bank discourse establishes the link between improved local livelihoods and the chances for biodiversity conservation and emphasises the need for active participation of local communities and non-governmental organisations at the project level (World Bank, 1995b).

Reflecting much of the discourse, the World Bank has developed over the past decade a series of specific environmental and social policies and operational directives to provide guidance to its staff and ensure quality and consistency throughout its investment portfolio. Among its mandatory operational policies and directives which have a direct bearing on biodiversity conservation are the Bank's policies on environmental assessments (OD 4.01), on natural habitats (OD 4.04), on forestry (OP 4.36) and on indigenous peoples (OD 4.20). Many of these policies require the informed participation of project-affected people and therefore fit into what Blaikie has called the 'neo-populist' approach to biodiversity conservation as distinct from the 'classic approach' with its roots in colonial administration and the use of state power as its main tool (Blaikie, 1995).

8.3.2 The largest source of financing for 'global' environmental projects

The Global Environment Facility (GEF) was established in 1991 as an international financial entity to provide funding for projects in four focal areas: climate change, biodiversity conservation and the protection of both the ozone layer and international waters. The financing of projects to protect biodiversity represent the largest section of the GEF's portfolio (Global Environment Facility, 1998).

The GEF was established at the initiative of northern governments in 1991 and its choice of focal areas reflects the perceptions of northern constituencies of what the most urgent global environmental problems are. The GEF's mandate expanded in 1992 when it was adopted as the interim financial mechanism by the United Nations Convention on

Biodiversity (CBD) to help developing countries meet their obligations under the Convention. The CBD became a legally binding international agreement which entered into force in December 1993 when, as stipulated by Article 36 of the CBD, 30 of the states which are signatories to the Convention, had passed national legislation to ratify it. The preamble of the CBD recognises that the conservation of biodiversity is a common concern to humankind and sets three goals that place the CBD squarely in the field of environment and development, namely: (1) The conservation of biodiversity; (2) the sustainable use of its components; and (3) the fair and equitable sharing of the benefits arising out of genetic resources (United Nations, 1992: CBD, Art. 1). The CBD also establishes that the GEF 'function under the authority and guidance of, and be accountable to, the Conference of the Parties of the Convention' (United Nations, 1992: CBD, Art. 21).

This stipulation puts the GEF on an unclear legal footing as to which guidelines ultimately apply to its projects because the GEF is not an independent entity, but a tri-partite arrangement co-managed by the World Bank, the United Development Programme and the United Nations Environment Programme. In this the World Bank exercises a dominant role as administrator of the GEF trust fund and as implementing agency for all GEF investment projects. Functioning under the authority of a United Nations-type body is not reconcilable with the World Bank's charter, which establishes that voting shares are proportional to the shareholders' financial contribution (World Bank, 1989a). The unsolved dilemma consists of a UN agreement, which is based on the principle of one country/one vote, attempting to have under its authority a financial mechanism largely identified with a Bretton Woods institution, in which the world's wealthiest ten countries have a majority of the vote.

So far this potential conflict has not come to the fore, as the Conference of the Parties of the CBD has limited itself to providing guidance to the GEF in only the most general terms. As a result, the fact that the decision-making procedures and internal policies of the World Bank apply to all GEF investment projects has not been subject to in-depth questioning. The World Bank itself emphasises that it administers GEF funds with the same care used for its own funds. Therefore, in addition to the more general guidance from the Convention on Biodiversity, World Bank policies and directives apply to all GEF investment projects (Shihata, 1994).

8.3.3 Documented practice: existing programmes

What can be said about the implementation of the institutions' biodiversity-friendly policies? Only the analysis of specific lending programmes and projects can shed some definite light on what the institutional adoption of the global environmental agenda has accomplished in practice. But there are few systematic, independent, field-based assessments of the effectiveness of the policies (Fox & Brown, 1998). Overall, implementation of the policies is thought to be uneven and their impacts quite limited (ibid.). Further, the institutions themselves are doing a poor job at supervising and monitoring the projects that they finance. According to the Operations Evaluation Department (OED), a semi-independent unit within the World Bank, the institution's monitoring and evaluation activities are weak and suffer from a lack of sustained attention (World Bank, 1995c).

In view of the difficulties in establishing the relationship between official policies and real existing development/environment programmes, it is helpful to review some of the World Bank's internal evaluation reports. One of the better known ones is the 1992 Wapenhans report, an official World Bank report named after then Vice-President, Willi Wapenhans. This report revealed a systemic failure within the Bank to monitor the implementation of its own projects, and found that 37.5 per cent of all recently evaluated World Bank projects were rated as unsatisfactory on Bank assessment criteria and that well over half of ongoing operations were not of 'likely sustainability' (Wapenhans, 1992). It attributed responsibility for this state of affairs to the institution's 'approval culture', a term which describes the Bank's emphasis on rapid loan approval and lack of attention to the actual implementation of its projects. Similarly, the World Bank-commissioned history of its first 50 years refers to the pressure on Bank staff to exhaust resources intended for its poorest member countries within three years, despite problems with the 'absorbability' of large amounts of funds given the often poor infrastructural and institutional contexts of these countries, in order to qualify for a replenishment of Bank resources by the major donor countries (Kapur *et al.*, 1997).

Following the Wapenhans report, the World Bank elaborated a plan to address some of the problems it had raised. Five years later, it undertook an internal evaluation of the effectiveness of its reform efforts. The synthesis of the evaluation revealed disappointing results and attributes much of the failure of the reforms to the persistent impact of the Bank's institutional culture: 'The lessons from past experience are well known, yet they are generally ignored in the design of new operations. This synthesis concludes that institutional amnesia is the corollary of institutional optimism' (The World Bank, 1997b: 15). The World Bank's official history reaches a similar verdict when it states that the institution had only given a bureaucratic response to the Wapenhans report (Kapur *et al.*, 1997).

With regard to the environmental agenda, the institution's performance cannot be considered as separate from findings concerning the Bank's overall performance: they are part and parcel of the same institutional culture, subject to the same pressures and lack of incentives to learn from past mistakes.

The World Bank's policy on environmental assessments is perhaps the most important of the institution's environmental policies. It also establishes apparently transparent and participatory procedures which require extensive involvement of local people. A 1996 report by the Bank's Operations Evaluations Department on environmental assessment concluded that the procedures led to greater attention to environmental issues in Bank projects, but that the often massive documents were of little use in project design and implementation and that Bank supervision was weak (World Bank, 1996). According to the report, information disclosure and consultation processes were most often pathetic: consultations, if they were held at all, were held too late in the process to have any meaningful impact and affected groups, including women and the poor, were rarely involved (World Bank, 1996). The difficulties of complying with the environmental assessment procedures in infra-structure development projects, where the impacts on ecosystems and biodiversity are immediate, make it a reasonable assumption that the policy commitments are not being adhered to in other types of programmes, such as structural and sectoral lending programmes, where the causality of the impacts is not so readily established.

Does the GEF fair differently? According to the GEF itself, as well as external researchers, it suffers from many of the problems of its principal parent-agency, the World Bank. They found that there is pressure on the GEF Implementing Agencies to prepare project proposals quickly, which is leading to the generation of hastily developed projects (GEF, 1994; Wells, 1994; Fairman, 1996).

Again, little is known about the actual impact of GEF biodiversity projects. According to a study commissioned by the GEF Secretariat, the budget of the GEF monitoring and evaluation office has not been sufficient to build monitoring and evaluation components into GEF projects and therefore the rating of a project's success is largely subjective and determined by the responsible implementing agency (Porter *et al.*, 1998).

In addition, the presence of the GEF may well reduce the pressure to redress the underlying causes of the depletion of biodiversity by focusing on a mostly traditional approach of setting-up and supporting protected areas. Not everyone, even in the large northern-based conservation organisations which are closely associated with the GEF, is enthusiastic about the GEF. According to one of its leading spokespeople: '[t]he GEF is a typical top-down, throwing-money-at-the-problem, dealing-with-symptoms-rather-than-causes solution to a very complex set of issues' (McNeely, 1993: 1).

These types of preoccupation are echoed within the GEF Secretariat and the GEF Implementing Agencies themselves. Social scientists inside the institutions are warning that the success of biodiversity conservation projects depends upon a thorough understanding and careful consideration of social, political and cultural factors and that these factors are often overlooked as project preparation concentrates on financial, technical and administrative aspects (Cruz & Davis, 1996).

8.4 Conclusion: a political economy of institutions

Despite the degree of uncertainty involved in scientific issues relating to the Earth's biodiversity, there is ample agreement in the literature that deforestation and the loss of biodiversity caused by human activities at different geographic scales are advancing at unprecedented rates. This chapter has reviewed contending approaches to biodiversity as represented by both the natural sciences and by a multi-dimensional approach which places local human activities and needs at the centre of biodiversity generation and conservation. It has then examined the role of the world's two leading public international financial institutions which have adopted biodiversity conservation as an institutional goal.

Although there are no systematic independent studies of the concrete impact of the institutions' development/environment programmes, internal evaluation reports make it clear that the transition from institutional policy to implementation has not been made in any systematic fashion. This transition, however, is especially important with regard to the public international financial institutions because the scale of their financial resources lends them the power to turn ideas and intentions into expenditure programmes.

Both institutions fall squarely into Max Weber's definition of bureaucracies as modern systems of large-scale administration in which the administrative staff is clearly distinguished from the governing body that employs it (Beetham, 1996). The governing body consists of the member states under the predominant influence of the northern countries, while the administrative staff consists of the institutions' management and staff. As Ascher points out, the paradox of international financial institutions is that they are both creatures of states and full-blown bureaucracies in their own right (Ascher, 1983). The analysis of the gap between discourse and implementation has to be carried out at both levels.

The neo-realist perspective of political science, which holds that international institutions are an instrument of the interests of their most powerful shareholder nations (see also Warner, Chapter 11 in this volume), offers further insights into how the environment and biodiversity were propelled to the top of the agenda of international financial institutions: namely, that pressure from environmental constituencies in northern countries led the World Bank and the GEF to adopt biodiversity conservation as a fundamental objective. Especially in the case of the World Bank, the placement of biodiversity at the centre of its development discourse represents a sharp departure for an institution which is closely associated with the traditional interpretation of development as resource exploitation through agricultural expansion, logging, mining and the like: in these the environment is largely considered to be an infinite resource and a free good.

But the northern governments' role in propelling the environment to a central role in public international financial institutions has largely been limited to superficial efforts. These efforts have added a new mission to the international financial institutions, but they do not link environmental degradation and biodiversity loss to the political and economic interests that are creating and perpetuating these very problems (Bryant, 1997). Member governments are not asking questions of how the pro-environment/biodiversity programmes they are supporting are related to the demands of the expanding global economy. Maybe such questions would be considered as too threatening for maintenance of the status-quo. Also, while northern donor governments favour a neo-populist discourse with its emphasis on local participation in decision-making and on local livelihoods, they do not question that their support finances state-centred activities (see Chapter 9, in this volume). Both the World Bank and the GEF work mostly through national governments, many of which have little interest in the participation of marginalised and disempowered people who are the inhabitants of remote biodiversity-rich areas.

The analysis of the influence of the governing body (i.e. the shareholding-governments constituting the World Bank), however, has limited explanatory power when it comes to the internal processes of the institutions. North–South bargaining and underlying tensions within the governing body increase the operational autonomy of the international financial institutions from both donor and recipient governments (Fairman, 1996). The resulting grey areas provide discretionary decision-making powers to the bureaucracies. It is important that the bureaucracies themselves be examined because they are actors with objectives and approaches that are not simply the vector of interests of their member states (Wade, 1997). Ultimately, the internal dynamics of institutions determine to a large degree how institutions will pursue a new set of goals and how these will become incorporated into institutional practice. While it is important to emphasise that the institutions are not monolithic and that their impact is not uniform, theories of organisation can offer important insights into their internal dynamics. For example, these theories make an important distinction between organisational adaptation and learning. While the latter leads to the adoption of qualitatively new objectives and priorities, the former involves changes brought about by new pressures or incentives but without adjustments in the organisation's underlying goals and priorities. According to this, adaptation more than learning appears to guide the activities of the international financial institutions. The World Bank and the GEF adopt new issues such as biodiversity protection and the promotion of local participation as gestures which are made for reasons of legitimacy but which are largely ineffective at the operational level (Wade, 1997). The search for legitimacy is a symptom of challenges which indicate, as Crush suggests, that development discourse is not hermetically sealed (Crush, 1995).

Increasingly, the World Bank and other development agencies are recognising that 'institutions matter' and that the role of institutions in development is likely to be more important than the role of public investment (Picciotto, 1995). This approach, known as new institutional economics, emphasises the importance of the design of responsible and accountable institutions in developing countries. It extends the scope of economics to include an exploration of 'opportunism', rationally self-interested behaviour and uncertainty (Toye, 1995). Turning the table around, an important line of inquiry for future research would be the internal dynamics of multilateral financial institutions themselves. Thus, international institutions cannot be assumed to be unitary rational entities always acting in the public interest (Vaubel, 1991). The fundamental goals they pursue are linked to their survival, control over resources and decision-making authority, which often may be divorced from the objectives for which the institutions were created (Le Prestre, 1986). In the case of the World Bank, Wade observed that the structure that is in place allows for a decoupling of discourse and practice (Wade, 1997).

The biodiversity-friendly discourse of the World Bank and the GEF serves multiple goals: to mobilise (funding), to reassure (create the perception that something is being done about the environment), and to manipulate (through the concealment of divisive issues) (Gasper, 1996b). The ability to conceal divisive issues depends on keeping the natural environment separate from political realities. Both international politics (avoidance of fundamental questions) and the internal political economy of the institutions (culture of approval) represent serious stumbling blocks for the necessary connection of ecology with political economy. Even incremental progress on establishing this connection would help puncture the global agenda set by the northern governments and the authoritarianism of many southern governments.

Acknowledgements

Grassroots and non-governmental organisations in southern countries are increasingly documenting the devastating environmental and social impacts of international investments including internationally-funded and ill-conceived development and environment programmes. The individuals in these organisations often work at considerable personal risk. I feel indebted to them. In addition, my special thanks go to Professor Tony Allan and Dr Kathy Baker at SOAS, and my colleagues Bruce Rich and Ken Walsh at the Environmental Defense Fund.

Note

1   Editors' note: we should be realistic, however, and recognise that in part this dependence on natural resources may reflect a lack of access to alternatives and may not correspond entirely to the material aspirations of 'indigenous peoples'.

References

Ascher, W. 1983: New development approaches and the adaptability of international agencies: the case of the World Bank. *International Organization* **37**(3), 415–39.

Bailey, R.C. 1996: Promoting biodiversity and empowering local people in central African Forests. In Sponsel, L.E., Headland, T.N. and Bailey, R.C. (eds), *Tropical deforestation*. New York: Columbia University Press, 316–34.

Balick, M.J., Elisabetsky, E. and Laird, S.A. (eds) 1996: *Medicinal resources of the tropical forest.* New York: Columbia University Press.

Ballie, J. and Groombridge, B. (eds) 1996: *1996 IUCN red list of threatened animals.* Gland, Switzerland: IUCN Publications.

Barraclough, S.L. and Ghimire, K.B. 1995: *Forests and livelihoods: the social dynamics of deforestation in developing countries.* London: Macmillan Press.

Beetham, D. 1996: *Bureaucracy.* Buckingham: Open University Press.

Bell, R. 1987: Conservation with a human face: conflict and reconciliation in African land-use planning. In Anderson, D. and Grove, R. (eds), *Conservation in Africa*. Cambridge: Cambridge University Press, 79–102.

Blaikie, P. 1985: *The political economy of soil erosion in developing countries*. London and New York: Longman.

Blaikie, P. 1995: Biodiversity and the politics of the local control of resources with a case study of Cameroon. Paper presented at the annual meeting of American Geographers, Chicago.

Blaikie, P. and Jeanrenaud, S. 1997: Biodiversity and human welfare. In Ghimire, K.B. and Pimbert, M.P. *Social change and conservation*. London: Earthscan Publications.

Boecklen, W.J. and Gotelli, N.J. 1984: Island biogeographic theory and conservation practice: species-area or specious-area relationships? *Biological Conservation* **29**, 63–80.

Brown, K., Pearce, D., Perrings, C. and Swanson, T. 1993: *Economics and the conservation of global biological diversity*. Working Paper Number 2, Washington, DC: Global Environment Facility.

Bryant, R.L. 1997: Beyond the impasse: the power of political ecology in Third World environmental research. *Area* **29**(1), 5–19.

Chambers, R. 1986: *Sustainable livelihoods*. Institute of Development Studies, University of Sussex, mimeo.

Chandler, P. 1991: The indigenous knowledge of ecological processes among peasants in the People's Republic of China. *Agriculture and Human Values*. Florida: Agriculture, Food, and Human Values Society, vol. VIII., Numbers 1 and 2.

Colchester, M. 1994: *Salvaging nature: indigenous peoples, protected areas and biodiversity conservation*. Geneva: United Nations Research Institute for Social Development (UNSRID), World Rainforest Movement and World Wide Fund for Nature.

Connolly, B. 1996: Increments for the Earth: the politics of environmental aid. In Keohane, R.O. and Levy, M.A. *Institutions for environmental aid*. Cambridge, MA and London: The MIT Press, 327–65.

Crush, J. (ed.) 1995: *Power of development*. London & New York: Routledge.

Cruz, M.C.J. and Davis, S.H. 1996: *Social assessment in World Bank and GEF-funded biodiversity conservation projects: case studies from India, Ecuador and Ghana*. Washington, DC: World Bank Paper.

Davis, S.H. (ed.) 1993: *The social challenge of biodiversity conservation*. Washington, DC: Global Environment Facility, Working Paper No. 1.

Diamond, J. 1976: Island biogeography and conservation: strategy and limitations. *Science*. **193**, 1027–9.

Ehrlich, P.R. and Wilson, E.O. 1991: Biodiversity studies: science and policy. *Science*, **253**(16) August 1991, 758–62.

Fairhead, J. and Leach, M. 1993: *Contested forests: modern conservation and historical land-use of Guinea's Ziama reserve*. Guinea: Connaissance et Organisation Locales Agro-Ecologiques, Working Paper 7.

Fairhead, J. and Leach, M. 1996: *Misreading the African landscape: society and ecology in a forest-savanna mosaic*. Cambridge and New York: Cambridge University Press.

Fairman, D. 1994: Review of the report of the independent evaluation of the Global Environment Facility pilot phase. *Environment* **36**(6), 25–30.

Fairman, D. 1996: The Global Environment Facility: haunted by the shadow of the future. In Keohane, R.O. and Levy, M.A. (eds), *Institutions for environmental aid*. Cambridge, MA and London: The MIT Press.

Flitner, M. 1998: Biodiversity: of local commons and global commodities. In Goldman, M. (ed.), *Privatizing nature: political struggles for the global commons*. London: Pluto Press.

Fox, J.A. and Brown, L.D. (eds) 1998: *The struggle for accountability; The World Bank, NGOs and grassroots movements*. Cambridge, MA and London: The MIT Press.

Gasper, D. 1996a: Essentialism in and about discourse. *European Journal of Development Research*, **8**(1), 149–76.

Gasper, D. 1996b: Analysing policy arguments. *European Journal of Development Research*, **8**(1), 36–62.

Ghimire, K.P. and Pimbert, M.P. (eds) 1997: *Social change and conservation*. London: Earthscan Publications.

Gilbert, F.S. 1980: The equilibrium theory of island biogeography: fact or fiction? *Journal of Biogeography* **7**, 209–35.

Global Environment Facility 1994: *Independent evaluation of the pilot phase*. Washington, DC: GEF.

Global Environment Facility 1998: *Annual Report*. Washington, DC: GEF.

Goodland, R. 1982: *Tribal peoples and economic development: human ecologic considerations*. Washington, DC: The World Bank.

Graham, R.L., Perlack R.D., Prasad, A.M.G., Ranney, J.W. and Waddle, D.B. 1990: *Greenhouse gas emissions in Sub-Saharan Africa*. Tennessee: Oakridge National Laboratory.

Graham, R.W. 1992: Late Pleistocene faunal changes as a guide to understanding effects of green-house warming on the mammalian fauna of North America. In Peters, R.L. and Lovejoy, T.E. (eds), *Global warming and biological diversity*. New Haven and London: Yale University Press, 76–90.

Gray, A. 1991: *Between the spice of life and the melting pot: biodiversity conservation and its impact on indigenous peoples*. Copenhagen: IWGIA Document 70.

Groombridge, B. (ed.) 1994: *Biodiversity data sourcebook*. Cambridge: World Conservation Press.

Hancock, G. 1989: *Lords of poverty*. New York: The Atlantic Monthly Press.

Harte, J., Torn, M. and Jensen D. 1992: Consequences of indirect linkages between climate change and biological diversity. In Peters, R.L. and Lovejoy T.E. (eds), *Global warming and biological diversity*. New Haven and London: Yale University Press, 325–42.

Hartshorn, G.S. 1992: Possible effects of global warming on the biological diversity in tropical forests. In Peters, R.L. and Lovejoy, T.E. (eds), *Global warming and biological diversity*. New Haven and London: Yale University Press, 137–46.

Harvey, D. 1996: *Justice, nature and the geography of difference*. Malden, MA and Oxford: Blackwell Publishers.

Horta, K. 1991: The plundering of Cameroon's rainforests. *The Ecologist*, **21**(3), 142–7.

Horta, K. 1994: Troubled waters – World Bank disasters along Kenya's Tana River. *Multinational Monitor*. July/August, 12–16.

International Alliance of Indigenous-Tribal Peoples of the Tropical Forests & International Work Group for Indigenous Affairs. No date. *Indigenous peoples, forest, and biodiversity*. London: The International Alliance of Indigenous-Tribal Peoples of the Tropical Forest International Secretariat.

Jeanrenaud, S. 1997: Perspectives in People-Oriented Conservation. *Arborvitae*, Supplement, WWF, IUCN (no page numbers)

Kapur, D., Lewis, J.P. and Webb, R. (eds) 1997: *The World Bank – Its First Half Century*. Washington, DC: The Brookings Institution, Vol. I (History), Vol. II (Perspectives).

Lawton, J.H., Bignell, D.E., Bonlton, B. *et al.* 1998: Biodiversity Inventories, indicator taxa and effects of habitat modification in tropical forest. *Nature*, Vol. 391, 1 January 1998, 72–76.

Leach, M. and Mearns, R. (eds) 1996: *The lie of the land: challenging received wisdom on the African environment*. London: The International African Institute.

Le Prestre, P.G. 1986: A problématique for international organizations. *International Social Science Journal*, **107**, 127–38.

Little, P.D. and Brokensha, D.W. 1987: Local institutions, tenure and resource management. In Anderson, D. and Grove, R. (eds), *Conservation in Africa: people policies and practice*. Cambridge: Cambridge University Press, 193–209.

Lonsdale. J. 1987: Consequences for conservation and development. In Anderson, D. and Grove, R. (eds), *Conservation in Africa*. Cambridge: Cambridge University Press, 271–6.

Lugo, A.E. 1988: Estimating the reductions in tropical forest species. In Wilson, E.O. (ed.), *Biodiversity*. Washington, DC: National Academy Press, 58–70.

Lutzenberger, J. 1985: The World Bank's Polonoroeste project: a social and environmental catastrophe. *The Ecologist* **15**, 69–72.

MacArthur, R.H. and Wilson, E.O. 1967: *The theory of island biogeography*. Princeton, NJ: Princeton University Press.

Machlis, G.E. 1992: The contribution of sociology to biodiversity research and management. *Biological Conservation* **62**, 161–70.

Mann, C.C. 1991: Extinction: are ecologists crying wolf? *Science* **253**, 16 August, 734–8.

Martin, P.S. 1996: Africa and Pleistocene overkill. *Nature* **331**, 16–17.

Martin, P.S. 1973: The discovery of America. *Science* **179**, 969–74.

Martin, P.S., Sabels, B.E. and Shutler, D. 1961: Rampart cave coprolite and the ecology of the Shasta ground sloth. *American Journal of Science*. **259**, 102.

McNeely, J.A., Miller, K.R., Reid, W.V., Mittermeier, R.A. and Werner, T.B. 1990: *Conserving the world's biological diversity*. Gland, Switzerland: International Union for the Conservation of Nature and Natural Resources, World Resources Institute, Conservation International, World Wildlife Fund-US and the World Bank.

McNeely, J.A. 1993: *Global Environment Facility: cornucopia or kiss of death for biodiversity?* Gland, Switzerland: IUCN Manuscript.

Moore, J.D., Chaloner, B. and Stott, P. 1996: *Global environmental change*. Oxford: Blackwell Science Ltd.

Myers, N. 1988: Tropical forests and their species. In Wilson, E.O. (ed.), *Biodiversity*. Washington, DC: National Academy Press, 28–35.

National Research Council 1996: *Lost crops of Africa*. Volume I. *Grains*. Washington, DC: National Academy Press.

Nelson, G.J. and Serafin, R. 1992: Assessing biodiversity: a human ecological approach. *Ambio* **21**(3) May, 212–18.

Norgaard, R.B. 1994: *Development betrayed*. London & New York: Routledge.

Norse, E.A. (ed.) 1993: *Global marine biological diversity*. Washington, DC: Island Press.

Pearce, F. 1997: Lost forests leave West Africa dry. *New Scientist* 15 January, 218.

Picciotto, R. 1995: *Putting institutional economics to work*. Washington, DC: World Bank Discussion Paper, No. 304.

Porter, G., Clemencon, R., Ofusu-Amaah, W. and Philips, M. 1998: *Study of the GEF's overall performance*. Washington, DC: GEF.

Raven, P.H. 1988: Our diminishing tropical forests. In Wilson, E.O. (ed.), *Biodiversity*. Washington, DC: National Academy Press, 119–23.

Redclift, M. 1987: *Sustainable development: exploring the contradictions*. London & New York: Routledge.

Richards, P. 1985: *Indigenous agricultural revolution*. London: Unwin Hyman Ltd.

Sachs, W. (ed.) 1992: *The development dictionary: a guide to knowledge as power*. London & New Jersey: Zed Books.

Schneider, S.H., Mearns, L. and Gleick, P.H. 1992: Climate-change scenarios for impact assessment. In Peters, R.L. and Lovejoy, T.E. (eds), *Global warming and biodiversity*. New Haven and London: Yale University Press, 38–55.

Secrett, C. 1986: The environmental impact of transmigration. *The Ecologist* **16**, 77–88.

Shihata, I.F.I. 1994: *The World Bank inspection panel*. Oxford and New York: Oxford University Press.

Shiva, V. 1992: Resources. In Sachs, W. (ed.), *The development dictionary: a guide to knowledge as power*. London & New Jersey: Zed Books, 206–18.

Simberloff, D.S. and Abele, L.G. 1976: Island biogeography theory and conservation practice. *Science* **191**, 285–6.

Simon J.L. and Wildavsky, A. 1993: Facts, not species, are periled. *New York Times*, 13 May 1993.

Skole, D. and Tucker, C. 1993: Tropical deforestation and habitat fragmentation in the Amazon: satellite data from 1978 to 1988. *Science* **260**, 25 June, 1905–10.

Smith, F.D.M., May R.M., Pellew, R., Johnson, T.H. and Walter, K.S. 1993: Estimating extinction rates. *Nature* **364**, 5 August, 494–6.

Smith, T.B., Wayne, R.K., Griman, D.J. and Bruford, M.W. 1997: A role for ecotones in generating rainforest biodiversity. *Science* **276**, 20 June, 1855–7.

Soulé, M.E. 1991: Conservation tactics for a constant crisis. *Science* **253**, 16 August, 744–50.

Soulé, M.E. 1992: The wrong time for climate change. In Peters, R.L. and Lovejoy, T.E. (eds), *Global warming and biological diversity*. New Haven and London: Yale University Press, xiii–xix.

Soulé, M.E., Wilcox, B.A. and Holtby, C. 1979: Benign neglect: a model of faunal collapse in the game reserves of East Africa. *Biological Conservation* **15**, 259–71.

Sponsel, L.E., Headland, T.N. and Bailey, R.C. (eds) 1996: *Tropical deforestation: the human dimension*. New York: Columbia University Press.

Srivastava, J.P., Smith N.J.H. and Forno, D.A. (eds) 1996: *Biodiversity and agricultural intensification*. Washington, DC: The World Bank, Environmentally Sustainable Development Studies and Monographs Series No. 11.

Stott, P. 1991: Recent trends in the ecology and management of the world's savanna formations. *Progress in Physical Geography* **15**(1), 18–28.

Stott, P. 1998: Biogeography and ecology in crisis: the urgent need for a new metalanguage. *Journal of Biogeography* **25**, 1–2.

Sullivan, S. 1996: Towards a non-equilibrium ecology: perspectives from an arid land. *Journal of Biogeography* **23**, 1–5.

Sullivan, S. 1999: Folk and formal, local and national: Damara knowledge and community-based conservation in southern Kunene, Namibia. *Cimbebasia* **15**, 1–28.

Sullivan, S. in press a: perfume and pastoralism: gender, ethnographic myths and community-based conservation in arid north-west Namibia. In Hodgson, D. *Rethinking pastoralism: gender, culture and the myth of the patriarchal pastoralist*. Oxford: James Currey and Ohio University Press.

Sullivan, S. in press b: How sustainable is the communalising discourse of 'new' conservation? The masking of difference, inequality and aspiration in the fledgling conservancies' of north-west Namibia. In Chatty, 1). (ed.), *Displacement, forced settlement and conservation*. Oxford/New York: Berghahn Press.

Terborgh, J. 1974: Preservation of natural diversity: the problem of extinction prone species. *BioScience* **24**(12), 715–22.

The Week 2000: Super-volcano threatens global chaos. *The Week*, 12 February.

Toye, J. 1995: The new institutional economics and the implications for development theory. In Harris, J., Hunter, J. and Lewis, C.M. (eds), *The new institutional economics and Third World development*. London & New York: Routledge, 49–68.

United Nations 1992: *Convention on biological diversity*. New York: United Nations Conference on Environment and Development.

United Nations Food and Agriculture Organization (FAO) 1993: *Forest resources assessment 1990: tropical countries*. Rome: FAO Forestry Paper 112.

Vansina, J. 1990: *Paths in the rainforests: towards a history of political tradition in equatorial Africa*. Wisconsin: The University of Wisconsin Press.

Vaubel, R. 1991: A public choice view of international organization. In Vaubel, R. and Willett, T.D. (eds), *The political economy of international organizations: a public choice approach*. Boulder, CO and Oxford: Westview Press.

Wade, R. 1997: *Development and environment: marital difficulties at the World Bank*. Geneva: Working Paper Series of the Economic and Social Research Council, No. 29.

Wapenhans, W.A. 1992: *A Report of the portfolio management taskforce*. Washington, DC: The World Bank.

Watson, R.T. and Heywood, V.H. (eds) 1995: *Global biodiversity assessment: summary for policy-makers*. Cambridge: Cambridge University Press for the United Nations Environment Programme.

Wells, M.P. 1994: Global Environment Facility and prospects for biodiversity conservation. *International Environmental Affairs* **6**(1), 69–97.

Western, D. and Ssemakula, J. 1981: The future of the savannah ecosystems: ecological islands or faunal enclaves? *African Journal of Ecology* **19**, 7–19.

Whittaker, R.J., Bush, M.B. and Richards, K. 1989: Plant recolonization and vegetation succession on the Krakatau islands, Indonesia. *Ecological Monographs* **59**(2), 59–123.

Wiens, J. 1984: On understanding a nonequilibrium world: myth and reality in community patterns and processes. In Strong, D.R., Simberloff, D., Abele, L.G. and Thistle, A.B. (eds), *Ecological communities: conceptual issues and the evidence*. Princeton, NJ: Princeton University Press, 434–57.

Williams, F. 1990: Forests. In Turner II, B.I. (ed.), *The earth as transformed by human action*. Cambridge: Cambridge University Press, 179–201.

Wilson, E.O. (ed.) 1988: *Biodiversity*. Washington. DC: National Academy Press.

Wilson, E.O. and Simberloff, D.S. 1969: Experimental zoogeography on islands: defaunation and monitoring techniques. *Ecology* **50**(2), 267–78.

World Bank 1982: *Tribal peoples and economic development*. Washington, DC: The World Bank.

World Bank 1987: *Annual report*. Washington, DC: The World Bank.

World Bank 1989a: *International Bank for Reconstruction and Development: articles of agreement. As amended effective February 16, 1989*. Washington, DC: The World Bank.

World Bank 1989b: *Sustainable growth with equity – a long-term perspective for Sub-Saharan Africa*. Washington, DC: The World Bank.

World Bank 1990a: *Annual environmental report*. Washington, DC: The World Bank.

World Bank 1990b: *Credit to Guinea for forestry and fisheries: official memorandum to Vice President*. Washington, DC: The World Bank.

World Bank 1992: *World development report: development and the environment*. Washington, DC: The World Bank.

World Bank 1995a: *Annual report*. Washington, DC: The World Bank.

World Bank 1995b: *Mainstreaming biodiversity in development*. Environment Department Paper No. 029. Washington, DC: The World Bank.

World Bank 1995c: *OED précis-monitoring and evaluation: making headway*. Washington, DC: Operations Evaluations Department, Number 83.

World Bank, Operations Evaluation Department 1996: *Effectiveness of environmental assessments and national environmental action plans: a process study*. Washington, DC: The World Bank.

World Bank 1997a: *Environment matters report: winter/spring 1997*. Washington, DC: The World Bank.

World Bank 1997b: *Office memorandum – portfolio improvement program: draft reviews of sector portfolio and lending instruments: a synthesis, 23 April 1997*. Washington, DC: The World Bank.

World Commission on Environment and Development 1987: *Our Common Future*. Oxford and New York: Oxford University Press.

World Resources Institute 1992: *Global biodiversity strategy: a policy-makers' guide*. Washington, DC: World Resources Institute, The World Conservation Union & the United Nations Environment Programme.

World Resources Institute, United Nations Environment Programme, United Nations Development Programme and the United Nations 1990: *World resources 1990–91*. Oxford and New York: Oxford University Press.

World Resources Institute, United Nations Environment Programme, United Nations Development Programme, World Bank 1996: *World resources: a guide to the global environment 1996–97*. Oxford and New York: Oxford University Press.

Wylie, J.L. and Currie, D.J. 1993: Species-energy theory and patterns of species richness: II. predicting mammal species richness on isolated nature reserves. *Biological Conservation*, **63**: 145–8.

Zerner, C. 1996: Telling stories about biodiversity. In Brush, S. and Stabinsky, D. (eds), *Valuing local knowledge: indigenous peoples and intellectual property rights*. Washington, DC: Island Press, 68–101.

World Wide Web resources

Tropical Ecology Web Site: URL: http://www.ecotrop.org, accessed 3 May 1999: 3 p.m.

9

Contesting the plot

Environmental politics and the urban allotment garden in Britain and Japan

Richard Wiltshire, David Crouch and Ren Azuma

9.1 Introduction

The 1992 Earth Summit in Rio de Janiero heralded the widespread expression of a new municipal environmentalism in economically advanced societies, manifested in the commitment (real or imagined) of many urban authorities to the promotion of 'sustainable development' at the local level. Ordinary people have in turn been urged to embrace more 'sustainable lifestyles' as their personal contribution to reducing pressure on the planet's resources. The outcomes of exhortations to alter personal behaviour to achieve impersonal environmental goals are frequently disappointing, however, in part because the working life of many city dwellers is one of 'virtual labour' executed by keyboard and telephone, wholly detached from the physical world. Yet within the modern city, people often make time to commune with nature as best they can – in public parks, in private back gardens, in tending bonsai and window boxes. The Confucian admonition to 'garden when the sun shines and read when it rains' seems as relevant to defining a healthy and sustainable lifestyle for the desk-bound worker in contemporary information society as to the cloistered scholars of old. And if it is in the garden that city dwellers come closest to the natural processes that sustain life, then perhaps it is in the garden that an effective municipal environmentalism might take root.

A high geographical density of urban living imposes limits, however, upon the opportunities available to residents to develop ecologically flavoured lifestyles through the direct medium of cultivation. High rise dwellings in the inner city divorce people from the ground in the most literal sense, while high land costs encourage developers to cram new homes on suburban sites. One outcome of the inevitable shortage of private space for active gardening and the limited, passive engagement afforded by the public park, is the demand for parcels of land suitable for recreational horticulture to be made available for ordinary citizens to rent; that is, for the creation or retention of urban allotment gardens, where people can deepen their association with the earth by growing a little of their own food – locally, and under their own control.

And yet it is here, on the urban allotment site, that a contemporary environmental logic has injected new life into what has been, in Britain and elsewhere, a long and bitter debate over the legitimacy of one of the most contested categories of urban land-use. A powerful narrative is deployed against the allotment garden, based on the economics of the urban land market and the politics of planning, in which the allotment is denigrated as an obsolete and uneconomic use of urban land, hindering the rational deployment of scarce public resources, obstructing the pursuit of private profit through development, and best sacrificed in the cause of protecting other open space of greater aesthetic and recreational value. In an uneven contest against this narrative, individuals with a passion for land which they do not own in any legal sense, but which easily becomes endowed with secret values and meanings generated by prolonged, personal and intimate contact, deploy whatever fragments of argument they can muster in the allotment's defence, from appeals to the ancient rights of the working man to tragic depictions of oppression and desecration by unscrupulous developers and fellow travellers. In these circumstances, engagement with the narrative of local sustainable development can be seen as an attractive option, combining a natural and genuine belief in the inherent social and environmental value of allotment gardening with the prospect of a new, coherent and powerful line of defence.

Our purpose in this chapter is to explore some of the political dimensions of the struggle to protect urban allotment land and allotment gardening, and to explore the impact on that struggle of sustainable development aspirations articulated at the municipal and personal level, not least as a means for individual gardeners to empower themselves in the battle to hold 'their' ground. The empirical context is provided by the British allotment garden, an institution with a long history but a troubled present, and by the Japanese *shimin noen*,[1] a comparatively recent invention with strong European (especially German) roots, which is confronting similar tensions in maintaining a secure place in the modern Japanese city, but from a position that is inherently weaker, and for which rather different solutions may be appropriate.

In Britain, the main vehicle for achieving sustainable development at the municipal level is the Local Agenda 21 process. The British Prime Minister has famously declared that by the year 2000 every local authority should have an agreed Local Agenda 21 strategy (Hams, 1997: 17), formulated in consultation with its citizens. In practice, Local Agenda 21 has provided a fertile arena for diverse environmental interest groups to promote their own agendas, not least because the meaning of 'sustainable development' at the local level has yet to be encapsulated with any conceptual rigour (Munton, 1997). Allotment gardeners, real or aspiring, have the opportunity to use this process as an instrument to achieve a more immediate end – security enhancement (Thompson, 1997) – by exploiting new channels of communication with their landlords, with local authorities, and with the general public. A moral basis for this instrumentalism is provided by genuine and objective environmental benefits (to the individual and to the community at large) inherent in what allotment gardeners do anyway (for which see Garnett, 1996 and Steele, 1999), and by the legitimate and deeply held values which ordinary people can discover through this pastime (Crouch and Ward, 1997).

Two of the present authors have argued the case elsewhere for Japan to seek a reinvigoration of its own allotment tradition by selective adoption of the ideas developed in Britain within the Local Agenda 21 process (Wiltshire and Azuma, 2000). Local Agenda 21 has yet to diffuse as widely in Japan as it has in Britain, but plans to improve the local environment, to promote sustainable lifestyles, and to mobilise the population to that end are commonly articulated by Japanese local authorities, with or without reference to Rio and its aftermath. As in Britain, therefore, the problem facing Japanese allotment holders is how best to take advantage of the opportunities for security enhancement which this situation presents.

In the following sections we explore four of the main dimensions of the struggle to create and retain urban allotments, namely the relationship of allotments to the urban land market, the role of allotments within urban land-use planning, problems inherent in the landlord–tenant relationship, and the roles and effectiveness of plotholder organizations. The division is artificial to some extent and there are significant overlaps, including those which result from the multiple roles of local authorities. As an ordering device, however, this approach allows us to tease out some of the ways in which sustainability arguments can be and have been employed to defend and promote the urban allotment garden.

9.2 The competition for urban land

The most obvious barrier to allotment provision in advanced capitalist economies, and the greatest threat to existing sites, stems from the logic of the urban land market, which allocates land to the uses which can pay the highest economic rent. This is a market in which even the most productive garden can scarcely compete on the value of its produce alone, and where the best hopes for the allotment gardener lie in evading competition through recourse to mechanisms which lie outside the market, in accepting inferior land with no other claimants, in agreeing to the temporary use of land otherwise held for speculation, or in seeking out land in a remote location where competition is weak. The alternative is to face continuing uncertainty over when and how the land will be converted to other uses, uncertainty which saps the will to invest (materially and emotionally) in the upkeep of soil fertility and the maintenance of facilities, and blights the land (House of Commons, 1998b: xxi).

Losses of urban allotment land in Britain and Japan have been most noticeable where development pressures are greatest, in the regions around the global cities of London and Tokyo, and where the legal owners of the land have a strong incentive to sell. In Britain, the influence of the land market can be most readily detected in the high rate of closure of private and temporary allotment sites, as compared with statutory sites which enjoy at least some insulation from arbitrary sale. In 1970 the numbers of statutory and non-statutory allotment sites in England were evenly balanced; by 1996 the latter were outnumbered by three to one (Crouch, 1997: 8). In Japan, the shortage of publicly owned land in urban areas (and the prohibitive cost of acquiring more), combined with the absence of a substantial inheritance of allotment land such as that enjoyed by many local authorities in Britain, means that most urban recreational horticulture inevitably takes place on privately owned land, on terms which offer little long-term protection to the cultivator. Thus, while allotment provision has grown substantially in the 1990s in rural areas remote from development pressures under the influence of much improved allotment legislation, these gains have been balanced by the steady erosion of provision in the areas where most people actually live (Aoki, 1996).

This divergence in the ownership pattern of allotment land between Britain and Japan creates a large difference in the effectiveness of sustainability arguments as a means of combating market forces, and the way such arguments are best deployed. In Britain, where the vast majority of sites are now on land under public ownership (House of Commons, 1998b: xix), the defence of allotments has traditionally turned on the statutory protection afforded by the Allotments Acts and sentimental appeals to the better nature of council members and officers, through the deployment of a tragic discourse of neglect and mistreatment. Local authorities, however, are under enormous financial pressure to manage their assets as effectively and productively as possible, or in other words, to pay more attention to the opportunity costs of not managing their estates (including allotment land) in line with market signals. Their freedom to act improved markedly in 1996, when the courts diluted the criteria applied to determine the adequacy of an alternative site offered to existing plotholders on a statutory site earmarked for closure, by eliminating the requirements for equivalence in facilities and convenience of location, and ruling that the relocation site need not have statutory status (Court of Appeal, 1996). Complaints over the weakening of statutory protection aired during the 1998 Parliamentary Inquiry into the Future for Allotments were met by a new obligation imposed by the Department for the Environment, Transport and the Regions on local authorities to demonstrate that they have 'actively promoted' their allotments before the Secretary of State will approve the disposal of statutory allotment land. But this helpful-looking provision could yet prove a double-edged sword for plotholders on under-used sites, because evidence of promotion (effective or otherwise) would undermine charges of wilful neglect, and thus the other traditional line of defence.

This leaves allotment gardeners in need of a new argument to encourage local authorities not to cave in to market pressures, and Local Agenda 21 is the best available, for two effective if cynical reasons. First, because local authorities have a vested (though not a statutorily defined) interest in achieving at least some successes which can be labelled as a contribution to sustainable development, and capitalising on the efforts of allotment gardeners is a quick way to register gains with minimum effort and expense. And second, because Local Agenda 21 can be exploited by plotholder groups to gain access to materials, money and publicity to improve the quality and appeal of their sites and attract new plotholders, thereby reducing the opportunity costs to the local authority of leaving the land under allotment use, since these newcomers would have to be accommodated somewhere else should the land be sold.

In the Japanese case, however, the prevalence of private landowners – ordinary farmers for the most part – renders these methods ineffective, since there is no obligation on the landowner's part to contribute to sustainable development or to find alternative accommodation for plotholders at the time of sale. In this respect, Japanese urban plotholders have more in common with the users of British inner city 'community gardens', whose interests lie in encouraging landowners to make available idle sites for temporary horticultural use pending redevelopment. The willingness of landowners to do this depends, of course, on the quality of the guarantees given that the land will be surrendered on demand. Wiltshire and Azuma (2000) have argued elsewhere, however, that the formation of legally defined allotment user associations at the municipal level in Japan dedicated to the achievement of sustainable development goals through horticulture could help to bring land into allotment use – and keep it there – through effective forward planning of provision based on access to an adequate number of sites, but not necessarily the same sites, to meet the needs of members. Plotholders would be guaranteed continuous membership of the association, and continuous provision of land somewhere, while landowners need worry less about resistance to the closure of specific sites, resistance which could jeopardise membership of the user association and access to its benefits. The user associations could also expect to enjoy support from local authorities, given that the associations' goals are fully compatible with policies to achieve local sustainable development, and could be instrumental in bringing those policies to a successful conclusion.

9.3 Allotments and land-use planning

In Britain, Japan and other advanced capitalist societies, urban land markets are regulated and distorted through land-use planning or zoning systems operating at a variety of spatial scales, from the very local to the national, the content of which is a compromise between technical possibilities defined by expertise and aspirations expressed through the political process. The interests of allotment gardeners lie in manipulating both expertise and the political system in a manner which creates a presumption in favour of the provision and protection of cultivable land for allotments, so that the planning system deflects land market pressures elsewhere.

Allotment gardening is deeply embedded in British urban planning theory. As far back as 1898, Ebenezer Howard's 'Garden Cities' concept gave prominence to allotments as a favoured land use on the immediate margins of new settlements. To be embedded, however, is not necessarily to be influential. At times during the twentieth century, allotment gardening has been favoured by wider political and economic events, and never more so than during the Second World War, when the Ministry of Food's 'Dig for Victory' campaign brought thousands of acres into temporary production. Post-war prosperity has long since rendered allotment provision marginal to planning thinking and as questionable a requirement within the modern urban land use plan as Howard's epileptic farms and homes for waifs. But a century on, sustainable development has breathed new life into the Garden Cities tradition, and with it a new focus on a place for horticulture in urban areas.

In their recent homage to Howard's influence on planning in Britain, Hall and Ward note the inherent sustainability of Howard's original concept, and in their quest for a model of sustainable urban development appropriate to the twenty-first century, they call for the incorporation into new residential developments of

> an allotment garden, which ideally would be provided in the communal open space in the middle of a superblock, entirely surrounded by houses and their own small private gardens. It would answer the insistent call for organic food from an increasingly sophisticated and worried public.
>
> (Hall and Ward, 1998: 206–7)

In reality, however, food production (and the many other benefits of allotment gardening) are bound to remain a peripheral concern even within a planning system tinged with green: the issue that will continue to dominate planning thinking well into the next century is where to put the millions of new homes required in Britain. At this point, the allotment risks falling victim to sustainability defined at a higher level: the optimum allocation of houses and population between town and countryside. At this level, there has been a strengthening presumption in favour of raising densities within cities, not only to defend the 'open' countryside and contain development within existing urban areas – a policy which enjoys strong and well-connected political support – but also to facilitate improvements in public transport. The result has been an increasing emphasis on the development of urban 'brownfield' sites. The fear for allotment gardeners is that their plots might look temptingly brown to developers seeking to avoid the high costs of reclaiming polluted industrial sites for housing and to cash-strapped councils charged with the task of identifying adequate supplies of housing land.

The political challenge, therefore, has been to secure a definition of 'brownfield' land which explicitly excludes allotment sites. Since local plans are subject to national planning policy guidance, it is at the national level that political action has been required. Hence the importance of the Parliamentary Inquiry into the Future for Allotments, which accepted evidence on the effect of development pressures from urban plotholders throughout the country, and called in its report for explicit protection for allotments within a revised Planning Policy Guidance Note (PPG3) on Housing (House of Commons, 1998b: xxiv). In the event, the public consultation draft of the new PPG3 issued in March 1999 explicitly excludes allotments from 'previously-developed land' (the formal definition of 'brownfield' sites), and goes further, in recommending that 'Other types of open space should also be protected against pressures for development, in particular allotments, which are important to local communities for both recreation and the provision of green spaces in urban areas' (Department of the Environment, Transport and the Regions, 1999: 15). This recommendation is situated in a section of the proposed PPG3 entitled 'Promoting sustainable patterns of development', which makes explicit the link between allotment gardening and the government's sustainable development agenda. And it is by continuing appeals to that agenda that allotment gardeners can bring political pressure to bear to achieve planning rules which steer the behaviour of local authorities in the 'right' direction, i.e. towards the protection of allotments for the purpose of achieving the goals of Local Agenda 21 in partnership with the local community and its allotment gardeners.

The Inquiry was one means to achieve this; another was the subsequent Early Day Motion on Allotment Gardening (EDM 1598, Session 1997–98), which flushed out substantial cross-party support amongst MPs for the role which allotments can play in the achievement of sustainable development objectives, particularly in urban areas. The motion read

> 'That this House welcomes the work done by local allotment groups; further welcomes their involvement in many areas with Local Agenda 21 initiatives, for example, Quality Environment for Dartford, notes the contribution that allotment gardening can make to the local environment through recycling, sheltering wildlife and conserving open spaces; further notes the benefits for health of allotment gardening through regular exercise and fresh fruit and vegetables; and calls on the Government to do everything it can to support local allotment groups.'

EDM 1598 was backed up by a national campaign (in which one of the present authors participated) to encourage individual allotment gardeners to write to their MPs and secure support, which has since drawn praise for its effectiveness (Flack, 1999). The reference to Dartford is significant, because Dartford lies at the heart of the region to the east of London known to planners as the Thames Gateway, which is scheduled to undergo the most intensive process of urban development in Britain over the next quarter century, and as Hall and Ward point out: 'Thames Gateway is thus a unique chance to design a model sustainable urban development on a huge scale, a model for the entire world' (Hall and Ward, 1998: 157).

There are signs that in Japan too, thinking in higher level planning circles is beginning to recognise the potential value of allotments in enhancing the environmental quality of urban areas. The National Land Agency's Fifth Comprehensive National Development Plan, published in 1998, reads in part:

> In order to create urban spaces where people can come into contact with nature, we need to plan the formation of networks of water and greenery linking waterside spaces along rivers and shorelines with urban parks and green spaces, to promote the consolidation of allotments, and to protect woodlands within our cities . . .
>
> (Kokudocho, 1998: 63, Authors' translation)

There is a notable similarity between this statement and the proposed revision to the British PPG3 quoted earlier. In practice, however, the opportunities for steering the Japanese planning system from below in directions favourable to urban allotment gardeners seem more limited than in Britain. Under the present system, land in and around Japanese cities is divided between Urbanisation Control Areas and Urbanisation Promotion Areas. Support for allotments under new laws introduced in 1989 and 1990 (Azuma, 1991) has proved of limited effectiveness within Urbanisation Promotion Areas, where the presumption is very much in favour of development. A new measure introduced in 1991, the Productive Green Space Law, was designed to protect farmland as a residual source of greenery within Urbanisation Promotion Areas, by reducing the inheritance tax burden on land which was to remain in agricultural production (Azuma, 1998: 62; Tashiro, 1995), and thus presented an opportunity to enhance the protection of allotment sites located on such land as well. Unfortunately, the opportunity was missed: if the landowner dies and the land is under allotments rather than ordinary cultivation, inheritance tax is payable on the market value of the land for urban uses, which is a powerful incentive for farmers not to make land available for allotment use – or to employ subterfuges to disguise the true use of the land. An example of the latter is the 'farm cramming school' charade employed in the Nerima Ward of Tokyo, in which the plotholders are officially students learning about horticulture – on land which therefore remains under agricultural use as far as the law is concerned (Azuma, 1998: 62–3). Had the government chosen instead to adopt an inheritance tax policy favouring allotment gardens over land kept under ordinary cultivation, then it could easily have stimulated a major expansion in the provision of legitimate allotment gardens in Urbanisation Control Areas – allotments which would then have enjoyed protection for 30 years, under the terms of the Productive Green Space Law. Any such move would have faced strong opposition from the Ministry of Finance, however, which has jurisdiction over the tax system – and little enthusiasm for creating new tax loopholes for the benefit of allotment gardeners. By contrast, problems of reconciling planning and taxation policy are not something which campaigners for British urban allotments commonly face, because most of the land concerned is already under public ownership.

Effective mobilisation of political support for urban allotments in Japan (were there bodies actually capable of attempting this) would also be more difficult than in Britain, given the reluctance of politicians to interfere with the rights of private landowners in general, whether through taxation policy or planning rules, and with the rights of farmers in particular, given the strong influence which farmers and their organisations have enjoyed within the Japanese political system since the post-war land reforms. Given the fact that allotment gardens are open to members of the public to enjoy, and in this sense have attributes which resemble those of a public park, it is difficult for politicians to favour allotments without also seeming to favour public interests over those of the farmer/landowner. There is also good reason to expect opposition to tax breaks for allotment gardens to be voiced by some city dwellers as well, especially aspiring but frustrated home-buyers, given that further constraints on the supply of developable land in Urbanisation Promotion Areas would only serve to put further upward pressure on land prices in residential areas.

It was partly in anticipation of these difficulties that proponents of an expansion in the supply of allotments in Japan adopted a strategy from the late 1980s onwards which sought to take advantage both of the politics of agricultural protection, by promoting allotments as a means of maintaining the fertility of under-utilised agricultural land, and of the interorganisational politics between the agencies responsible for agricultural and planning policies, by advocating the use for allotments of land otherwise strictly reserved for agriculture under agricultural land zoning laws, and tapping into the public funds already available to support the farming sector as a means to finance the infrastructure that allotment sites require (Azuma, 1991). It was certainly intended that the new allotment laws of 1989 and 1990 would generate an expansion in the supply of allotment gardens in and around Japanese cities, but in practice these laws have been most effective in remote rural areas, where farmers lack a viable alternative to making land available for this purpose, and it is in rural areas that most of the contemporary models of good practice have been established, rather than in urban areas as in Britain.

On the other hand, the strident defence of 'open' countryside in Britain exemplified by the strength of support for the Metropolitan Green Belt translates badly into the Japanese context, where ex-urban land-use patterns are frequently of the mixed *desakota* type so characteristic of much of East Asia (McGee, 1989). And besides, the Japanese agricultural landscape has traditionally been full of people, unlike the post-enclosure rural landscapes of urbanised Britain. Attempts to promote ex-urban allotments in Urbanisation Control Areas are therefore far more likely to attract sympathetic support from politicians, landowners and the public in Japan than in contemporary Britain, Howard's 'Garden Cities' model notwithstanding. The disadvantage of this solution, in environmental terms, is the increased travel involved in visiting the allotment site, given that the land most likely to be made available for vegetable cultivation is that formerly occupied by dry fields or uneconomically small paddy fields in upland areas. A compromise worth exploring might be to convert land closer to the city into 'paddy field allotments' (*suiden kuraingaruten*), allotments devoted solely to rice production, and thus requiring fewer visits from users over the course of the year. In historical terms paddy rice fields have long supported a high population density in Japan on a sustainable basis, particularly when combined with woodlands on adjacent high ground as a source of fuel and green manures. In addition to their advantages measured by practicality and sustainability, therefore, paddy field allotments could be promoted by exploiting the strong sentimental appeal of Japanese rural traditions.

9.4 Relationships between landlords and tenants

In principle, the relationship between the allotment gardener as tenant and the local authority or private landowner as landlord is governed by the terms of the rental or use agreement, the content of which is constrained by relevant legislation which may or may not give the landlord room for discretionary content as well. In Britain, for example, rental agreements typically require the land to be used predominantly for the cultivation of food crops, specify the period within which the land must be brought into full cultivation, and set out the circumstances under which rents must be paid and notice to quit may be given, in language tailored to the requirements of the Allotments Acts. Discretionary elements include rules over such things as whether fruit trees are permitted and the colour and dimensions of sheds.

Whatever the details of the agreement, however, and notwithstanding the fact that rental agreements are freely entered into, they do remain one of many potential sources of tension between landlord and tenant, due to the difficulties of policing agreements when tenants develop an affection for the land and a deep sense of 'ownership' which transcends legalities and invest the plot with their own creative energies and individual conceptions of the way an allotment garden should be cultivated and plants cared for. Another source of tension arises from the way other people's plots are cultivated – or not cultivated as the case may be, and the effort that landlords put into the maintenance of vacant plots and public areas that lie outside the responsibilities laid down by individual tenancies. When handled well, through a genuinely participatory and holistic regime of site management and community relations, differences over details such as this can help to deepen the appreciation on both sides of the importance of having rules and the need to interpret those rules with broader consequences in mind. A well-structured scheme for investigating cases of non-cultivation, and negotiating a resolution which takes into account the plotholder's individual circumstances, for example, is more likely to be accepted as fair by a tenant in difficulty than an unheralded disciplinary notice from the local authority's legal department. Schemes such as this are possible under devolved management regimes (see next section) where allotment societies are responsible for agreeing and implementing management policies (see, for example, Dartford Road Allotments Association, 1998), but are otherwise far too demanding of officer time to be a practical solution for most local authorities.

By far the greatest source of tension, however, lies in the absence of any basis for a relationship of trust between landlord and tenant, under circumstances where the tenant is aware of the implications of the land market, and has no guarantee that the landlord will not give in to pressures for development, whatever the consequences for sustainability and without reference to the wishes of individual allotment gardeners. Where the landowner (if not the immediate landlord) is a private individual, as in the case of most Japanese sites, plotholders are in a weak position, and have little choice but to adjust their own behaviour to the rules, but where the landlord is the local authority, the option is open for plotholders to complain about poor service from 'their' council, an avenue which can lead easily to a form of rentierism. In the face of unreasonable complaints, unreasonably phrased, and rents which often do not cover the landlord's operating costs, let alone provide a reasonable rate of return on the land relative to other (and more deserving) uses, councils may be forgiven the temptation to turn a deaf ear to complaints – and thereby inflame matters further, to the point where relations are conducted by megaphone. These are not circumstances under which a local authority is likely to adopt a positive strategy to promote allotment gardening; rather, it may prefer to look for ways to abandon its involvement in the provision of allotments, including 'benign' neglect and failure to advertise vacancies. Allegations to this effect were made to the recent parliamentary inquiry, and led the government to introduce the new requirement discussed earlier (see Section 9.2). That local authorities must demonstrate that they have 'actively promoted' their allotments before any disposals of statutory land will be approved.

The chances of a local authority withdrawing active support for allotments depend in part on the underlying value of the land and pressures for development, which are higher in the southeast of England than in many northern cities, and are accentuated by urban containment policies which require local authority planners to concentrate their search for new housing land on 'brownfield' sites within existing urban areas (see Section 9.3). Also relevant is the political willingness of the local authority to maintain support for its own reasons, including (in wealthy suburbs) the desire to prevent any further residential development. Not all local authorities find themselves in a state of undeclared war with their tenants. Allotment strategies such as that proposed for Bristol strike a careful and overt balance between development opportunities and site improvements based on well-informed public consultation exercises (Bristol City Council, 1998). And allotment associations, particularly those which accept a degree of responsibility for the management of specific sites, can play a useful role in improving the flow of information between local authorities and their tenants. Nevertheless, even the briefest inspection of allotment news items in the British popular gardening press reveals how poor relations between plotholders and their landlords can become, an impression readily confirmed by the evidence offered to the recent parliamentary inquiry.

The potential contribution of the new municipal environmentalism to the resolution of problems arising from the landlord–tenant relationship is that it opens up a new avenue for communication between plotholders and the local authority which does not depend on the legalities of that relationship, and in the success of which both the local authority and the allotment gardeners have a vested interest. Shared interests are a rational basis for trust, and thus for allotment gardeners to become 'trusted partners' in delivering local sustainable development.

At a superficial level, this partnership may amount to little more than an opportunity for some cheap green relabelling by the local authority, but there are greater rewards on offer. Crouch and Ward note that 'The most remarkable result of the cultural changes of the post-war years is the sheer diversity of today's allotment-holders' (Crouch and Ward, 1997: 80). In taking advantage of Local Agenda 21 by, for example, receiving waste materials for recycling, allotment gardeners become active participants in environmental activities which extend beyond the allotment into the broader community, bringing into the Local Agenda 21 process a wide variety of ordinary people whose personal concerns (beyond gardening) are likely to range across many local environmental issues and to whom Local Agenda 21 can give a legitimate 'voice'. As Goodwin (1998) points out, many areas of local environmental action are dominated by professional discourses, fuelled by lottery cash and led by paid 'experts', which leave no space for the expression or validation of local environmental values. In the next section, we address the 'problem' of weak user organisations among allotment gardeners at anything above the very local level; in the present context, however, this weakness is a source of strength, for it is difficult to detect any 'professional' discourse on allotments which demonstrably over-rides preoccupations with local issues. Indeed, the last serious attempt to impose a 'professional' image on allotments by reinventing them as 'leisure gardens' in the image of the orderly German *kleingarten*, in line with the recommendations of Professor Harry Thorpe and his Committee (Thorpe, 1975), largely foundered on a combination of hostility and indifference amongst ordinary allotment holders, who remained attached to the traditional vernacular landscape of the allotment (Crouch, 1989). It is essential, of course, that advocates of participation in sustainable development initiatives do not fall into the same trap of imposing an exclusive – and exclusionary – vision of their own; Thompson's work on 'security enhancement' demonstrates the importance of a diversity of views and strategies if a long-term relationship with the environment is to be maintained, no matter how circumstances change (Thompson, 1997).

Turning to the Japanese case, we noted earlier that plotholders are in a weaker position when the landowner is a private individual, and indeed, the fact that terms of rental agreements for Japanese allotments tend to be very restrictive, particularly as regards the length of tenancy, might be judged essential if land is to be made available for urban allotments in the first place. Nevertheless, the argument that local authorities have a vested interest in cooperating with allotment gardeners in seeking to achieve the goal of sustainable development holds true for Japan as well as for Britain. The pay-off for allotment gardeners is more likely to come in a different and indirect way, however, through a higher level of interest amongst local authorities in encouraging farmers to make land available (and keep it available) for use as allotments, and in promoting methods of site management and use which maximise environmental benefits. Participation in Local Agenda 21 is a way to reduce the costs of establishing and operating an allotment site (Wiltshire and Azuma, 2000), and these savings should also appeal to site owners and allotment gardeners in Japanese urban areas. Where the mode of participation involves an input of time and effort by the individual plotholder, through for example the construction of a shed using recycled materials, then there are grounds to expect the terms of the rental agreement either to be softened or interpreted more leniently, but it is also possible to conceive of linkages developing within a Local Agenda 21 framework which do not involve plotholders, such as the provision of subsidised materials to a site owner/operator for site improvement works, which would have no effect on the operation of the landlord/tenant relationship.

9.5 Plotholder organisations

In their treatment of the theory and practice of citizen participation in local government in Britain, Burns *et al.* make explicit reference to the plotholder organisation as an ideal:

> Consider an allotments society, for example. Its membership will typically be drawn from allotment holders who share a particular site and who are therefore in a number of ways dependent on one another. The fact that most membership organisations are built around shared interests or identities does not mean that they have to be exclusive ... Such organisations therefore belong to their membership in a tangible and concrete way [and] ... while they sometimes provide a means for political participation, they are nearly always also engaged in providing services or running activities for their own membership. Such organisations, along with the more informal end of the voluntary sector, constitute the bedrock of civil society and participatory democracy.
>
> (Burns, *et al.*, 1994: 274)

From a local authority's perspective, an allotment society like this must sound like the ideal 'trusted partner' in a sustainable development initiative, while for plotholders, the society can act as a focus for their broader sense of 'ownership' of the allotment site. During the 1990s, the pressure on local authority budgets in Britain has encouraged a trend towards varying degrees of 'devolved management' (Wiltshire, 1998b), under which allotment societies assume an agreed share of the responsibility for site management, including in some cases actual responsibility for the issuance and enforcement of rental agreements. Devolved management can be interpreted as a means for local authorities to capitalise on the plotholders' sense of ownership, by substituting voluntary effort for costly council-provided services. In a more positive sense, however, the trend towards devolved management is very much in line with the emphasis on 'empowerment through the diffusion of responsibilities and resources to local levels' which Munton and Collins (1998: 346) identify as essential to establishing the political legitimacy of sustainable development, and compatible with the current drive for 'best value' in local government.

Devolved management can give a participating allotment society an element of control over recruitment and the external image of the site, enhancing the site's popularity and hence the political pressure which can be exerted to protect it from the pressures of the urban land market. Devolved management can also be more sensitive to the need to police compliance with the terms of rental agreements in a manner that is acceptable to the majority of plotholders, since managers are directly accountable to the plotholders themselves, a factor which can help reduce the irritations which normally arise from landlord–tenant relations. Much depends, however, on whether the allotment society has the vision, confidence and capacity to accept a higher level of responsibility for the site.

When the objective of the local authority is purely to offload responsibilities, then there is little incentive for it to invest in the capacity of plotholder organisations to manage a site's affairs, and indeed the local authority has a vested interest in seeing devolved management fail – as another excuse to sell the land off. Which is not to say that a society will shy away from devolved management under these circumstances: there is nothing like the threat of closure to get plotholders organised. But when devolved management is combined with the promotion of sustainable development, an incentive is created for the local authority to assist wherever it can in building up the capacities of site managers, and devolved management is thus more likely to succeed. The chances of success also depend, however, on whether the membership of the society includes people who are responsive to the notion of sustainable development, and who can provide sustained leadership in this direction, but who can also maintain cohesion within the society by respecting alternative voices.

At a higher level, plotholder organisations at the regional and national level have the potential to influence allotment legislation, strategic planning policies and government attitudes towards allotments, and to reinforce the efforts of local societies and individual plotholders to defend allotment sites in urban areas. In practice, the main organisation in Britain – the National Society of Allotment and Leisure Gardeners (NSALG) and its regional divisions – has long been severely weakened by recurrent and fractious internal disputes and by the unwillingness of local societies to provide an adequate level of funding to support activities which are not of immediate and obvious benefit to their members: strong localism is so easily wedded to extreme parochialism. The NSALG now finds itself in an interesting position. The 1998 Parliamentary Inquiry for which it lobbied drew from the government a commitment to work with the Local Government Association (LGA) to define and advocate a best practice regime for allotment management, and the deliberations of the working party which has advised the LGA on this regime have leaned towards a strong endorsement of participation in Local Agenda 21 initiatives, an endorsement which is closely aligned with the government's own position that allotment issues are best resolved locally and through initiatives such as this (House of Commons, 1998a). The challenge for the NSALG is to rise above its own internal factional politics and take a constructive role in the diffusion and implementation of the best practice regime, not just because of any merits that the regime may have, but also because a successful effort in this direction will enhance the probability that the NSALG's voice will be influential in future political debates over the status of allotments. In this respect, the high profile given to Local Agenda 21 in recent issues of the NSALG's journal, the *Allotment and Leisure Gardener*, is a hopeful sign.

In Japan, however, the articulation of plotholder concerns at site, regional and national levels is far weaker than in Britain. Japanese tenancy agreements usually have a duration of around one year, which matches the period of notice built into many British agreements. The key difference, however, is that while in Britain there is a presumption that tenancies can continue indefinitely if the terms are otherwise adhered to and in the absence of an alternative use for the site, in Japan there is no such presumption. Even if a tenant is successful in securing a plot for a second year, it may well be a different plot on the same site. In part, this insecurity of tenure is a reflection of the overriding importance of encouraging landowners to make land available which has already been alluded to above. But where public funding has been employed, it also can reflect the desire of the local authority to counter the potential criticism that it is inappropriate to grant exclusive rights to the use of a public facility on anything other than a very short-term basis (Azuma, 1991: 53–5). As a result, it is difficult for Japanese allotment gardeners, particularly in urban areas, to develop anything like the sense of ownership which comes from prolonged cultivation of a specific plot of land and thus the motivation to organise collectively with others to defend it. This does not mean that Japanese allotment gardeners are insensitive to the threats which overhang their plots: one site manager in Tokyo's Setagaya Ward, for example, complains that the hardest part of his job is having to explain the reasons for this underlying insecurity to individual plotholders (Anon., 1996). The problem is the lack of an effective means to articulate such concerns as they materialise. And while many sites incorporate 'club houses' to facilitate social events and relaxation, there is a desire on the part of many landowners not to encourage the development of allotment societies that could give plotholders an effective voice in the management – and eventual disposal – of the site. Local organisation is therefore sparse and politically weak, and without effective local organisation there is nothing to support a Japanese equivalent of the NSALG at the national level.

A solution to this problem may lie in the formation of legally defined user associations at the municipal level as advocated above, which could draw strength not only from involvement in ensuring the supply of adequate quantities of land to satisfy the needs of users, but also from engaging in an organised and coherent way with municipal environmental agendas. These associations could then federate with advantage to influence national legislation and political attitudes toward allotment gardening. In effect, the resulting national body would more closely resemble the British Henry Doubleday Research Association (HDRA) or the Soil Association (which both support organic gardening) in being defined by an interest in a way of gardening rather than in the defence of particular geographical sites. This need not be a second-best solution: it could certainly be argued that in recent years the HDRA and Soil Association have been as effective in promoting the interests of allotment gardening at the national level in the United Kingdom as any other bodies.

9.6 Conclusion

The analysis presented in this chapter suggests that urban plotholders and plotholder organisations can gain significant political advantages by aligning themselves with municipal 'sustainable development' initiatives, advantages which strengthen their position in the struggle to obtain and retain land for allotments in urban areas. Land market pressures can be deflected by increasing the popularity and value of allotment gardening to the community. Greater protection for allotments can be sought from within the land-use planning system. The tensions in the landlord–tenant relationship which can make allotment gardeners unpopular with local authorities can be ameliorated. And allotment societies can operate more effectively in their members' interests, particularly if they also accept devolved management. In Britain these advantages seem reasonably achievable, given the overt support for Local Agenda 21 proclaimed by governments at all levels, the close involvement of local authorities in the provision of land for allotments, and the strong tradition of plotholder organisation at site level. Japanese plotholders face a much harder task: private landowners dominate provision, and plotholder organisations are weaker. We have argued that intermediate plotholder organisations operating at the municipal level could help promote allotment gardening and assist Japanese local authorities in the attainment of sustainable development objectives. There is also one other compromise open to Japanese plotholders, however, a geographical compromise in which allotments are displaced beyond the immediate suburbs to ex-urban agricultural areas in which urbanisation pressures are legally controlled. While less acceptable than immediate local food production on environmental grounds, given the additional travel involved, this may yet prove the least worst alternative – and one which allows many of the other benefits of the sustainable development agenda to be realised.

Note

1   The term 'allotment' has been used throughout this chapter as a convenient shorthand for the Japanese *shimin noen* although many of the newer Japanese allotment sites are much closer to *kleingarten* in design. The first *shimin noen* to be founded by a local authority was established in Kyoto in 1925, and was actually based on the British model (Kinoshima, 1994). A set of illustrative images of British allotments and Japanese *shimin noen* can be found at http://www.btinternet.com/~richard.wiltshire/le1.htm

References

Anon. 1996. Toshi noen no yukue [Which way next for urban allotments?]. *BIO-City* **9**, 61.

Aoki, S. 1996: Chiho ni okeru kuraingaruten no kanosei: Nihon-gata kuraingaruten no genkyo to hatten hoko [The potential for kleingarten in the provinces: current situation and development trends of Japanese-style kleingartens]. *BIO-City* **9**, 38–43.

Azuma, R. 1991: *Ekorojikaru raifu: Midori to hito ga fureau shimin noen* [Ecological life: allotment gardens putting people in touch with nature]. Tokyo: Ie no Hikari Kyokai.

Azuma, R. 1998: Toshi jumin ni yoru nochi no rekurieeshiyonteki riyo no kanosei: nochi no tamenteki riyo seisaku no Ohnichi hikaku [The potential for recreational use of agricultural land by urban residents: a comparison of policies to promote multiple use of agricultural land in Europe and Japan]. *Nogyo Mondai Kenkyu* **34**(3), 32–9.

Bristol City Council 1998: *Living Bristol allotment strategy* (draft document). Bristol: Bristol City Council.

Burns, D., Hambleton, R. and Hoggett, P. 1994: *The politics of decentralisation: revitalising local democracy.* London: Macmillan.

Court of Appeal 1996: *R v Secretary of State for the Environment, ex parte Gosforth Allotments and Gardens Association.* 43 EG 153. London: Court of Appeal.

Crouch, D. 1989: The allotment, landscape and locality: ways of seeing landscape and culture. *Area* **21**(3), 261–7.

Crouch, D. 1997: *English allotments survey: report of the joint survey of allotments in England.* Corby: National Society of Allotment and Leisure Gardeners and Anglia Polytechnic University.

Crouch, D. and Ward, C. 1997: *The allotment: its landscape and culture.* 3rd edition. Nottingham: Five Leaves Publications.

Dartford Road Allotments Association 1998: *Management policies.* Dartford: Dartford Road Allotments Association, mimeo. (http://www.btinternet.com/~richard.wiltshire/draa4h.htm).

Department of the Environment Transport and the Regions 1999: *Revision of planning policy guidance note 3 housing: public consulation draft.* London: Department of the Environment Transport and the Regions.

Flack, K. 1999: Writing to MPs. *Allotment and Leisure Gardener* **2**, 18.

Garnett, T. 1996: *Growing food in cities.* London: NFA/Safe Alliance.

Goodwin, P. 1998: 'Hired hands' or 'local voices': understandings and experience of local participation in conservation. *Transactions, Institute of British Geographers* NS **23**(4), 481–99.

Hall, P. and Ward, C. 1998: *Sociable cities: the legacy of Ebenezer Howard.* Chichester: John Wiley & Sons.

Hams, T. 1997: Was UNGASS all hot air? *EG: Local Environment News* **3**(7), 16–18.

House of Commons, Environment Transport and Regional Affairs Committee 1998a: *The future for allotments: minutes of evidence.* HC560-iii, 67–75. London: The Stationery Office.

House of Commons, Environment Transport and Regional Affairs Committee 1998b: *The future for allotments: fifth report of the House of Commons Environment, Transport and Regional Affairs Committee*. Volume I. HC560-I. London: The Stationery Office.

Kinoshima, H. 1994: Nihon ni okeru saisho no shimin noen [The first community garden in Japan]. *Japanese Journal of Agricultural Education* **25**(2), 101–8.

Kokudocho 1998: *21-seiki no kokudo no gurando dezain* [Grand design for national land use in Japan in the 21st century]. Tokyo: Kokudocho [National Land Agency].

McGee, T.G. 1989: Urbanisasi or kotadesasi? Evolving patterns of urbanization in Asia. In Costa, F.J., Dutt, A.K., Ma, L.J.C. and Noble, A.G. (eds), *Urbanization in Asia: spatial dimensions and policy issues*. Honolulu: University of Hawaii Press, 93–108.

Munton, R. 1997: Engaging sustainable development: some observations on progress in the UK. *Progress in Human Geography* **21**(2), 147–63.

Munton, R. and Collins K. 1998: Government strategies for sustainable development. *Geography* **83**(4), 346–57.

Steele, J. 1999: Agenda 21. *Allotment and Leisure Gardener* **1**, 27–8.

Tashiro, Y. 1995: Toshi nogyo to tochi mondai [Urban agriculture and the land problem]. *Toshi Mondai* **86**(12), 17–28.

Thompson, M. 1997: Security and solidarity: an anti-reductionist framework for thinking about the relationship between us and the rest of nature. *Geographical Journal* **163**(2), 141–9.

Thorpe, H. 1975: The homely allotment: from rural dole to urban amenity: a neglected aspect of urban land use. *Geography* **268**, 169–83.

Wiltshire, R. 1998a: *Allotments in Local Agenda 21: a brief prepared for the Local Government Association's working group on a best practice regime for allotments*. Dartford: QED Allotments Group, mimeo. (http://www.btinternet.com/~richard.wiltshire/lga3.htm).

Wiltshire, R. 1998b: *Devolved management for allotments: a brief prepared for the Local Government Association's working group on a best practice regime for allotments*. Dartford: QED Allotments Group, mimeo. (http://www.btinternet.com/~richard.wiltshire/lga4.htm).

Wiltshire, R. and Azuma, R. 2000: Rewriting the plot: sustaining allotments in Britain and Japan. *Local Environment* **5**(2), 139–51.

10

Environmental refugees

The origins of a construct

Patricia L. Saunders

10.1 Introduction

The 1999 *World Disasters Report* of the International Federation of Red Cross and Red Crescent Societies (IFRC, 1999) claims that there were 25 million 'environmental refugees' in 1998 – 53 per cent of all refugees. The source is a report for The Climate Institute by Norman Myers, who defines 'environmental refugees' as migrants who have sought sustenance elsewhere because they

> can no longer gain a secure livelihood in their traditional homelands because of environmental factors of unusual scope, notably drought, desertification, deforestation, soil erosion, water shortage and climate change, also natural disasters such as cyclones, storm surges and floods.
> (Myers and Kent, 1995: 18–19)

According to the IFRC, the environment 'has joined politics and economics as a major force behind migration'. Myers forecasts that the number of 'environmental refugees' will double by 2010 and if 'global warming' causes a rise in sea level their numbers could reach 150 million by 2050, far outnumbering refugees as traditionally defined. Industrialised countries have a choice: 'export the wherewithal for sustainable development for communities at risk – or import growing numbers of environmental refugees' (ibid.: 13).

10.1.1 Key documents

Myers and others (Ramlogan, 1996; Jacobson, 1988) believe the construct 'environmental refugees' to have originated in a booklet by Essam El-Hinnawi (1985) for the United Nations Environment Programme. Others (Kibreab, 1997; Black, 1998) acknowledge an earlier report for Earthscan by Timberlake and Tinker (1984). However, although the El-Hinnawi study is indeed the first to weave together the construct's many strands, the term 'ecological displaced persons' was employed in an environmental classic, *Road to Survival*, by William Vogt (1949), and the concept has Malthusian antecedents. This chapter analyses its history from Malthus, through 30 'key documents', to its construction in the late 1980s and concludes that it is Lester Brown and the Worldwatch Institute that should be identified as its true originator. It then discusses the implications of these origins for the current debate on the usefulness of the construct in analysis and policy-making, suggests areas for further research and draws preliminary conclusions.

10.1.2 Methodology

This analysis is founded on document-based research. The 30 'key documents' which emerged from a wide-ranging examination of the literature and the relationship between them and the principal components of the construct are modelled in Figure 10.1. The bibliography lists those referenced in this chapter from among the many more consulted. Most were known to the author through her work in the British NGO community over the past 20 years, building links between development, environment and peace movements. Worldwatch and Earthscan publications were systematically reviewed. Norman Myers supplied copies of his publications. The Refugee Studies Centre at Oxford University supplied material from its documentation centre. Others references were located by systematically tracing sources cited in these and other documents found in library, BIDS and Internet searches. The author would be grateful to have any sources that were none the less overlooked drawn to her attention.

10.1.3 A note on terminology

My practice is to refer throughout to *migrants* or *displaced persons* and to reserve the word *refugee* for migrants who satisfy the legal definition employed by the United Nations High Commission for Refugees (UNHCR). Where I use a term in a way which differs from this usage I will employ single quotation marks, hence 'environmental refugees'. Where I am quoting a source that uses the terms in a different way, I draw attention to this in the traditional manner [*sic*].

10.2 Origins

The construct 'environmental refugees' is complex. Tracing its origins is difficult, because it depends upon most of the other elements in the 'environmental orthodoxy' (cf. Leach and Mearns, 1996). This section will trace this history via a chronological description of the findings from the 'key documents' supplemented with observations from supportive and contemporary material.

10.2.1 Malthus (1798, 1826, 1830)

10.2.1.1 Checks to population

All 'key documents' are Malthusian in their emphasis on population growth as the root cause of forced migration. Malthus (1798, 1826, 1830) believed that *if unchecked*, population could double every 25 years, growing geometrically. Food production, even if all land were farmed by the most enlightened methods, could only grow arithmetically. It was evident, therefore, that population growth was being checked. Those 'preventative' checks which a clergyman at the turn of the nineteenth century could advocate, namely, celibacy and the postponement of marriage, were ineffective, in part because the English Poor Laws

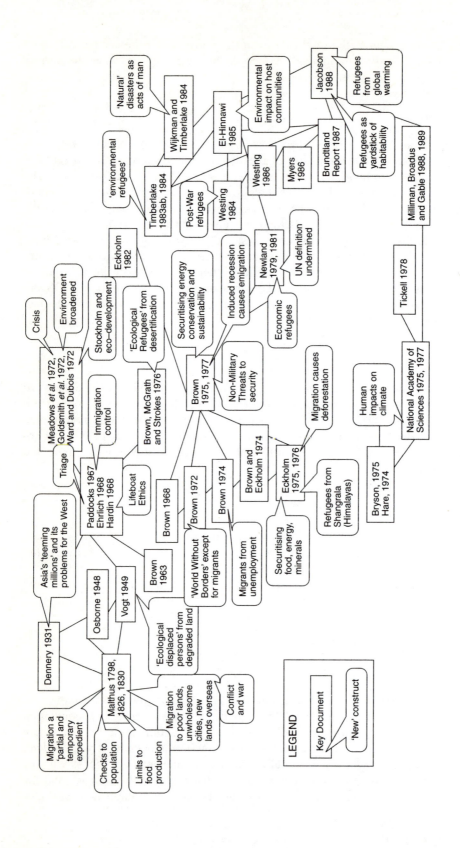

Figure 10.1 Relationship between key texts and 'new' elements of the construct 'environmental refugees'

prevented the poor from suffering the full consequences of their excessive fecundity and thus inhibited the requisite forethought. Experience showed that the 'positive' checks – diseases, epidemics, wars, infanticide, plague and famine – had operated over time and throughout the world to keep population at or near the means of subsistence. Poverty was therefore inevitable and benefits (*sic*) from the operation of the positive checks would be short-lived. Thus:

> the traces of the most destructive famines in China and Indostan are by all accounts very soon obliterated. It is very much to be doubted whether Turkey or Egypt are upon an average much less populous for the plagues that periodically lay them waste ... The most tremendous convulsions of nature, such as volcanic eruptions and earthquakes, if they do not happen so frequently as to drive away the inhabitants, or to destroy their spirit of industry, have but a trifling effect on the population of any state.
>
> (1798: 107–8).

10.2.1.2 Limits to the expansion of agriculture

Malthus did not share his contemporaries' optimism regarding the potential for agricultural innovation. He was a pioneer political economist, the first to articulate the law of diminishing returns, arguing that yields would 'after a short time, and independently of new inventions, be constantly decreasing till, in no very long period, the exertions of an additional labourer would not produce his own sustenance' (1830: 243). Additions of capital for drainage, dressing or machinery would also be subject to diminishing returns either because of the 'comparative exhaustion of the soil' or because returns to labour or capital were insufficient (ibid.: 247). Uncultivated land was probably infertile and would require 'laborious effort' for a small increment. *New* land overseas could be settled but would eventually reach the same point of diminishing returns since what applied to a single farm must be true of 'an extensive territory or the whole earth' (ibid.: 244). Eventually population would increase up to the level of subsistence unleashing the unavoidable – and divinely ordained – positive checks.

10.2.1.3 Migration a 'partial and temporary expedient'

Malthus observed two ways in which the operation of the positive checks was postponed. In Switzerland, when mountainous pastures

> have been once fully stocked with cattle, little more can be done; and if there be neither emigration to take off the superabundant numbers, nor manufacturers wherewith to purchase an additional quantity of food, the deaths must equal the births.
>
> (1830: 261)

This 'emigration to take off superabundant numbers' was seen as the traditional method employed by shepherds in primitive societies since Lot parted from Abraham. In civilised countries it operated to delay the operation of the positive checks by forcing migration to 'unwholesome cities', poor land, or the colonies. However, emigration as a solution was at best 'a partial and temporary expedient' (1826, vol. 2: 36). Disease, epidemics and plague were endemic in cities because of crowding; poor lands produced little additional food and migration to the colonies was risky, especially for pioneers, and involved conquest and the subjugation of native peoples. It was also expensive since the poor would need assisted passage and military protection. Emigration to America had enabled the opening up of vast new productive lands, but freed from the positive checks, population was doubling every 25 years, and would soon exceed food production. Furthermore, much land overseas 'has a great barrenness upon it'. Thus, although emigration could offer relief in the short term and offered benefits to both sending and receiving regions, eventually population would reach the level of subsistence, leading to poverty and the inevitable positive checks.

10.2.2 Dennery (1931)

10.2.2.1 Asia's 'teeming millions' and its problems for the West

Dennery claims that 'appalling visions of a sudden eruption of Asiatic peoples on to the white man's country have haunted the minds of the West since the days of Attila and Genghis Khan' (Dennery, 1931: 229). This echoes Malthus who attributed the collapse of the Western Empire to a 'want of subsistence' among the Huns (1798: 83). Dennery describes the way emigration from China, Japan and India relieves over-population. Emigration is an 'economic necessity' for India. However, although others fear the 'yellow peril', he does not regard emigration as an immediate threat since 'Overwhelming numbers of destitute, unemployed and unskilled, are a source of exhaustion, rather than strength for a country' (1931: 239). Should these nations overcome their present disorder, however, 'who can foresee the perils which a peace-loving world would have to endure from these hostile masses, so densely packed, which strive to break down the barriers which imprison them' (ibid.). Initially, most migration will be to neighbouring Asian countries. However, resentment against the West, like that occasioned by American barriers to Japanese immigration, may unite them in future. 'What force, then, will be able to retain the masses of the east and prevent them from seeking outside their own Continent the resources which they must possess if they are to live?' (ibid.: 243).

10.2.3 Osborn (1948), Vogt (1949)

10.2.3.1 Efforts to expand food production are destroying the land

Malthus does not examine the effect of efforts to increase yields beyond the point where diminishing yields commence. However, this theme pervades American literature in the aftermath of the 1930s' dust bowl. Steinbeck's Okies are frequently described as fleeing human-caused soil erosion (Osborn, 1948) and soil degradation, deforestation and desiccation are central themes in Jacks and Whyte's agricultural surveys (1938, 1939) which influenced the understanding of processes of soil erosion world-wide, especially in Africa (cf. Hailey, 1938). Osborn documents the way two billion people are wantonly destroying the earth's resources, eroding soils and destroying forests. In China, he argues, the 'needs of the teeming millions are being met at the expense of the future of the land', while in India man is 'ever increasing in numbers, ruining himself and the earth on which and by which he must live (1948: 86, 87).

William Vogt (1949), in his classic study of 'excessive breeding and abuse of the land', develops this analysis. As with Osborn, soil falling from the sky due to the human-caused dust bowl portends imminent disaster. We are exceeding the carrying capacity of the land. To ignore these warnings has created problems in the past (Craven, 1925) and could create a disaster that wipes out three-quarters of humanity (1949: 17). Vogt classifies land into eight natural types and a ninth that is newly-created desert and argues that the poorest five should remain uncultivated. Unfortunately, however, excessive populations in El Salvador, Haiti and the Punjab (*sic*) prevent this, since grain must be grown or man will starve. Thus though farmers innovate, their terraces or chemicals only postpone famine until the land's productive capacity has been outbred.

10.2.3.2 'Ecological displaced persons'

Vogt presents the first clear antecedent of 'environmental refugees'. Farmers fleeing eroded land, degenerated forests and overgrazed ranges are 'ecological displaced persons'. They are displaced persons:

> in a much more serious sense than the few hundred thousands in European refugee camps. They are displaced in the ecological sense. They can feed and clothe themselves, and supply food, fibers, charcoal, and wood to cities *only by destroying the land on which they live and the resources associated with it*. It is they who wreck forests, start soil erosion, exterminate wildlife, set the flood crests rolling . . . Scores of millions of them must be moved-down the eroding slopes, out of the degenerating forests, off the overgrazed ranges – if they are not to drag ever lower the living standards of their respective countries – *and the world*.
>
> (Vogt, 1949: 107, italics mine)

Note the introduction here of an important element of the environmentalists' construction, namely, that of the peasant as perpetrator of *local* environmental degradation which affects the *global* community.

10.2.4 The 1960s' environmentalists: Brown (1963, 1968); Paddock and Paddock (1967); Ehrlich (1968); Hardin (1968)

10.2.4.1 Technological innovation will buy time and allow population to stabilise

This environmental pessimism continues to pervade the American environmental literature into the 1960s despite two technological innovations, namely, contraceptives which enabled 'preventative checks' other than 'sexual restraint and the postponement of marriage' and the agricultural revolution in Mexico and Asia which promised that yields could match population growth until the latter stabilises. In addition, Boserup (1965) was writing about the positive role of population growth in stimulating technological change.

10.2.4.2 Poor countries have become dependent on the US for grain

Lester Brown (1963), then with the US Department of Agriculture (USDA), is associated with this optimism. Nevertheless he brought one disturbing development before the American foreign policy community, namely, that many poor countries which had formerly been food exporters were now net importers *primarily because of their growing populations*. Brown projected global supply and demand and predicted a disastrous shortfall by 1984.

10.2.4.3 Broadening of the word 'environmental'

A number of populist neo-Malthusians countered the technological optimism by stressing several emerging ecological problems. Carson (1962) punctured confidence in chemical fertilisers, pesticides and herbicides. Ehrlich (1968) emphasised the development of resistant pests and weeds, waterlogging and salinization from irrigation, accelerating soil erosion, falling water tables, the detrimental downstream impact of big dams, eutrophication in lakes and atmospheric oxygen depletion. When atmospheric pollution from industry and cities is added, it was alleged that human activity could significantly affect the climate. Thus by 1970, concern about the impact of over-population on soil fertility had evolved into a wide-ranging, global environmental crisis.

10.2.4.4 Triage

In *Famine 1975!* the Paddock brothers brought Brown's predicted shortfalls forward to the mid-1970s, prophesying massive famine in 'hungry nations' and 'a mounting increase of civil tensions, riots and military take-overs as the growing scarcity of food forces prices higher and higher' (Paddock and Paddock, 1967: 205). American food aid will be insufficient during this 'time of famines' and the Paddocks' response mirrors that of Malthus towards the Poor Laws. They sub-title their book *America's Decision: Who Will Survive?* arguing that the US should allocate food according to the rules of 'triage'. Countries should be divided into (a) the 'can't be saved' for whom sending food is pointless; (b) the 'walking wounded' who will be able to buy food; and (c) the 'should receive food' for whom the imbalance of food and population is only manageable if they receive aid. Libya and Venezuela are 'walking wounded' because they can buy food; Haiti, Egypt, India and East Pakistan 'can't be saved'; and The Gambia, Tunisia and West Pakistan, 'should receive aid'. Panama, the Philippines and Bolivia qualify as 'can't be saved' under the triage rules, but should be treated as exceptions due to political or strategic factors, or the presence of raw materials.

For the 'should receive aid' group, American grain will buy time to introduce family planning programmes and modernise agriculture. It will ensure the relative prosperity and economic stability of both America and the world as a whole during the 'time of famines' and help create a better world thereafter. Since Americans will need to forego meat consumption during this period, they need to be assured that triage policy will deliver their 'money's worth'. The title of the final chapter encapsulates such a commitment: 'The time of famines can be the catalyst for a period of American greatness' (Paddock and Paddock, 1967: 230).

10.2.4.5 Population and immigration control

Ehrlich, in *The Population Bomb* (1968), supports the Paddocks' recommendations, adding one rider: food aid should be limited to that which can be produced without damage to the North American ecology. In his 'cheerful' scenario for 'time of famines', he postulates a 'die back' in the *un*developed countries in which 500 million people, one seventh of world population, die from famine, disease and local warfare. A decade later, when the 'die back' is over, a broad plan can be introduced to stabilise world population at 2 billion by 2025 and 1.5 billion by 2100 (Ehrlich, 1968: 44). The US and other developed countries, through the United Nations, can then create 'area rehabilitation' programmes whose bedrock is 'population control, *necessarily including migration control to prevent swamping of aided* *areas by the less fortunate'* (Ehrlich, 1968: 101, italics mine). Educational programmes via satellite TV should combine 'straight' programmes and 'cleverly devised entertainments', emphasising the prospect of affluence rather than threat of starvation and warning that food supplies are conditional on progress in family planning and food self-sufficiency (ibid.: 102).

10.2.4.6 Lifeboat ethics

The success of high-yielding grains and extensive irrigation projects in West Pakistan had encouraged the Paddocks and Ehrlich to exclude it from the 'can't be saved' category to which they consigned the remainder of South Asia. For Hardin (1968, 1972), however, 'the population problem has no technical solution'. His two metaphors, the 'Tragedy of the Commons' and Planet Earth as an overcrowded lifeboat, attempt to capture the ethical challenge presented by overpopulation. The lifeboat is sinking. Adding more people will clearly cause it to capsize. Migration off-planet is no solution. Similarly, those with grazing rights on an English commons will overstock since it is communally owned. Each commoner will pursue his own self-interest, adding livestock until the carrying capacity of the common has been exceeded. Hardin argues that private ownership could solve this problem but was not an option for air and water. Nor was the right to reproduce. 'To couple the concept of freedom to breed with the belief that everyone born has an equal right to the commons is to lock the world into a tragic course of action' (Hardin, 1968: 258).

10.2.5 Brown (1972)

10.2.5.1 Interdependence and a truly transnational world

Lester Brown moved to the Overseas Development Council (ODC) in 1967, 'an independent non-profit organization established to increase American understanding of the economic and social problems confronting developing countries and of the importance of these countries in an increasingly interdependent world' (Howe, 1974: 212). The ODC had close connections with the Council for Foreign Relations and the influential journal *Foreign Affairs* and was clearly of significance within the Atlanticist foreign policy community.

Among Brown's publications are a paper for *Foreign Affairs* on the agricultural revolution in Asia (1968) and a book, *Seeds of Change* (1970). Both express continued optimism about the potential for the new hybrid seeds and advocate an active role for American aid which, he argues had successfully enabled India to survive the poor monsoons of 1965–6. The USAID 'short-tether' policy, whereby 'food-aid agreements are of short duration and renewal depends on local effort and performance', had obliged India, Pakistan and the Philippines to transform their agriculture (1968: 689). He does not anticipate that the 1970s will be a 'time of famines' but rather a period for eradication of hunger, expanding employment and trade confrontation (1970).

10.2.5.2 A world without borders (except for migrants)

In *World Without Borders* (1972) Brown envisages a truly unified, transnational world to facilitate economic interdependence, heal the East–West divide and enable the transfer of resources from the military to agricultural development and poverty alleviation. It is a blueprint for globalisation. Developing countries must *sacrifice sovereignty*. In exchange, they will obtain access to technology, energy supplies, raw materials and foreign markets. 'If West Germany and Belgium recognize that they are anachronisms as independent economic entities, then the Philippines, Ghana, Colombia and scores of other developing countries whose economies are far smaller must eventually take note as they strive to modernize' (ibid.: 188). New international infrastructure is required to facilitate this integration, including a much stronger UN, a global environmental agency, an international currency and the replacement of *multinational* (MNCs) with truly *transnational* corporations (TNCs). Regional economic groupings are encouraged.

A *World Without Borders*, according to orthodox economic theory, should enable free movement of capital, technology, resources and labour. However, Brown's enthusiasm for the market does not extend to immigration. He identifies three ways to resolve the imbalance between labour shortages in Europe and Japan and high unemployment in poor countries: (a) import labour into rich countries; (b) invest in labour-intensive activities abroad; or (c) import labour-intensive products such as textiles or fruit. His recommendations focus on the latter two (1972: 235).

The demographic pressures which forced 'marginal men' to exchange rural unemployment for social disintegration, poverty and extreme crowding, e.g. in Calcutta and Bangladesh, encouraged migration from more to less densely populated countries. Even Americans are migrating to Canada to escape social disintegration and recover personal security. Political repression is also creating the desire to migrate (e.g. from East Germany). Legislation in Australia and Britain is clearly designed to restrict, if not prohibit, such immigration. 'Though clearly racist in its thrust, [the new British immigration bill] nonetheless reflects increasing sensitivity to crowding' (ibid.: 139). 'In a world in which man is becoming increasingly mobile, these pressures to emigrate could create an entirely new source of difficulties in international political relationships' (ibid.: 140).

10.2.6　Limits to Growth, A Blueprint for Survival and Only One Earth (1972)

10.2.6.1　*Eco-development as a response to a global crisis*

The early 1970s witnessed significant changes in the geopolitical context of this debate. Three books published before the United Nations Conference on the Human Environment in Stockholm in June 1972 reflected these changes. *Limits to Growth* (Meadows *et al.*, 1972) and *A Blueprint for Survival* (Goldsmith *et al.*, 1972) were the most influential; the more balanced *Only One Earth* (Ward and Dubos, 1972) less so. All stressed the threat to global survival of a deteriorating environment and the necessity for rich countries to limit their growth and poor countries to limit their population, in order to survive within the constraints imposed by a finite biosphere. *Limits to Growth* substituted concepts of limits for Malthus' checks, exponential curves for his geometric ones, and the goal of an equilibrium society for one in which large numbers are trapped in perpetual poverty. *Blueprint's* vision for a stable society included immigration control and a halt to rural–urban migration in poor countries. *Only One Earth* expressed concern, *inter alia*, about the increasing numbers who were being displaced by large dams and other development projects. The Stockholm conference brought environment and development activists together, popularised the construct eco-development and led to the establishment of the United Nations Environment Programme (UNEP) the following year.

10.2.7 Lester Brown (1974) and Brown with Eckholm (1974)

10.2.7.1 Securitising food, energy, minerals

Two books, *In the Human Interest* (Brown, 1974) and *By Bread Alone* (Brown and Eckholm, 1974), illustrate the Worldwatch interpretation of the global economic problems in the early 1970s. Prices of all commodities were rising due to the imbalance between growing demand from increased population and superaffluence and tight supply due to ecological deterioration and incipient resource depletion. Soviet mismanagement of agriculture necessitated massive purchases of American grain in 1972, leaving no affordable imports to meet shortfalls in India and Bangladesh. International price increases for soya beans and animal feed led America to impose export restrictions to contain domestic inflation. High demand for rice in the newly affluent Middle East, the collapse of the Peruvian anchovy fishery, fertiliser shortages and the US abandonment of the gold standard, also forced up prices and revealed the fragility of international food markets, the vulnerability of food-importing developing countries and the importance of North American food exports. Thus food scarcity is emphasised, a Food Security Index devised and arguments for interdependence from *World Without Borders* used to promote the underlying ecological problems as central to foreign policy discourse. Brown's emphasis changes from 'buying time' to 'opportunity lost'. 'Gains will be short-lived', he writes, 'if the population problem is not solved soon' (Brown with Eckholm, 1974: 140).

The 1973 Arab oil embargo and the escalation in petroleum prices sent a similar shock through energy markets not just because of the perceived scarcities described in *Limits to Growth* but because of the recognition by developing countries that they possessed leverage over the West. Consequently, there are calls for an NIEO by the G7 and threats to withhold supplies of oil and other commodities unless Western policies towards Israel and South Africa changed. Brown's emphasis is on the depletion of these reserves and the power this confers on the exporting developing countries. As *Limits* had illustrated, it was not just oil, but also copper, tin, rubber, bauxite, coffee and timber cartels, which threatened America's economy and thus her security.

Thus the three regions – North America with food, the Middle East with oil, and developing countries with minerals – are each dependent on the others for key imports. Interdependence is the solution for this uneasy balance of power.

10.2.8 Brown (1975); Brown *et al.* (1976); Eckholm (1975, 1976)

In 1975, the Worldwatch Institute is founded with Lester Brown as its president and Eckholm as senior researcher. An initial project, jointly sponsored with UNEP, investigated 'the ecological undermining of food production systems caused by overfishing, deforestation, overgrazing, desert encroachment, soil erosion and the silting of irrigation systems' (from Brown's introduction to Eckholm, 1975). Four publications – *The Other Energy Crisis* (Eckholm, 1975), *The Politics and Responsibility of the North American Breadbasket* (Brown, 1975), *Losing Ground* (Eckholm, 1976) and *Twenty-two Dimensions of the Population Problem* (Brown *et al.*, 1976) – include descriptions of the relationship between these environmental problems and increased internal and cross-border migration. Underpinning their analysis is the Malthusian concern with population growth and the resulting growth in the labour force. Since this labour cannot be absorbed by agriculture, given degraded lands, unequal land tenure and inefficient agriculture, it migrates to urban areas, into rainforests, up hillsides, to land unsuitable for agriculture, to areas at risk from natural disasters, to neighbouring countries and to the West. Figure 10.2 models these relationships.

10.2.8.1 *Migration into tropical forests as a cause of deforestation*

Tropical deforestation is now perceived as a major threat. The hopes of Vogt and others for a new breadbasket in Amazonia are dashed because of poor soils and ecological costs. Replacing forests with cropland or cattle ranches is seen to be benefiting a local élite, while the costs – erosion, reduced streamflow, dry season droughts, increased siltation, loss of species, global warming – are perceived to be borne by everyone (Eckholm, 1975, 1976: 155–74).

10.2.8.2 *Refugees from Shangri-La*

This literature is the source of the influential theory of 'Himalayan Environmental Degradation' (cf. critique by Ives and Messerli, 1989). Migration up hillsides is seen to increase population and livestock density and thus the demand for food, fuel, fodder and timber. Firewood shortage results in the burning of cow dung previously used as fertiliser and thus fertility, already declining due to soil erosion, falls sharply. Lower output leads to the 'clearing of ever larger, ever steeper tracts of forest, intensifying the erosion and landslide hazards'. Deforestation increases run-off of water and sediment, which exacerbates flooding in India and Bangladesh. The additional sediment blocks irrigation channels and silts up dams, generating further migrants. Thus 'mountain people have little choice but to follow their soils down the slopes' (Eckholm, 1976: 75). Other examples are given for the Andes and the Horn of Africa.

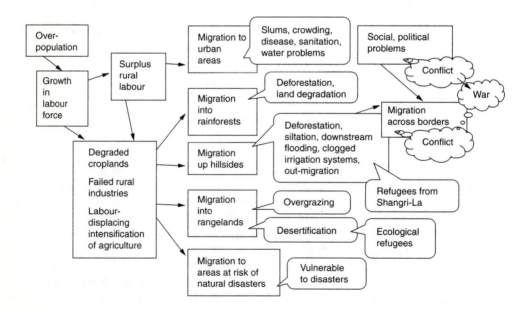

Figure 10.2 The Worldwatch construction of environmental degradation as a source of migrants, 1974–76. *Source:* Eckholm (1975), Eckholm (1976), Brown, McGrath and Stokes (1976)

10.2.8.3 'Ecological refugees' from desertification

Migration to farm unsuitable drylands is said to have created the US dust bowl, the degradation of Russia's 'virgin lands' and the southward expansion of the Sahel.

> As human and livestock populations retreat before the expanding desert, these *'ecological'*
> *refugees* create even greater pressure on new fringe areas, exacerbate the processes of land
> degradation, and trigger *a self-reinforcing negative cycle of overcrowding and overgrazing in*
> *successive areas.* When the inevitable drought sets in, as happened in the early seventies, this
> deteriorating situation is brought to a disastrous climax for the humans who perish by the
> hundreds of thousands; for livestock, which die in even greater numbers; and for productive
> land, which is destroyed.
>
> (Brown, *et al.* 1976: 39; italics mine)

The related constructs of 'overgrazing', 'carrying capacity' and 'desertification' are central to this analysis.

Migration to areas at risk from natural disasters is seen to follow from several components of this construction of environmental knowledge. In Bangladesh people move on to the Ganges floodplain where the risk of flooding is said to have increased. In Java they move up volcanic slopes. Coastal areas, often subject to natural disasters, also exert a strong pull (Brown *et al.*, 1976: 42).

Migration is often across borders to nearby countries experiencing similar environmental pressures. This causes conflict as, for example in the 1969 'soccer war', whose underlying cause was 'the wholesale migration of Salvadorans from their crowded country into less-populous Honduras' (ibid.: 56). Migration – both legal and illegal – is also to the less densely populated West whose economies require temporary labour. This too often results in conflict.

10.2.9 Brown (1977)

10.2.9.1 Non-military threats to security

In the late 1970s, this emphasis on conflict because of environmental degradation becomes a major theme in Worldwatch literature. Some of the causal links are direct, as in the alleged relationship between overfishing and the 1960s', UK–Icelandic 'cod war'. Others are mediated through constructions of 'environmental security'. An important Worldwatch Paper, *Redefining National Security*, provides a comprehensive treatment of this issue (Brown, 1977) and *Rays of Hope: The Transition to a Post-Petroleum World* (Hayes, 1977) elaborates on the energy implications. The essential components of this construct are displayed in Figure 10.3.

The three imperatives of the new geopolitical realities referred to in section 10.2.7 – North American dominance in grain exports, Middle Eastern control over oil, and developing country power in minerals markets and their calls for a NIEO – become three of the four causes of insecurity in the world, namely, the deterioration of biological systems, the depletion of petroleum reserves and the depletion of mineral resources. The construction reflects, therefore, the dominant political interests of the United States, but all are defined as environmental concerns. The fourth cause, the preoccupation with national (and military) security, is seen as obviating against the recognition that the real dangers are both non-military and global, and usurping resources that should be directed against these threats.

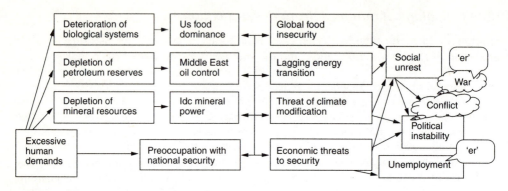

Figure 10.3 Worldwatch construction of non-military threats to security (1977). *Sources:* Brown (1977, 1978). *Note:* 'er' means 'environmental refugees' created indirectly as a result of the environmental root causes mediated by the modelled factors

10.2.9.2 *Energy conservation as short-term solution to all four threats*

The four non-military threats to security are linked by a common factor: the need to reduce demand for petroleum to undermine OPEC. Thus the analysis of 'global food insecurity' is similar to that already described with a new concern to reduce the high-energy inputs to agriculture (Hayes, 1977: 89–104). Similarly, the need to move to alternative sources of energy is constructed as an environmental problem – the 'lagging energy transition' from fossil fuels to 'non-renewable' resources. The long-term solution is seen as a transition to alternative energy sources before energy supplies peak and then decline, anticipated in the 1990s. Nuclear power is no longer recommended because of the risks of accidents and its association with weapons; coal is polluting and its emissions of CO_2 may contribute to global warming; solar technology is undeveloped; large dams are dangerous (Freeman, 1977). Thus the short-term solution, a dramatic conservation programme, is combined with a 'broad-based global effort to develop the entire range of renewable energy sources' (Brown, 1977: 13).

Mitigating the 'threat of climate modification' also necessitates the conservation of fossil fuels. Thus, the first serious discussion of 'global warming' in Worldwatch literature, emerges as a security problem within a document emphasising energy conservation as a means to weaken OPEC. Thus 'the primary limiting factor on energy production from fossil fuels over the next few centuries may turn out to be the climatic effects of the release of carbon dioxide' (NAS, 1975 in Brown, 1975: 22).

10.2.9.3 *The induced recession as a cause of emigration*

The focus for the 'economic threats to security' is the undermining of the biological foundations of the economy (see also Brown, 1978) and the impact of higher prices for food, petroleum, minerals and other commodities on inflation. Inflation weakens economies and reduces living standards, especially of the poor. 'Efforts to cope with inflation by slowing economic growth' (Brown, 1977: 33) have induced a recession. This slowdown itself reduces the demand for petroleum products and thus OPEC's hold over the US economy. However, costs include increased unemployment at a time when the global labour force is experiencing unprecedented growth. Hence 'the quest for jobs is driving people across national borders at alarming rates' (ibid.: 35). US borders are insecure, having been penetrated by 8 to 12 million illegal immigrants, principally from Mexico. European guestworkers are surplus to requirements and are being sent home. '[E]xpanding unemployment constitutes one of the world's gravest social ills' (ibid.: 36).

Among the conclusions is that these 'non-military threats to security' cause the wars that create refugees:

> The military threat to security is only one of the many that governments must now address. The numerous new threats derive directly or indirectly from the rapidly changing relationship between humanity and the earth's natural systems and resources. The unfolding stresses in this relationship initially manifest themselves as ecological stresses and resource scarcities. Later they translate into economic stresses – inflation, unemployment, capital scarcity and monetary instability. Ultimately these economic stresses convert into social unrest and political instability.
>
> (ibid.: 37)

It is clear from the context and earlier examples in this chapter that strikes and protests over high food prices are turning violent (ibid.: 33) and that rivalry over resources is leading to civil and international conflict (ibid.: 23). These wars will later be deemed 'proximate causes' that force the migration of 'environmental refugees' whose 'root causes' lie in overpopulation and the undermining of biological systems.

10.2.9.4 Sustainability as the key to global security

Finally, it should be noted that the construct 'sustainable' is securitised in this paper.

> In the late twentieth century the key to national security is sustainability. If the biological underpinnings of the global economic system cannot be secured, then the long-term economic outlook is grim indeed. If new energy sources and systems are not in place as the oil wells begin to go dry, then severe economic disruptions are inevitable.
>
> (Brown, 1977: 41)

Achieving a 'sustainable society' will later become the unifying theme for all Worldwatch analysis and recommendations (Brown, 1978, 1981, 1982; Eckholm, 1979).

10.2.10 Newland (1979, 1981)

10.2.10.1 The political construction of 'economic refugees'

Two papers by Kathleen Newland provide the first full-length studies of refugee issues by the Worldwatch Institute. The first examines the 20 million 'economic refugees', plus their defendants, who 'have pulled up stakes to escape hardship and to better their standard of living' (Newland, 1979: 5). The second focuses on the 16 million political refugees 'adrift in the stormy sea of world politics' (Newland, 1981: 5). Both categories are growing and Newland predicts that the 1980s will be a 'decade of refugees' (1979 : 6).

'Economic refugees' are distinguished from migrants forced to leave home because of wars, ecological catastrophes, invasion, enslavement, tyranny or persecution. They are considered 'refugees' because although their migration may appear voluntary, it is motivated by desperation and lack of alternatives: 'the force that expels them is usually not the force of arms but rather the force of circumstance' (Newland, 1981: 6). Countries with low incomes, youthful populations, high birth rates and overcrowded job markets will produce growing numbers of 'economic refugees'. Examples include migration from El Salvador into Honduras; from Bolivia, Colombia and Paraguay into Argentina and Venezuela; from Upper Volta into the Ivory Coast; and from all developing countries into Western Europe, North America and the Middle East. (Note, however, that there is no reference to the fact that these are the same factors and case studies said to produce 'ecological refugees' in Eckholm, 1976).

10.2.10.2 The Malthusian construction of 'political refugees'

A political refugee is one who has been forced to migrate because of a

> well-founded fear of being persecuted by means of race, religion or political opinion, is outside the country of his nationality, and is unable, or owing to such fear is unwilling, to avail himself of the protection of that country or who not having a nationality and being outside the country of his former habitual residence as a result of such events, is unable, or owing to such fear, is unwilling to return to it.
>
> (UN, 1951, 1967)

The presence of these refugees is characteristic of violent conflicts today, because 'the world has *become more densely populated* . . . [catching] larger numbers of people in the cross-fire wherever shooting starts'. Other causal factors include competition for land, 'spurred to satisfy the requirements and aspirations of *growing populations*', unequal distribution of land and wealth, and disputes over international boundaries. Poverty holds more people than ever in its grip, providing a 'fertile breeding ground for tensions that can erupt into violence between or within countries'. Thus refugee crises should no longer be treated as temporary aberrations. Modern warfare uses control over civilians as a tactic. Human greed, betrayal of popular will, lust for power and ethnic hatred combine with ethnic stress to ensure that refugee numbers will grow. Some national leaders are seeking to exploit this instability. The world community must 'convince these few how dangerous and futile such a notion is in a '*crowded*, complex and highly interdependent age' (Newland, 1981: 6, all italics mine).

10.2.10.3 Undermining the UN definition of refugee

Both papers emphasise the problems in differentiating between political and economic refugees. The distinction is not simply academic. There are major legal and resource implications once an individual or a group are designated refugees under the UN Conventions. Both sending and receiving countries strive to have asylum seekers defined as voluntary economic migrants rather than refugees; the former to evade charges of persecution; the latter the financial and other statuary obligations of asylum provision. Central to case studies is the necessity to transcend a convention designed for post-Second World War refugees and establish one appropriate to much larger numbers of mainly Third World refugees. The pool of possible economic migrants is vast, containing more than 350 million unemployed, or underemployed, people world-wide. This has 'explosive potential that could turn millions more into political refugees' (Newlands, 1981: 13).

Finally, Newlands argues, there is no preventative action specific to refugee problems.

Solutions lie in resolving the problems that drive people to migrate including the unresolved boundary disputes that are the legacy of the colonial period. An international consensus is needed to define 'acceptable norms of behaviour for nation states', as is a more modern concept of nation state 'as an association for the mutual benefit of various people, dedicated to more abstract principles than race or language' (ibid.: 29). States that oppress one tribe, linguistic group, region or class, precipitating a mass exodus of their citizens, commit actions which can no longer be tolerated. They 'infringe on the sovereignty of other countries by destabilizing the international system and by flooding other countries with refugees' (ibid.: 31). Newland argues that the international community has an obligation to respond. These 'large issues' resonate with problems facing the international community today. *Inter alia*, they illustrate the profound *political* significance of the Worldwatch constructions of 'refugees'.

10.2.11 Timberlake (1983a,b) and Timberlake and Tinker (1984)

10.2.11.1 'Environmental refugees' in the Caribbean

Lloyd Timberlake wrote two Earthscan briefing documents about the Cartenage Treaty, the first treaty to be negotiated under UNEP's regional seas convention (1983a, 1983b). These press releases popularise the Worldwatch construction linking environmental degradation, mass migration and conflict. In the first, *The Improbable Treaty*, the focus is on the environmental problems of the Caribbean and the benefits that will accrue from the treaty. The second, *Environmental Wars and Environmental Refugees*, highlights the political, economic and social factors which have created these problems. For Timberlake, a 'neo-feudal social and political system' has 'a profound effect on the physical environment'. He cites draft environmental reports by the USAID stating that 'the fundamental causes of the present conflict in El Salvador are as much environmental as political, stemming from problems of resource depletion in an overcrowded land' (Timberlake, 1983b: 10, citing Durham, 1979; Anderson, 1982). Similarly, in Haiti, the social and political structure, widespread landlessness and environmental degradation create social unrest and political repression. While this cycle had not yet caused an 'environmental war', it had resulted in a massive stream of 'environmental refugees' (citing Haiti Outreach Project, 1981). Thousands had fled from oppression in Port-au-Prince (800,000 to other islands plus 20,000 to the US since 1972). Environmental problems were also responsible for the emigration of Jamaicans to the US and the UK and the thousands of Mexicans fleeing to the US (Timberlake, 1983b: 10).

10.2.11.2 Environmental factors in the peace and conflict studies literature

The peace studies community began to link environmental degradation, underdevelopment, conflict and war in the 1980s (Galtung, 1982; Ullman, 1983; Arthur Westing, 1984, 1986). Worldwatch publications continued to develop this theme, applying geopolitical theory to 'whole earth security' (Deudney, 1983). British Quakers were also exploring these links (QPS, 1983). An Earthscan briefing document, *Environment and Conflict*, was an early attempt to synthesise many of these emerging insights, sub-titled 'links between ecological decay, environmental bankruptcy and political and military instability' (Timberlake and Tinker, 1984). It is clearly influenced by Worldwatch publications (Eckholm 1976 and 1982 while a visiting fellow with Earthscan). It argues that conflicts due to environmental degradation and competition for renewable resources will accelerate, creating 'bloodshed – riots, guerrilla movements, revolutions, wars' and further migration. Where governments give little priority to the rural sector,

> people seeking livelihoods leave the land in uncontrolled waves to: move across national boundaries as *refugees or migrant workers*, creating tension between states; move into regions of better agricultural land creating *conflicts with people already settled* there; convert forests to fields, disrupting the societies of, and often *fighting with forest people*; and move into swollen cities . . . [causing] a deep effect on *urban political stability*.
>
> (Timberlake and Tinker, 1984: 10, italics in original)

Examples are described from Peru, Poland, Horn of Africa, Iran, Afghanistan and Bangladesh where illegal immigrants from Bangladesh into Assam are said to have resulted in 3,000 deaths in 1983 during clashes between Hindus and Muslims. Competition for land and resources is considered responsible, not religion. They report chronic conflict between nomads and forest peoples in Ethiopia and suggest that the 1984 violence in the Punjab was precipitated by the expansion of the Thar desert and that in Bihar by pressure on forests by migrants seeking cropland. Similarly the Indonesian programme of transmigration is interpreted as a response to environmental degradation on Java, and the conflict in the Chittigong Hill Tracts to displacement of tribals by the Kaptai hydroelectric scheme and the resettlement of land-hungry Bengalis.

'Environmental refugees' are seen as 'fleeing environmental degradation which undercuts their ability to survive in their native lands' (Timberlake and Tinker, 1984: 21). They were not able to 'go home'. Durable solutions were needed. The Indian and US governments would 'find it more cost-effective to help their neighbours tackle the environmental degradation which drives the refugees to leave, rather than build vast preventative barriers?' (ibid.: 79). The authors comment on fears that immigrants will change and destabilise US society, arguing that both American society and the immigrants are resilient. Initially immigrants perform useful but low paid, dirty jobs; ultimately they become valued citizens (see also Galbraith, 1979). In addition, their numbers are small relative to the 10 million 'official' refugees fleeing to neighbouring Third World countries.

10.2.12 Wijkman and Timberlake (1984)

10.2.12.1 'Natural disasters' as acts of man

A joint publication of Earthscan and the International Red Cross, *Natural Disasters: Acts of God, Acts of Man?*, identifies two ways whereby people make 'natural disasters' more frequent and dangerous.

> First, people can alter their environment to make it more *prone* to certain disaster triggers, mainly to drought and flood. Second, people (and it appears from fatality statistics to be mainly poor people) can live in dangerous structures on dangerous ground, making themselves more exposed and *vulnerable* to disaster triggers.
>
> (Wijkman and Timberlake, 1984: 29, my italics)

Examples of the former include the ubiquitous link between erosion and deforestation in the Himalayas and downstream flooding; droughts exacerbated by the removal of vegetation and soil; and cyclones and tsunamis whose effects are worsened by the removal of barrier reefs, coastal mangroves and inland forests. Examples of the latter include: population pressure which forces more people to live in coastal areas or flood plains; increased population density which reduces flexibility and the option to migrate; government policies which replace subsistence agriculture with mono-culture, increasing susceptibility to pests; and poverty which denies people access to food during droughts and to the earthquake-proof structures available to the rich.

10.2.13 El-Hinnawi (1985); Westing (1984)

10.2.13.1 *The UNEP construction of 'environmental refugees'*

El-Hinnawi defines 'environmental refugees' as those people who have been forced to leave their traditional habitat, temporarily or permanently, because of a marked environmental disruption (natural and/or triggered by people) that has jeopardised their existence and/or seriously affected the quality of their life. He defines 'environmental disruption' as 'any physical, chemical and/or biological changes in the ecosystem (or the resource base) that render it, temporarily or permanently, unsuitable to support human life.' It excludes 'those displaced for political reasons or migrants seeking better jobs on economic grounds' (El-Hinnawi, 1985: 4).

El-Hinnawi defines three broad categories of refugees according to the duration of their expulsion from their original habitat: those temporarily displaced because of short-term environmental stress; those permanently displaced because of development projects such as large dams; and those temporarily or permanently displaced because of the degradation of their resource base (ibid.: 4–5). He identifies five causes of migration: namely, natural disasters, land degradation, large dams, environmental accidents and degraded and/or mined environments as a result of war. Figure 10.4 models the relationship between these two sets of parameters, with the boxes representing the latter, and the bubbles depicting the 'environmental refugees'.

El-Hinnawi's sources include Eckholm (1976, 1982), Eckholm and Brown (1977) and Newland (1981) – all Worldwatch publications. The source for the material on natural disasters is primarily Wijkman and Timberlake (1984). His treatment of land degradation is as described above and reflects UNEP's perception that '[d]esertification is caused almost entirely by human misuse of the environment' (El-Hinnawi, 1985: 26). Most case studies are also those cited by earlier authors with the exception of that on large dams which is based on earlier published research by UNEP (El-Hinnawi and Biswas, 1981). With the exception of the treatment of the socio-economic and environmental consequences for host countries, therefore, most is derived from key documents; however, the construction, since it includes a sensitive treatment of the temporal scale of the displacement and all five of the 'push' parameters, is original.

10.2.13.2 *Post-war refugees*

The residual impact of the Vietnam War was still severe over a decade after American withdrawal. Quoting Westing (1984), El-Hinnawi refers to the 'massive bombing of rural areas, the excessive mechanical and chemical destruction of forests, large-scale chemical and mechanical destruction of crops, wide-ranging chemical anti-personnel harassment and isolation, and the massive forced displacement of people. In short, the tragedy represented the intentional destruction of both the natural and chemical ecologies of the region'

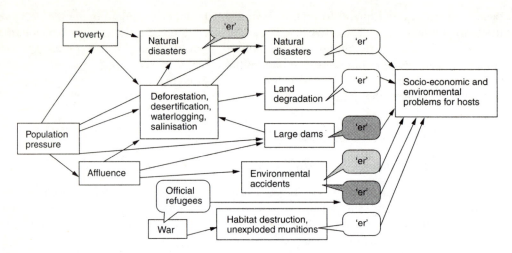

Figure 10.4 'Environmental refugees' as constructed by El-Hinnawi. *Source:* El-Hinnawi (1985). *Note:* 'er' refers to 'environmental refugees'. Light shading indicates that they are assumed to be of short duration, returning when the emergency is over. Dark shading indicates that the displacement is permanent. No shading indicates that the displacement is a complex pattern of seasonal, nomadic and permanent displacement

(El-Hinnawi, 1985: 38). He also cites areas of Egypt and Libya still closed to nomads by Second World War mines and similar situations in the Middle East and Africa.

10.2.13.3 The environmental impact of refugees on host communities

Finally, El-Hinnawi discusses the socio-economic and environmental problems created by refugees on their host country, particularly the conflict over scarce land and other resources. Examples include the cattle-owning Afar in Ethiopia, driven by drought to Wollo where they came into conflict with settled farmers where they are said to have accelerated environmental degradation. This allegation becomes an important theme in later constructions where refugees are perceived as 'exceptional' degraders of host environments (cf. Leach, 1992), a contention challenged by specialists in refugee studies (Kibreab, 1997; Black, 1998).

10.2.14 Jacobson (1988)

10.2.14.1 Refugees from global warming

The treatment of climate change in 'key documents' has so far been muted. In the 1970s, the scientific community was uncertain whether dust-induced cooling or CO_2-induced warming would dominate. Concern focused on the negative effects of increased variability upon agricultural systems developed during the preceding, relatively stable period in earth's climatic history (Bryson, 1975; NAS, 1975, 1977; Tickell, 1978). However, the late 1980s saw widespread acceptance of 'global warming' as the dominant influence. An influential paper from the Woods Hole Oceanographic Institute (Milliman *et al.*, 1989) predicted that millions would be displaced by a combination of subsidence and sea level rise in Egypt and Bangladesh (see critique by Bradnock and Saunders, Chapter 3, this volume). A draft was cited in a Worldwatch Paper by Jodi Jacobson (1988). She estimates current 'environmental refugees' at 10 million and suggests that the number of permanently displaced refugees be used as a yardstick to measure global environmental decline (ibid.: 39). Numbers would increase even in the absence of global warming. Using the 'worst' and 'really worst' projections of the Woods Hole research, Jacobson predicted that 'environmental refugees' from all causes, including sea level rise, would exceed the current number of refugees from all causes by a factor of six (ibid.: 38). Of Bangladesh she wrote, 'Eventually, the combination of rising seas, harsher storms, and degradation of the Bengal delta may wreak so much damage that Bangladesh as we know it may virtually cease to exist' (ibid.: 35).

10.3 Discussion

10.3.1 The changed geopolitical and intellectual context

This history traces the origins of the construct 'environmental refugees' to 1988, by which time all of the elements in the mature construct have appeared. Its history after this point should therefore be seen as describing its spread. Other changes reinforce this date as appropriate for a move from origins to spread. The geopolitical context changes dramatically with the fall of the Berlin Wall the following year. Since then, although few of the demands for economic justice embedded in calls for a NIEO have been realised, some of the new institutions recommended by Brown in *World Without Borders* (1972), e.g. the World Trade Organization (WTO), reflect moves towards his 'truly unified, transnational world'. The numbers of official refugees have fallen dramatically since the 1991 peak, with those from Eastern Europe the only category that is growing. The majority of refugees are 'internally displaced persons' since most wars are now civil, not interstate, wars (UNHCR, 1999). The global community now cites state persecution of minorities resulting in the mass exodus of a people as justification for military intervention (e.g. Kosovo, East Timor). Oppression of one segment of a state's population is now seen as a war crime. The geopolitical context is thus very different.

Furthermore, environmental issues have become mainstream concerns of civil society and public policy since the late 1980s. The 'take-off' for this fundamental change in worldview can be traced to the publication of the Brundtland Report in 1987, the popularisation of the construct 'sustainable development' and Hansen's statement that the 1988 drought in the North American breadbasket was evidence for 'global warming'. Pressure from the UNCED process has forced nation states and UN agencies, including UNHCR, to delineate the environmental implications of their activities. IPCC terms of reference coupled with considerable finance for related research have shaped the debate about 'global warming' and persuaded policy-makers and the media of the need for mitigating action.

However, the growth in popular acceptance of the environmental orthodoxy has been paralleled by academic research that has challenged both its theory and its application. Professional ecologists now question the theory underlying conceptions of carrying capacity, equilibrium and balance of nature (Cohen, 1995; Wu and Loucks, 1995; Sullivan, 1996; Saunders, 1999). There is now a growing body of research which questions much of the environmentalists' construction of soil erosion (Stocking, 1996); deforestation (Fairhead and Leach 1996; Stott, 1999); Himalayan degradation as a cause of downstream flooding (Ives and Messerli, 1989; Hofer, 1999); overgrazing (Behnke *et al.*, 1993; Scoones 1996); desertification (Swift, 1996); global warming (Moore *et al.*, 1996; Bradnock and Saunders,

Chapter 3, this volume); global security (Werner, 2000, Chapter 11, this volume). Assessment by academics directs closer attention to spatial and temporal scale and eschews global generalisations.

Also, there is a new consensus regarding the Malthusian belief that population must inevitably expand up to the level of subsistence. It is now anticipated that population will level off in the twenty-first century without draconian measures of birth or immigration 'control' (Harrison, 1993; Cassen and Bates 1994; UNFPA, 1999). And although there are serious concerns about regional water shortages, demand- and supply-based solutions are available which could enable the meeting of the need for sustenance by the projected population (Dyson, 1996; Allan, Chapter 5, this volume). That is not to deny that there are regions where high population density poses severe threats: with half a million people now living on the active flood plain in Bangladesh, it would be irresponsible to dismiss the significance of severe demographic pressure (World Bank, 1995). However, it is country-specific analysis and policy which is needed, not global generalisations and in the absence of a (highly unlikely) dramatic, non-linear shift in global climate, any massive increases in mortality will be the result of political failure, not natural, inevitable, divinely sanctioned Malthusian checks.

Finally, there has been a commensurate growth in refugee studies research, some of which addresses environmental deterioration as part of a complex package of root and proximate causes for forced migration (McGregor, 1993; Clear, 1997; Kibreab, 1997). Black (1998) analyses contentions that (a) environmental degradation is a cause of forced migration; and (b) refugees are 'exceptional degraders' of host environments and finds little evidence for either. He reviews the literature deconstructing the environmental orthodoxy and concludes, *inter alia*, 'If one accepts the argument that desertification itself is largely a myth, then it is not perhaps too great a step to suggest that desertification-induced migration is a myth too' (Black, 1998: 26).

10.3.2 Relevance to the current debate

None the less, the history of the construct 'environmental refugees' is relevant to the current academic debate about the root causes of forced migration. First, it is important to set the record straight about its origins. Timberlake (1983a, 1983b; Timberlake and Tinker, 1984) and El-Hinnawi (1985) appear to have been the first to use the words, 'environmental refugees', but as this research has shown, many of its constituents are present in embryo in Malthus, and that similar terms have been used to describe migrants from degraded land since Vogt's 'ecological displaced persons' in 1949. All the environmental 'push' factors are to be found in Worldwatch publications of the 1970s and early 1980s. Thus, although El-Hinnawi's construction consolidates them and gives it the UNEP imprimatur, which has aided its spread, I would argue that Lester Brown and the Worldwatch Institute are its original source.

Second, it enables a distinction to be drawn between a strong and a weak definition of the construct. Figure 10.5 is my attempt to describe the construct as of the late 1980s. It brings the concepts from all 'key documents' into one representation and is heavily dependent on the Worldwatch construction since it includes insights from Brown's 'non-military threats to security' absent from the El-Hinnawi construction. Thus the bubbles marked 'er' in Figure 10.5 are shown as emanating directly from several stages of the process and indirectly from others, so that some 'official refugees' are also 'environmental refugees' since they emerge during the later stages of a process which begins with population pressure, and moves

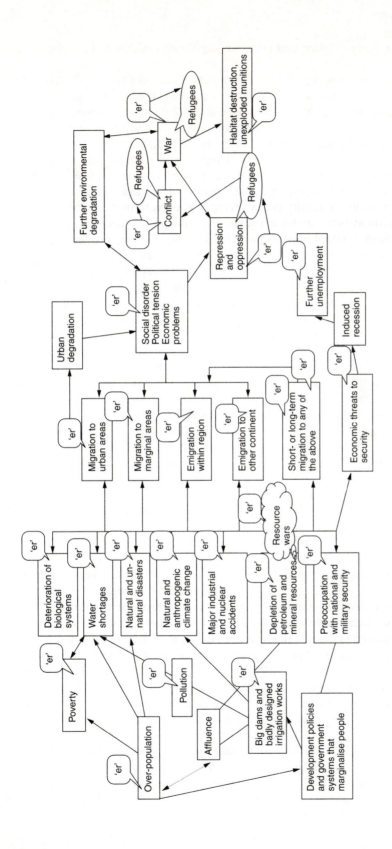

Figure 10.5 Strong construction of 'environmental refugees' by the late 1980s. *Sources:* Brown (1975); Brown *et al.* (1976); Brown (1977); Newland (1981); Timberlake and Tinker (1984); El-Hinnawi (1985); Jacobson (1988). *Note:* 'er' is 'environmental refugees'

through environmental degradation and resource depletion, undermined economies, social disorder, conflict and war.

This representation highlights two important aspects of the construction: first its ubiquity; and second, in consequence, its lack of explanatory power. All advocates acknowledge that the environmental root causes of forced migration are difficult, if not impossible, to isolate. However, since it is employed to designate migration from such a wide range of root and proximate causes, over such varying spatial and temporal scales and with varying degrees of significance, it means that *virtually all migrants meet the definition to some degree or other*. It is therefore *incapable of discriminating* between 'environmental refugees' and those designated as 'official' refugees under the UN definition of 'economic migrants' who cross borders seeking work or a higher standard of living. I interpret this as a 'strong' version of the construct and would argue that its inability to discriminate renders it useless.

A 'weak' version, which would mesh easily with weak and welfare-oriented definitions of sustainability (cf. Black, 1988: 5–6), might, however, be retained as an appropriate means of constructing those ecological factors which can be identified as part of the causal package at the local scale. I would suggest that it retain the older title 'ecological refugees' and that it refer exclusively to those abandoning regions where there is evidence that ecological deterioration, whether natural and/or anthropogenic, has occurred and is the primary factor compelling migration. I would treat separately 'oustees' displaced by development projects (Kane, 1995), chemical and nuclear accidents, such post-war factors as residual munitions and those that may or may not occur through 'global warming'. These distinctions are essential if there is to be conceptual clarity when analysing remedies for forced migration. In those cases where population density is a factor underlying internal or external migration it is essential that it be recognised as such and its implications analysed (cf. FAO, 1984). Care should be taken to ensure that a rejection of the strong construction does not hinder this analysis.

Third, Kibreab (1997: 21) argues that 'the term "environmental refugees" was . . . invented at least in part to depoliticize the causes of displacement, so enabling states to derogate their obligation to provide asylum.' Chimni (1998: 351) identifies the creation of a 'myth of difference' between European and Third World refugees which 'went hand in hand with an internationalist interpretation of the root causes of refugee flows which squarely laid the blame of post-colonial societies and states, undermining the significance of external factors'. Identifying Brown as its author highlights 'environmental refugees' as politically constructed 'environmental knowledge' (Bryant and Bailey, 1997). It is deeply embedded in the globalisation agenda of its American originators and contemporary geopolitical preoccupations. The construct 'environmental security' which develops later (Galtung, 1982; Westing, 1986, 1989; Matthews, 1989; Myers, 1989, 1995) contributes little but a new title to the ideas of Brown (1977), which are essential to the argument that there are deep-rooted environmental causes propelling economic and political refugees. The Worldwatch logic is compelling, and I suspect that those responsible for both immigration and military policy have been concerned about the threat of 'environmental refugees' ever since the neo-Malthusians identified it, and that this has contributed to the tightening of immigration and asylum law (cf. Golub and Townsend, 1977). Further work is required to test this hypothesis.

Fourth, the construct is the product of the environmental and, to a lesser extent, the conflict studies communities, not that of development or refugee studies. It has been promoted in papers and editorials in *Environmental Conservation* (Myers, 1987; Westing, 1992), in a recent book edited by its late editor (Polunin, 1998), by *The Guardian's* environmental correspondents (Brown, P., 1999), and in *The Ecologist* (Foley, 1999); though interestingly, the current issue of the Worldwatch Vital Signs has ceased to use the term (Brown, Renner and Halweil, 1999). Galtung (1998) and Homer-Dixon (1999) are among peace and conflict analysts who discuss these issues but Galtung's primary category is massive migration not 'environmental refugees', which play a relatively minor part in his analysis, and Homer-Dixon does not use the term and rejects the generalised analysis of its promoters. An explanation for the reasons for the rejection of the construct by academics outside the environmental and population disciplines is beyond the scope of this chapter. However, it is important to note that those authors who are promoting the construct have not yet incorporated insights from the deconstruction of the environmental orthodoxy referred to above, nor do they appear to recognise the relevance of either the refugee studies or the development literature. Moreover, they remain doggedly Malthusian in their emphasis on population growth as the ultimate cause (see Myers, 1998).

Fifth, international organisations are under pressure to employ environmental constructions in their literature and policies. Three have recently employed the term 'environmental refugees' in their annual reports (IFRC, 1999; UNEP, 1999; UNFPA, 1999), although the major refugee organisations appear to have reservations related to its potential to undermine asylum provision (UNHCR, 1999; USCR, 1999). Individuals such as Norman Myers are actively promoting it. Media reports are popularising it (the earliest that I have found is an article in June 1989 in the *New Scientist* (Anon, 1989)). It is therefore likely that it will become an integral component of the environmental orthodoxy.

10.4 Further research

The process whereby the construct 'environmental refugees' spreads through literature other than that of the environmental and peace studies communities should be monitored while it is happening, assessing the role of academic journals, international organisations, think tanks, funding agencies, individuals and the media. Treatment by academic journals should compare those representing the development, environment, peace, refugee studies and climate change communities and contrast Western and Southern perspectives. The research should assess the impact of international organisations upon the debate. The role of think tanks, especially the Worldwatch and Climate institutes, should be studied and the influence of funding agencies evaluated. The influence of individuals should be monitored, ideally incorporating interview-based research with both advocates and opponents. Finally, the role of the media should be evaluated, perhaps using methods similar to those used by Chapman *et al.* (1997).

10.5 Conclusion

It is evident that the construct 'environmental refugees' has its origins in the neo-Malthusian literature of the United States. It has been systematically promoted by Lester Brown and the Worldwatch Institute within an agenda that has been solutions within a sustainable, interdependent, global society. It is becoming an integral part of the environmental orthodoxy. The importance of its origins in this literature cannot be over-emphasised as it is now being actively and effectively promoted by its advocates and widely publicized in the press and adopted by individuals and organisations who would reject many of the assumptions of its originators. It will probably become an integral part of the environmental orthodoxy in the near future. This process should be monitored and the nature of the political construction of this component of current environmental knowledge assessed.

Acknowledgements

I am grateful to the advice and guidance received from my supervisor, Professor Philip Stott, and for insights gleaned during conversations with others, particularly Robert Bradnock, Norman Myers, Carole Rakodi, Sian Sullivan and Martin Evans. I am also indebted to staff at the International Federation of Red Cross and Red Crescent Society, the British Refugee Council, the Refugee Studies Centre in Oxford, the SOAS and University College Libraries, and perhaps most important, to Edward Saunders, my supportive and long-suffering husband.

References

Allan, P.A. 2000: 'Contending environmental knowledge on water in the Middle East: global, regional and national contexts'. Chapter 5, this volume.

Anderson, T.P. 1982: *The war of the dispossessed: Honduras and El Salvador 1996*. Lincoln: University of Nebraska Press.

Anon 1989: Eco-refugees warning. *New Scientist* 10 June, 1989.

Behnke, R.H., Scoones, I. and Kerven, C. (eds) 1993: *Range ecology at disequilibrium: new models of natural variability and pastoral adaption in African savannas*. London: ODI and IIED.

Black, R. 1998: *Refugees, environment and development*. Harlow: Longman.

Black, R. and Robinson, V. (eds) 1993: *Geography and refugees: patterns and processes of change*. London and New York: Belhaven.

Boserup, E. 1965: *The conditions of agricultural growth*. Chicago: Aldine.

Bradnock, R.W. and Saunders, P.L. 2000: Subsidence, submergence and sea-level rise: the political ecology of environmental change in the Bengal delta. London: SOAS, in press.

Brown, L.R. 1963: *Man, land and food*. US Department of Agriculture, Economic Research Service, Foreign Agriculture Report No. 11, November 1963.

Brown, L.R. 1968: The agricultural revolution in Asia. *Foreign Affairs* **46**(4), 688–98.

Brown, L.R. 1970: *Seeds of change: the Green Revolution and development in the 1970s*. New York and London: Praeger and Pall Mall (for the Overseas Development Council).

Brown, L.R. 1972: *World without borders*. New York: Random House.

Brown, L.R. 1974: *In the human interest*. Oxford: Pergamon (for Overseas Development Council and Aspen Institute).

Brown, L.R. 1975: *The politics and responsibility of the North American Breadbasket*. Washington, DC: The Worldwatch Institute, Worldwatch Paper 2 (October).

Brown, L.R. 1977: *Redefining national security*. Washington, DC: Worldwatch Institute, Worldwatch Paper 14.

Brown, L.R. 1978a: *The global economic prospect: new sources of economic stress*. Washington, DC: Worldwatch Institute, Worldwatch Paper 20.

Brown, L.R. 1981: *Building a sustainable society*. New York: Norton.

Brown, L.R. 1982: *Six steps to a sustainable society*. Washington, DC: Worldwatch Institute, Worldwatch Paper 48.

Brown, L.R. 1999: More now flee environment than warfare. *The Guardian*, 24 June, 16.

Brown, L.R. and Eckholm, E.P. 1974: *By bread alone*. New York: Praeger for Overseas Development Council.

Brown, L.R., Flavin, C., French, H. and ten others 1999: *State of the world 1998*. Washington, DC: Worldwatch Institute.

Brown, L.R., Renner, M. and Halweil, B. 1999: *Vital signs: the environmental trends that are shaping our future*. London: Earthscan for the Worldwatch Institute.

Brown, L.R., McGrath, P.L. and Stokes, B. 1976: *Twenty-two dimensions of the population problem*. Washington, DC: Worldwatch Institute, Worldwatch Paper 5.

Bryant, R.L. and Bailey, S. 1997: *Third world political ecology*. London and New York: Routledge.

Bryson, R.A. 1975: The lessons of climate history. *Environmental Conservation* **2**, 163ff.

Carson, R. 1962: *Silent spring*. Boston MA: Houghton Mifflin.

Cassen, R. and Bates, L.M. 1994. *Population policy: a new consensus*. Washington, DC: Overseas Development Council.

Chapman, G., Kumar, K., Fraser, C. and Gaber, I. 1997: *Environmentalism and the mass media: the North–South divide*. London and New York: Routledge for the Indian Institute of Advanced Study, Shimla.

Chimni, B.S. 1998: The geopolitics of refugee studies: a view from the south'. *Journal of Refugee Studies* **11**(4), 350–73.

Clear, S. 1997: Migration and the environment: a review of recent literature. *Social Science Quarterly* **78**(2), 606–18.

Cohen, J.E. 1995: *How many people can the earth support?* New York: Norton.

Craven, A.O. 1925: Soil erosion as a factor in the agricultural history of Virginia and Maryland, 1606–1860. *University of Illinois studies in the social sciences* **13**(1), 1–179.

Dennery, E. 1931: *Asia's teeming millions and its problems for the west*. London: Jonathan Cape.

Deudney, D. 1983. *Whole earth security: a geopolitics of peace*. Washington, DC: Worldwatch Institute, Worldwatch Paper 55.

Durham, W.H. 1979: *Scarcity and survival in Central America: ecological origins of the soccer war*. Stanford, DCA: Stanford University Press.

Dyson, T. 1996: *Population and food*. London and New York: Routledge.

Eckholm, E.P. 1975: *The other energy crisis: fuelwood*. Washington, DC: Worldwatch Institute, Worldwatch Paper 1, September.

Eckholm, E.P. 1976: *Losing ground: environmental stress and world food prospects*. New York: Norton for Worldwatch Institute.

Eckholm, E.P. 1979 *The dispossessed of the earth: land reform and sustainable development*. Washington: Worldwatch Institute, Worldwatch Paper 30.

Eckholm, E.P. 1982: *Down to Earth: environment and human needs*. London: Pluto Press.

Ehrlich, P.R. 1968, 1971: *The population bomb*. London: Ballantine for Friends of the Earth (British edition 1971).

Ehrlich, P.R. 1990: *The population explosion*. New York: Simon and Schuster.

El-Hinnawi, E. 1985: *Environmental refugees*. Nairobi: UNEP.

El Hinnawi, E. and Biswas, A.K. 1981. *Renewable sources of energy*. Dublin: Tycooli International.

Fairhead, J. and Leach, M. (eds) 1996: *The lie of the land: challenging received wisdom on the African environment*. London, Oxford and Portsmouth: The International African Institute, James Curry & Heinemann.

Fairhead, J. and Leach, M. 1998: *Reframing deforestation: global analysis and local realities: studies in West Africa*. London and New York: Routledge.

Foley, G. 1999: The looming environmental refugee crisis. *The Ecologist* **29**(2), 96–7.

Food and Agricultural Organization 1984: *Land, food and people*. Rome: FAO (based on the FAO/UNFPA/IIASA report *Potential population-supporting capacities of lands in the developing world* (1983).

Freeman, P.H. 1977: *Large dams and the environment: recommendations for development planning*. Washington, DC: IIED.

Galbraith, J.K. 1958: *The affluent society*. New York and Toronto: Mentor.

Galbraith, J.K. 1979: *The nature of world poverty*. Harmondsworth: Pelican.

Galtung, J. 1982: *Environment, development and military activity: towards alternative security doctrines*. Oslo: Universitetsforlaget.

Galtung, J. 1998: Global migration: a thousand years' perspective. In Polumin, N. *Population and global security*. Cambridge: Cambridge University Press, 173–84.

Goldsmith, E., Allen, R., Allaby, M., Davull, J. and Lawrence, S. 1972: *A blueprint for survival*. London: Tom Stacey.

Goldsmith, E. and Hildyard, N. 1984, 1986, 1992: *The social and environmental effects of large dams*, Volumes I, II, III. Wadebridge: Wadebridge Ecological Centre.

Golub, R. and Townsend, J. 1977: Malthus, multinationals and the Club of Rome. *Social Studies of Science* 7, 201–22.

Hailey, Lord 1938: *An African survey: a study of the problems arising in Africa south of the Sahara*. Oxford: Oxford University Press.

Haiti Outreach Project 1981: Project paper (Project S21–0122).

Hardin, G. 1968: The tragedy of the Commons. *Science* **162**, 1243–8.

Hardin, H. 1972: *Exploring new ethics for survival*. New York: Viking Press.

Hardin, H. 1993: *Living within limits: ecology, economics and population taboos*. New York and Oxford: Oxford University Press.

Harrison, P. 1993: *The third revolution: environment, population and a sustainable world*. London and New York: Tauris.

Hayes, D. 1977: *Rays of hope: the transition to a post-petroleum world*. New York: W.W. Norton for the Worldwatch Institute.

Hofer, T. 1988: *Floods in Bangladesh: a highland–lowland interaction*. Berne: Institute of Geography, University of Berne.

Homer-Dixon, T. and Blitt, J. (eds) 1999: *Ecoviolence: links among environment population and security*. Maryland: Rowman and Littlefield.

Howe, J.W. 1974: *The US and the developing world: agenda for action 1974*. New York: Praeger for the Overseas Development Council.

International Federation of Red Cross and Red Crescent Societies (IFRC) 1999: *World disasters report 1999*. Geneva: IFRC.

Ives, J.D. and Messerli, B. 1989: *The Himalayan dilemma: reconciling development and conservation*. London and New York, Routledge.

Jacks, G.V. and Whyte, R.O. 1938: *Erosion and soil conservation*. London: Imperial Bureau of Soil Science, Technical Communication No. 36.

Jacks, G.V. and Whyte, R.O. 1939: *The rape of the earth: a world survey of soil erosion*. London: Faber and Faber.

Jacobson, J.L. 1988: *Environmental refugees: a yardstick of habitability*. Washington, DC: Worldwatch Institute, Worldwatch Paper 86.

Kane, H. 1995: *The hour of departure: forces that create refugees and migrants*. Washington, DC: Worldwatch Institute, Worldwatch Paper 125.

Kibreab, G. 1997: Environmental causes and impact of refugee movements: a critique of the current debate. *Disasters* **21**(1), 20–38.

Leach, M. 1992: 'Dealing with displacement: refugee–host relations, food and forest resources in Sierra Leonean Mende communities during the Liberian influx, 1990–1991. Brighton: Institute of Development Studies, IDS Research Reports No. 22.

Leach, M. and Mearns, R. 1996: *The life of the land: challenging received wisdom on the African environment*. London: The International African Institute in association with James Currey and Heinemann.

Malthus, T.R. 1798, reprinted 1970: *An essay on the principle of population*. Harmondsworth: Penguin. Usually referred to as the *First Essay*.

Malthus, T.R. 1826, 6th edition, being fifth edition of *Second Essay*, reprinted 1958: *An essay on population*. London: Dent/Everyman, two volumes.

Malthus, T.R. 1830, reprinted in 1970 with the 1798 essay, see above: *A summary view of the principle of population*. Harmondsworth: Penguin, 1958.

McCormick, J. 1995: *The global environmental movement*. London: Wiley.

McGregor, J. 1993: Refugees and the environment. In Black, R. and Robinson, V. (eds), *Geography and refugees: patterns and processes of change*. London and New York: Belhaven, 157–70.

Meadows, D.H., Meadows, D.L. Randers, J. and Behrens, W.W. Jr 1972: *Limits to growth: a report for the Club of Rome's project on the predicament of mankind*. New York: Signet.

Milliman, J.D., Broadus, J.M. and Gable, F. 1989: Environmental and economic implications of rising sea level and subsiding deltas: the Nile and Bengal examples. *Ambio* **18**(6), 340–45.

Moore, P.D., Chaloner, B. and Stott, P.A. 1996: *Global environmental change*. Oxford: Blackwell.

Morris, J. 1995: *The political economy of land degradation*. London: Institute of Economic Affairs.

Myers, N. 1986: The environmental dimension to security issues. *The Environmentalist* **6**(4), 251–7.

Myers, N. 1987: Population, environment and conflict. *Environmental Conservation* **14**(1), 15–22.

Myers, N. 1989: Environmental security: the case of South Asia. *International Environmental Affairs* **1**, 139–54.

Myers, N. 1993: Environmental refugees in a globally warmed world. *Bioscience* **43**(11), 116–18.

Myers, N. 1995: *Ultimate security: the environmental basis of political security*. New York and London: Norton.

Myers, N. 1998: Global population and emergent issues. In Polunin, N. *Population and Global Security*. Cambridge: Cambridge University Press, 17–46.

Myers, N. with Kent, J. 1995: *Environmental exodus: an emergent crisis in the global arena*. Washington, DC: The Climate Institute.

National Academy of Sciences 1975: *Understanding climate change*. Washington, DC: National Academy of Sciences (Panel on Climate Variation).

National Academy of Sciences 1977: *Energy and climate*. Washington, DC: National Academy of Sciences.

National Park Service/US Man and the Biosphere Secretariat (1982) *Draft environmental profile of El Salvador*. Washington, DC: Bureau of Science and Technology, USAID.

Newland, K. 1979: *International migration: the search for work*. Washington, DC: Worldwatch Institute, Worldwatch Paper 33.

Newland, K. 1981: *Refugees: the new international politics of displacement*. Washington, DC: Worldwatch Institute, Worldwatch Paper 43.

Osborn, F. 1970: *Our plundered planet*. New York: Pyramid Books.

Paddock, W. and Paddock, P. 1964: *Hungry nations*. Boston: Little, Brown & Co.

Paddock, W. and Paddock, P. 1967: *Famine 1975! America's decision: who will survive?* Boston and Toronto: Little, Brown & Co.

Polunin, N. 1998: *Population and global security*. Cambridge: Cambridge University Press.

Quaker Peace and Service 1983: Quaker Conference 'Environment, Disarmament, Development – Linked Paths to Peace'.

Ramlogan, R. 1996: Environmental refugees: a review. *Environmental Conservation* **23**(1), 81–8.

Renner, M. 1989: *National security: the economic and environmental dimensions*. Washington, DC: Worldwatch Institute, Worldwatch Paper 89.

Richmond, A.H. 1994: *Global Apartheid: refugees, racism and the new world order*. Toronto, New York, Oxford: Oxford University Press, Chapter 4.

Saunders, P.L. 1999: Savanna systems are non-equilibral but persistent. Unpublished essay, London: SOAS.

Scoones, I. 1996: Range management science and policy: politics, polemics and pastures in Southern Africa. In Leach, M. and Mearns, R. (eds), *The lie of the land: challenging received wisdom on the African environment*. Oxford, James Curney, 34–53.

Shaw, R.P. 1989: Rapid population growth and environmental degradation: ultimate *versus* proximate factors'. *Environmental Conservation* **16**(3), 199–208.

Shepherd, J. 1975: *The politics of starvation*. Washington, DC: Carnegie Endowment for International Peace.

Smith, J.W. 1998: *Global meltdown: immigration, multiculturalism and national breakdown in the new world disorder*. Westport, CT: Praeger.

Stocking, M. 1996: Soil erosion: breaking new ground. In Leach, M. and Mearns, R. (eds), *The lie of the land. challenging received wisdom on the African environment*, Oxford: James Currey, 140–54.

Stott, P.A. 1999: *Tropical Rain Forest: a political ecology of hegemonic myth-making*. London: Institute of Economic Affairs.

Sullivan, S. 1996: Towards non-equilibrium ecology: perspectives from an arid land'. *Journal of Biogeography* **23**, 1–5.

Swift, J. 1996: Desertification: narratives, winners and losess. In Leach, M. and Mearns, R. (eds), *The lie of the land: challenging received wisdom on the African environment*. Oxford: James Currey, 73–90.

Tickell, C. 1978: second edition 1986: *Climate change and world affairs*. Oxford: Pergamon.

Timberlake, L. 1983a: *The improbable treaty: the Cartagena Convention and the Caribbean environment*. London: Earthscan Press Briefing Document No. 34A.

Timberlake, L. 1983b: *Environmental wars and environmental refugees: the political background to the Cartagena Convention*. London: Earthscan Press briefing Document No. 34B.

Timberlake, L. and Tinker, J. 1984: *Environment and conflict: links between ecological decay, environmental bankruptcy and political and military instability*. London: Earthscan Briefing Document 40.

Trolldalen, J.M., Birkeland, N.M., Borgen, J. and Scott, P.T. 1992: *Environmental refugees: a discussion paper*. Oslo: World Foundation for Environment and Development & The Norwegian Refugee Council.

Ullman, R.H. 1983: Redefining security. *International Security* **8**, 129–53.

United Nations 1951: *Convention relating to the status of refugees*. Geneva, 28 July 1961, as amended by the protocol relating to the status of refugees, New York, 31 January 1967.

United Nations Environment Programme 1999: *Global environmental outlook 2000*. New York: United Nations.

United Nations Fund for Population Activities 1999: *The state of world population 1999: six billion, a time for choice*. New York: United Nations.

United Nations High Commission for Refugees 1999: *The state of the world's refugees 1998*. New York: United Nations.

USAID/MAB (1992): draft environmental profiles quoted in Timberlake, and 1983a, 1983b, 1984.

US Committee for Refugees 1999: http://www.refugees.org

Vogt, W. 1949: *Road to survival*. London: Gollancz.

Ward, B. and Dubos, R.H. 1972: *Only one Earth*. London: André Deutsch.

Werner, J. 1999: Global environmental security: an emerging 'concept of control'. Chapter 11, this volume.

Westing, A.F. 1984: *Herbicides in war*. London: Taylor and Francis.

Westing, A.F. 1986: *Global resources and international conflict: environmental factors in strategic policy and action*. Oxford: Oxford University Press.

Westing, A.F. 1989: Comprehensive human security and ecological realities. *Environmental Conservation* **16**, 295.

Westing, A.F. 1992: Environmental refugees. a growing category of displaced persons. *Environmental Conservation* **19**(3), 201–7.

Wijkman, A. and Timberlake, L. 1984: *Natural disasters: acts of God, acts of Man?* London: Earthscan.

World Bank 1995: *Staff appraisal report: Bangladesh river bank protection project*. Washington, DC: The World Bank.

World Commission on Environment and Development (WCED) (Brundtland Commission) 1987: *Our common future*. Oxford and New York: Oxford University Press.

Wu, J.G. and Loucks, O.L. 1995: From balance of nature to hierarchical patch dynamics: a paradigm shift in ecology. *Quarterly Review of Biology* **70**(4), 439–66.

11

Global environmental security

An emerging 'concept of control'?

Jeroen Warner

11.1 Introduction

In spite of apparently declining public interest in environmental issues, a concern with 'environmental security' seems to be growing at the state level. But is this just hype, or is there a lasting significance to concepts of 'environmental security'? Here I argue that while it is underscored by a significant intellectual effort, it remains significant for reasons other than its intellectual merits. In particular, 'environmental security' seems to serve the same kind of unifying and self-reinforcing discursive strategy that launched 'sustainable development'. Given that the idea of 'security' implies that something requires protection, the implementation of protection in the name of environmental security can be constructed as essential by those asserting environmental security concerns. While International Relations (IR) has been staunchly materialist in its Realist and Political Economy interpretations, it is now increasingly realised that ideas themselves are among the interacting social currencies influencing International Political Economy (van der Pijl, 1992). Given that ideas do not simply float around in space, disconnected from the circumstances surrounding their production, it is impossible to separate knowledge production from the realisation and definition of material interests. And given that material interests do not exist in a vacuum of power relations, the latter play a crucial, if not *the* crucial, role in determining what knowledge is sought, how it is judged and how it is applied in practice.

In this context, various actors struggle for the upper hand in defining state policies, and do so by coercive as well as discursive means. The Amsterdam, or 'concepts of control' school of international relations, has been looking into the way various economic interests have influenced outlooks. Drawing on the writings of Antonio Gramsci (e.g. Gramsci, 1971), they argue that conflicting material interests stemming from different relations to the means of production unsurprisingly can be linked to different political agendas. While this approach acknowledges that it is too simple to portray the executive of government as the handmaiden of an economic élite, this school of thought maintains that the outcomes of political processes do tend to favour the dominant of society via more subtle mechanisms. In particular, it is suggested that if political dominance cannot be achieved by coercive means, then instead interests are advanced by discursively co-opting the goals of contenders in a blanket reformulation of the 'common good'. In this context environmental concerns are simply a new arena for the enacting of this process.

Neo-Marxists are not the only ones to reappraise the importance of the 'management of meaning'. A group of Neo-realist political scientists (the 'Copenhagen School') has come to acknowledge the process of apparent depoliticisation in decision-making and have developed what has become known as 'securitisation theory' (Buzan *et al.*, 1995), which, given a climate of concern regarding environmental issues and 'securitisation' discourse as a 'speech act',[1] invokes 'existential threats' as a means to release and legitimate financial and political resources. In governance and international relations a key issue is that *a successful 'securitisation' strategy helps legitimise state intervention and, as a consequence, the state*. This is particularly important in the context of a key area of contention in governance; namely the degree of state intervention and protection versus free operation of market forces.

It will be argued, then, that 'securitising' the environment can be understood as an effort to prop up a beleaguered Westphalian state system, as well as acknowledging the economic interests underlying that effort. In this sense, my approach constitutes a Gramscian account of securitisation in relation to 'environmental security', notably in the context of agriculture, with a brief excursion into energy policy. To this end I first outline a brief history of concepts of security, leading to the rise and prominence of environmental security in current policy debate. I then propose a non-traditional explanation for this prominence with the help of (slightly modified) Gramscian ideas about comprehensive concepts of control as developed by the 'Amsterdam school' of thinking regarding international relations. I also add elements from other schools of thought in emphasising the role of the state: particularly in thinking about how institutions shape actions and how issues can be apparently depoliticised and at the same time 'securitised'. In closing I make some observations regarding the theories employed to justify the salience of environmental security, as well as on the role of intellectuals in disseminating these theories.

11.2 Changing conceptions of security – a brief history

Today's society of states was shaped 350 years ago with the Peace of Westphalia which introduced the idea of state sovereignty and territorial integrity. Before Westphalia, city-states, commercial federations and other private entities, empires and bishoprics were players in the patchwork of Renaissance politics. Today's system of international security is still roughly based on the Westphalian arrangement, even though the unitary state remains a legal fiction. States are formally independent, endowed with absolute sovereignty – i.e. the supreme, independent and final authority – are clearly separated by borders and are obliged to follow a path of non-intervention in the domestic affairs of other states. In other words, we have a powerful image of states as unitary, impenetrable billiard balls. From this perspective, state acts are driven by the desire to protect and maximise the national interest. The state's key interest is seen as safeguarding its *security* in direct ratio to perceived threats to state survival. Since there is no superordinate authority to ensure order, each state must look after its own security needs.

While the Westphalian order brought clarity concerning who was entitled to what, it did not bring peace. Ever since 1648, the international state system has remained highly prone to conflict. In this context, and until recently, the study of International Relations has been primarily concerned with war and conflict. The Westphalian paradigm clearly gave priority to military security and diplomatic relations between states (*high politics*) over development issues, including economic and environmental issues (*low politics*), and it is inferred from the priorities of these issues in governance that states which fail to solve high political differences are unlikely to co-operate on low politics issues (Lowi, 1993).

Until 1945 this Westphalian scene was dominated by multipolarity, as the Five Great Powers carved up the globe between them. In the post-war era the Cold War redefined the international arena. The former Great Powers gradually shed their colonies. A bipolar world emerged, dominated by superpower rivalry, each with complex patron–client relations between states which gave newly decolonised states an opportunity to play off the two superpowers against each other. In the post-colonial era, and given an international aid and trading system which underspins colonial patterns of state centrality (Ayoob, 1997), new states have not been able to challenge the Westphalian order.

The fall of the Berlin Wall in 1989, however, has changed this state of affairs. Even prior to this, the traditional concerns of Security Studies had started to crumble. Foreign affairs agendas had become larger and more diverse, the traditional hierarchy among issues seemed to be steadily falling away and 'low politics' started to creep up the policy agenda. Robert Keohane and Joseph Nye (1977), for example, observed that '[n]o longer can all issues be subordinated to military security'. In particular, the 'energy crises' of the 1970s drove home to policy-makers that resources could very well be a high politics issue. As Japan's economic power grew to rival American hegemony in the mid-1980s, and as trade wars with the European Union became commonplace, students of International Political Economy started to focus on *economic security*, propelling a formerly 'low-politics' issue into the domain of 'high politics'.

The demise of the Soviet Union and the end of the Cold War opened the door to still more concepts of security. Cold War strategists found themselves looking for new significance. It dawned upon them that most conflicts are not battled out between states but *within* states: the number of civil wars outnumbers violent interstate exchanges. It was noted that, world-wide, governments do not so much fight each other as confront domestic opposition, and that not infrequently these conflicts involve 'natural resources' (Buzan *et al.*, 1995).

The principle of non-intervention between states came under fire when it became clear that local actions could easily spill over into international conflict and migration (see Saunders, Chapters 10, this volume). This gave rise to a debate about how environmental resources may become the objects of security strategies. Strategic natural resources in international conflict have been used as instruments and targets of war since time immemorial (Gleditsch, 1997). The new element in the alarmist publications of the early 1990s was the connection between resource scarcity and regional (and global!) *instability* – i.e. resource scarcity as a threat to *international security*. In the media John Bulloch and Adel Darwish and Joyce Starr sounded early alarms over impending 'Water Wars', and a deep nerve was struck by Robert Kaplan's article 'The Coming Anarchy' in *Atlantic Monthly* (1994), which linked concerns over environmental degradation, inner-city crime and drugs trafficking with alarm over state overload and ungovernability. Environmental degradation seemed sure to trigger conflict, notably in the developing world.

Academic scepticism about the concept of environmental security, however, is rather widespread. Authors such as Daniel Deudney have tried to prove the 'futility of the concept of environmental security' and Gleditsch (1997) provides an excellent critique of this literature. For example, it has been argued that prioritising environmental security overburdens states, would give them Orwellian powers, and is methodologically flawed because it takes the future as evidence: i.e. the incidence of 'water wars' and other resource degradation narratives is no more testable than the prediction that 'Jesus Christ will return soon'. Rather than dwell on the issue of whether or not we are in the throes of environmental catastrophe, I would like instead to venture an hypothesis on how the environment has come so close to the top of the security agenda by drawing on some Gramscian-style thinking about issues.

11.3 A neo-Gramscian approach

Let me first place Gramscian-thinking in its International Relations context. In simplified form, International Relations can be seen to harbour three competing paradigms: Realism, Pluralism and a smattering of critical schools such as *dependencia*, structuralists and post-positivists. In keeping with the old Westphalian order, the dominant strand in IR, Realism, starts from the idea of self-interested states vying for a dominant place in an inherently conflictual international system. Game theory (Prisoners' Dilemma theory), a favourite realist tool, predicts a great measure of non-cooperation. Realists will readily agree that, internally, the state represents the interests of the dominant power élite; accepting this state of affairs as normal. Regime theorists ('international relations pluralists') do not see the state as unitary, however, and instead view it as allowing national as well as sub-, inter-, supra- and transnational actors on the international scene. In particular, they recognise that the explosive, accelerating mobility of information, capital, commodities and people makes the billiard-ball metaphor more and more irrelevant. Instead of a unitary state, Pluralism pictures the state as a fragmented multiplicity of actors, with multiple state–society and translational relations both significant such that state and non-state entities are increasingly linked with foreign counterparts. This 'complex interdependence' in turn leads to increasing inter-national co-operation. Regime theory is a theory of convergence which, in its underlying functionalist logic, is seen as inevitable: the shadow of the future is long enough to make it worthwhile for states to work together on common problems and forgo short-term interests. However, while they may successfully minimise the potential for violent conflict, they are likely to leave underlying problems intact. Note that Pluralism has no problem accepting inequality within a society or a regime; indeed, to many American regime theorists the existence of a hegemony is the prerequisite for a regime.

Both Realism and functionalism have a limited, one-dimensional concept of power. A third school of International Relations, however, examines how overt and covert (Lukes, 1974) or structural power translates into social inequality. This approach, which after Murphy and Tooze can be labelled the new International Political Economy, views the international system as a product of the historical expansion of capitalism as an economic and social system. Similarly, in Marxist thought, a society is not conceived as a homogeneous whole, as Realists would have it, but as a differentiated reality of social strata. Power is not just used by states but extends to all social relations. In this amalgam, the capitalist class exerts 'structural power' over state and society. Structural power can be defined as an 'enduring capacity to act, which may or may not be exercised on any particular occasion' (Isaac in Sklair, 1998); in fact it may be the power not just to set the rules but to call the type of game.

All this will come as no surprise to the reader. The insights of the Amsterdam regulation school, however, stem from the realisation that within any dominant élite there is a necessary division of interests, strongly correlating with the business orientation of its constituent members. They analyse the divisions within the capitalist class to see which calls the shots at a certain moment in history. These fractions constantly realign along axes of conflict, predominantly over the *degree* and type of trade protection exerted by the state (for example, through creating quasi-monopolies, imposing tariffs, restriction on capital mobility and trade, discrimination against foreign capital) as opposed to free trade. With respect to disposition, two ideal-type orientations are identifiable: the view of productive, fixed capital and that of circulating, highly mobile capital. The material, soil-bound nature of productive capital (agriculture, industry) implicates a more entrenched outlook – industries are less flexible and more concerned with availability of labour, regional markets, recouping sunk costs and protection from foreign competition. Circulating capital (banks, financial services) thrives with open frontiers, allowing money to find its way to the highest rate of return.

Of course these main fractions are themselves fractured, reflecting different stages of developing capitalism, e.g. traditional agrobanks vs. speculative offshore capital. They are also *dynamic*, and the changing 'risk horizons' of their actors are influenced by the process of virtualisation, i.e. the disembedding or 'removal of economic activities from the social and other [environmental] relationships in which they had occurred' such that they are carried out 'in a context in which the only important relationships are those defined by the economic activity itself' (Carrier, 1998: 2). Although Marxian economic theory presupposes productive capital to be the logical basis for any circulatory activity, the functions may become geographically dispersed. A historic instance began in the 1970s, when tiny, sandy Kuwait could mobilise its oil resources to expand its industrial activities (steel production) in Germany, and then become a financial portfolio: an almost 'virtual state', i.e. the KIC (Kuwait Investment Company), which you can pick up and take somewhere else. The age of the Internet takes the virtualisation of money and matter to even more baffling extremes, enhancing the dominance of financial interests over everything else supported since 1972, with the end of Bretton Woods, via which the international balance of forces gave much more autonomy to the banking and financial system relative to corporate, state and personal financing. This has made the system more crisis-prone, but also enabled financial institutions to move capital around 'almost oblivious of the constraints of time and space that normally pin down material activities' (Harvey, 1989).

How is it possible that increasingly unequal social power relations and conflicting interests continue to exist while the consent of subordinate groups is gained? This can be explained by the way structural power is embedded in social constructs. In researching this structural power, the 'Amsterdam School' in International Political Economy draws heavily on the work of Antonio Gramsci, notably his *Prison Notebooks*, written in 1922 during his incarceration in Fascist Italy (a selected translation appeared in 1971). Gramsci, an Italian Marxist, was disenchanted with the determinism and materialism in Marx's work. He rehabilitated the power of ideas and knowledge in historic developments, recognising they are never neutral, but always 'for someone and for some purpose' (Gill, 1993). Thus ideas legitimise, cement and perpetuate political control structures.

Gramscian concepts-of-control theory usefully fuses the material and ideational. Meaning is not the automatic outcome of material interests, but can be managed and manipulated; as can theories about the future including future environments. Gramsci draws an important distinction between coercive (dominance) and consensual (legitimacy) leadership. Following Sklair (1998: 150),

> [t]he mobilisation of the active consent of peripheral groups to a given order, . . . is more effective than coercion. Hegemony is achieved by core interests (in the form of classes, states, transnational actors) through a combination of coercive and consensual means. The latter is built on a system of alliances which must be continually readjusted and renegotiated to prevent peripheral groups from forming a potentially counter-hegemonic movement.

From this view, as global capitalism evolves, it is considered to change power relations between various production-related interests, with corresponding changes in social organisation seen to be the dependent variable. Thus we can look at the outcome and see what material interests (hegemonic coalitions) benefit, and thereby arrive at a political explanation for a particular set of economic and ideological interrelationships. While domination can be effected through coercion it is also achieved through hegemony. This requires a combination of coercive and consensual means, the latter 'built on a system of alliances which must continually be readjusted and renegotiated to prevent peripheral groups from potentially forming a counter-hegemonic movement'. Hegemony is not dominance: it is legitimated leadership. It allows me to go ahead with a social or political project that may be manifestly not in your material interests, but make you accept it regardless, perhaps even whole-heartedly, as I have persuaded you that it is only in your best interests.

At the ideas level, *hegemony* is found in groups of every size and ilk. I can persuade you that my interest is really the common good by taking into account those aspects of your interests that suit me – I may even compromise on aspects that are less essential to my interests. Of course a real or imagined external threat ('they are out to destroy us!') always comes in useful in this kind of team building. But where there's hegemony, there is a niche for counterhegemony, a counter-coalition intent on overthrowing the ruling coalition. The coalitions are forever shifting and may even be composed of some of the some actors. Ultimately, a synthesis will be arrived at, in which parts of both merge.

Antonio Gramsci was the first major figure to look seriously into the 'ideational superstructure' of Fordism. The Amsterdam School, led by Kees van der Pijl and Henk Overbeek, together with like-minded Canadian scholars based in York University (Robert Cox, Stephen Gill) and others (e.g. Sol Picciotto), have since been active in exploring and applying a Gramscian view of hegemony to various domains of International Relations. Hegemony implies a certain degree of legitimacy: leadership is accepted if only because an unpopular leader is preferred to instability and chaos. Hegemonic actors can afford to embark on a goodwill strategy to integrate centrifugal forces in their political project. When that strategy is too obviously self-interested, these forces may not be so forthcoming.

Following Stephen Gill (1993), Gramsci's theory can be said to have three main characteristics:

1   Agent and structure are both recognised – social relations consist of historic structures. A historically specific ensemble of social structures and forces produce the progressive globalisation of the international political economy.
2   It is post-positivist in that it holds that social reality and knowledge production are interdependent. The latter, in turn, cannot be separated from how concrete material interests are defined and realised.
3   Acknowledging that the role of the scholar cannot be separated from the social context s/he studies, scholarship should further debates on social justice, legitimacy and moral credibility.

In this chapter these three elements are explored in relation to ideas of 'environmental security' by pursuing the following themes:

(a) capital fractions and the state;
(b) hegemonial projects and concepts of control related to interests;
(c) the role of theories and who frames them.

11.4 Capital fractions and the state

There are different paths in state-making. The earliest states arose in semi-arid regions to regulate and harness water resources. These states required a great amount of control and were extremely authoritarian. In the pre-industrial world, agriculture dominated human life, first of autonomous villages, but soon the scale increased. In China, India, and the Middle East in 4000 BC people learned to master flood control, which required large-scale organisation. In these redistributive 'hydraulic states', wealth flowed from the outbacks to the centre, and water flowed back again. The irrigation state had to be defended against, among others, marauding nomads. States want control not transhumance. Nomads unwittingly cross borders and are hard to keep track of. So, to this day, states have tried to delegitimise the nomadic style (Bryant and Bailey, 1997) and provide a material incentive for the settlement of nomads by supplying water at a fixed point and fixed time. An example is the way in which pastoralists were settled on a large scale in Saudi Arabia in the 1920s. This reduced nomadic uncertainty in finding water (obviously very important in Saudi Arabia), and the state's uncertainty in administratively controlling them. The interests seem symmetrical but they are not: the state's control of nomads easily can be extractive, while the nomads' control of the state in terms of obstructive power (non-compliance) is extremely limited.

Modern (industrial) capitalism began in England, the cradle of free trade and internationalism, and expanded to America. In both countries an entrepreneurial, free trade-oriented middle class soon dominated the state, while competing continental states tended to be protectionist. The later a country industrialised, the larger and more obtrusive its state institutions became. As Feigenbaum *et al.* (1998) note,

> [w]ith surplus capital a rare and highly dispersed commodity in agricultural societies, those countries which had, or could create, institutions for gathering and centralizing capital were more likely to develop competitive industries. Thus, Germany and France had greater public sectors than Britain and the USA, Japan more so than Germany and France, and Russia the largest and most repressive of all.

In recent years the globalisation of economy has seen Germany, Japan and France move towards a model of facilitation while authoritorian states now are predominantly in the 'South'.

After van der Pijl (1992) the latter may be termed 'Hobbesian'-type states and the former 'Lockeian'. Indeed van der Pijl builds his whole historical model on competing Lockeian and Hobbesian political theories and configurations. Thomas Hobbes postulated the war of all against all, and advocated the absolutist state (the Leviathan) as the only way to safeguard individual securities. For him, the state needed to be absolutist, if derobed of the earlier transcendental overtones of church and empire. John Locke, on the other hand, being a strong believer in the self-regulating power of civil society, postulated total freedom and independence. Private property needed to be safeguarded by the state, nothing more. Interestingly, the 'use it or lose it' frontier ideology is very apparent in his writing.

In Gramscian theory, the existence of a *state class* and an underdeveloped social base characterises the authoritarian Hobbesian state. Competing against advanced Lockean states, they will have to undergo a 'passive revolution', i.e. to hold on to their power, they have to impose a 'top-down' revolution that contains some elements of the original 'revolution'. This goes some way to explaining the enthusiasm with which some Southern élites accepted Chicago economics and Structural Adjustment Programmes in the post-Fordist 1980s and 1990s (i.e. the age of 'flexible accumulation', Harvey, 1989).

In Europe, crucially, the modern state arrived with a vigorous middle class, defeating complex feudal structures and dual allegiances of church and state. There was (and still is) a clear symbiosis between states and economic actors: states provide economic actors with security, stability and protection, while they rely on the economic surplus generated by the capitalist class for their tax base.

States are not simply political bodies, however; they are also institutions: they are Weberian machine bureaucracies geared to standardisation, predictability and, especially, legal–administrative control over resources and people. Institutions as well as states compete for discretionary power but as the formal monopolist on the means of violence the state will not tolerate competing power centres. Because of their nature, then, many states have tried to mould the economy in their image to make it 'manageable'. States are likely to make a better 'fit' with place-bound, sedentary agriculture and industry, as those bound to the soil have predictable inputs and markets. As noted, the interests of agriculture and industry are informed by their sunk costs – they cannot move their units of production as easily as financial institutions can. As a result, they are more inclined to serve a home market and be concerned with a minimum degree of employment as a basis for purchasing power. States, then, have been very helpful in facilitating the process of enclosure, here and in developing countries because this creates clarity of property rights and thus lays the basis for taxability. But as the industrial sector has become increasingly mobile, financial capital strengthened its hand and the overlay of global competition has made itself felt: in this context the sovereignty of the state has started to fall apart at the seams from the inside as well as the outside.

True, the relative strength of economic actors *vis-à-vis* states is important here. In earlier days, some entrepreneurial states even engaged in commodity trade and piracy, striking deals with formal and informal enterprising sectors. Until recently, the East Asian tigers could feel strong enough to impose controls on capital, i.e. could (threaten to) regulate it. But following the 1997 speculation concerning the Malaysian ring, states have increasingly lost control and are now forced to liberalise their economies, thus facilitating rather than dominating the private sector. The public sector is at risk of becoming, as it were, a sector among many, and it is this situation which provides the background to my exploration of increasing environmental security concerns.

11.5 Securitisation: three cases

I now add a 'neo-realist' flavour to the account by introducing and drawing on securitisation theory. My primary concern is the observation that the presentation of environmental issues under a security flag promotes a 'low-politics' issue to high politics. Through doing this it helps exact the commitment of exceptional political action and resources. And, given that knowledge is never value-neutral, the thinking, theorising and 'evidence' used in support of environmental security arguments end up underpinning political arguments for hegemonic strategies which tend to serve some groups more than others.

Something is deemed a strategic/security good when it is essential to (personal or state) survival: oil, food, and water are examples. Buzan *et al.* (1995) have come up with the word 'securitisation' to describe this process. It can become a strategic (state) interest that transcends politics. For example, in the Middle East, water is considered of such strategic importance that it is 'securitised': it is elevated to the level of the undebatable and takes on a 'pre-political immediacy' – in other words, it is *depoliticised* (see Allan, Chapter 5, this volume). Importantly, there is always an 'absolute' element involved that renders the issue area well nigh non-negotiable. Thus, when we say that a resource is *securitisable* we are providing 'an excuse for bending the rules' in terms of how state resources are utilised: invoking a justification for the release of 'necessary' monetary amounts to, for example, the arms industry (Red Scare), coastal defence (water scare) and even literacy programmes for backward children in the 1950s under the Defence Act. An example of tagging an issue on to (inter)national security is the legitimation of intervention, e.g. securitising oil to legitimise intervention in Iraq. Basically, securitisation is a way of 'jumping the queue of political priority' (Buzan *et al.*, 1995).

NGOs can perform the same trick: securitising the salmon to release energy for cleaning up the River Rhine and speeding up the drafting of the Rhine Action Plan, or securitising the seas to stop Exxon's decommissioned Brent Spar platform being dumped into it. NGOs such as Greenpeace are highly aware of the power of this mechanism. During the Brent Spar affair, they got the facts wrong but when that surfaced, the general public just didn't mind. It had been swayed by an emotional argument: the 'securitisation' of the sea. Representing a commodity (food, water, oil) as scarce, or a country as 'underdeveloped', then invoking the relevant theory, seems an effective lever for releasing resources for exceptional measures. Of course, you need sufficient clout to be able to call a crisis.

Securitising Spaceship Earth has proved more difficult than securitising the salmon. Despite the 'Limits to Growth' scare coinciding with the oil crisis and NIEO optimism of the early 1970s, securitising the *environment* did not quite take off first time around, although in the 1990s things seem to be on the move. For the purposes of this chapter, my perspective on securitisation is to try and understand it as a management-of-meaning mechanism for some material interest: that is, to illuminate the way that coalitions of capital fractions are cemented to help depoliticise an issue and present it as the 'general interest'. It is this process which is explored in the account which comprises the next section.

11.5.1 Securitising agriculture

Keynesian Fordism, supplanting Taylorism and now superseded by 'neo-liberalism', has become the most well-known comprehensive concept of control. Fordism takes its name from car-maker Henry Ford who, at the turn of the century, improved working conditions in his factory by famously offering a $5-a-day minimum wage which provided both workers with purchasing power and industrial producers, such as himself, a market, as well as with stable labour relations. This arrangement was taken up to the federal level (Keynesian mode of state regulation) in the face of emerging socialism to prevent the serious destabilising potential of *Verelendung* (immiseration, now known as 'social exclusion'). Franklin D. Roosevelt's New Deal not only created jobs in infrastructural works and agriculture, it legitimised Big Government.

American Fordism was exported to Europe after the Second World War. A Depression ideology, the Marshall Plan, prevented immiseration and ensuing socialist sympathies. Securitising the whole of the West (the Cold War) freed up unthought resources for technological progress – the famed military–industrial complex. But it can be argued that Fordism had a strong agricultural component that was internationalised after 1945. In the face of post-war hunger and destitution, international agricultural efforts were directed at the creation of a World Food Board. As Carrier (1998: 88) argues, during the Second World War governments on both sides had undertaken:

massive, co-ordinated efforts to direct the production and distribution of food. The Allies continued to control food after the war for relief and rehabilitation of war-torn countries. . . . In the United States, organised farm lobbies gained support for farmers in the form of government purchases to support prices, as well as controlled imports. In Great Britain, the home of Free Trade, bread rationing was introduced a year after the war ended.

Government had to bridge the conflict of interest between high producer prices and low consumer prices. The resulting regime was the most intensely state regulated of all the 'Fordist' sectors (Carrier, 1998: 88). Surpluses were disposed of through food aid, first to Europe and Japan, then to the Middle East and the Third World and China, finally even to the Soviet Union. The response of other states was to regulate agriculture just as intensely as the United States.

At the start, the regime was modelled on small farms that would no doubt have had to succumb to unregulated competition. But as technological advances continued, producers were increasingly subordinated to industrial and financial capital. Third World countries were encouraged to boost their own agriculture by adopting Green Revolution technologies – the key sponsor of which happened to be the Rockefeller Foundation (which of course was totally unrelated to Rockefeller's agrochemicals interest!). In the process, small farmers were simply pushed aside to make way for efficient export-oriented cash cropping. 'Development' became a sacred cow – another instance of successful 'securitisation' – with handsome profits for Western exporters of expertise and technology. But there were winners in the South, too. As Tony Allan cogently argues, the availability of cheap, subsidised food in the international agromarket bailed out wealthy states in arid climates who found it increasingly hard to feed their rapidly growing population (see Allan, Chapter 5, this volume).[2] The welfare system wasn't there for everybody, however. Food *exporters* who happened not to be strategic to US foreign policy or 'Lomé' countries ran up against stiff import tariffs: ironically, they were the ones to advocate freer trade to exploit what seemed to be their comparative advantage.

In Europe, agricultural Fordism had created an elaborate subsidy system to maximise food production that favoured farmers, industry and traders. European agriculture has a highly productive, large-scale and intensively farmed north-west (Benelux, Ile de France, England, North Germany) and a not-so-productive, small-scale, extensively farmed Central and Southern region. The Common Agricultural Policy was largely formulated in the image of the hi-tech, land-poor Netherlands. In 1968, the Mansholt Plan had basically concluded small farms had to go, but compensated the inefficient South in a Europe-wide welfare system. In the early 1990s the international scene had changed – massive transfers of income were no longer acceptable in the age of neoliberalism. Jacques Delors' 'Social Europe', portraying agriculture as an essentially social (cohesive) and environmental activity, was challenged by Margaret Thatcher's free-trade Atlanticism, which perceived agriculture as the production of tradable commodities like any other industry (industrial farming). This time, the MacSharry plans for CAP reform came from an Irishman – a Commissioner from a land-rich, not so high-tech country. It stressed the social and ecological necessity of keeping people on the land. The new compromise hammered out now conveniently included environmental concerns: the most competitive producers (English, Benelux, French) were encouraged to compete, with grant aid shifting to more environmentally sensible set-aside schemes, while the weaker ones had to reinvent themselves as stewards of nature or accept a generous early retirement provision. This seemed like a conditional victory for the environmental lobby. Ultimately, though, big business had won the game – international agrofood corporations such as Monsanto had outgrown the national regimes that set them up. Agriculture had always constituted the main exception to GATT, at the instigation of the US but enthusiastically condoned by Europe and Japan, taking away a sector where Third World countries traditionally enjoyed a competitive advantage. Now the same Americans forced the abolition of agricultural tariffs. Agribusiness operating in trade, processing and supply of farm inputs successfully defeated protectionists, even getting seats at the food safety standards (*Codex Alimentarius*) board (Ritchie, 1991).

11.5.2 Securitising the environment

We have seen how the environmental issue became part of the package to rescue the compromise between different economic interests. Let us now see how the environment entered the debate. The 'first wave of environmentalism' took place in the context of a Fordist hegemonic world order and coincided with the transnationalisation of production and the internationalisation of the state. In this process of consensus formation, the main countries of the West and their structure of negotiation were most influential, transferring the settlement to Third World states, co-opting Third World élites, and together constituting a 'transnational managerial class'. The development of transnational *banking* changed the international 'content' of the transnationalisation, if not the 'form', and encouraged the 'transition to neo-liberalism', a 'doing away with ideas on the necessity of state regulation of economy and society' (Kolk, 1994; Cox, 1987) and a phasing out of the independent role of the state.

The 1970s Club of Rome reports had sent shockwaves through international societies, but due to its radical 'zero-growth' demands it largely failed to make a political impact. But in the 1980s, the less influential but still important regulationist coalition in international organisations examined the environmental problems in terms of international solidarity and 'a common future' – this time coupled with an economic growth imperative. Sustainable development seemed a 'metafix' that will unite everybody. A kind of *environmental Fordism* seemed to emerge but how to depoliticise it and turn it into an hegemonic strategy? Teaming up environmentalists with economic protectionists seemed to work at first, but this alliance foundered when free-traders gained the upper hand in GATT. GATT ruled that local environmental policies, not international trade policies should be toughened up: import restrictions on commodities produced by environmentally unsound production process were now banned.

11.5.3 Securitising the Westphalian order?

GATT seemed a defeat for the attempts to construct an environmentalist hegemony, but meanwhile something else reared its head: the return of global environmental threats in the shape of global *risk*. This was the outcome of a change in perception rather than a scientific breakthrough: some of the same information climatologists presented to demonstrate a global cooling effect was now recycled in evidence of global warming (cf. Adams, 1995: 161)! Still, the perception of global risk shook the financial sector with assertions that '[t]he bond uniting the "coolers" and the "warmers" is *instability*' (Adams, 1995: 167). While speculative capital thrives on instability, reinsurance companies became apprehensive – particularly with the dramatic downfall of some Lloyds underwriters still relatively fresh in our memory. The predicted increase in the incidence of disasters led Swiss Re, one of the biggest firms, to take the worst-case scenario very seriously, and it responded by adopting the precautionary principle (Leggett, in Prins, 1993). The turnaround is potentially important as insurance companies not only have the leverage to demand and realise change in the 'wiring diagram of global energy use' (Prins, 1993) but to force decisions in other areas as well. However schizophrenically detached from the 'real economy', this part of the financial sector is not immune from global misfortune, and increasingly realises the degree to which 'natural disasters' might be human-made.

Of course the energy industry was having none of it. The 'Seven Sisters', who 'first blocked and then determined the content of environmental regimes on maritime (oil) pollution' (Buzan *et al.*, 1995) started harnessing scientific evidence against the greenhouse effect. By the mid 1990s, the Global Climate Coalition, a vehicle for the oil industry, had spent over a million dollars to downplay the threat of climate change (Gelbspan, 1995). As a 'veto actor' (Porter and Welsh-Brown, 1995) the energy sector has every motive to 'undersecuritise' and depoliticise environmental issues, which they can because of their monopoly or oligopoly on economy – and technological knowledge (Buzan *et al.*, 1995).

This development can change the line-up of hegemonic alliances, unless actors reinvent themselves. With oil prices sinking deeper and deeper. Royal Dutch Shell is already hedging its bets and investing heavily in renewable sources of energy (Shell Solar),[3] a major diversion of capital away from carbon-fuel technologies. In itself, institutional adaptation is a normal, secular process in the course of history. Just as species adapt to their environment until they are outcompeted, sectors may respond to developments in the global economic system by changing their outlook. As capitalism develops, some modes of production risk becoming increasingly marginalised, even irrelevant. While hanging on to a cherished discourse of food security, farmers have long exerted political influence way beyond their number and contribution to GNP, but in the late twentieth century, the sector had the choice either to reinvent themselves or disappear: back to 'niche agriculture' (regional produce), turning 'eco', or virtualising by letting the biotechnology industry take over (GMOs).

But an important new window of opportunity in promoting the environmental agenda was the fall of the Berlin Wall in 1989 which left the security community without a rationale. For the first time since 1917, the state itself has come under attack and may need to reinvent itself. A 'crisis of hegemony, or "general crisis of the state" (Gramsci, 1971: 210) is a regular feature of capitalism – in Gramsci's day it was the crisis resulting from the First World War and the ascent of Communism (Sklair, 1998: 151).

In the 1980s, Thatcherism eroded industry, labour unions and local government in favour of financial services, but it stopped at eroding central government. In the early 1990s, however, the state itself became increasingly perceived as threatened by erosion, not just from the outside (globalisation) but from the inside as well (NGOs, alternative power centres). As the Communist threat had gone, the defence budget was under pressure. History itself seemed to have come to an end (Fukuyama, 1992) – the rationale for the state seemed archaic. The hegemony of international (investment) capital and obsolescence of financial controls rendered the state toothless. But if it fell, it would drag down with it the interests that depend on its protection. World agricultural prices were predicted to rise after the phasing out of US and EU subsidies, which would badly affect states like Egypt. Already whole parts of the world (notably Africa) were close to being written off and the US increasingly seemed to turn inward to its domestic problems.

As military budgets are increasingly diverted from Cold War hardware to more conventional 'peacekeeping' packages, a new arrangement of international clientelism seems to be emerging. Especially in the US, alarm over possible 'resource wars' hit a raw nerve and there is a tendency to see the allocation of development funds for sustainable development in the light of security (Duffield, 1998).

There is a 'supply' and a 'demand' side to this. As security institutions set about reinventing themselves, they are looking for new relevance in the world, and identify new dangers and protectable interests to lavish their resources on. Having lost its obvious necessity, security sectors must have been keen to identify new, vital post-Cold War threats: organised crime, terrorism, cyber-sabotage, drug trafficking, migration, terrorism, uncontrollable violence in rundown inner cities. Instability through civil war and migration made countries less safe for investment. So the logical solution seems to be: invent new essential threats. The war on drugs, terrorism, traffic in Soviet nuclear material and, last but not least, environmental degradation might rehabilitate the state. The alarm bells over 'water wars' in the Middle East aroused some US officials. And lo and behold, the defence budgets were on the rise again, even before 'Kosovo'.

On the demand side, recipient states, no longer automatically supported by East or West for ideological reasons, need to find new reasons for attracting strategic funds and international back-up, as they see their power eroded from various sides: externally, the forces of globalisation, internally, the popularity of non-state contenders for power. Now Bolivia joins the war on drugs, its biggest export. In the security studies community, the erosion (failure, or collapse) of the state as the monopolist on the means of violence, and resulting *ungovernability*, are portrayed as the key threat to international stability. Indeed, African 'warlords' may seek to control strategic resources (including water) to advance their power base; the resulting struggles, it is feared, may spill over into international conflicts. The use of the state machinery for private (illegal) enrichment is another such factor (Frerks, 1998). But ultimately it means the erosion of the Westphalian system and the scope for its control by a transnational coalition.

What seems to be portrayed as *scarce* here is not food or water but *regulatory capacity*. Such observations give rise to an intensified call for propping up states to restore a semblance of international order and stability in a turbulent world. Cloaking this concern in neutral environmental terms and not in the need to protect naked business interest is likely to improve its wider acceptability. The Hobbesian Leviathan is now dressed in green.

11.6 Theories of environmental insecurity

So far we have looked at 'states' and 'sectors' as having 'political projects'. But where do the underpinnings of these projects come from? In formulating political programmes, intellectuals have always played an important role, especially political philosophers.

Theories of International Relations, like all theories, bear the hallmark of their creators. It can hardly be coincidental that American authors, Neo-realists and Regime theorists alike, currently dominate the field. In Neo-realist analysis hegemonic states are seen to create and maintain a particular form of order in the international economy. Realism is based on Hobbesian (Darwinian) philosophy: the survival of the fittest. The toughest billiard ball gains the upper hand. Ideas do not count for much in traditional Realism; they are subservient to the power interests of the (American) state.

Functionalism (regime theory), on the other hand, explains why it became 'logical' and 'useful' to converge on rules, which in terms are based on values. (Even liberal regime theory is not as 'ideas-based' as it seems: it readily acknowledges the utility of side payments and a bit of coercion to maintain hegemonic power). Interestingly, one strand of regime theory explicitly singles out scientists as actors in international policy formation. *Epistemic communities* may provide crucial information to overcome co-operation deadlocks (Haas *et al.*, 1993). Haas acknowledges the possibility of mutually opposed epistemic communities, but still seems to believe in 'objective', impartial science.

For Gramscians there can be no such thing. A Foucauldian perspective identifies a mutually reinforcing triangle of institutions, intellectuals and ideology. The processes by which certain intellectual figures become regarded as experts whereas other voices get marginalised has been theorised in Tuathail *et al.* (1998: 7–8). Gramsci attributes an active role to intellectuals in the creation and sustenance of hegemonic formations. Any developing social group that has an essential function in economic production will itself give rise to one or more strata of intellectuals that lend it homogeneity and consciousness of its function, in an economic as well as a social and political sense. Locke, Hobbes and those preceding and succeeding them were not, of course, writing class manifestos but their philosophical ideas helped create the intellectual resource base of the emergent bourgeoisie. As van der Pijl (1992: 2) states: '[a]ll political theory can be seen as a recommendation to think in a certain direction which, through a process of mutation and selection became part of a concrete power constellation between classes and between states and nations'. They are alternative concepts, one of which temporarily approaches the general interests, but may be superseded by another without it leading to a total crisis of the social system.

It would be hopelessly naïve, therefore, to suggest that academic ideas are quite separate from global politics. On the contrary, the symbiosis between university professors ('organic intellectuals'), government and private interests can be striking – there is always a shortage of money and the lure of prestige. Political scientists, regrettably, are among the worst culprits, trying to get very close to the seats of power. Ever since Machiavelli lent his Advice to the Prince, inciting him to ignore basic human rights when it was convenient to do so (Machiavelli, 1952 [1532]), things seem to have gone pretty much downhill. Notably in international politics, subsidising and made-to-order research have taken on abhorrent forms (van der Pijl, 1992). The Vietnam intervention, for example, in part designed to save Vietnam for the free market, was dreamt up by such behaviouralists as Asia specialist Staley who thought they could capture the 'hearts and minds' of the Viet Cong by force of liberal constitutionalism and forced labour in 12,000 'strategic hamlets' (van der Pijl, 1992: 239). Notably in the United States, political scientists have seen fit to frame their research 'in the American interest' (Strange, 1982, see also below). Just like the economic interests of some can be conflated to the interest of all, the particular American interest is easily conflated to the interests of the global population.

It does not seem entirely fortuitous that the ascent of theories of co-operation has coincided with the rise of international (neo)liberalism, ending the 'domestic class compromise and turning the financial world into the organising force of the global system of production' (van der Pijl, 1992: 262, my translation). This world-view was strongly advocated in the 1980s by those looking for a breakdown of protectionism, notably *vis-à-vis* Japan. Their 'cobweb' view of the world offers a different perspective on the role of the state. The power of complex interdependence, the theory predicted, would slowly but surely erode the centrality of the state, which was regarded as positive. The 'invisible hand' of interdependence thus promotes integration, reduces nationalism and promotes stable peace. As a consequence, government will become smaller. (Note that this prediction, despite widespread liberalisation, has not yet been borne out in practice – liberalised economies seem to give rise to bigger rather than smaller states as there is more to 'regulate'.)

Revealingly, the security concerns of the 1990s see Realist hegemonic theory interspersed with greentalk. Norman Myers, to quote one respected American environmental author, can claim without any eyebrows raised that peace in critical regions will depend on

an open global economy with particular respect to US access to important markets and key resources, safeguarding the political and economic stability of American allies and of nonaligned nations, preventing undue expansion of nations and influences opposed to American values, and fostering orderly relations among the community of nations.

(Myers, 1994)

He adds to these familiar American concerns the protection of the global environment, thereby promoting sustainable development throughout the world. Underlying his argument are two theories. First, 'security = stability' (as the sub-title to his book attests). Strange (1982) has argued in her critique of regime theory that obsession with order and stability completely overlooks the equally legitimate need for radical change to redress economic imbalances, thereby increasing the economic security of the disadvantaged (security = change). Second, Myers approvingly quotes World Banker McNamar's Lockeian belief that '(s)ecurity is development, and without development there can be no security. Our [American] security is related directly to the security of the developing world.' It will be interesting to see what ideas American Vice-President A1 Gore, the 'Green' candidate for the Presidency in the year 2000, will develop on 'green' American leadership in the international community.

Robert Kaplan – a journalist, not a scholar – recently has become the darling of the establishment. The reason may be the simplicity of his argument. His persuasive article (1994), as it were, rolls environmental degradation, inner city crime, drug and nuclear trafficking into one security concern: *ungovernability*. While advanced with panache, Kaplan's argument basically revives the (Neo)-Malthusian thesis, then couples it with Hobbesian state theory, i.e.:

population growth => increased competition for resources => Tragedy of the Commons => acute resource conflict

The underlying notion in environmental security thought is that resource scarcity leads to conflict. Each individual competes with other individuals for scarce resources; this creates a situation of mutual rivalry and threat characterised by chronic uncertainty and the perception of others as potential enemies. Only a strong state can counter this permanent state of nature. By way of example, Kaplan notes the loss of control in Western African states following the collapse of the cocoa market. But as James Tansey (1999) points out:

Kaplan describes this as a metaphor for the 'Coming Anarchy' in the light of population growth. In reality it is probably more useful as an example of how economic interdependence can have malevolent consequences . . . [t]he point is *not* that in the face of G[lobal] E[nvironmental] C[hange], societies will necessarily collapse but that by failing to provide basic security, the legitimacy of a nation state may be undermined.

This last point touches on the more recent work of Thomas Homer-Dixon, who emerged as the main advocate of positing natural rather than social causes for socio-political changes: '[n]ature is coming back with a vengeance, tied to population growth. It will have incredible security implications.' This is to forget to question how people came into this position and if they might not co-operate rather than fight. To be fair, however, Homer-Dixon allows for *values and politics* as intervening variables, has now discredited the water wars theory, and has become increasingly careful in drawing direct relations, wondering, for example, whether the resilience of social institutions may be an important intermediary variable. As he states, 'For every one environment-conflict case study presented, we can probably find several other global examples where situations with ecologically similar conditions did not result in conflict' (Homer-Dixon, 1994). But judging by the number of writers quoting him (Homer-Dixon, 1999), the damage has already been done.

It is interesting that there has not been much of a counter-attack to Environmental Security publications. While there have been isolated outcries to environmental protectionism (Baghwati, 1993 is an example) there is no uniform free-market, Cornucopian opposition to it mobilising scientists the way the energy industry is mobilising to disprove the greenhouse effect. It is true, however, that the work of the darling of neoliberal America, Fukuyama, is sponsored by the Olin Foundation (founded by an American gunpowder manufacturer), which was especially set up to circulate certain ideas among intellectuals (van der Pijl, 1992: 265–6) and in doing so to legitimise neoliberalism. Fukuyama's 'End of history' (1992) is a globalised marketplace where the Hobbesian state, with its politicians and generals, has given way to predominantly economic activities – as Carrier might phrase it, the ultimate disembedding of global society. The lack of an outspoken anti-Environmental Security school seems slightly worrying to me: it would only join the debate if it felt itself to be under threat.

11.7 An afterthought

I have refrained from presenting 'environmental security' as a new 'comprehensive' concept of control, on a par with Keynesian Fordism and flexible accumulation (Neo-liberalism). At most, it can make an important component of one – the actual packaging will change in accordance with whatever seems strategically useful, as the political struggle in the arena of meaning continues. Where there is hegemony, there is always a locus for counter-hegemony. Finally, in true dialectic fashion, hegemonial and counterhegemonial ideas may fuse into a synthesis, taking the process to a higher, more comprehensive stage.[5]

What is this synthesis? How will 'state-first' environmental protectionism and 'market-first' neo-liberalism melt into one? A possible, cynical thesis is that states are increasingly adapting to an informalisation of the world economy. In this hyperreal, hyper-liberal world, place-bound territory and regulatory capacity are already an anachronism in a world characterised by what Timothy W. Luke calls the 'flow', an endless turbulence where '(h)aving open and unconstrained access to the flows, not closed domination of places, perhaps becomes as crucial an attribute as sovereignty in informationalised societies' (Luke in Tuathail *et al.*, 1998).

All of this should make political ecologists (as an epistemic community in their own right) think of for whom or what they are writing and doing research from their (our?) ivory towers – the forces of sovereignty or the forces of access. The recent controversy over genetically modified organisms ('Frankenfood') already seems to have moved away from the original outrage over repeated attempts to silence, then discredit whistle-blowing Professor Pusztai for the sake of key biotech players such as Monsanto and retailers such as J. Sainsbury. We would do well to keep reminding ourselves of episodes like these everytime we hear the phrase 'objective science'.[6]

Notes

1   Editors' note: Following Cilliers (1998: 55) 'speech-act theory' argues 'that the meaning of an utterance depends on the context in which the speech act is performed, where 'context' includes

the social conventions pertaining to the act ... the success of the act is determined by the congruence of the intentions of the speaker and the given circumstances or context'. In this case, the language of 'environmental security' *works* because it is invoked in a context of widely held concerns regarding environmental degradation and ecological sustainability.

2   This 'water welfare system' effectively redistributed root-zone water, so plentiful in temperate-zone Western Europe and the US, to the water-poor Middle East. Thus recipient states could claim that there was enough water and hold on to their tenuous legitimacy bases (e.g. Allan, 1997).

3   My 1960s' generation grew up in the absolute confidence that oil stocks would be running out in 50 years from then. But as it looks now, stocks will last for the next 200 years. Have our insights been improved on the basis of new methods or were we fooled? Similarly, the 'oil crisis' supposedly created scarcity in the global energy market. Now it turns out that even at the climax of the 'oil crisis' there was never a question of scarcity – in Holland, oil tankers were queuing in Rotterdam causing a (navigational) traffic nuisance (Hellema *et al.*, 1998). Experiences like these teach one to be distrustful of 'scarcities' and 'objective information'.

4   'Theory' of course has different meanings. Here it is loosely used in the sense of 'pre-assumed model'.

5   For purposes of clarity it could make sense to separate 'inside' counterhegemonies that share the discourse and interest in a certain mode of social organisation yet differ on the preferred degree of state regulation (e.g. liberal vs. conservative) from 'outside' (dissident) coalitions that question both.

6   Editors' note: paradoxically, it is now acknowledged that the media's use of Pusztai's work was not 'objective' either. Every 'scientific' attempt to discredit biotechnology in agriculture has to date proved unsubstantiated.

References

Adams, J. 1995: *Risk*. London: University College London.

Allan, J.A. 1997: 'Virtual water': a long-term solution for water short Middle Eastern economies. Paper presented at the 1997 British Association Festival of Science, University of Leeds, 9 September.

Ayoob, M. 1997: Defining security: a subaltern realist perspective. In Krause, Keith and Williams (eds), *Critical security studies: concepts and cases*. London: UCL Press, 121–48.

Baghwati, J. 1993: The case for free trade. *Scientific American*, November, 42–9.

Bryant, R.L. and Bailey, S. 1997: *Third World Political Ecology*. New York: Routledge.

Buzan, B., Waever, O. and de Wilde, J. 1995: *Security: a new framework for analysis*. Boulder, CH: Lynne Rienner.

Carrier, J.G. and Miller, D. (eds) 1998: *Virtualism: a new political economy*. Oxford and New York: Berg.

Carrier, J.G. 1988: Abstraction in Western economic practice. In Carrier, J.G. and Miller, D. (eds), *Virtualism: a new political economy*. Oxford and New York: Berg, 25–49.

Cilliers, P. 1998: *Complexity and postmodernism: understanding complex systems*. London: Routledge.

Cox, R. 1987: *Production, power and world order: social forces in the making of history*. New York: Columbia University Press.

Crush, J. 1995: *Power of development*. London and New York: Routledge.

Duffield, M. 1999: *Globalisation and war economies*. Paper presented at the 1999 Spring Seminar, Development Studies Association, Conflict and Security working group, 26 March 1999, South Bank University, London.

Frerks, G. 1998: Omgaan met rampen [Dealing with disaster]. Inaugural lecture, Wageningen: Agricultural University Wageningen, 3 December.

Friedmann, H. 1998: 'A sustainable world food economy.' In Kei, R. *et al.*, (eds), *Political ecology: global and local*. London and New York: Routledge.

Feigenbaum, H., Henig, J. and Hammett, C. 1998: *Shrinking the state: the political underpinnings of privatization*. Cambridge: Cambridge University Press.

Fukuyama, F. 1992: *The end of history and the last man*. New York: Free Press.

Gelbspan, R. 1995: The heat is on. *Harper's Magazine*, December, 31–7.

Gill, S. 1993: *Gramsci, historical materialism and international relations*. Cambridge: Cambridge University Press.

Gleditsch, N.P. 1997: Armed conflict and the environment: a critique of the literature. Proceedings, KNAW Workshop on Environmental Change and International security, Amsterdam, 20 January, 65–81.

Gleick, P.H. 1994: Water and conflict: freshwater resources and international security. *International Security* **18**(1), 79–112.

Gramsci, A. [1922], 1971: *Selections from the prison notebooks*. Edited and translated by Q. Hoare and G.N. Smith, London: Lawrence and Wishart.

Harvey, D. 1989: *The condition of postmodernity*. Cambridge: Blackwell.

Haas, P.M., Keohane, R.O. and Levy, M.A. 1993: *Institutions for the earth: sources of effective international environmental protection*. Cambridge, Mass., London: MIT Press.

Hellema, D., Wiebes, C. and Witte, T. 1998: *Doelwit Rotterdam: Nederland en de oliecrisis 1973–1974*. Den Haag: Sdu Uitgevers.

Hobbes, T. [1651], 1968: *Leviathan*. Harmondsworth: Penguin.

Homer-Dixon, T.F. 1994: Environmental scarcities and violent conflict. *Scientific American*, Summer 1994, 5–40.

Homer-Dixon, T.F. 1999: The myth of global water wars. *Forum*, International Committee of the Red Cross (ICRC), **1**(1), 10–13.

Kaplan, R.D. 1994: The coming anarchy. *Atlantic Monthly*, February, 44–76.

Keohane, R.O. and Nye, J.S. 1977: *Power and interdependence: World Politics*. Boston: Little & Brown.

Kolk, A. 1994: *The formulation of a political economy perspective for international environmental politics*. Amsterdam: Amsterdam International Studies Paper No. 32, University of Amsterdam, March.

Locke, J. [1690], 1965: *Two treatises on government*. New York: Mentor.

Lowi, M.R. 1993: *Water and power: the politics of a scarce resource in the Jordan river basin*. Cambridge: Cambridge University Press.

Lukes, S. 1974: *Power: a radical view*. London: Macmillan.

Machiavelli, N. [1532] 1953: *The Prince* [Il Principe]. New York: Mentor.

Merrett, S. 1997: *Introduction to the economics of water resources: an international perspective*. London: UCL Press.

Myers, N. 1994: *Ultimate security: the environmental basis of political stability*. New York and London: W.W. Norton.

Pijl, van der, K. 1992: *Wereldorde en machtspolitiek: visies op de internationale betrekkingen van Dante tot Fukuyama* [World order and power politics: perspectives of international relations, from Dante to Fukuyama]. Amsterdam: Het Spinhuis.

Porter, G. and Welsh-Brown, J.W. 1991: *Global environmental politics*. Boulder, CO: Westview Press.

Politi, A. 1997: *European security: the new transnational risk*. Paris: Chaillot paper No. 29.

Prins, G. (ed.) 1993: *Threats without enemies: facing environmental insecurity*. London: Earthscan.

Ritchie, M. 1990: GATT, agriculture and the environment. *The Ecologist* **20**(6), 214–21.

Sklair, L. 1998: 'The transnational capital class. In Carrier, J.G. and Miller, D. (eds). *Virtualism: a new political economy*. Oxford and New York: Berg, 135–61.

Strange, S. 1982: Cave! Hic dragones: a critique of regime analysis. *International Organisation*, **36**(2), 337–54.

Stripple, J. 1998: Securitizing the risks of climate change: institutional innovations in the insurance of catastrophic risk. IIASA Interim Report 98–098.

Tansey, J. 1999: Understanding risk and danger. PhD dissertation, University of East Anglia.

Tuathail, G.O., Dalby, S. and Routledge, P. (eds) 1998: *The geopolitics reader*. London and New York: Routledge.

Vogel, E.F. 1979: *Japan as number one*. Cambridge, MA: Harvard University Press.

Worster, D. 1985: *Rivers of empire: water, aridity and the growth of the American west*. New York: Pantheon Books.

Index